Thomas Nemeth
Philosophy in Imperial Russia's Theological Academies

Thomas Nemeth

Philosophy in Imperial Russia's Theological Academies

DE GRUYTER

ISBN 978-3-11-221486-2
e-ISBN (PDF) 978-3-11-100286-6
e-ISBN (EPUB) 978-3-11-100325-2

Library of Congress Control Number: 2023932878

Bibliographic information published by the Deutsche Nationalbibliothek
The Deutsche Nationalbibliothek lists this publication in the Deutsche Nationalbibliografie; detailed bibliographic data are available on the Internet at http://dnb.dnb.de.

© 2025 Walter de Gruyter GmbH, Berlin/Boston
This volume is text- and page-identical with the hardback published in 2023.
Printing and binding: CPI books GmbH, Leck

www.degruyter.com

Contents

Introduction —— IX

Acknowledgments —— XVI

Chapter 1
The Early Kyiv and Moscow Theological Academies —— 1
1.1 The Late Seventeenth Century —— 2
1.2 Philosophical Instruction in Kyiv and Moscow —— 9
1.3 Lopatinskij's Defense of "Two Truths" —— 13
1.4 Peter the Great's Ideologist —— 16
1.5 From a "Second Scholasticism" to Wolffianism —— 19
1.6 The Reign of Wolffian Philosophy in the Academies —— 25

Part I: Under the First Charter

Chapter 2
The St. Petersburg Academy Under the First Charter —— 33
2.1 First Turbulent Years —— 33
2.2 Sidonskij's *Introduction* and His Fate —— 39
2.3 Three Epigones: Drozdov, Nadezhin, Kedrov —— 44
2.4 Karpov's Psychologism and Defense of Orthodoxy —— 48

Chapter 3
The Moscow Academy Under the First Charter —— 61
3.1 Philosophy's First Steps in Moscow – Kutnevich —— 61
3.2 Golubinskij – A Founder of Russian Religious Philosophy —— 63
3.3 Kudrjavcev on the Concept of God and Evolution —— 72
3.4 Kudrjavcev on Cognition and Comtean Positivism —— 79

Chapter 4
The Kyiv and Kazan Academies Under the First Charter —— 88
4.1 Skvorcov's Philosophical Theology —— 88
4.2 Innokentij on Three Kinds of Knowledge —— 94
4.3 Avsenev on Three Approaches to God —— 98
4.4 Jurkevich as Conduit from the Academy to the University —— 103
4.5 The Seemingly Tortuous Start of the Kazan Academy —— 109

4.6   The Teaching of Logic in the 1850s —— 114

Part II: Under the 1869 Charter

Chapter 5
The St. Petersburg Academy Under the Second Charter —— 122
5.1   Chistovich's Psychology —— 122
5.2   Svetilin's Logic and the Question of Psychologism —— 125
5.3   Debol'skij's Theistic Phenomenalism from Kant to Hegel —— 128
5.4   Debol'skij's Right Hegelianism and Nationalism —— 134
5.5   Karinskij on the History of Modern Philosophy —— 139
5.6   Karinskij's Proto-Phenomenological Inquiries —— 145

Chapter 6
Philosophy at the Moscow Academy Under the Second Charter —— 150
6.1   Potapov's Understanding of Gravitational Attraction —— 150
6.2   Kudrjavcev on the Nature of Philosophy —— 153
6.3   Kudrjavcev on Philosophical Method —— 159
6.4   Kudrjavcev on the Traditional Proofs for God's Existence —— 163
6.5   Kudrjavcev on Modern Science —— 166
6.6   Kudrjavcev on Morality —— 169
6.7   Roman Levickij on the Morality of Christianity —— 171

Chapter 7
Philosophy at the Kyiv and Kazan Academies Under the Second Charter —— 175
7.1   Olesnickij's "Protestant"-Oriented Ethics —— 176
7.2   Linickij's Ambiguous Conception of Philosophy —— 181
7.3   Linickij on Cognition —— 184
7.4   Snegirev and Miloslavskij Confront Psychology —— 190
7.5   Archbishop Nikanor and His Positive Philosophy —— 198

Part III: Under the 1884 Charter

Chapter 8
Philosophy at the St. Petersburg Academy Under the Third Charter —— 211
8.1   Karinskij on Kant —— 212
8.2   Akvilonov on Proving God's Existence —— 217

8.3   Khrapovickij and Gribanovskij: A Turn to Self-Consciousness —— 220
8.4   Serebrenikov on Psychology and Mirtov Against Nietzsche —— 226

Chapter 9
Philosophy at the Moscow Academy Under the Third Charter —— 232
9.1   Ostroumov and Sokolov on German Idealism and Faith —— 233
9.2   Three Moral Theorists in Moscow —— 241
9.3   Two Historians of Philosophy in Moscow —— 252

Chapter 10
Philosophy at the Kyiv and Kazan Academies Under the Third Charter —— 261
10.1. Linickij Under the Third Charter —— 263
10.2   Linickij's Successors: Bogdashevskij and P. Kudrjavcev —— 266
10.3   Snegirev Under the Third Charter —— 272
10.4   The Summit of Imperial Russia's Academic Religious Philosophy —— 276

Part IV: **Under the 1910 Charter**

Chapter 11
Philosophy at the Academies Under the Fourth Charter —— 291
11.1   Philosophy at the Petersburg, Kyiv, and Kazan Academies —— 293
11.2   Philosophy at the Moscow Academy: Glagolev —— 298
11.3   Florenskij's Critique of Kant —— 303
11.4   Florenskij's *Magnum Opus* —— 308
11.5   Florenskij's Critics —— 313

Chapter 12
Concluding Remarks —— 318

Bibliography —— 322

Index —— 339

Introduction

As a scholarly topic, the study of the quiescence of the Russian Orthodox Church, both politically and, most importantly for our purposes here, intellectually during the years of late Imperial Russia is still very much in its infancy. Whereas research into the ideas and personalities involved in Russian revolutionary movements abound, largely owing to the historical impact of the events of 1917 and their aftermath, there are relatively few monographs concerning the philosophical trajectories emanating from representatives of Orthodoxy even in the Russian language, let alone in the West. The reason for this, understandably, is not hard to ascertain and fathom. Unlike the supposedly revolutionary theories of the 1825 Decembrists and the "Men of the Sixties," representatives of and within Orthodoxy had little direct political impact unless, of course, we take their very passivity as a bolstering of the given state of affairs, which in fact is what they did and sought to do. As Richard Pipes noticed some decades ago now, the basic feature of Orthodox Christianity – indeed, of most eschatological religions with the exception of certain Protestant forms of Christianity – is resignation in confrontation with earthly misfortunes. One *could*, of course, trace such an attitude back to the Biblical sayings of Jesus of Nazareth. But since not all forms of Christianity have historically opted for open political passivity, it alone cannot completely account for the *Russian* Church's attitude. We should also add, perhaps most importantly, that the Russian Church did not appeal to Jesus's avowed political quiescence to justify its own attitude. No, the Russian Church to an uncommon degree in Christianity abandoned its institutional distinction within society without resistance and allowed itself already with Peter the Great to become a branch of the state apparatus, a role it has seemingly forever since *de facto* if not *de jure* warmly embraced including to the present day. Having abandoned their status as an autonomous estate equal to or above the state, the Russian Orthodox clergy neither as a group nor certainly on the individual level could count on the Church's institutions to serve as a bulwark against any attempt to encroach on its perceived prerogatives, most noteworthy of which was the safeguarding of what it considered to be eternal and immutable truths. To a large extent, then, as an appendage of the state it saw its continuance and expansion as dependent on the endurance and vitality of the state. Thus, it served for much of its modern existence not merely as in passive compliance with the state's wishes, but as actively endorsing and promoting government policies. The Russian state during the late Imperial era, for its part, was happy to let the Church tend to the safeguarding of ethereal timeless and inviolable truths, seeing these as buttressing the established social and political order, which itself was such a truth.

Another factor, however, influencing the relative neglect of scholarship on institutionalized Orthodox thought was that thought's *intended* unoriginality. Why would scholars, whether in Russia or in the West, investigate theological deliberations and speculations that purposely offered nothing new, that in effect offered an apology for the existing state of affairs. To an extraordinary degree, Russian Orthodox theologians and philosophers of religion safely ensconced in their own separate educational establishments saw their purpose to be a defense of traditional Church teachings, particularly as set against a perceived corrupting influence of modernism and Western Christianity. Unlike in much of Europe where philosophically-minded clerics reared in the Latin language could conceivably look upon a body of works in that tongue going back more than a millennium, Russian theologians, many even at the highest levels, remained largely ignorant of the Greek language, which was that of their revered intellectual ancestors. Even the most fundamental of all Christian texts, the Bible, did not receive a complete Russian translation until well into the nineteenth century.[1] Given this fact, Russian religious philosophers could not reference many historical treatises when writing their own scholarly works yet had to be circumspect when handling Latin-language texts out of fear of "contagion," of having their own theological viewpoint infected by Western treatments. When possible, they referred to the writings of the Eastern Church Fathers, which only reinforced their estrangement from the West. The result was the historical insularity of their community. The Orthodox Church's reliance on Old Church Slavonic, a language developed in Bulgaria, for its religious services, rather than Latin as in the West, also contributed to its isolation from much of Europe. As Gustav Shpet wrote, "We were baptized in Greek, but the language given to us was Bulgarian. What could the language of a nation devoid of cultural traditions, literature, and history bring along with itself?"[2]

Another factor in the development of the Russian Orthodox religio-philosophical outlook was its emerging (cultural) nationalism. The autocephaly of the Russian Orthodox Church entailed a separation not just from Western Christianity, but even from other national Orthodox churches. Given the sheer expanse of the Russian Orthodox lands with their low population density compared to Western Europe, there was no compelling reason for the Church to reach out beyond its borders, which in any case would have been difficult. The effect of this was to encourage an insular sense of nationhood within the Church. For all of these rea-

---

[1] This late date can be compared unfavorably to the appearance of translations into German, French, and English in the sixteenth century. The first book printed in Hungary was a translation of the Bible in the middle of that century, and a Dutch translation became available around the same time.

[2] Shpet (2008), 55.

sons the Orthodox Church in Russia saw itself as the *Russian* Orthodox Church. This cultural nationalism is reflected also in the neglect by those we shall examine in the pages ahead of other philosophically-minded Orthodox theologians from outside Imperial Russia.³ Whereas those who taught philosophy at the theological academies certainly thought of themselves as Orthodox Christians, they appear never to have given more than a tacit acknowledgment to their co-religionists in a number of Eastern-European lands, such as Bulgaria, Romania, Serbia, and, most importantly, Greece.⁴ Thus, they never drew inspiration or guidance in their own intellectual quests from beyond the political borders of their own country.

One of the most notable features of Imperial Russian religious philosophy within the academies was the constant attempt by its representatives to set it apart from Western philosophical systems. We find within the academies an incessant distancing of their philosophies from modern Western thought spanning from Descartes to Kant. Whereas many figures within these religious establishments were undoubtedly influenced by their readings of Western thought, this influence could hardly be acknowledged explicitly. We find no acknowledged Cartesians or Kantians within the academies. All philosophical writings emanating there as a rule had to be harshly critical of Western ideas even while implicitly absorbing many of them. All of this surely was only to be expected given the mission of the Imperial Russian schools. More surprising, however, is the sheer silence throughout by these religious philosophers on medieval scholasticism. With their gaze fixed, as it were, on modern thought, they had scarcely a word to say about the immense philosophical corpus left by Thomas Aquinas or that by such figures as Duns Scotus and William of Ockham. Why this was so is less obvious. They certainly could have aimed their barbs against the implicit rationalism of the Western medievalists, but they, to a man, remained silent. Yes, the Russians finally did address the traditional rational proofs for God's existence in the nineteenth century, but they did so uniformly without direct reference to the respective

---

3 The nationalism of Imperial Russia's Orthodox theologians was surely not a form of political nationalism, but a religious nationalism seen as a subset of cultural nationalism. They saw *their* understanding of Orthodoxy to be an essential feature or component of Russian culture and sought to defend and promote it whenever necessary and possible. Certainly, ethnic Ukrainians were culturally Russian in the eyes of these theologians, but whether other ethnic groups in the Asiatic expanses of Imperial Russia could belong to the cultural Russian nation was not an issue they addressed in their theoretical writings even though they sent missionaries to those lands seeking conversions.
4 A qualified exception here is Vladimir Solov'ëv, who maintained warm relations with clergy in Orthodox Serbia – and Catholic Croatia. The qualification is necessary here, since he was not a professor at a theological academy.

arguments' original formulation. There was no textual exegesis as such on scholasticism, arguably again for fear of some intellectual contagion. Whereas we can find commentaries on Kant's *Critique of Pure Reason*, e.g., in the works of Gogockij, Jurkevich, Archbishop Nikanor, and Bogdashevskij, we find nothing similar on Thomas Aquinas or, for that matter, any other medieval philosopher of Western Christianity. Moreover, prior to the establishment of the academies, the Russian Orthodox clergy displayed no interest at all in the theoretical grounding of their faith and doctrines comparable to what we find in the West.

The overt hostility of the philosophical tracts emanating from Imperial Russia's academies against Western philosophy was aimed at the pernicious "subjectivism," as they saw it, of modern Western philosophy.[5] Thus, since medieval philosophy had little trace of this evil, there was no particular need to address it. However, we cannot help but observe that just as in Western Europe philosophy professors in Russia's academies had to contend with the emergence of psychology as a distinct branch of knowledge, a discipline that by its very definition dealt with the human individual. This posed a challenge. How could one avoid subjectivism with its attendant relativism while engaging in research on the individual mentality? Few, if any, of those engaged in psychological queries pursued their investigations to explicitly psychologistic conclusions even though some did hold even logic to be an empirical science.

Such, then, is the principal motivating factor behind the following pages, namely, to help fill in a distinct gap in the history of Russian philosophy and in that way to help understand Russia itself, its people and its culture. Make no mistake, the reader should not expect and will not find in the following pages philosophical arguments to compare with Kant's transcendental deduction of the categories or Husserl's inquiries into inner time-consciousness. But he/she will find much that will lead the thoughtful person to reflect upon and to help realize that certain issues remain interesting and vital across national cultures. Nevertheless, the investigations that follow illuminate a widespread type of mental outlook that persists to this day and, thus, can help us understand the emergence of a character trait that lay dormant under an official ideology that proclaimed the universality of human interests and goals.

We shall proceed chronologically in the pages that follow with the caveat that we are dealing with four different religious higher-educational institutions dubbed

---

[5] The present study focuses, unquestionably, on the Imperial Russian context. However, it was not only the Russian Orthodox Church that reacted in horror to the subjectivism of modern philosophy. The Catholic Church, for example, had placed Hume's works on its *Index Librorum Prohibitorum* in 1761 and Kant's first *Critique* entered the list in July 1827. Even the devout Catholic Descartes had his books so honored in 1663.

theological academies, one each in St. Petersburg, Moscow, Kyiv, and Kazan. These four academies were governed by charters, which stipulated the common set of rules they were expected to follow. As the reader will also notice, there were four charters over the course of the existence of the academies up to the revolutionary events in 1917. Rather than examining each academy separately over the course of their roughly century-long existence, we shall see how each fared under the various charters. Thus, the narrative that follows will be divided into four parts. Of course, since we are dealing with the thoughts and works of human individuals whose profession was for the most part the teaching of philosophy as that discipline was understood at the time, their careers may have extended over more than the span of a single charter. This is particularly the case with the second charter, which was in effect for only fifteen years. Many professors, then as today, had teaching careers lasting much longer than that. Another caveat in our story is that in order to avoid extending it beyond manageable bounds, we shall limit our discussion to the works that appeared in print while the respective individual was associated with one of the four academies. This is important in that some figures still published philosophical tracts after leaving, for whatever reason, a teaching position at one of the academies. A prominent example is Pamfil Jurkevich, who taught at the Kyiv Academy in the 1850s, but then accepted the professorship in philosophy at the secular Moscow University, when instruction in philosophy was again permitted under Tsar Alexander II after it had been forbidden with the exception of psychology and elementary logic in 1850. Thus, we shall leave aside his numerically meager but important writings composed during the decade following his departure from Kyiv.

We begin naturally with the pre-history, so to speak, of the theological academies, with the time when the lands comprising Imperial Russia lacked not just institutions of higher education but had barely any fully formed educational establishments at all. Such was a confusing time in western Russia with vying political and religious allegiances. A number of centuries earlier the land of the Rus' officially adopted Christianity from Constantinople, not Rome as did their Slavic folk in neighboring Poland. A fact that, from the Western viewpoint, was to have over the centuries the most disquieting effects. The ambassadors of Kyivan Rus' surely were astonished by the apparent wealth of tenth-century Byzantium with its magnificent churches and Constantinople's enormous fortifications, but what they did not see was a civilization well into its decline and isolation in every noteworthy respect. Rus' inherited a form of Christianity, but not a spirit of inquiry, which was already largely absent in Byzantium.

As we shall see, whereas in the West the Roman Church confronted the rise of the empirical sciences and thereby the role of reason in affirming religious tenets and in resolving metaphysical disputes, similar conflicts were largely absent from the Orthodox Church in Rus' and later Imperial Russia. At no time did the Church in those lands look to rational inquiry and criticism in order to understand the theological tracts that were available to them. The Russian Church produced not a single priest who through his writings challenged the rational mind to understand that Church's theological tenets. Instead, it largely opted for an appeal to tradition and to a mystical intuitivism, an alleged direct insight into what it took to be religious truths at the expense of logic and deliberation. Already in 1840, Arkhimandrit Gavriil (1795–1868), who taught at Kazan University, wrote, "All that does not agree with the true reason of Sacred Scripture is essentially false, a delusion, and without any mercy must be rejected."[6] We can hardly be surprised, then, that education beyond immediate practical needs was not merely disparaged, but even too often seen as a step leading to heresy. Another consequence that we see even today most vividly is Russia's sense of isolation from the West culturally and Western civilization intellectually and in values. When confronting the rationalism of Western Christian philosophy, Russia's Orthodox thinkers, almost uniformly, chose to re-affirm ever more strongly their retreat from reason into a personal and even social intuitivism that simply skirted rational elaboration and analysis. They saw themselves, the preeminent Slavic nation, as having insight into truths that other political nations or ethnic groups – it is not clear which – being blinded by their false faith, whether Christian or not, could neither see nor grasp. Gavriil expressed in the sixth volume of his *History of Philosophy* that each nation has its own special character and with it its own philosophy.[7] The relativistic consequences of such a position are all too obvious to need elaboration.

The original motivation behind the undertaking of the present study was not merely to write a long neglected history of philosophical thought in the Imperial Russian theological academies, but also to see whether the late nineteenth-century German debate on psychologism impacted or even had any resemblance to a similar controversy in the Russian philosophical scene. The importance of this inquiry is not only to determine the intellectual relationship between Germany and Russia in the nineteenth century, but also whether the latter with its insular conception of philosophy also maintained a preference for psychologism. The following pages will show that ultimately psychologism by no means exercised a hegemonic control over philosophy in the academies despite its forceful advocacy by some. In this lies the hope – however slim – that the heirs of Russian thought will finally emerge from their self-imposed philosophical isolation in asking such a xenopho-

---

6 Gavriil (1840), 22.
7 Gavriil (1840), 3.

bic question as Russia's place in history and instead share in the pursuit of answers to the same queries as their colleagues in America and western Europe.

Most, if not all, scholarly studies of Russian thought, regardless of how broadly or narrowly they are conceived, have to contend with how to render Russian names. Various systems have been employed over the decades. Although the range of choices has decreased, no single one has yet won universal acceptance among all the peoples employing the Latin alphabet in writing. Moreover, since different transliterations have been used in the past, the scholar is virtually forced to be somewhat familiar with all of them. An obvious example of this is the rendering of Solov'ëv, as used in this present work, but which has also been rendered as Soloviev, Solov'ev, and Solovyov. Since a number of the names and terms mentioned here have also appeared in the author's previous studies, rendering them differently now could only lead to further confusion and bewilderment. Some readers, surely, would prefer a different spelling, but hopefully they will recognize the names and terms found in these pages and not misidentify the individuals and concepts intended.

Acknowledgments

A study such as this could not be possible without the resources of numerous libraries. I am as always deeply appreciative of the remarkable collection housed in the New York Public Library, access to which is open to all regardless of one's home residence. I would also like to acknowledge the assistance in my research of New York University and, in particular, its Jordan Center for the Advanced Study of Russia, at which I was a visiting scholar for two years. As for individuals, I would like to thank my wife Anne for her understanding each and every day while I secluded myself in my study researching and writing the work before you. I particularly appreciate the many observations and suggestions made on this work in manuscript form by the blind reviewers. If these lines should pass before their gaze, please be assured that even though I, of course, cannot acknowledge them by name, I am deeply thankful for their efforts and assistance. I especially would like to express my gratitude to all those at the publishing house of Walter De Gruyter who helped make possible the appearance of this work, in particular Christoph Schirmer, whose thoroughness and promptness are, to say the least, exemplary, and Mara Weber along with the entire production team, whose exactitude and courtesy are much appreciated. Lastly, the vast bulk of Chapter 2 previously appeared under this author's name as "Philosophy in the Early St. Petersburg Theological Academy: toward the roots of classical Russian Idealism." *Studies in East European Thought* 73(2021): 495–515. Permission to reprint is graciously acknowledged.

Chapter 1
The Early Kyiv and Moscow Theological Academies

Any investigator of the history of higher education in general, whether secular or clerical, and not just of philosophy, in the lands that comprised "Imperial Russia" cannot but be startled, perhaps even perplexed, at first sight at how late such education arrived there. In the lands of western Europe, numerous universities had already existed for centuries before Russia established a single one. The University of Bologna in Italy dates from the late eleventh century. The University of Oxford was founded shortly afterward, and the University of Cambridge dates from the following century. The University of Paris was officially chartered in 1200. In central Europe, Prague's Charles University, modeled on that in Paris, was founded in the late 1340s with four faculties, and Jagiellonian University in Krakow was established in 1364. Even the British colonies in North America saw the establishment of Harvard College in 1636 and that of the College of William and Mary in 1693. In contrast, Imperial Russia established in Moscow its first university only in 1755. This is not to say, of course, that there were no institutions of higher education at all prior to that date in Russia. There were, but their curricula were quite narrow and as such far from what we today conceive as typical of a university. Whether the course of study in Imperial Russian schools provided instruction at a level comparable to that offered in western Europe is difficult to determine with confidence. One possible measure would be to look to the general attitudes expressed at the time and at the cultural and scientific accomplishments, broadly speaking, both of the society in which the various schools were located as well as, but principally, of the instructors and their graduates. Another conceivable objective measure would lie in comparing the classroom texts in terms of their level of difficulty and comprehensiveness. Such a measure, however, could be deceptive in that two quite distinct schools may employ the same text but not utilize it to the same extent or to the same degree of depth.[1] As our concern here is with philosophy as a scholarly discipline, viz., its teaching, propagation, and original development, within Imperial Russia's clerical or theological schools, let us look first at

---

[1] The global ranking of universities is today rather commonplace taking into account such factors as the size of the respective libraries, international reputations, the number of international awards received by faculty members, and citations of writings by a school's staff in established scientific/scholarly journals. Unfortunately, none of these criteria is suitable in judging eighteenth-century universities.

how the country's nascent educational institutions evolved into the theological academies found in nineteenth- and early twentieth-century Imperial Russia.

1.1 The Late Seventeenth Century

Imperial Russia traced its origin back to Kyivan Rus', which existed from the ninth century to the Mongol conquest in the mid-1200s. Accepting Christianity from Byzantium rather than Rome in the year 988, Rus' looked first to Eastern Christendom for religious and intellectual models. Unfortunately, as Gustav Shpet, remarked, the appeal of Kyivan Rus' to Byzantium was at a time when the once glorious Eastern Roman Empire and its civilization were already in marked moral and intellectual decline.[2] Nevertheless, Kyiv, which in the decades following its adoption of Eastern Orthodoxy was a large and vibrant cultural and trading center, should have had, in theory, access to the intellectual treasures of Greek antiquity and, though admittedly to a decidedly lesser extent, of medieval Islam.

Of course, having rich stores of philosophical and scientific works available to a person – or a nation – does not mean availing oneself of them. Kyivan Rus' demonstrated no particular interest in Greek philosophy or even in more recent theological subtleties, political theories, or scientific developments. To be sure, Rus' had as yet no developed educational system populated with competent individuals who could utilize what they could have possessed. But this simply begs the question: Why did the embrace of Eastern Christendom by Rus' not induce the establishment of such a system and prompt individuals to avail themselves of the newly available resources? What we do find is a smattering of translations of maxims from the Church Fathers, lives of saints, and basic edifying texts. Whatever dissemination did occur of ancient philosophy, it did not stimulate philosophical inquiry, let alone creativity. We find no interest in a theoretical grounding of their Orthodox Christian faith comparable to that found at the time in western Europe.[3] There,

---

[2] Shpet (2008), 55. Whereas Shpet was correct from his perspective in the early twentieth century, the ambassadors of Rus' certainly would have been impressed by the apparent wealth of Byzantium as compared to the lack thereof of Rome. The conversion of Rus' to Orthodox Christianity instead of to Roman Catholicism, in the worlds of Richard Pipes, "was perhaps the single most critical factor influencing that country's destiny." By doing so, "Russia separated itself from the mainstream of Christian civilization which, as it happened, flowed westward." Pipes (1979), 223.

[3] Many foreign travelers to Russia noted this general apathy and even hostility to intellectual inquiry. Johann-Georg Korb, a member of the Austrian embassy at the end of the seventeenth century, remarked, "In their schools positively the only labour of the schoolmasters is to teach the children how to write and shape their letters. ... They despise liberal arts as useless torments of youth,

the so-called recovery of Aristotle in the Middle Ages led in short order to the huge corpus of Thomas Aquinas, but we find nothing at all similar to that in Kyivan Rus' or even the early Russian Empire.

Although this broadly painted, negative portrayal of the intellectual atmosphere in medieval Kyivan Rus' is correct, it fails to convey a full picture of the state of affairs. To be sure, "Athenian wisdom" was taken during these centuries in Rus' as a form of Western rationality, fundamentally incompatible with the people's religious faith. Yet, based on mentions in their own writings there were some who had a degree of familiarity with philosophical works from antiquity. The mid-seventeenth-century poet-monk Symeon of Polotsk (1629–1680) promoted an acquaintance with Greek works and referred to Aristotle. His intellectual debt to the latter was primarily through his ethics, which Symeon saw to be of the highest importance, writing: "Nature gives us life; philosophy teaches the good of life. ... Just as medicine heals a disease, philosophy corrects the soul's disposition to evil."[4] However, a century earlier Andrej Kurbskij (1528–1583), a one-time friend of Ivan the Terrible and later a political opponent in self-imposed exile, recognizing the ignorance of the Orthodox community, urged his co-religionists to study the patristic tradition, which he saw as a continuation of a tradition that stemmed from the Greek philosophers. "Of the latter," remarked the noted twentieth-century Orthodox scholar Georges Florovsky, "he [Kurbskij] mainly read Aristotle (*Physics* and *Ethics*), probably under the influence of St. John of Damascus and Cicero, from whom he derived a Stoic conception of natural law."[5] We should bear in mind, though, that these manifestations of Kurbskij's intellectual interests originated from after his emigration from Ivan's Russia to neighboring Lithuania, where access to Western literature was much greater than in his homeland. To be sure, some information about philosophical ideas from antiquity, both Greek and Roman, was in the hands of a small handful of individuals in Rus'.[6] Whether they made use of it in any concrete fashion is another matter.[7]

---

they prohibit philosophy, and they have often publicly outraged astronomy with the approbrious name of magic." Korb (2013), 196.

4 Simeon (1953), 70, 71.

5 Florovsky (1979), 40. Florovsky notes that Kurbskij drew up an ambitious plan to translate the Church Fathers of the fourth century, but the translations were to be done based on Latin, not Greek, texts. The project never reached completion.

6 Shakmatov wrote that Plato was known almost from the very beginning of written documentation in Rus' with sayings attributed to him or excerpts from his works. Shakmatov (1930), 55.

7 In an essay immediately following that of Shakmatov in the same collection, the noted Ukrainian scholar Dmitrij Chizhevskij asked us to cautiously bear in mind what Shakmatov had unearthed: "Even a cursory glance at the material will convince us that we are by no means dealing with independent philosophizing, affiliated with Plato or emanating from him ... but only information re-

The expanding and concomitantly contracting borders of central and east European political states at this time brought into contact peoples who had previously been culturally and religiously isolated from one another. The incorporation of lands into the burgeoning Lithuanian state in the second half of the sixteenth century and the first half of the following century brought Orthodox believers into direct contact with Western European culture, religions, and institutions, where Latin typically was the *lingua franca*. Whereas the Thomistic-Aristotelian tradition of educated religious discourse dominated in the West, particularly in Poland, a more symbolic and figurative understanding of Christianity dominated in the Eastern, Orthodox lands. In order to protect and defend their faith – and concomitantly their trade and pecuniary interests – the Orthodox believers within the expanding states formed "brotherhoods," consisting of laymen and clergy. Although the origin of these brotherhoods is unclear, they appear to have had their roots in the Middle Ages with the purpose of maintaining and supplying churches with the necessities for religious services.[8] These brotherhoods provided youth with the means and at least a modicum of education in Orthodox doctrine.

At least one of, if not, the oldest brotherhood, that in Lviv arose already in the fifteenth century. However, with its weak organizational structure and little financial resources, it played but a small role in historical terms during these early years. The Union of Lublin in 1569 creating the Polish-Lithuanian Commonwealth accelerated the creation and involvement of Orthodox brotherhoods in the field of education as a bulwark against Jesuit encroachments from Poland. In 1615 shortly after the founding of the Kyiv Epiphany Brotherhood a school was created and quickly established itself placing it in a leading position vis-à-vis the other schools. Drawing its instructors from Lviv and elsewhere, the school provided a general education that included grammar and history as well as, reportedly, philosophy![9] The initial attraction of the brotherhood schools began to dim in the early decades of the seventeenth century owing to scarcity of resources and competition with Jesuit

---

ported by chance, on the basis of one or another theological question or scattered among other historical data." Chizhevskij (1930), 71. After summarizing Shakmatov's information and evaluating comparisons between Plato's writings and the treatments of it in antiquity, Chizhevskij concluded that Shpet's judgment of the "ignorance" of philosophical education in ancient Rus' was overly harsh. Nevertheless, "one can perhaps remark that the comparisons show that in ancient Rus' there was only a very superficial, inaccurate and unclear acquaintance with Plato, that Plato's positions were often tendentiously distorted in order to exalt Plato through an alleged proximity of his positions to those of Christianity, or vice versa, in order to refute them, emphasizing the moments of Platonism that are unacceptable to Christianity." Chizhevskij (1930), 80.

8 Subtelny (2009), 97. Florovsky places their origin in "probably" the 1580s as parochial organizations that went on to become "corporations of the defense of the faith." Florovsky (1979), 56.
9 Sukhova (2013a), 8.

institutions. Those who sought a higher caliber of teaching opted for the latter despite the threat of "infection" from western Catholicism.

In the late 1620s, Petro Mohyla (1597–1647) was appointed archimandrite of the Kyivan Cave Monastery. Although himself educated at the Lviv Brotherhood School and possibly in France and the Netherlands, Mohyla remained firmly within the Orthodox Christian camp. Shortly after securing his new position and recognizing the ignorance of the youth and even of the clergy, he decided to establish a school near the monastery. Whether intended or not, it clearly stood in competition with the Kyiv Brotherhood School. When Mohyla's school opened in 1631 with more than one hundred pupils, it was met with rumors and suspicions of promoting pro-Uniate doctrines. To dispel the charges, Mohyla agreed to merge his school with the Kyiv Brotherhood School.[10] Nevertheless, the resulting Kyivan Mohyla College or Collegium[11] was organized around the principles of the Jesuit colleges, which would remain the model for more than a century afterward. Apart from catechism and Slavic grammar, the basic disciplines were taught in Latin.[12] Although one might think the school would place an emphasis on the Greek language, the teaching of it and of the Slavonic language soon decreased. Some classes were even taught in Polish. Aristotelian philosophy and Thomist theology were introduced in 1689 with the former divided into three parts: logic, physics, and metaphysics. Aristotle's writings themselves penetrated into Rus' in Latin and Polish translations.[13] The Kyivan Mohyla professors consistently over the next half century identified themselves exclusively with Aristotle, whereas western European logic courses at the time appealed to a variety of other thinkers in addition to Aristotle.[14] Nevertheless – and this cannot be stressed enough – neither originality nor critical thinking was either the stated goal or tolerated in classroom instruction. We should add, though, that critical thinking was also not the goal at the time in Western educational institutions, where, as in Russia, philosophy was taught using manuals as texts, which students were expected to learn much as they would hard facts in history or natural science.

---

10 Charipova (2006), 46–49. Charipova writes that the two surviving manuscript courses of philosophy from 1639–1640 serve as evidence that "at least an incomplete philosophical curriculum was already taught at the time." Charipova (2006), 52.
11 The title of "Academy" came later. In 1635, the king of Poland confirmed the school but not yet as an academy. Ševčenko (1985), 14. The first surviving written instance of the Kyivan school being called an "Academy" dates from 1701. Sukhova (2013a), 15.
12 "Latin was revered as the most important language, which is why it flourished from the first years of the school." Bulgakov (1843), 75.
13 Ovchinnikova (2012), 33.
14 Simchich (2016), 15.

Learning for its own sake was certainly not welcomed in much of seventeenth-century Russia regardless of its source. Instruction in languages and even of the grammar of one's own tongue had a purely utilitarian goal. The Church needed those who could compose liturgical literature, and the state needed clerks with a mastery of foreign languages to deal with trade and diplomacy. However, apart from these basic needs many members of the clergy regarded an aspiration for knowledge as amounting to a betrayal of religious faith. The cultivation of the mind, they held, was at the expense of the soul. The desire for knowledge was to know the mind of God and as such represented an example of the sin of pride, a sin that the Orthodox Church charged the Roman Church of having committed. An additional fear on the part of a powerful segment of the former was that the use of the Latin language and Latin-language literature would destabilize the commitment of Orthodox believers to their faith. Such a fear surely lurked behind the tension between a "Latin party" and a "Greek party" that would in time play out in Moscow.

As a result of the Russo-Polish War (1654–1667) the city of Polotsk in present-day Belarus fell into Russian hands. Tsar Aleksej (1629–1676) visited there in 1656 and was introduced to Symeon of Polotsk, who presented to him several panegyrics. Impressed with Symeon's ideas, the Tsar invited the monk, a graduate of the Kyiv-Mohyla Collegium and of a Jesuit school in Vilnius, to Moscow in 1664. Symeon organized an unfortunately short-lived school in the Zaikonospasskij monastery and was appointed tutor to the Tsarevich Aleksej and after his death to Tsarevich Fedor in addition to other children of the royal family.[15]

Tsar Fedor III (1661–1682) in 1679 requested Symeon to write a charter for what became the Slavic-Greek-Latin Academy, the ancestor of the Moscow Theological Academy. Unfortunately, Symeon's death the following year halted these plans for the time being. Symeon's student Sil'vestr Medvedev obtained permission from the new regent Sophia, who was among those tutored by Symeon to renew the school started by Symeon in the Zaikonospasskij monastery in 1682. To be sure, the clash between the Greek and the Latin parties, the latter being those who favored teaching in Latin against those who placed an emphasis on Greek, had not abated and the plan to open the school stalled.[16] The patriarch of Moscow Joachim, thinking that the new school would surely be modeled on the one in Kyiv and in-

---

[15] Korzo (2011), 137. Symeon was reproached for harboring a secret Catholicism but was saved by having Aleksej's favor.

[16] Medvedev's story is quite tragic, even bizarre. Harmlessly enough it would seem, he took the "Latin" position regarding a purely theological point concerning the Holy Spirit. But after losing his job, rumors began swirling that he wished to kill the patriarch. He was alleged to be part of a political conspiracy, jailed, tortured, and, after two years in prison, executed.

fused with the spirit of Catholicism, revised the charter so that prospective teachers would have to prove their adherence to Orthodoxy. In addition, Joachim requested of his counterparts in Constantinople and Jerusalem to find teachers for the new school that he proposed to establish. It would be purely Orthodox with an emphasis on Greek and Slavonic, not Latin. Sophia, seeking not to challenge the patriarch, acquiesced.

The Leichoudes (Likhud) brothers, Ioannikios (1633–1717) and Sophronios (1652–1730), arrived in 1685. Although Greek monks, they were educated in Rome and the University of Padua. Their instructions for the Slavic-Greek-Latin Academy were to strengthen the Hellenic trend at the expense of a Polish-Latin one. The school opened in 1687, albeit without a charter.[17] In its first decade the school stressed the study of Greek, but curriculum changes would eventually make Latin the predominant language of instruction.[18] The brothers, to no surprise given their educational background, taught in the same scholastic spirit as in Italy. Their instructions in logic and science were drawn from Aristotle mediated through medieval philosophy and more recent advances in natural science, though their understanding of the latter was still framed in qualitative rather than quantitative terms.[19]

The Leichoudes brothers benefited from the patronage of Patriarch Joachim, but they began to lose support with his death in 1690. Beset with enemies in Moscow, the brothers also encountered an attack by the patriarch of Constantinople, who, in a letter in 1693, remonstrated them for teaching not just in Greek, but also in Latin, thereby "introducing Latin iniquities into simple minds."[20] To whatever extent they taught and inspired their students with philosophy, it could not have been significant. The brothers were dismissed from their positions the following year and the school declined rapidly thereafter.[21] The immediate successors to

---

[17] To date the Moscow school from 1687 is not undisputed. The completion of a building to house the school on the grounds of the Zaikonosplasskij monastery occurred in 1687, but the school was officially recognized by Patriarch Joachim already at the end of 1685. Panibratcev (1997a), 14.
[18] Michelson (2020), 96.
[19] "The Leichoudes' Aristotle was not simply the original Aristotle (*pace* Leichoudian assurances to this effect) or the Aristotle of the Byzantines; rather it was a Jesuit Aristotelianism, Thomist in its basic interpretative approach but also eclectic in that it incorporated elements from other philosophical systems." Chrissidis (2016), 76.
[20] Quoted in Pavlov (2017), 16.
[21] The brothers first taught Italian to a group of people in accordance with a decree from Tsar Peter, but they continued to be charged with heretical views and exiled to a monastery in Kostroma. Later, in 1706, they were summoned by the bishop of Novgorod, who requested that they establish a school like that in Moscow. In that year they also completed an anti-Protestant treatise *Luther's Heresies*. They also occupied themselves, one might say, with translations from Latin

the Leichoudes, Nikolaj Semenov and Fedor Polikarpov, both of whom were students of the two brothers, taught neither philosophy nor theology. Their classes were given entirely in Greek.

The school changed rapidly under Peter I (the Great). He issued a decree in June 1701 to start teaching in Latin and invited instructors from the Kyiv Academy based on their scholarly rather than religious credentials. As "protector" of the Moscow School, Metropolitan Stefan Javorskij (1658–1722), who had himself previously taught, albeit briefly, at the Kyiv Academy, expanded the course of study and introduced the teaching of German, French, medicine, and physics.[22] These changes were of course consistent with Peter's intent to Europeanize his country. The invitation extended to the Kyiv Academy for instructors was prompted by pragmatic considerations and not meant as a slight to other institutions. Only those from Kyiv were thought to have the requisite academic background including knowledge of Latin to fill the vacancies in Moscow. The newly-arrived instructors brought along their Kyiv texts imbued with the spirit of scholasticism. The study of Greek fell into disfavor until 1738, when it was again introduced, along with Hebrew, but the Academy's authorities displayed little interest in it. Only at the end of the century (1798) was a study of Greek and Hebrew made mandatory. Until then, even theology was taught in Latin.

---

and Italian. The following year Sophronios went to Moscow on an assignment from the bishop to retrieve fonts from a printer in Moscow. He, however, stayed on to teach Greek. Ioannikios remained in Novgorod, running the school along with former students. It along with all the other newly created lower-level schools was closed in 1708. He returned to Moscow to help his brother teaching.

22 Pavlov (2017), 17. Pavlov writes that Peter the Great invited teachers from the Kyiv-Mohyla Academy to Moscow; Sukhova writes that it was Stefan Javorskij who called teachers from Kyiv. See Sukhova (2013b), 31–32. Shpet, settling the dispute even before it arose, wrote that Peter's decree was based on a suggestion from Javorskij. Shpet (2008), 88. On Javorskij's meteoric rise to administrative power in Peter's Russia, see Collis (2012), 211–214. Javorskij studied for five years in Polish Jesuit schools but re-converted to Orthodoxy on his return to Kyiv in 1689. He was appointed professor of philosophy at the Kyiv Collegium two years later. His lectures there on "natural philosophy" included astrological interpretations of Biblical depictions. Collis writes that Javorskij's sermons also displayed a "distinctly mystical and astrological bent." They "drew extensively on the mystical and emblematic writings of a number of prominent seventeenth-century Jesuits." Collis (2012), 215. Prior to approximately 1690, Javorskij displayed no firm commitment to any particular career. "In this period of his life, Javorskij appears before us as a completely secular man, close to the secular interests of the higher aristocratic circles of the Ukrainian social elite. ... One can even say that in Javorskij's literary works of the time there was no hint of his categorical desire to dedicate himself to the Church and even less to a monastic life style." Chechin (2005), 81. In any case, he decided to be a monk in late 1689-early 1690.

1.2 Philosophical Instruction in Kyiv and Moscow

Before turning to a sketch of the philosophical and intellectual environment in Russia's nascent Kyiv and Moscow theological academies in the eighteenth century, let us first look at their economic condition. Until Peter I (the Great), the Russian Orthodox Church enjoyed a considerable degree of autonomy from the state. The implementation of the reforms Peter had in mind required a considerable amount of money, and he resented that the clergy not only avoided taxation but also played only a small, insignificant role in furthering state interests.[23] The age-old custom among those with means to bequeath a portion of their wealth to the Church in their will further irritated Peter.

The Tsar's perception of the Church's wealth, whether real or imagined, was not reflected in the financial condition – and therefore stability – of the theological academies and seminaries. The academies, standing as they were at the summit of the education system, were held in higher esteem by both the Church and the secular authorities and thus were assured of preferred financial treatment compared to the seminaries. However, that was not saying much. Subsidies for compensating the teaching staff and for the basic needs of the students came only irregularly. For example, monies for the upkeep and repair of the buildings of the Moscow Academy would remain a constant and insoluble issue throughout the eighteenth century. Moreover, teachers' salaries were quite low even when they were paid. Food and firewood were often given instead of cash. The situation was even much worse in the Kyiv Academy, where many of the instructors were monks who received compensation in the form of the bare necessities, such as housing, food, firewood, and candles. Despite the seemingly constant requests by the teachers for payment of their salaries, these came generally only on holydays, such as Christmas and Easter. Given these conditions, we can hardly be surprised that many students, who, unless they came from a prosperous family, had to literally beg in town, work in the fields, or say prayers in exchange for money.[24] There was, not surprisingly, a significant turnover of instructors who found they could make a better living in other ways, including even teaching in secular schools when their superiors approved. In 1736, the Moscow Academy had only seven teachers. Admission to the theological schools was not, in principle, restricted to sons of clergy. Children from a bourgeois background, as well as the service nobility, and even peasants could attend. Javorskij, for example, came from a poor noble family. However, given the manner in which clerical vacancies were filled, those from a secular

---

23 Pipes (1979), 240.
24 Charipova (2006), 56.

background were at a decided disadvantage. Moreover, throughout much of the century there was determined resistance on the part of the academic authorities to this class-blind admission policy. The Moscow Academy, for example, did become a closed institution later in the eighteenth century allowing only those from the clerical estate to enroll officially.[25]

Philosophy became a required course of study at the Kyiv Mohyla Collegium in 1632, the first in the Russian Empire. The depth of these courses can only be imagined. Fortunately, lecture material dating from a number of years later in that century and into the next has survived. Students at the Collegium studied philosophy for two years, the general topic being divided as mentioned above into logic, physics, and metaphysics. Starting in the 1730s, the study of ethics was systematically introduced into the curriculum. Training in "dialectic," the first of the two parts into which logic was divided, concerned the three alleged activities of the understanding: the use of concepts, judgments, and inferences.[26] This was the focus of study for one to two months at the start as a statement of principles. Then, the subject matter of the course turned to the other topics discussed in Aristotle's *Organon* including his thoughts on interpretation.[27] Also among the first topics to be discussed was the problem of universals and issues associated with it. The aim was to teach the fundamentals of Aristotelian logic in its medieval interpretation along with some of the later additions made during that period. Javorskij, for example, who taught logic from 1691–1693 specifically stated that the material he was presenting was drawn from Aristotle as viewed through medieval eyes and as preached by Jesuits.[28] This is not to say that each instructor of logic merely presented the material using the same text. By no means was this the case. Based on the evidence in the form of surviving archival sets of notes, most instructors composed – and were expected to do so – their own lectures, differing to various degrees in detail from each other while remaining within an accepted Aristotelian framework.[29] These differences, stemming, most likely, from differences in the Jesuit teaching of logic elsewhere in Europe, has led recent investigators to conclude

---

[25] Generally regarded as the first step in this process was Peter's decree through the Holy Synod – effectively the ministry of religious affairs – in November 1721 that the sons of clergymen should study in the religious schools.
[26] Bulgakov (1843), 67.
[27] Simchich (2016), 17–18; Simchich (2009), 77.
[28] "Javorskij's scholarship was purely scholastic. ... He knew the classics well, but he was much more attracted to medieval and modern Jesuit scholasticism, from which he borrowed his preaching style with its rhetorical effects, historical anecdotes and fantastic references to natural history." Pypin (1902), 194.
[29] Simchich writes that there are approximately 80 such specimens that have been taken to be student notes. Simchich (2009), 34.

that there was more originality in those courses than was really the case.[30] The instructors at the Kyiv Academy, where there was a high turnover, attended various Jesuit-led institutions in Europe.[31]

The next topic of concern after logic, extending for approximately ten months, was physics, which formed the largest component of the two-year philosophy course. Again, the lectures were structured in accordance with Aristotle's treatment of the same as found, not surprisingly in his *Physics, On the Heavens, On Generation and Corruption, Meteorology*, and *On the Soul*. Of particular interest were issues associated with matter, form, and privation (for example whether matter can exist without form). This discussion was drawn largely from the first book of the *Physics*. The second book of Aristotle's *Physics* formed the basis of the lectures dealing with the Greek philosopher's definition of nature, asking, for example, whether nature itself is an active or passive principle. After this, the course typically turned to an analysis of cause – what is it and what are the types of causes. Among other topics addressed were the essence of motion, whether an infinite could exist and whether an infinite division is possible. However odd it may appear to us today, metaphysics was the briefest part of the two-year philosophy course lasting as it did less than one month. Judging from the surviving manuscript-notes, the topics addressed were again drawn from Aristotle's *Metaphysics*, for example, the difference between being and essence, substance and accident.[32]

The regular and systematic teaching of ethics in Kyiv actually began relatively late – only in 1737. Naturally, this is not to say that it was not touched upon earlier than this in other courses, and we should note that Feofan Prokopovich, a major figure whom we shall discuss shortly in more detail, was the first to teach ethics at the Kyiv Academy, which he did in the 1706–1708 academic sequence and that Stefan Kalinovs'kij (1700–1753) also taught an idiosyncratic ethics course in 1729–1731.[33] Ethics in the early eighteenth century was not a required component

---

[30] For example, one historian writes, "The professors of the Kyiv-Mohyla Academy in the eighteenth century tried to take into account the experience of their predecessors ... seeing the anti-scholastic orientation of their utterances, the often dualistic nature of their philosophical views. Thus, the democratic tradition of teaching generated in the listeners' minds a steady desire for independent thinking, from time to time a push to a different mind-set, to a critical attitude toward Orthodoxy, and even to a departure from faith." Shkurinov (1992), 45. There is little basis for this author's claims. In fact, the opposite is evidenced not just by the surviving notes but also by the number of prominent clerics that emerged from the Kyiv Academy.

[31] Simchich (2009), 76, 89.

[32] Simchich (2016), 20–22.

[33] Simchich, possibly in contradiction with his later statement, wrote that ethics "was taught systematically only after 1729 starting with Stefan Kalinovs'kij." See Simchich (2009), 48. To be sure 1737 was later than 1729, so it is possible there is no contradiction here. Kachuba writes that

of the philosophy course. Consequently most professors simply ignored it or did not see the need to introduce it. Others managed to devote some attention to the topic if there was free time after the presentation of dialectic, logic, and natural philosophy. Consistent with what we just saw, the ethics that was taught not only contained many Aristotelian elements – a concentration on virtues and vices, but to be sure also of the moral good and of happiness and bliss – but was also structured along Aristotelian lines. Whereas Kalinovs'kij taught ethics in the spirit of scholastic Aristotelianism while trying to cover as much as possible all topics mentioned in the *Nicomachean Ethics,* Prokopovich held that ethics is the study of customs. The purpose of ethics as a subject matter in school was to teach the rules of good behavior.[34] Since ethics was taught by various individuals and, unlike the course in logic, varied considerably over the years, the time spent on the subject could vary from one to three months.

The dispute between the Latin and the Greek "parties" continued to play out in Moscow in the early eighteenth century with the forceful addition of another "party," a Protestant-oriented theological direction. Nonetheless, the general picture concerning the teaching of philosophy was much the same in these early years in Moscow as in Kyiv. Sophronios Leichoudes in 1690–1691 taught a course in philosophy, which, as in Kyiv, consisted of logic and natural philosophy. And as in Kyiv the presentation of logic contained problems connected with the theory of argumentation, i.e., the rules of dialectical disputation and the skillful framing of questions and answers. A second section on the treatment of logic was specifically entitled "Preliminary Questions Concerning the Entirety of Aristotle's Logic," which included a discussion of the significance of logic and its divisions. The third section was entitled "Explanations and Questions on Porphyry's *Introduction,*" which was a standard logic textbook in medieval Europe. This section ended with a look at Aristotle's *Categories* and the first chapters of the first book of his *Analytica.*[35]

In his course on "natural philosophy" presented in 1691 the other brother, Ioannikios, spoke of problems associated with matter and motion, causality, space and time, finitude and infinity, continuity and discontinuity drawing his information from both physics and chemistry. Make no mistake, though, these presentations were not abstract, narrowly focused treatments of the subject matter

---

based on archival material ethics was taught to some extent by Kalinovs'kij in 1730, Eronim Mitkevich in 1734, and Syl'vestr Kuljabka in 1739. See Kashuba (2006), 100. Cracraft writes, "Prokopovich appears to have been the first and for a century almost the only professor of philosophy at Kiev to teach the subject." Cracraft (1978), 56.
34 Semikras (2019), 37.
35 Panibratcev (1997b), 9.

as we find them in university classrooms today. Ioannikios made it clear at the start that whereas his lectures were in accordance with the doctrines of Aristotle they were being presented with the help of the Holy Spirit so as to be fully in accordance with Orthodox Christianity.[36]

1.3 Lopatinskij's Defense of "Two Truths"

Peter the Great's 1701 decree shifted the center of Russia's education system, such as it was, from Kyiv to Moscow even though the school in the former continued for a time to supply Moscow with personnel for both the academy there as well as for the Church's administrative units.[37] All of the instructors at the Moscow Academy were graduates of Kyiv, but one of the earliest, who stands out, in particular, for special attention was Fedor (Feofilakt) L. Lopatinskij (~1680–1741). After studying at the Kyiv Collegium, he reportedly went for additional study to Poland, Italy, and Germany. He possibly returned to teach at his alma mater in Kyiv, but his stay there in any case had to have been rather brief. In 1702, he appeared in Moscow and began lecturing in philosophy in 1704 as well as theology in later years. He also served as rector for a time.[38]

Lopatinskij structured his philosophy course along the traditional lines of the time to include "dialectic" or logic, natural philosophy (i.e., physics), metaphysics, psychology, and mathematics. He banished ethics to a third year of philosophical studies, which, as mentioned, was previously only a two-year sequence at the academies. Lopatinskij's course reflected his training in scholastic Aristotelianism and followed it in terms of both style and content.[39] His division of philosophy into theoretical and practical may not be surprising, but his inclusion of logic in the latter certainly is unusual to the contemporary reader. The reason given for this is that logic provides information about the structure of our mental activity, which in-

---

36 Smirnov (1855), 61.
37 Sukhova (2013a), 25.
38 Panibratcev (1997b), 14. The very first years of the new century before Lopatinskij's arrival were dismal for the effectiveness of philosophical instruction. The rector of the Academy from 1703–1704, Iosif Turobojskij, another graduate of Kyiv and who taught philosophy there, probably did not teach philosophy in Moscow. In fact, remaining in Kyiv he visited Moscow only for short stays. His presence in Moscow was on an invitation from Peter as part of the 1701 decree.
39 "We will not slavishly adhere to the ancients, although we respect all philosophers, in particular Aristotle. Accordingly, we do not swear allegiance to anyone. We are all friends, but truth is dearer. The philosopher is obliged to rationally state his opinion and not rely on authority." Lopatinskij (1997), 213.

cludes the human will. Our minds are by nature prone to delusion and oscillate regularly between truth and falsehood. The task of logic is to get the mind oriented to affirming the truth. It is comparable to a tool that allows us to distinguish truth from falsehood. But the point of knowledge is to motivate us to act. Thus, practical philosophy had, in his eyes, a priority over theoretical philosophy.[40]

As we might expect from those writing at this time, their works were by no means strictly secular. Indeed, Lopatinskij held to a doctrine of "two truths," a position widely attributed to Averroës, although whether Lopatinskij was aware to any extent of the pedigree of his belief is unknown. In any case, he held that there is one truth given to us from Scripture and Revelation and another acquired through reflection. Theologians are concerned with the former; scientists, in a broad sense, with the latter. In this, Lopatinskij hoped to stake out for himself a measured independence from religious dogma. But he cleverly avoided transgressing the scientific sphere when discussing religious dogmas. We need not try to determine how closely he adhered to or departed from strict Thomism, but Lopatinskij certainly was aware of such later medieval philosophers as Duns Scotus and William of Ockham. We should bear in mind that Lopatinskij's writings were not intended to be original works that contributed to world philosophy. His intent was merely to teach established thought. Although today we look on rationalism and empiricism as contending expressions of modern European philosophy, we should not forget that the representatives of both philosophical directions were not academics and their writings played only a marginal role in the academic world in their own time. Rather than being surprised by Lopatinskij's admission of seemingly old-fashioned Aristotelianism, we should be struck by his frank mention and therefore awareness, although perhaps only cursory, of Descartes. Yet what is surprising is that although Lopatinskij acknowledged Descartes' position in the forefront of the "newest" philosophical directions, his overt concern is not with Descartes' subjectivist stand, but with the Frenchman's natural philosophy. Lopatinskij saw Descartes as an advocate of Democritus' atomism with the proviso that Descartes differed on whether atoms are divisible. Unfortunately, Lopatinskij's notes end here after writing that he would return later to the issue of whether Descartes succeeded in amending the Greek's conception of matter.[41]

Lopatinskij served for a comparatively lengthy period as rector of the Moscow Academy persevering through crises including the high turnover in instructors and acute deficiencies in the number of staff. He cooperated over many years with So-

---

40 Lopatinskij (1997), 209. He structured his argument along scholastic lines with theses and contrary theses.
41 Lopatinskij (1997), 213.

phronios Leichoudes in preparing a Slavic translation of the Bible. Like Javorskij, Lopatinskij generally supported the reforms of Peter and delivered patriotic sermons in connection with hostilities against Sweden, then a major European power. However, a gulf began to widen between those who could and those who could not abide what they considered to be secular interference in ecclesiastic matters. Peter indulged to the end Javorskij's criticisms out of consideration of the latter's rigorous defense of Peter's military exploits.[42] Javorskij additionally voiced support for the content of Peter's reforms, just not for the manner in which they were being carried out. However, neither Javorskij nor Lopatinskij chose to remain silent over the pro-Protestant inclinations of Peter and his leading ideologist Prokopovich. At the time of his death in 1722 Javorskij left behind an anti-Protestant tract *Kamen' very* [*The Rock of Faith*], aimed chiefly at Prokopovich and which attempted to rebut Protestantism's objections to Orthodoxy and Catholicism by appealing to Scripture, tradition and the resolutions of Church councils. Lopatinskij took it upon himself to edit and publish this work in 1728.[43] Whereas Javorskij never fully encountered the wrath of Peter and his associates, a gradual estrangement between the two resulted from the former's protest against state intervention in the Church's fiscal affairs and his speech in 1712 in praise of the Tsarevich Aleksej Petrovich, who was not, to say the least, on the best of terms with his father. As a result of that speech Javorskij was forbidden to preach.

Lopatinskij's own anti-Protestant outlook did not sit well with the German court circles after Peter's death. He was arrested in May 1735, though released after interrogation on condition of house confinement and forbidden to conduct religious services. He was arrested a second time in December 1738, accused of malicious, obscene, and impudent reasoning and criticism, and kept in a gloomy dungeon in the Vyborg castle north of St. Petersburg for three years. Upon his release, he returned to St. Petersburg, where he lived in the archbishop's residence until his death six months later.[44]

---

42 Florovsky (1979), 121. This is not to say that all was well between Javorskij and Tsar Peter. A gradual estrangement between the two started already in 1712 when the former denounced among other things Peter's divorce and marriage to his mistress, showing support for the Tsarevich Aleksej.
43 Gary Hamburg accurately summarizes, "In form, the book owed much to the Scholastic tradition of theological inquiry; in content, its greatest debt went to post-Tridentine Western thinkers who spelled out Christian teaching on issues of dogma, and defended those dogmas against the 'heretical' beliefs of Protestant theologians." Hamburg (2016), 261.
44 Lopatinskij's successor in the role of teaching philosophy at the Moscow Academy was Stefan Pribylovich (?-?). A Pole by birth, Pribylovich taught for four years, after which he lived in a Kyiv monastery. There, in 1716 the monks accused him of heresy. Instructed to go to St. Petersburg to translate or correct some ecclesiastic works, he was again charged with heresy.

1.4 Peter the Great's Ideologist

The most influential and thus most important figure from the first estate in Petrine Russia was undoubtedly Feofan Prokopovich (1681–1736), a Ukrainian raised by his uncle, who was a rector of the Kyiv Collegium, where the young Feofan studied until 1698.[45] He then went for additional study to Poland and subsequently Rome, returning to Kyiv in 1702 after a pause in Protestant Germany that remains controversial today. We mentioned above that Prokopovich taught a somewhat innovative course in ethics already in the first decade of the eighteenth century. He also taught a course in rhetoric and hermeneutics, for which a manuscript entitled "De arte rhetorica" has survived and which relies fundamentally on Aristotle, particularly his *On Interpretation*.[46] Prokopovich's writing style, understandably, was heavily indebted to scholasticism even when he departed from scholastic doctrine and, in particular, Aristotle to whom he frequently referred regardless of the topic and whose views he virtually always summarized before engaging in any discussion.

In 1708, Prokopovich taught a course on natural philosophy and in 1712–1716 theology. Not all of the notes for these courses have survived intact, but based on what has we can come to an overall picture of his teaching and overall philosophical conception.[47] In the years 1705–1706, Prokopovich taught philosophy, which at the time uniformly started with dialectics. Not unlike earlier and later professorial manuals or notes preserved at the Kyiv and Moscow Academies, Prokopovich's texts cover such basic topics as the rules of elementary logic, the division of concepts and judgments, rules of debate, the types of argument, and how to conduct an argument. There is little controversial or interesting in this.[48] However, we can tentatively conclude that he, in effect, dismissed what today we call "psycholo-

---

[45] The first name "Feofan" was his chosen monastic name in honor of his uncle Feofan. The family name "Prokopovich" was his mother's maiden name as well as that of his uncle. The real name of the young "Feofan" appears to have been Elysei Tsereis'kyi. See Ivanov (2020a), 60. Much has been written over the years about Prokopovich, undoubtedly, owing not just to his theological positions, but to his political allegiance with Tsar Peter and the reformist official circles. For this reason, we need not linger long on him apart from his position in the history of Russian non-secular philosophy.
[46] For the Latin text, see Prokopovich (1961), 228–333.
[47] Cracraft has urged a bit of caution here, writing "Prokopovich's supposed philosophy lectures, on the other hand, have only been printed in translated extracts without indication of the state or provenance of the manuscript sources." Cracraft (1981), 189.
[48] In their introductory essay to the Ukrainian translation of Prokopovich's philosophical works, the editors remark regarding this logic, "In its structure and problems, it resembles the logic of Melanchthon, a famous Protestant scholar and theologian." Kirik and Nichuk (1979), 61.

gism." The formal object of logic, he affirms, is "the operations of the mind directed toward the correct approach in a dispute."[49] The utility of logic is to help the human mind, so that it can reason without falling into error.

Of more interest than his dry exposition of logic is Prokopovich's physics. More than most professionally-trained philosophers even today, Prokopovich hailed the study of physics. Philosophy and physics complement each other, and he found it unsurprising that historically the two disciplines were not viewed as separate. Most historically eminent philosophers engaged in investigations that belong to what we now ascribe to the discipline of physics. Indeed, "the ancients respected physics more than any other part of philosophy, and only those were called philosophers who found happiness in the careful observation of nature."[50] As an Orthodox clergyman, he stressed the link between physical investigation and his religious beliefs and found no conflict lurking between them. Not only must physics be considered of use to moral philosophy, but "only with the help of physical observations can one know God, who judges people by merit."[51] Prokopovich, certainly, did not want to depart from Scripture, but the divine revelation given in antiquity was to those with a low level of scientific knowledge compared to today. Such revelation needs constant improvement and, when necessary, correction from science. Since God created the laws of nature as well as gave the Scriptures, there can be neither conflict nor contradiction between the two. Neither is to be accepted at the expense of the other. A perceived conflict means that the Scriptural text is to be interpreted allegorically. We can find a concrete example of this approach in Prokopovich's treatment of the heliocentric model of the solar system, which, as we know, was controversial in early modern Europe and proscribed in Kyiv and also at the Moscow Academy, where Javorskij taught.[52] Prokopovich in the mentioned course briefly described the models of Ptolemy, Copernicus, and Brahe. He voiced distinct reservations about the Copernican system for its apparent conflict with Scripture and expressed tepid approval of Tycho's.[53] "Most modern philosophers have adopted this system, precisely because it is the easiest to solve many complex questions of astronomy and in turn does not contradict Scrip-

---

49 Prokopovich (1980), 50.
50 Prokopovich (1980), 116.
51 Prokopovich (1980), 117.
52 Ivanov (2020b), 50. In 1704, Javorskij came out against Copernicus, who preached, according to the former, that "the heavenly wheels do not lie, stand, or come to a stop" as he falsely claims. Quoted in Morozov (1971), 42.
53 Obolevitch (2015) provides much general information on the reception of Galileo's conception of the solar system in Russia.

ture."⁵⁴ In this, we see Propokovich's melding of science with theology, of observation with the sacred text.

Prokopovich's position developed gradually toward an acceptance of the heliocentric model and with it of an allegorical interpretation of the Bible. In his theology course given in the second decade of the eighteenth century, he announced that he was willing to accept Copernican heliocentrism despite a literal reading of the Bible if scientific evidence supported the former. "If," he said, "the disciples of Copernicus as well as other scientists, who defend the movement of the earth, can bring valid physical and mathematical arguments to prove their opinion, then the texts of Sacred Scripture that speak of the movement of the sun cannot serve as obstacles. These texts should be understood not in a literal, but in an allegorical sense."⁵⁵ Prokopovich, in time, fully accepted heliocentrism as he himself was able to utilize a telescope in Russia. Make no mistake, though, already upon his return from abroad, Prokopovich firmly rejected scholasticism and sought to replace the Aristotelian Thomism in Kyiv's curriculum with essential elements drawn from Protestant authors.

Prokopovich's prominent position in Russian intellectual history has little to do with his "innovative" theological positions but much to do with his political thought and defense of Peter the Great's reforms including those of the Church. Since these relevant documents stem from after his call to St. Petersburg after leaving the Kyiv Academy in 1715, they are not germane to our topic here. Nevertheless, if their traditional attribution to Prokopovich is correct, they further enhance our understanding of his idiosyncratic Protestant-oriented Orthodoxy. Peter commissioned Prokopovich to compose the *Dukhovnyj reglament* [*Spiritual Regulation*], which was published and enacted in 1721. This document led to the creation of the Holy Synod, which in effect made the governance of the official Orthodox Church a governmental department with the tsar at its ultimate head.

Typically thought to be of more interest and importance, however, is the *Pravda voli Monarshej* [*The Right of the Monarch's Will*] of 1722, which sought to ground the monarch's absolute rule.⁵⁶ Set in opposition to what he viewed as Catholicism's Papocaesarism, Prokopovich defended Caesaropapism as sacred and absolute. Peter had previously that year decreed that the reigning monarch had the sole

---

54 Prokopovich (1980), 290.
55 Quoted in Pypin (1902), 201. Pypin observed, "Here for the first time Prokopovich recognized the position of science, which then was considered a great heresy (as we saw was Javorskij's opinion)."
56 To what extent Prokopovich single-handedly, if at all, wrote this tract has been questioned recently. See Cracraft (1981).

and absolute right to declare a successor, a stand that departed from Russian tradition. Prokopovich's text, thus, can be seen as an apology by drawing on Biblical sources and European political philosophy.[57] He understood the social contract between the tsar and the people as the transference of all power and the bestowal of unlimited rights from the latter to the former. The endowing of this authority is sanctioned by the Deity.[58] And after quoting Hugo Grotius's definition of sovereignty, Prokopovich added, "Thus, every Autocratic Sovereign need not keep to human law, since he is not to be judged for transgressing it. He must adhere to God's commandments, and for their transgression he will answer only to God. He cannot be judged by man."[59] In short, all political power in Prokopovich's scheme comes from God.

Through his service to Peter and advocacy of reform, Prokopovich's "star" rose quickly. Even before the death of Javorskij, who as president of the Holy Synod nominally was the highest figure in the Church, Prokopovich, as vice president, was the de facto head. With Javorskij's death, Peter delegated authority to Prokopovich, leaving the highest office nominally vacant. From his position he was able to exercise enormous influence. Later, during the comparatively brief tenure of Peter II (1727–1730) and with Javorskij's posthumous charges in his *Rock of Faith*, Prokopovich's position became increasingly tenuous. However, with Peter II's death and the elevation of Tsarina Anna, Prokopovich acquired virtually dictatorial power, filling the Synod with subordinates. His policy of subordinating the Russian Church to state interests continued past his death and, in fact, strengthened.

1.5 From a "Second Scholasticism" to Wolffianism

Whereas Peter Mohyla in seeking to staff his Collegium with competent teachers had little choice but to encourage the best and the brightest to study at Jesuit-run institutions in the near-abroad, the need to continue the practice became less acute with the gradual maturation of the Kyiv and Moscow Academies. This coupled with Prokopovich's infectious disdain for scholasticism and sympathy for Protestant attitudes toward physical science and Biblical-interpretation meant fewer and fewer students went to the predominantly Catholic countries of Europe for further study. Indeed, by the mid-eighteenth century the practice be-

---

57 The seminal examination of *Pravda voli* is Georgij Gurvich's work, written while still a law student at Jur'ev (Dorpat) University.
58 Gurvich (1915), 15
59 As cited in Bugrov (2020), 102.

came rather uncommon. Instead, study at universities in Protestant-dominated locales became favored.[60] Already under Prokopovich's influence, the professorial manuals began to introduce questions and concerns that Lutheran theologians, in particular, had been raising. Now, there was greater emphasis on questioning accepted tenets such as, for example, whether natural religion was sufficient for salvation. The study of philosophical ethics, which, as we saw, had been quite neglected, also drew more attention by mid-century.

There were, of course, those who fundamentally adhered to Aristotelianism. One of the last was Vasilij Kryzlanovskij (?-1760), who has come down to us by the name Vladimir Calligrapher, owing to his work in the Moscow Academy's calligraphy shop. Calligrapher was a converted Jew and a graduate of the Kyiv Academy. He taught theology there for a time starting in the mid-1750s. Although he often referred to Leibniz, his own position harkened back to an earlier era. Owing to criticism in one sermon of the Moscovite reliance on icons and prayers to the apostles rather than to Jesus, Calligrapher was accused of heresy (of Lutheran and Jewish "prattle") and transferred to the Yaroslavl Theological Seminary, where he too ran into conflict being charged with teaching Protestantism and Judaism. Nonetheless, his course and text at the Moscow Academy were virtually the last expressions of scholasticism there. Henceforth, the Wolffian system as presented by Friedrich Baumeister came to be taught.[61]

Although there were signs of dissatisfaction with scholastic Aristotelian philosophy in the first half of the eighteenth century, the speed with which its teaching was abandoned at both the Kyiv and Moscow Academies was amazing. We can see this evolving trend arguably most distinctly from the titles of the philosophy courses at the Kyiv Academy. In a course beginning in September 1743 the philosophy professor Mykhailo Kozaczynski specifically stated that his intent was to lead a course in Aristotelian philosophy using "the model of the peripatetic school."[62] His successor for the two-year philosophy sequence in 1745–1747 was Gideon Slo-

---

[60] Ivanov (2020a), 48. We should not overlook, though, that the Catholic Church began questioning the value for itself of allowing Orthodox students to temporarily convert in order to attend Catholic schools only to find them reverting to Orthodoxy once back in their homeland. Protestant universities in Germany had no religious requirement, thereby obviating the charade the eastern Orthodox students had to play. Ivanov (2020a), 74.

[61] "In general, the textbooks of Baumeister on logic, metaphysics, moral philosophy, and physics were known in Russia from the middle of the century." Pavlov (2017), 79. Indeed, a translation from the Latin of his *Institutiones metaphysicae* was published in 1764. Another translation of his ethical thought appeared in the 1780s.

[62] Simchich (2009), 223. Simchich, however, also states that Kozaczynski used as his textbook at this time one by the Capuchin friar Gervasius Brisacensis. He adds that although the work was written by a Franciscan it was not typical of someone who was in the mold of Duns Scotus.

mins'kiy, who in the title of his own course specifically stated that it would be set out as much as possible in conformity with the logic commentary of Bartholomäus Keckermann (c. 1572–1609), a German Calvinist.[63]

Continuing in rapid succession, the successor of Slomins'kiy was Hryhoriy (Georgij) Konys'kiy (1717–1795), who taught philosophy from 1747–1751. Konys'kiy taught the two-year philosophy course twice, the first of which we know only by its title but which clearly referenced the "peripatetics" and Aristotle.[64] The title of the second variant, from 1749–1751, the notes for which have survived, makes no mention of Aristotle or the "peripatetics" but wishes to present the course merely as a general introduction in philosophy. We can tentatively conclude from this alone that by 1749 Konys'kiy became dissatisfied with a strict adherence to Aristotelian scholasticism, even though the influence remained. He structured his course along the lines of late scholasticism but acquainted his students also with the ideas of Descartes, Leibniz, Wolff, and Baumeister. As with the Aristotelians, he ascribed great importance to sensory perception, i.e., to observation and experience, but the goal of knowledge of truth, he held, cannot be achieved without the natural light of reason, an expression we will come across again. Konys'kiy placed great trust in this "natural light" to lead us to a correct view of possibly disputable problems. "If you ask him [an uneducated person] about things that are simple and familiar to him, then the power of natural light will lead him to the right answer even concerning those matters about which he never thought."[65] However, Konys'kiy rejected the Platonic doctrine of recollection as being counterintuitive, writing "If knowledge were acquired by means of recollection, then a blind person could acquire knowledge about flowers."[66]

Konys'kiy was aware of the Copernican model of the solar system and found it compelling. But as with the early Prokopovich, Konys'kiy ultimately sided with Tycho Brahe's model, seeing in it a way to account for observation without introducing a conflict with Scripture. Konys'kiy stated, "it is considered to be more useful in solving astronomical difficulties and does not contradict the Holy Scriptures, or, probably, it is safer, since it approaches the solution more cautiously."[67] He recognized the issues that arose from an acceptance of the geocentric model that re-

---

[63] Simchich writes that Keckermann was much closer both in terms of content and style to the Aristotelianism presented in the courses given by Jesuits than that of many of the other Protestant academics. Simchich (2009), 143.
[64] Kashuba (1979), 32.
[65] Quoted in Kashuba (1979), 99.
[66] Quoted in Kashuba (1979), 98.
[67] Quoted in Kashuba (1979), 78.

quired numerous movements of celestial bodies, but in the end he preferred to remain agnostic.

Unusual for the time, Konys'kiy taught ethics immediately after logic, seeing the former as a practical application of the latter, and his treatment of ethics displayed a great debt to Aristotelianism, while condemning "the rubbish of Aristotle's interpreters."[68] Unlike some at this time, he held ethics to be the "science" of morality, one that could be discussed in a secular context. Its purpose is to teach the rules of good behavior, and elaborating rules ethics seeks and proves conclusions utilizing principles and axioms.[69] Consistent with virtue theory, he held that such qualities as dignity and honor are not innate, but that they were developed in one's personality through gradual improvement and work. Indeed, one purpose of education is specifically such a development. Nevertheless, unlike some narrowly focused theologians, Konys'kiy thought that the greatest happiness in earthly life, a state of bliss [*blazhenstvo*], could be a goal in life and thus be discussed in ethics, even though the lasting attainment of such bliss is difficult owing to a human trait to be ceaselessly dissatisfied with all goals once obtained.

Unfortunately, Konys'kiy's teaching career came to an abrupt halt with his appointment to a bishopric in what is today Belarus, where he found the local priests had little education and whose ability to write was sorely deficient and then only in Polish. Inquiring further, he sought assurance in time that all priests had in his view at least a minimal ability to read and preach the Christian message.

Konys'kiy's abrupt departure from the Kyiv Academy left Grigorij Shcherbac'kij (1725–1754) to teach philosophy there from 1751 to 1753. Shcherbac'kij had himself studied at the Academy from 1737–1743 and had been already teaching other subjects since 1749. His tenure in Kyiv is notable for his shift to a pronounced Cartesian orientation in his philosophy lectures with a focus on the textbook of the Sorbonne professor Edmond Pourchot. As was traditional, Shcherbac'kij's course consisted of logic, physics, metaphysics, and ethics. His innovation was his support for a Cartesian foundationalism, holding that our knowledge must be more firmly secured than sensual evidence permitted. This foundation was the natural light of reason, and in this we see a continuation of an aspect of Konys'kiy's viewpoint, only with greater emphasis on this "light." Unlike Konys'kiy, Shcherbac'kij was willing to entertain the concept of innate ideas, which "by the will of God is given to our thinking from birth."[70] Although these ideas are always at our disposal, they need to be

---

68 Kashuba (2006), 103.
69 Kashuba (2014), 227.
70 Shcherbac'kij wrote, "Descartes in his Third Meditation deduces the existence of God from the fact that all people have by nature an innate conception of God, which can come from nowhere except from God Himself." Quoted in Latin as well as rendered into Ukrainian in Stratij (2002), 167.

brought forth and substantiated by the correct method, i.e., by whether they meet the test of being clear and distinct. As with Descartes, Shcherbac'kij held that the *cogito ergo sum* was unquestionably true. In Shcherbac'kij's phrasing, this statement became: "Because we cannot doubt the fact of doubting or thinking, we exist."[71] Following the Cartesian method of affirming the existence of what is a clear and distinct idea, Shcherbac'kij believed that on reflection we can substantiate the existence of the self, of God, and of the external world. The attainment of clarity and distinctness of an idea insures its veracity. Thus, the first step in philosophy is to isolate clear and distinct ideas from those that are doubtful. Not only is the idea of my existence one such clear and distinct idea, but so is that of God. He wrote,

> The idea of God, though imperfect, is clear and distinct, because we know God as the highest perfect being. Our conception has attributes that can answer to God alone and not to another, namely, to be infinite, eternal, omnipotent, etc. Thanks to these attributes, it is possible to picture God clearly and distinctly, but not to know God so perfectly as to understand. Finite thinking cannot comprehend the infinite perfections of God.[72]

In short, we understand an idea when we are able to "picture" it clearly and distinctly. And as with Descartes, Shcherbac'kij held that God is the guarantor of the objective significance of our thinking. The subjective counterpart of this significance is, again, clarity and distinctness. The most important element in his position for the future development of Russian religious philosophy is Shcherbac'kij's belief that the mind can directly connect to a "natural light" within us and thus to God. As a member of the Orthodox clergy, we should not be surprised that he tied his understanding of Cartesianism to his theistic position. A correct understanding of the "natural light" of reason, namely, that ideas are clear and distinct, is insured by God, Who placed them originally in our mind. Since these ideas correspond to reality, they have ontological significance.[73]

Shcherbac'kij had little confidence in sense data to provide truth. Although it is needed for much knowledge, it is also the source of error. For that reason, he was dismissive of scholasticism owing to its alleged reliance on empirical data. Scientific work in the true sense should not be aimed at the gathering of information from the senses, but at developing and substantiating our innate ideas, which when clear and distinct cannot err. Discursive cognition, he held, only creates the requisite conditions for the cognition of divine ideas, which must be realized

---

71 Stratij (2002), 157–158.
72 Quoted in Stratij(2002), 161.
73 Stratij (2002), 164.

intuitively by illumination from reason. This illumination is primary, but analysis is necessary for a more complete understanding. Shcherbac'kij additionally added that there is knowledge that is both obvious and indubitable but yet incomprehensible. We can, for example, know the veracity of the Holy Trinity with its three hypostases but have little understanding of it. Such religious truths are given to us through divine suggestion.

Shcherbac'kij appealed to Descartes' ontological argument for the existence of God arguing that since we have a clear and distinct idea of a supremely perfect being and since necessary existence is contained in this idea, God exists. Nevertheless, Shcherbac'kij was unwilling to jettison scholasticism in its entirety, for he also adduced Thomistic arguments as well. Referring to Aquinas, Shcherbac'kij wrote, "Since all beings cannot be contingent, one must be absolutely necessary, independent, and on which all depend, in other words, God."[74] Having thereby established God's existence and being certain of his moral perfection, we can conclude that the persistent phenomena of other beings similar to us cannot be illusory, for God would not so deceive us.

Shcherbac'kij's advocacy of Cartesian foundationalism was short-lived. In 1753, the Holy Synod ordered him to take up a position as professor of theology at the Moscow Academy. His death the following year meant he exercised virtually no lasting influence there. However, even if he had not come to a premature end, it is doubtful that his Cartesianism would have found welcoming soil in Moscow. Even his teaching in Kyiv gained no recognizable following. His departure brought to the fore David Nashchins'kij (1720–1793), who had attended the Kyiv Academy and then had studied with Baumeister during his stay in Saxony. Nashchins'kij at first used the Wolffian textbook of Johann Winkler, *Institutiones philosophiae universae*, which contained a somewhat complete exposition of Wolff's general philosophical system including physics.[75] However, due to Shcherbac'kij's intervention, Nashchins'kij changed to a 1744 edition of Baumeister's *Institutiones philosophiae rationis: method Wolfii conscriptae*, which became a popular text, thus, again narrowing the gulf between philosophical education in Imperial Russia and western Europe. Baumeister's text became generally accepted for a considerable time thereafter and mandatory from 1764 upon the instruction of Samuil Mislavskij.[76] This popular presentation of the Wolffian system did not include physics, which

---

74 Stratij (2002), 167–168. Stratij again provides the quotation in Latin as well as in Ukrainian.
75 Simchich (2009), 143. Kozlov'skij (2011), 55.
76 Shpet (2008), 87. As with many other figures mentioned in this chapter, Mislavskij is a subject of some controversy. Later in life, he helped with the publication of Prokopovich's works and promoted the Russification of the Kyiv Academy.

as we saw occupied a prominent position in the two-year academic sequence. As a consequence, physics was taught using various other texts.

1.6 The Reign of Wolffian Philosophy in the Academies

The teaching of philosophy in the second half of the eighteenth century has received far less scholarly attention than the first half of the century. The pedagogical hegemony of scholasticism dissolved, being replaced by a Wolffian rationalism. Baumeister's books were accepted as suitable textual guides at the Moscow Academy owing to their expository clarity and good use of Latin, qualities that made for their wide acceptance in Germany as well. The shortage of available copies, however, became an obstacle, calling for a remedy to be sought in the local publication in 1777 of a compendium entitled *Baumeisteri Elementa philosophiae recentioris*.[77] Yet despite the supposed advantages of Baumeister's texts and system over the displaced scholasticism, which Prokopovich had earlier denounced for its intrinsic difficulty and "empty disputes,"[78] their success was questionable. The archbishop of Moscow Platon Levshin (1737–1812), who certainly did not look kindly on Aristotle and scholasticism, remarked that in his eight years of managing the Moscow Academy "he had not encountered among the students of philosophy a single one worthy of it."[79] Levshin appears to have concluded from this that a habitual attachment to scholasticism prevented the students from seeing the advantages of the new system.[80]

The inadequacy of Baumeister's texts to provide a complete picture of philosophy, as that was understood at the time, was a matter of concern for the rector and professor of philosophy at the Moscow Academy from 1775 Dmitrij E. Semenov-Rudnev (1737–1795), who came from the first estate, studied at the Moscow Academy and later in 1766 was one of the four Academy students to be sent for additional training to the University of Göttingen for several years. Upon his re-

---

77 Concerning the availability of Baumeister's texts, Chizhevskij states, possibly on the contrary, that at the Kyiv Academy, "in the second half of the eighteenth century Aristotle was finally expelled from the Academy by the Wolffian School, especially Baumeister, whose textbooks were imported in large quantities from Germany." Chizhevs'ki (2005), 110. The basis of Chizhevskij's statement, originally from 1927, is unclear, but it may well have been Shpet, who wrote several years earlier that Baumeister was so popular that his work was reissued in Moscow in 1777. Shpet (2008), 89. We have just indicated that this indeed was the case.
78 Smirnov (1855), 157.
79 Smirnov (1855), 299.
80 On what basis young students could come to the Academy with an "habitual attachment to scholasticism" [*privychnaja privjazannost' k skholastike*] is unclear.

turn, he became first a tutor and then a professor. As with many of the other figures we have seen, his teaching career lasted only a short time. During his time teaching, he, as well as the others, was a professional educator, not a professional philosopher in the contemporary sense of a researcher. However, he was surely interested in career advancement and as a cleric that meant advancement in the ranks. He was appointed to a bishopric in 1782, but during his time at the Moscow Academy he introduced a number of recent German-authored works, such as Samuel C. Hollmann's *Jurisprudentiæ naturalis prima*, Georg Bilfinger's *Dilucidationes philosophicae*, and Israel Canz's *Meditationes philosophicae*. He also lectured for the first time on the history of philosophical systems using Brucker's text, *Historia critica philosophiae*.[81] Semenov-Rudnev was obviously deeply indebted to Wolffian philosophy. Over the coming years and decades, philosophy instructors at the Moscow Academy used a series of Wolffian works such as Ludwig Philipp Thümmig's *Institutiones philosophiae Wolffianae*. Curiously, another book also mentioned in these academic reports is the Jesuit Berthold Hauser's *Elementa philosophiae ad rationis et experientiae*.[82]

The status of ethics, which was introduced late into academic instruction, as a sub-discipline in philosophy, remained ambiguous. The Holy Synod in 1786 instructed morality to be taught along the lines of Samuel Pufendorf's *On the Duty of Man and Citizen*, which already had been translated into Russian in 1724. Levshin, apparently, considered this to be sufficient for Academy students, and there was no further need for separate secular instruction in morality, since it was to be gleaned from Scripture and was subject matter for a theology, not a philosophy, class.

By end of the eighteenth century, the teaching of philosophy in the academies was firmly established along Wolffian lines. The Holy Synod in 1798 decreed that the subjects to be taught in philosophy would consist of a short history of philosophy, logic, metaphysics, morality, natural history, and physics. Baumeister's textbook was to be used for teaching logic, metaphysics, and the history of philosophy. A text by the Dutch scientist Pieter van Musschenbroek was first used late in the century for teaching physics, but changed in the early nineteenth century to a

---

[81] Smirnov (1855), 300. A Russian translation appeared in Moscow in 1788. Concerning Brucker's history, Lewis White Beck wrote: "Though episodic rather than developmental in its structure, Brucker's work tended, nevertheless, to evaluate other systems of philosophy by the standards of Wolffianism." Beck (1969), 277–278.

[82] To what extent any of the philosophy instructors availed themselves of Hauser's massive seven-volume, 5213-page work is unclear. Most likely, it was simply glanced at and included in a report for embellishment.

quite general text by the French "natural philosopher" Mathurin Jacques Brissonc.[83]

By the end of the century, the Orthodox Church saw the need to reform and systematize education in the theological schools in the Russian Empire, which in addition to the two academies had a number of lower-level seminaries. Philosophy was offered, however, in only four of the twenty-six seminaries before 1750. Only in the 1780s did the other seminaries begin to offer a full course in philosophy and theology.[84] The aim of introducing philosophy into the seminaries was merely to acquaint students with basic terminology. Only later in the next century was a course on the history of philosophy introduced into the curriculum and this merely to provide some sense of the spirit of philosophical discussion.

Change came slowly, but in 1797 the seminaries in St. Petersburg and Kazan were transformed into theological academies. The Holy Synod took up the general issue of education in the theological institutions, the result being a decree that then served as a charter for the schools. Although the document did not envision any specific reforms, it enshrined that philosophy was to be taught for two years, theology for three, and the academies were to hold open debates on philosophical and theological topics twice per year. Yet, the need for reform lingered and was further agitated by the creation of a secular educational system in the early years of Tsar Alexander I's reign. A commission was formed headed by Mikhail Speranskij in November 1807 and presented in six months a general plan, which received confirmation by the Tsar and which called for a hierarchical system of parish schools – district schools – seminaries – academies.[85] A permanent commission established in June 1808 developed a charter to be implemented on a trial basis in 1809 at the St. Petersburg Theological Academy. Based on input from the Academy's rector and the experience of the first graduating class, an amended charter was adopted and confirmed in 1814.[86] The intention all along had been to open one academy at a time in recognition of the shortage of qualified teaching staff and in order to avoid the huge anticipated cost of the transformation. Thus, the Moscow Academy opened in 1814 under the new charter. The Kyiv Academy opened only in 1819. The opening of the fourth of the planned academies was delayed until 1842.

The intent behind this reform program was to raise the educational level of the theological academies up to that found in other European countries. Among those on the commission, there was no uniform opinion concerning the role of phi-

---

[83] Nikol'skij (1907), 354. Unfortunately, Nikol'skij does not provide the specific titles.
[84] Pavlov (2017), 22.
[85] Florovsky (1979), 177.
[86] Pavlov (2017), 137.

losophy in the future academies. Speranskij, on the one hand, advocated for a "reawakening of reason," for a "lively" discussion of religious topics and of the philosophical problems associated with them. The powerful Archbishop Feofilakt (Rusanov) (1765–1821), on the other hand, believing that the fundamental questions that Speranskij had wished to be discussed had already been resolved by religion and earlier philosophy, advocated for a stress on aesthetics and literature.[87] Speranskij's withdrawal from the commission could have resulted in Feofilakt gaining the upper hand in the ultimate outcome of the deliberations had not Speranskij succeeded in securing a professorship for the Hungarian-born Ignaz Fessler, a fellow freemason, whose knowledge of philosophy far surpassed Feofilakt's.[88] All of the mentioned parties, however, soon disappeared from the scene. According to the final revised charter signed by Tsar Alexander, the teaching of philosophy in the academies was to present and compare the most well-known philosophies, coming to some common principle, one that those in the academies already knew. The charter read:

> The professor must be quite confident that neither he nor his students will see the light of a higher philosophy, of a one, true philosophy, if he does not find it in Christian teaching. Only those theories are fundamental and correct that are rooted, so to speak, in the truth of the Scriptures. For truth is one, but delusions are innumerable. ... Everything that does not agree with the true reason of the Holy Scriptures is essentially false and a delusion and must be rejected without mercy. Those, so to speak, who split reason from faith enter into a false philosophy.[89]

In this way, the hope was to maintain the level of philosophical education as to be on a par with western Europe while remaining true to the mission of the Orthodox academies. This was understandable given that the schools were theological institutions. Of more interest to us here is its condemnation of the divorce between faith and reason which rationalism had one-sidedly overcome but which was unjustified. "Those who split reason from faith enter into a false philosophy." The philosophical remedy was to be sought in antiquity.

---

87 Cvyk (2013), 45–46; Nichols (1978), 81.
88 Fessler's tenure at the St. Petersburg Academy was brief. For more information on this, see Nemeth (2017), 85–86. Fessler taught metaphysics and logic for a time at the university in Lemberg (today's Lviv), where one of his students was another Hungarian-born, Petr Lodij, who recommended him to Speranskij. See Avgustin (2018) for much more information.
89 Proekt (1823), 54, 5.

> Among the ancient writers, Plato is the first pillar of true philosophy. The professor is to seek a solid philosophical doctrine in his works and in the best of those of his followers. Among the latest philosophers, those who adhere closest to him should be preferred.[90]

This ultimate reliance on Plato and Neoplatonic philosophy would remain central not only to the philosophical doctrines emanating from the Russian theological institutions, but to all of classical Russian idealism until its termination with the Bolshevik *coup d'état*.

---

[90] Proekt (1823), 54–55. Plato is the only philosopher specifically mentioned by name in the charter. Gavriil in his *History of Philosophy* would repeat the same words with regard to Plato as found in the charter. See Gavriil (1840), 21.

Part I: **Under the First Charter**

Chapter 2
The St. Petersburg Academy Under the First Charter

At the start of the nineteenth century, Imperial Russia had four theological academies and thirty-five seminaries. Although the level of instruction at the academies and seminaries differed, they were intentionally organized along the same lines. The St. Petersburg Academy, being located closest to the seat of governmental power, was chosen as the first of the four academies to be remodeled precisely owing to its proximity to the seat of power. Unlike earlier, the four-year academic course was to have the first two years devoted to philosophy, literature, history, and mathematics, whereas the third and fourth years were to be devoted to theological subjects (dogmatic and moral theology, canon law, church history, etc.) and the study of languages. The principal purpose of this school as with so much of higher education in Russia, theological as well as secular, from the government's viewpoint, was to provide a thorough training for young men in order for them to enter into administrative positions in the church and the government.

2.1 First Turbulent Years

The St. Petersburg Theological Academy, like those in Kyiv and Moscow, could trace its origin back to an educational institution that predated its official designation as an academy. In 1721 – and thus during the reign of Peter the Great – a school was founded at the Alexander Nevsky Monastery and reorganized first in 1725 as the Slavic-Greek-Latin Seminary with enrollment approaching one hundred. It was renamed in 1788 simply as the Main Seminary with the best students from the other seminaries being sent to it. In 1797, it was again renamed as the Alexander Nevsky Academy. The transformation of the Nevsky Academy into the St. Petersburg Theological Academy did not mean that it became "overnight," as it were, a western research university, albeit with an underlying religious foundation. With the arguable exception of the first philosophy professor with professorial credentials, the Academy after this transformation saw a series of caretakers as professors and instructors who contributed little to nothing of note to philosophy. Upon its opening, Fr. Evgenij (Andrej E. Kazancev) was appointed to teach philosophy.[1] However, with Fessler's arrival from Berlin and his demonstrated knowledge of philosophy, Evge-

---

[1] Fr. Evgenij had previously served as an instructor of philosophy at a seminary.

nij was shifted aside to allow Fessler to teach philosophy in addition to Hebrew. Unfortunately, Fessler's six-month tenure at the Academy was too short to leave much more than an impression on his students of what a knowledgeable professor in his subject matter should be. Accused of atheism and of teaching unsanctioned philosophical directions, Fessler, not being a member of the Orthodox Church, was indeed an anomaly in an explicitly Orthodox religious educational institution.[2]

With Fessler's forced resignation in 1810, Johann von Horn, a graduate of Jena, received the appointment as professor of philosophy. He taught at first in accordance with the accepted Wolffian texts of Brucker and Winkler. However, von Horn found these guides to be inadequate in part owing to their age and supplemented them in his lectures with his own "reasoning."[3] Professor von Horn's dissatisfaction with Winkler's text led the supervisory commission to instruct the rector Filaret (Vasilij M. Drozdov) along with von Horn to find a suitable text. The search settled on Franz S. Karpe's Latin text *Institutiones philosophiae dogmaticae*.[4] Alas, this quest was resolved only in 1814 just when von Horn had departed. Owing to Napoleon's invasion of Russia, the situation in St. Petersburg was some-

---

[2] To be fair, Fessler was neither a rationalist nor a Kantian. There were distinct traces of mysticism both in his writings and reportedly in his lectures. Chistovich (1857), 193. Called before the official supervisory Commission, it found Fessler's summary to be obscure and in April 1810 demanded another, clearer one set out along Wolffian principles and terminology. Archbishop Feofilakt (Rusanov) found Fessler's summary to be quite understandable but based on principles "harmful to the Church, to the fatherland, and dangerous to students." Speranskij defended Fessler, remarking that the summary was completely consistent with the academic charter concerning the teaching of philosophy. He told Fessler to defend himself by citing passages from the Church Fathers supporting all the points made in his summary. This proved to be of no avail. Fessler was accused of idealism and pantheism and dismissed in July 1810. Avgustin (2018), 184–185. Shpet, commenting on this incident, wrote that Feofilakt's remarks on Fessler's summary were "a vivid indication of the philosophical ignorance at even the highest ranks of the Russian clergy." Shpet (2008), 190.

[3] He expressed himself in an official report: "As for a philosophical system, I had to explain the limitations of Winkler's textbook to the students. As soon as I became convinced that to achieve the goal of the Academy, which is oriented to the education of clergy and teachers in religious institutions, I recognized the need to do more than was demanded. ... Philosophy today is almost completely different from what it was one hundred years ago." Quoted in Chistovich (1857), 199.

[4] Chistovich (1857), 200. Concerning Karpe's book, Filaret wrote, "I, a professor of philosophy and Greek literature, have examined Karpe's book and found it to be useful for theological schools. ... This book was first supposed to be used in the seminaries. However, since the lack of a textbook is now even more noticeable in the Academy than it is in the seminaries, Karpe's book can be used as a classical text in the academies, leaving the old one [Winkler's] for the seminaries." Filaret (1885), 115–116.

what chaotic, and von Horn in any case was often absent from the capital during the final two years of his appointment.[5]

The successor to von Horn was Irodian Ja. Vetrinskij (1787–1849), a former student of Fessler's. Awarded a *magister*'s degree in 1814, Vetrinskij was one of twelve graduates of the St. Petersburg Academy to be retained as an instructor.[6] In 1819, he was promoted to full professor. Vetrinskij's principal contribution to philosophical education was his Latin text *Institutiones metaphysicae*, published in the capital in 1821. In the meantime, the choice of Karpe's book was deemed inadequate, and Winkler's text was once again resurrected.

Vetrinskij explained that his own text on metaphysics, the first such text under the new academic charter, was an attempt to determine its principles in the face of Kant's assault on the very possibility of metaphysics. "As far as the issues under consideration allow, I have decided to follow in Kant's footsteps not with the aim of swearing to his ideas, but in order to restore in part the rights and power of reason."[7] Vetrinskij asserted that there are three "transcendental" ideas: the world, the soul, and God. The aim of metaphysics, which proceeds from the idea of an absolute being, is to show the complete harmony of all things in the universe despite their apparent contradiction.

Composed under the watchful eyes of the commission, we can hardly expect Vetrinskij's text to be an original work or to depart significantly from the general thrust of Wolffian philosophy.[8] What it does offer and show is an officially sanctioned train of thought, or philosophical outlook, that was totally in keeping at the time with Russian Orthodoxy. In Vetrinskij's telling, the idea of harmony found in rationalism and even in Kant is the source of the principles that allow

---

[5] The brief (five pages of text) autobiographical sketch von Horn later published of his time in Russia merely mentions his employment as a professor of philosophy, providing no details. De Horn (1843), 3.

[6] At this time at the Academy, there were three degrees offered: *kandidat, magister,* doctor. Unlike later, the *magister*'s degree was awarded not based on separate written work or the completion of extra course work, but on the reports of reviewers without the active participation of the student. The awarding of a doctoral degree was also based on reviewers' reports as well as on a decision of the Commission of Theological Schools. See Sukhova (2010a), 22.

[7] Quoted in Pocci (2018), 58; Pozzi (2017), 73.

[8] According to the academic charter, "No new book may appear in the theological schools that does not adhere to the usual classical teaching except with the approval of the academic administration and with the knowledge of the supervisors." *Proekt* (1823), 8. Much of Pozzi's work is devoted to displaying Vetrinskij's debt to a 1807 text *Elementa metaphysices* by a now forgotten Gottfried Immanuel Wenzel (1754–1809). She writes, "A comparison of the texts also shows how relevant the Wenzelian meditation was for the Russian author, who seems to have been inspired by Wenzel in determining the same internal articulation in his own *Institutiones*. Pozzi (2017), 79.

for the construction of, for example, geometrical figures that apply so readily to nature. These principles lie within us *a priori* and stem from a higher mental power (*superior quaedam vis animi*)⁹ than that of representation or imagination. This higher "power" is what Vetrinskij called "reason" (*ratio*), which is concerned not with existence, but with possibility. If reason offers ideas that yield harmonious knowledge, they should be held to be reliable principles upon which the sciences, i.e., empirical knowledge, can build. If these "rational" ideas have explanatory power but still leave room for doubt concerning them, we call them "hypotheses."

The apparent contradiction between the two general principles underlying materialism and idealism, viz., that all is matter and that all is ideal respectively, must not distract us from conceiving the world as a unity. Despite the fact that many philosophers historically chose one path or the other, they err in that "one cannot in any way know what the human mind is, if one does not establish at the same time what the material world is, and how the spiritual world together with the material constitute a unity."[10] Whereas it may appear that Vetrinskij concluded with a unity, he actually believed metaphysics as an ideal construction starts with the idea of an absolute being. In his mind, pursuing either materialism or idealism merely illustrates the indispensability of the highest idea, that of the absolute being. Owing to the universal harmony of the universe, philosophy of nature cannot be divorced from philosophy of the mind and vice versa. "Although it has objective nature as its main concern, the philosophy of nature cannot be completely abstracted from subjective nature. Objective nature must be constructed so that it includes at the same time subjective nature."[11] It must follow the law of continuity so that there are no breaks, ascending from the formless in nature to where the subjective begins. In reverse, the philosophy of mind should be constructed, again according to the law of continuity, starting from the summit of the universe and descending to where objective nature begins.

Vetrinskij began his metaphysics with a conception of the universe as a synthesis of the objective and the subjective into a unity of a higher order, not a purely formal unity in which, to use Hegel's well-known expression against Schelling, all cows are black, but a unity that can be understood. There are limits, however, to what can be understood. The concept of an infinite being cannot arise from finite impressions stemming from our ordinary experience. Rather, it is based on principles and laws within the mind itself. The concept of an infinite and perfect

---

9 Pozzi (2017), 77.
10 Quoted in Pozzi (2017), 81.
11 Quoted in Pozzi (2017), 83.

being and our certainty in that concept's objective veracity follows from a "principle" [*principio*] of existence by virtue of a necessary argument. Here, we find an affirmation of the nexus between ontology and what the author takes to be a logically necessary conclusion of an argument. Vetrinskij affirmed, "The concept of existence arises not from the senses and not from experience. It is found originally in the very nature of the intellect. Therefore, it is not *empirical*, but *pure*."[12] In this, we see that Vetrinskij, unlike Kant, did not hesitate to determine existence from the intellect alone without the least contribution from empirical means.

Since all of the phenomenal world is finite and yet we have a notion of the infinite, viz., of infinite space and time, their origin must be ascribed to a spontaneity of cognition in contrast to a receptivity of impressions. On the other hand, Vetrinskij withheld extending space and time beyond the phenomenal world. "The idea of space and time can have no other origin than spontaneity and efficacy. ... However, they are inapplicable beyond the phenomenal world, i.e., beyond the limits of the sensible. Consequently, they cannot be applied to absolute entities."[13] Here, we see a possible debt to Kant.

Vetrinskij's text, though suitable for the Academy in terms of sheer content and for its lack of originality, had limited success. It serves us as an indication of what was allowed. With a tightening of the censorship in the years ahead, it undoubtedly would have been deemed unacceptable.[14] The mathematician Dmitrij I. Rostislavov (1809–1877) described in his memoirs that although instructors had borrowed material from Vetrinskij's text, the text itself was a testimony more to its author's wish to be pedagogically effective and love of the discipline rather than to its advancement. Having spent a decade at the Academy, Vetrinskij conclud-

---

12 Quoted in Pozzi (2017), 96.
13 Quoted in Pozzi (2017), 87.
14 Shpet wrote, "Professors, and especially professors of philosophy, were subjected to the stupidest censorship, and their pitiful teaching was conducted in an atmosphere of denunciations, persecutions, and absurd references to the true direction to which they must hold." Shpet (2008), 67. The law in force at this time reads: "The Censorship has the duty to examine books and writings of all kinds meant for public consumption. The chief object of this examination is to furnish society with books and writings contributing to a true enlightenment of the mind and the education of morals and to remove books and writings contrary to this intention. ... The Censorship Committee and in particular each censor in examining books and writings is to observe that there is nothing in them contrary to Divine Law, the Government, morality, and the personal honor of any citizen. A censor, having approved a book or writing that is contrary to this prescription, having broken the law, is liable to the extent of the importance of the violation." *Sbornik postanovlenij* (1862), 85, 88. Thus, the censor himself bore a legal obligation to enforce the censorship law lest he be charged with a criminal offense.

ed that philosophy there could only play the role of a servant to theology. Finally in the mid-1820s, bored with his teaching at the Academy, which Rostislavov stated Vetrinskij did not conceal, he left the Academy for a position as a censor for a time.[15] Nevertheless, he continued to publish much over the coming years, albeit outside the confines of the Academy.

During much of the 1820s, Vetrinskij was assisted and succeeded by several individuals, none of whom published on philosophy perhaps for fear of retribution. Rostislavov summed up the atmosphere at the St. Petersburg Academy at the end of Tsar Alexander I's reign in 1825.

> The reactionaries primarily attacked philosophy, forbidding instructors from employing their own notes for teaching and designated Baumeister's text for use in the seminaries and Winkler's at the academies. In my opinion, this was worse than if the teaching of philosophy were completely eliminated. The students ultimately did not know what philosophy as a discipline was, and the texts of Baumeister and Winkler aroused an aversion to it.[16]

Aleksandr Vvedenskij, who much later taught at St. Petersburg University, wrote concerning the atmosphere in the late 1820s,

> It got to the point that one professor of philosophy was afraid to read his own notes (although he actually could do so) and deliberately read directly from the book without providing explanation and in a monotone voice, this to avoid persecution from less talented colleagues.[17]

Several individuals taught philosophy at the Academy in the second half of the decade, none of whom produced – or perhaps more accurately were able to produce – any philosophical treatises. Andrej S. Krasnosel'skij (1796–1830) served as an instructor from September 1823 and then was promoted to ordinary professor, teaching the history of philosophy. His premature death from tuberculosis cut short the promise that Rostislavov saw in him owing to his knowledge of the German language.

Krasnosel'skij was succeeded by his own brother, although with a different family name (!), Dmitrij A. Vershinskij (1798–1858). A graduate of the St. Petersburg Academy, the first in his class, he taught Greek for a time before transferring to philosophy. His contribution to Russian scholarship lies in having translated Georg Ast's *Grundriss einer Geschichte der Philosophie*, Heinrich Ritter's *Geschichte*

---

[15] Rostislavov (1872), 181. A Soviet-era encyclopedia entry states that Vetrinskij "was forced to leave" the Academy. Nikolaev (1989), 438.
[16] Rostislavov (1872), 178.
[17] Vvedenskij (1901), 12–13. Vvedenskij did not name the individual.

der pythagorischen Philosophie, and Carl Bachmann's *System der Logik.*[18] In 1835, he was appointed to serve as the priest at the Russian embassy's church in Paris, where he remained until 1846.

2.2 Sidonskij's *Introduction* and His Fate

The only too obvious intellectual straitjacket imposed on philosophical instruction could not last long and gradually the instructors introduced their own comments again in class. Of course, these were guarded in full recognition that should they veer far from the sacrosanct texts of Baumeister and Winkler, introducing some bit of novelty whether orally or in writing, the consequences would be severe. The clearest and most well-known example of this is the fate of Fedor F. Sidonskij (1805–1873), a graduate in 1829 of the St. Petersburg Academy, who was given an appointment the following year to teach philosophy. Sidonskij reportedly lectured in Russian, rather than Latin, which was an unheard of novelty at the time.[19] At first, he taught the history of philosophy, then later metaphysics, moral philosophy, and natural law. Already in the first instance, he lectured using his own notes, finding the approved guides unsatisfactory. This soon aroused the ire of the authorities, namely the Academy's rector Venedikt Grigorovich and Vasilij Kutnevich, a member of the commission supervising the theological academies. Sidonskij was forced to defend his teaching at a public examination, which allegedly turned into an "ugly scene."[20] In Rostislavov's opinion, Sidonskij's principal crime, however, was that he presented his lecture with enthusiasm and thus aroused within the students a desire to think for themselves.

Had Sidonskij been fired or simply shifted away from teaching philosophy, his name would hardly be remembered today. However, in 1833 he published a book, *Vvedenie v nauku filosofii* [*Introduction to Philosophy*], which Mikhail Vladislavlev (1840–1890), the future son-in-law of Dostoevsky and a later professor of philosophy at St. Petersburg University, characterized as "the first, independent work of a Russian scholar in the field of philosophy."[21] For this work, Sidonskij was given that year the secular Demidov Prize, an annual award by the Russian Academy

---

[18] Chistovich (1857), 318.
[19] Rostislavov (1872), 179.
[20] Poljakova (2009), 29.
[21] Vladislavlev (1874), 51. Shpet too had high praise for Sidonskij's book writing that it was "positively the best book on philosophy to appear in Russia up to 1833. It is distinguished by its originality and stands in general alongside some of the tendencies of contemporary German philosophy." Shpet (2008), 178.

of Sciences.²² That Sidonskij, a priest, should receive such a prize and for an independent work in philosophy only further added to the fury of his superiors and aggravated his already tenuous position. Further irritating those in the clerical estate was the fact that Sidonskij had submitted his manuscript for censorship approval not to the sanctioned theological committee, but to a secular censor.

In his *Vvedenie,* Sidonskij saw philosophy as concerned with determining the ultimate and final truths as well as the rules for human action. But because of the sheer scope of its task, Sidonskij held that philosophy must be open to modifications. Whereas it formulated the ultimate problems, it had not found a satisfactory solution to them. The various methods posed by recent German philosophers – Fichte, Schelling, and Hegel – could not stand up to a rigorous comparison with those employed by natural scientists. To come to a correct conception of the task of philosophical investigation, we must, on the one hand, look at how that task has been conceived historically, the "abstract speculations" offered in both antiquity and modernity.²³ Sidonskij recognized that Russia has had in its history sparse instances of genuine philosophizing. When it began to turn to doing so in earnest, Russia became carried away by the "transient West."²⁴ On the other hand, we must recognize that we cannot limit our investigation to the opinions of a single individual or even a single school of thought. Our disciplines can also aid us. Sidonskij singled out, in particular, theology. Without recognizing the truths contained in divine revelation, philosophy's path is long, extremely tedious, and hardly secure. Yet, theology also needs firm philosophical foundations in that without them the educated and curious mind cannot be satisfied and will wander.²⁵

---

22 Later recipients of the prize were the mathematician Chebyshev and the chemist Mendeleev. In awarding the prize to Sidonskij for his book, the Academy wrote, "His style is everywhere noble, consistent and fully corresponds to the dignity of the subject. In terms of oratorical eloquence and strong expression of feelings, it rises in places even above simple didacticism. But most of all we praise his style for its clarity and correctness, especially since these qualities are so rarely found in philosophical works proper." Quoted in Poljakova (2009), 90. The competition for the prize at the time was Aleksandr Galich's 1834 *Kartina cheloveka.* Galich at the time was at St. Petersburg University but was stripped of teaching duties owing to his alleged preference for German Idealism over the accepted Christian doctrines. The Academy turned for a decision to Adam Fischer, who held the chair of philosophy at St. Petersburg University, who wrote, "Galich's anthropology certainly does not belong, as does Sidonskij's work, among those books that elevate and ennoble the entire literature of some discipline. ... If the former belongs primarily to philosophy, the latter is intended for readers who have had no education in philosophy. Consequently, these works must be judged by different standards." Otchet (1835), 104–105.
23 Sidonskij (1833), 10.
24 Sidonskij (1833), 314.
25 Sidonskij (1833), 289–290.

Sidonskij tells us that even though we can say philosophy is the scholarly or systematic solution to the chief tasks of the cognizing mind, this definition or determination of philosophy is vague. For we do not know what these tasks essentially (*suschchestvo*) are.[26] This did not prevent him, however, from affirming that the three basic (*korennykh*) tasks of philosophy are:
(1) the "determination of the mode of being of the entities in the real world,"
(2) "an explanation of the validity and formation of our cognitions," and
(3) "an indication of the fundamental laws of our activity."[27]

We can easily recognize that these three tasks encompass the subdisciplines of ontology, epistemology, and ethics, although Sidonskij did not describe them as such.

Sidonskij asked us to notice that the three tasks, which are so important in life, do not have equal primacy. Being an Orthodox priest, we might think that he would accord priority to ethics as did, in a sense, both Kant and Solov'ëv. However, despite expressly acknowledging morality as of the greatest importance in our lives Sidonskij believed we must "concede the right of primacy to the question of the nature of what is," i.e., to ontology. The reason he gave is that any treatment of ethical issues "depends, or at least should depend, on a particular view of the life of the universe and of mankind's place in it."[28] This awarding of primacy to ontology over epistemology and ethics will be a characteristic feature of much of Classical Russian Idealism, and not just in the theological schools. Sidonskij, in contrast, accorded a measure of primacy to epistemology over ontology in writing that to solve ontological problems we must turn to a "rigorous examination of the nature of the mind before [*do*] determining the laws by which our human actions must be conducted."[29] This proposed sequence of philosophical tasks must have shocked Sidonskij's ecclesiastic superiors.

Another item that surely must have angered Sidonskij's superiors, arguably above all others, was his advocacy of philosophy as a discipline independent of others including theology. For Sidonskij, this "freedom" meant that not only must it be conducted apart from theological considerations – though it certainly may lead to

---

26 Sidonskij (1833), 23.
27 Sidonskij (1833), 20.
28 Sidonskij (1833), 22.
29 Sidonskij (1833), 24. Disagreement exists concerning how to understand Sidonskij's three basic tasks. Jakovenko asserted that for Sidonskij "the human mind constantly concentrates on three problems: natural laws, the laws of human activity and, nature and the objective significance of human knowledge." Jakovenko (2003), 47. Jakovenko wished us to understand that these are Sidonskij's three tasks, but it is hard to see how one could derive the problem of natural laws from these tasks either individually or even together.

them and be in congruence with established tenets of theology – but its concerns and problems arise naturally and not as a result of religious ponderings. The danger Sidonskij posed from the perspective of his superiors was that officially the goal of teaching philosophy was to show the impotence of the human mind "to discover truth by its own means without the light of Revelation."[30] For Sidonskij, philosophy's independence is one of its two characteristics or traits, the other is a detachment from and an ascendance over the objective, thereby allowing for a clear consciousness. Sidonskij used the term "loftiness" [*vysprennost'*], which Shpet understood as transcendentality in a pre-Kantian sense.[31] Sidonskij somewhat explained this characteristic as allowing philosophy "to rise above everything objective."[32] This coupled with his idea that philosophy seeks that which is constant and aspires to perfection forms the work needed to accomplish the first basic task, the determination of what is. Sidonskij recognized, though, that it will remain an ultimately doomed goal. Its achievement would require a perfect, God-like mind. But this goal of philosophy, however noble and unachievable in practice, yields fruit of no less significance, viz., self-consciousness, making it worth all human efforts over the millennia.[33]

Just as Descartes held that preconceived opinions had to be set aside in order to lay the foundations for rigorous philosophy, so Sidonskij thought ideas held to be true at the outset of a philosophical inquiry can pose an obstacle to determining truth. We must turn to doubt, just as did Descartes, in order to proceed. Doubt is both necessary and useful in philosophy as a device. Nonetheless, there are limitations. Doubt serves at the start to clarify and expand our efforts to find firm truths, but it must not attack anything sacred – doubting without restraint.[34] The question, then, turns to where can our inquiry start, where can we find what is indubitable and requires no proof. For Sidonskij, there is no surer starting point than the ordinary experience of the world. "The point of view of ordinary (especially) empirical understanding, the world of experience perceptible to everyone, seems to me the best foothold, the most reliable starting point for philosophical thought."[35] Sidonskij recognized that his proposal is contentious, that he could well be criticized from both a philosophical as well as a religious standpoint. But he was convinced that sincere philosophical investigations will yield the truths of Christianity and that a reliance on reason alone at the expense of experience will

---

30 Chistovich (1857), 295.
31 Sidonskij (1833), 201; Shpet (2008), 181.
32 Sidonskij (1833), 201.
33 Sidonskij (1833), 127–128.
34 Sidonskij (1833), 155.
35 Sidonskij (1833), 345.

yield only skepticism and atheism. "The mind has its laws, its ideas, but a difference between these ideas, particularly correct ones, would be impossible without the guidance of experience. Experience must confirm the validity of speculative representations."[36] The mind and external nature are inseparable in that without externality the mind would be unable to recognize that its concepts have an objective significance and, consequently, would not know them.

Make no mistake, Sidonskij's *Vvedenie*, as Vladislavlev pointed out, is not a philosophical treatise, but only an introduction to genuine philosophizing. "No system or specific doctrine is expounded in it. It provides an indication of different paths of human thought and of possible directions in developing philosophical questions."[37] Sidonskij recognized and appreciated that there were different paths toward the goal of truth. Philosophy is one, and religion is another. Despite their differences, these paths should not be set against each other as if in opposition. Writing to and for his expected audience of theologians and theology students, he admonished his readers not to fear philosophical inquiry as though that would lead the mind to delusions and the heart to evil. The normal development of the mind, undoubtedly, will lead to the true faith, and, given the importance and necessity of that faith, the mind will not reject it. On the contrary, the human mind will appreciate all the more the truths of religious faith after an independent investigation arrives at them.[38]

Clearly, Sidonskij's superiors were not impressed with his argument. A review committee was established to examine the *Vvedenie*. However, since it had been approved by the secular censorship and had won the Demidov Prize, Church administrators feared that drastic action would only exacerbate relations with the secular authorities. Sensing his tenuous position, Sidonskij requested a transfer in mid-1835 to teach Hebrew at the expense of philosophy, but the request was denied.[39] By an act of the most influential figure in the Russian Orthodox Church at the time, Metropolitan Filaret (Drozdov) (1782–1867), Sidonskij was banned from teaching henceforth at Church schools.

Sidonskij's dismissal and assignment to a parish church in St. Petersburg did not mean he entirely abandoned either his standpoint or his philosophical activi-

---

36 Sidonskij (1833), 362.
37 Vladislavlev (1874), 51.
38 Sidonskij (1833), 188–189.
39 Even earlier, Sidonskij had been transferred to teaching French, but this failed to mollify his critics. They charged him with indulging in philosophy while translating French pieces. See Poljakova (2009), 30. That there are many more details concerning Sidonskij's tenure at the St. Petersburg Academy hardly needs to be stated, none of which are pleasant. Still, they add little to the overall picture of the nature and quality of philosophy propagated at the time there.

ties. Shortly after publishing his *Vvedenie*, he published a translation of Schultze's *Psychische Anthropologie*. He continued to support various scholarly activities connected with the Theological Academy and the Academy of Sciences, to which he was elected as a full member in 1854. Most importantly, when the teaching of philosophy was reinstated at St. Petersburg University after a decade of banishment, he was invited to an instructorship and awarded an honorary doctorate by the University in early 1864.

2.3 Three Epigones: Drozdov, Nadezhin, Kedrov

In 1835, there appeared a small volume on moral philosophy written by a former Academy classmate of Sidonskij's, Aleksej Drozdov. Whether the position advocated in the *Attempt at a System of Moral Philosophy* represented Sidonskij's own views on the topic is unclear, although his name listing him as the editor prominently appeared in it. This alone may lead us to think that he had a hand in the formulation of the stance taken therein. The volume neither attracted much attention upon its publication nor did it garner much subsequently – arguably for good reason.[40] Nevertheless, it stands in sharp relief to Sidonskij's reasoned plea for the pursuit of philosophy independently of religion and its concerns.

Drozdov distinguished what he called "active philosophy," i.e., ethics, from "speculative" or theoretical philosophy. The former is concerned with the idea of the moral good in humanity, whereas the latter deals with the idea of truth. Active philosophy deals with eternal and invariable laws of morality and right (*pravo*); speculative philosophy deals with eternal truths. Despite distinguishing active from speculative philosophy, they are merely two forms of one and the same discipline related to each other on the basis of a "so-called coordination."[41] Owing to this stand, each of them can independently strive for independence and completeness. It is in these ideas of coordination and independence that we can see, as it were, the hand or at least the touch of Sidonskij. Owing to them, Drozdov refused to grant primacy to speculative, theoretical philosophy over active, moral philosophy or vice versa, thereby refusing Kant's position according primacy to the latter.

Whereas from Sidonskij's viewpoint we may cautiously applaud Drozdov up to this point, he decisively links the development of modern moral philosophy to the

---

[40] The posthumously celebrated literary critic V. G. Belinskij reviewed the work, saying he had not read anything about it prior to his accidental discovery of it. Belinskij (1941), 84. Of course, given its contents he lambasted it for what he took to be its contradictory stances.

[41] Drozdov (1835), 4.

Christian religion. He wrote, "Modern moral philosophy owes its highest articulation and direction primarily to Christianity. If we would wish to remove from it everything that it has borrowed from Christian morality, we would rob it of all its strength."[42] However, if moral philosophy is to refrain from historical experience, as Drozdov proclaimed, how can it possibly "borrow" from Christianity, the appearance and rise of which is undoubtedly a historical phenomenon? Drozdov continued, claiming that moral philosophy is merely a systematic presentation of Christian morality, the goal of which is to raise the moral level of humanity. Drozdov's message was a purely religious one. The source of the moral good is not pure reason, but God, Who is also the original source of truth and beauty. The moral good is manifested in us as a love for God and humanity. Thus, a morally good act is at the same time a true and beautiful act.

Belinskij's observation that Drozdov's slim book received little notice is understandable. It broke no new ground and largely merely repeated the lessons its author had heard in Academy lectures. If philosophy were to continue along these lines, it would have no need of independent argument and reasoning. Christian doctrine has already indicated the path to truth and the moral good.

Another historically minor figure who felt some influence from Sidonskij was his former student Feodor S. Nadezhin (? – 1866),[43] who taught for a time at one of the theological seminaries and then went into the civil service. In his 1837 history of philosophy, he remarked that only in Germany do we find philosophy fully flourishing as a separate, forceful discipline. Only there do we find independent philosophical thinkers. And in Russia itself, what philosophy is taught is dictated by German philosophers. Nevertheless, Nadezhin found kind words for his former teacher, writing that Sidonskij's *Vvedenie* demonstrates independence, extracting philosophy's proper subject matter and particularly the solutions to its problems, from its history. "Having shown the methods involved in solving these problems as well as the nature of philosophical investigations along with their relation to other disciplines, Sidonskij establishes reason as the means to their solution."[44]

Nadezhin's subsequent (1845) work *An Attempt at a Science of Philosophy* demonstrated again the author's debt to Sidonskij, finding the basic traits of philosophizing to lie in its "loftiness (*transcendentalitas*) and independence."[45] Only by

---

42 Drozdov (1835), 8.
43 This figure should not be confused with Nikolaj I. Nadezhdin (1804–1856), who as editor of the journal *Telescope* was responsible for the publication of Chaadaev's "Philosophical Letter" and for which he was sentenced to internal exile.
44 Nadezhin (1837), 238.
45 Quoted in Kruglov (2009), 368.

distancing oneself from particulars can one judge the whole and direct one's philosophizing to what is common throughout, to laws and principles.

Belinskij, in an exceedingly short review, turned to Nadezhin's latest *opus*, and in his customary biting, but frank and accurate, style recognized its sterility and insignificance, features he found common to Russian philosophy books. Nadezhin had invited two contrasting principles into philosophy: the principle of authority and that of free rational thought. But he failed even to suspect that the two principles are diametrically opposed.[46] Belinskij surely would have found Drozdov guilty of the same oversight. The appeal to reason was half-hearted from the start. In Tsar Nicholas I's Russia, the principle of authority loomed supreme, whether in politics or thought, much as it would a century later under an even more ominous ruler.

A third disciple of Sidonskij was Ivan A. Kedrov (1811–1846), who received his degree from the St. Petersburg Academy and then taught philology at the Jaroslavl Theological Seminary. Just as Sidonskij, Kedrov thought "loftiness" to be the distinctive characteristic of philosophy that distinguishes it from other disciplines that study nature. This "loftiness" elevates it over all that is temporal and spatial. He saw the philosophies of the German Idealists (Fichte, Schelling, and Hegel) as leading to atheism or pantheism. Schelling's philosophy of nature, in fact, "is obviously a pantheistic doctrine," and pantheism is one of the greatest delusions of the human mind.[47] Kedrov read Schelling as promoting the idea that a single life pervades the universe and rejecting thereby the distinctiveness of human existence in creation and of our aspiration for moral or intellectual perfection. This, Kedrov could not countenance. Pantheism would strip us of our soul, but everything proves that we have one, particularly the moral law within us. Our very self-consciousness coupled with our innate feeling for other creatures like ourselves shows us that we have duties and responsibilities to them.

In addition to the empirical, we find the super-sensible, both in externality and within us. Kedrov held that we have a desire for this non-empirical, the "Infinite," presumably his expression for God, a desire "indelibly imprinted in the depths of our being" and which due to our physical limitations cannot be directly communicated to us.[48] Our a priori forms of thought prevent us from representing the Infinite, and our empirical senses cannot directly and immediately yield It. However, our understanding together with observation provide an excellent guide to discern

---

[46] Belinskij (1955), 643.
[47] Kedrov (1838), 37.
[48] Kedrov (1838), 63.

the ends, the purpose of everything, though we cannot penetrate into the essence of nature and grasp the Divine through the understanding.[49]

Kedrov could not believe that the Creator of the universe would have given us an irresistible and incomprehensible desire for truth and yet torment us by not ever allowing us to find it.[50] Such would be counter to God's fundamental goodness. But more important than the quest for scientific knowledge, for truth, is our moral sense, which lies in our soul and which alone can reveal the true significance of all of our theoretical questions. Morality alone provides our scientific investigations with worth. Kedrov, therefore, advised us to recognize that the fundamental task of our empirical studies is not to understand the essence of the universe, which is itself an impossibility, but to acquire the proper information that would allow for our moral development and perfection.[51] Kedrov, certainly then, accorded some priority to the empirical sciences over purely metaphysical speculation, but even those disciplines are to be conducted from a moral point of view. The human mind confined to the investigation of natural phenomena will often lose sight of their importance and meaning and will fail to recognize their source. Human indecision will result. Kedrov's 1844 *Course in Psychology* only reaffirmed his Christian ethicism.[52] A textbook intended for secondary schools, it, understandably sought not to derive metaphysical and theological insights, but presupposed them. The goal of life is moral perfection, which will be accompanied by a state of bliss. Although such perfection and bliss are unattainable in our earthly lifetime, we can and must strive as mightily as possible for them. Shpet ranked Kedrov's works below not just Sidonskij's, but also those of Nadezhin and Drozdov in philosophical value.[53]

---

49 Kedrov (1838), 15.
50 This view presumably would apply to all varieties of skepticism, but also to Kant's transcendental idealism.
51 Kedrov (1838), 17. In the sixth and final volume of his *History of Philosophy*, which was devoted to Russian philosophy, Arkhimandrit Gavriil (Vasilij N. Voskresenskij), a professor at Kazan University, summarized an unpublished text by Kedrov. Gavriil wrote that in it Kedrov, like Sidonskij, called "loftiness" the distinctive feature of philosophy, raising it "above everything spatial and temporal." Gavriil (1840), 156. We can look upon nature in two ways: either as limited or from a metaphysical viewpoint. Both are necessary. Without the infinite, there would be chaos. Since Gavriil wrote these lines during Kedrov's lifetime, he must have had privileged access to Kedrov's writing and been on familiar personal terms with him. Philosophically, much is presupposed in Kedrov's position as formulated by Gavriil. In any case, these thoughts had no discernible direct influence on subsequent Russian thought.
52 See Kedrov (1844).
53 Shpet (2008), 193.

2.4 Karpov's Psychologism and Defense of Orthodoxy

The most enduring professor of philosophy thus far at the St. Petersburg Academy was Vasilij Karpov (1798–1867). He completed his studies at the Kyiv Theological Academy in 1825 and then taught German and Greek for several years at the Kyiv Theological Seminary. He then taught French at the Kyiv Academy, doing so for two years before obtaining a position as instructor in philosophy and psychology there. In October 1833, he accepted a position as an instructor of philosophy at the St. Petersburg Academy on the invitation of the rector and in 1835 was appointed professor of philosophy, thereby becoming Sidonskij's successor. Karpov held this position until his death.

Apart from his Russian translations of Plato, on which he worked for decades, Karpov is best known – insofar as he is known, that is – for his 1840 *Introduction to Philosophy*.[54] He believed that in such an "introductory" text he could convey his own general position along with his conception of philosophy and its tasks. Karpov opined that the individual natural sciences investigate particular aspects of nature, but philosophy, unlike them, has no particular select domain of objects and topics of its own. Unlike the sciences, philosophy seeks to construct a general unified portrayal of all that is. To do so using the results of the sciences requires establishing the place of each vis-à-vis the others, the respective significance of each, and the connection between each so that they together form a harmonious whole.[55] In attempting to bring scientific results into a whole, the individual facts are still present, but their importance is diminished. What is of the greatest importance are the connections between these facts. Whereas in experience everything is isolated, a properly conducted philosophy rises above this isolation into the sphere of what Karpov called the "metaphysical." We see in this Sidonskij's conception of loftiness implicitly reintroduced and developed, albeit without a mention of either Sidonskij or even the term "loftiness" as such. Lest we misunderstand, Karpov distinguished the "metaphysical" from the "spiritual." The latter is that which does not manifest itself physically, and the two spheres, that of the physical and the spiritual, are set against each other with no bridge between them. Nevertheless, human experience shows that both are reflected and restrict each other in us.

---

54 Many, but not all, of the Platonic dialogues appeared in a Russian translation already in the 1780s, but with a small print-run. A translation of *Philebus* appeared in 1826 and of *Laws* in 1827 in a translation by Vasilij I. Obolenskij, a secondary school teacher of Greek. Karpov published a two-volume set of translations in 1841–1842. In 1863, he began to publish a corrected set of translations that included more but still not all of the dialogues. The four volumes that appeared then were followed by two published posthumously in 1879.
55 Karpov (1840), 24–25.

2.4 Karpov's Psychologism and Defense of Orthodoxy — 49

The third sphere or realm is that of the "metaphysical." It is neither physical nor spiritual. The "metaphysical" realm is not a thing in itself, but is the "kingdom of thought," organized from the purely formal representations of our I, or ego.[56] Since our cognitions stem partially from our I and partially from externality, respectively the purely subjective and the objective, cognitions combine the realities of both. Karpov ended his first numbered section of the *Introduction* with another philosophical somersault, saying that the object of philosophy is self-cognition (*samopoznanie*) and the investigation of everything on the whole as one being.

Karpov stated that in looking for the method(s) to be employed in the pursuit of philosophy we finally come to the truth that the "form" of philosophy is to be deduced from the very idea of philosophy, an idea acquired from an immediate and veridical intuition. In this respect, his train of thought bears a similarity to the "*cogito ergo sum*" of Descartes and to Frege's general properties of geometry.[57] Karpov himself likened his notion of intuition to the intuition of the moral force of Plato's idea of justice.[58] Had he said no more, we could ascribe to him a standard foundationalism. Karpov claimed that the fundamental principle can be neither a feeling nor even the idea of God. It must be a fundamental truth to which all agree; he proposed consciousness. "Consciousness, understood in a theoretical and moral sense (conscience) can rightfully be called the first truth. For everything that enters into the sphere of human life and that appears in it as ours, becomes so only under the condition of consciousness."[59] Of course, there is much here that needs elaboration. It is not evident, in the first place, how consciousness can be taken as a principle. The temptation to proceed from a disembodied or a transcendental consciousness is clearly not Karpov's intent. For he was highly critical of all such attempts, claiming that they lead to skepticism or pantheism.[60]

Despite Shpet's tepid praise for Karpov's work – he called it "fresher" than earlier tracts[61] – it is at best a mediocre undertaking. Karpov characterized his position as "synthetism" as against Kant's rationalism, Schelling's pantheism, and G.E.

---

56 Karpov (1840), 32. In order for these ramblings to be understood at all, they must be set against Schelling's speculations. So much is clear from Karpov's footnote: "Schelling, looking at the world from the side of Absolute Being, came to the conclusion that Divine thought is already being. In contrast, seeing the world in the human being, we must say the contrary, that being itself for us in matters of cognition is only *conceivable*." Karpov (1840), 32 f.
57 "In geometry, therefore, it is quite intelligible that general propositions should be derived from intuition." Frege (1986), 19–20.
58 Karpov (1840), 39.
59 Karpov (1840), 54.
60 Karpov (1840), 70.
61 Shpet (2008), 195. This faint praise is undoubtedly due to Karpov's elevation of consciousness, which conceivably, however incorrectly, could be construed as a step toward phenomenology.

Schulze's naturalism. Karpov revealed his real intent in writing that the one-sided conclusions and contradiction in the pantheistic and naturalistic systems show their hostility to the fundamental dogmas of Christianity and to astute political decisions based on natural moral demands. What relevance such hostility would have is not clear unless one presupposes that that hostility already precludes veracity. Of course, Karpov would hold precisely that presupposition. In Karpov's eyes, rationalism, in elevating the mind above truth, despotically pronounces on the place of the human mind in the universe. The goal of philosophy, understood as synthetism, is to determine the situation and the meaning of the human being in the world. In fact, "the goal of philosophy is to determine the place, significance, and relation of the human being in and to the harmonious being of the world."[62] This goal can be achieved only by first determining that universal harmony, by investigating the correlations between all that exists. Although couched in secular language – a quest for the all-encompassing law thanks to which everything exists – Karpov's conception was religious, not philosophical.

To his credit, Karpov avowedly was not averse to the sciences. He realized that their work would and had to continue. This did not mean that their endeavors were futile, but a sign that there was always more to be done. Likewise, that philosophy cannot attain its final goal is not to be taken as a sign of failure. "The triumph of the mind consists not in achieving final results, but in ceaseless striving for them."[63] Philosophy's unending quest for ever-elusive answers is already a sign of its triumph.

If Karpov had written no more than these extremely vague statements, he could easily have been neglected even in the annals, such as they are, of Russian philosophy. However, his turn to consciousness is of note, even though he understood it in a purely mundane sense. Yet, just as for the transcendentalists the essential structure of consciousness is the object of philosophical inquiry, so for Karpov the structure, though not essential, of the embodied consciousness is the key to all further philosophical study and branching from it the individual sciences. "A philosophical view puts its stamp on all the particular sciences that develop under its influence."[64] Whereas for Husserl the phenomenology of perception "sets forth the *necessary* system of structures without which it is *not possible* to think a synthesis of manifold perceptions as perceptions of one and the same thing,"[65] Karpov was content with a social-psychologistic view of consciousness

---

[62] Karpov (1840), 100–101.
[63] Karpov (1840), 104.
[64] Karpov (1840), 118.
[65] Husserl (1997), 93. Emphasis added. We see here that whereas Husserl was interested in the essentials of the perceptual process, this was totally absent in Karpov.

in which the philosophy of each cultural society puts its stamp on all particular sciences. From the formulation of a distinctively Russian philosophy will flow Russian sciences. This has happened already time and again in world history. "The moral-poetic frame of mind of Socrates and Plato was reflected in the Greek science of the day and subsequently, but also in the very style of its fine arts."[66] Likewise, the rationalist spirit of Kant, Fichte, and Hegel was impressed into the character of all North German scholarship. Karpov, then, drew a conclusion for Russian science. "A theory, regardless of the object of its investigations, will acquire a truly Russian character only when it arises from an original Russian philosophy."[67] This, however, leaves open the question whether the national character determines the nation's philosophy or vice versa. Karpov's answer, however implicit, at this point should not surprise us.

Karpov published during the previous year, 1839, a translation of the first volume of Heinrich Ritter's *Geschichte der Philosophie*. In his short translator's "Preface," Karpov admitted that philosophy in Russia did not have a long history, and it could not have been otherwise. Philosophy "has always been the highest limb of a nation's education and the final effort of its mind."[68] Russia, like any nation undertaking the discipline of philosophy, must first tackle its general historical development. Only having done so will Russia be able to add its own moral character and way of thinking to philosophy and thereby produce an original philosophy.[69] Clearly for Karpov, philosophy, whatever else it might be, is a reflection of the nation in which its developers toiled. A nation's philosophy – and Karpov was by no means averse to the idea that that made sense – was a part of its culture. Thus, for Russian philosophers to adopt the ideas expounded, say, in Germany or France would be akin to adopting the way of thinking or feeling there and amount to preaching a different way of life than one's own.

Karpov's *Introduction* did not go unnoticed in the Russian press, though there was little recognition of the nationalist tone of its message. A short, and unsigned notice in the well-known journal *Syn Otechestva* [*Son of the Fatherland*] remarked that it was "one of the few intelligent and well-written books" to have appeared that year in Russia, and the reviewer commented that he recommended it "especially to the youth imbued with fervor and pure love for intellectual work."[70] The

---

66 Karpov (1840), 118.
67 Karpov (1840), 120.
68 Karpov (1839), iv.
69 Karpov (1839), v.
70 [Anonymous] (1840), 723. A far more substantial piece dealing with Karpov's *Introduction* immediately preceded the just mentioned review. Its author Aleksandr Nikitenko, a freed serf and a literature professor at St. Petersburg University, found Karpov's conclusion concerning the fun-

literary critic Vissarion Belinsky also thought well of Karpov's book, finding it to be a "comforting phenomenon" that treats philosophy with respect and "not something to be trifled with as most of our home-grown philosophers do."[71]

In April 1841, Archbishop Afanasij (Aleksandr V. Drozdov) was appointed rector of the St. Petersburg Academy. Seeking to "protect" the Academy, Afanasij forbade Karpov from teaching philosophy using his own notes and charged him with holding firmly to Winkler's text. Karpov did indeed follow his orders, but taught Winkler with a "critical" eye and then turned to the history of philosophy.[72]

Karpov's instructional method in philosophy met with some displeasure. As a consequence, he began to teach logic in 1843, and the teaching of general philosophy was placed in the hands of Adam Fischer, a graduate of the University of Vienna. Fischer, who also taught at the secular university in the capital, obviously was thought to be unobjectionable. In his career in Russia, Fischer quickly learned both the language and how to avoid controversy. However, he plays only a minor role in both the history of Russian philosophy and the development of Russian thought in the theological schools. His own views in epistemological matters were reportedly close to those of Friedrich Jacobi, a sharp critic of German Idealism. When dealing with metaphysical issues, Fischer chose as his guidebook a text *Metaphysik als Rationale Ontologie* by a fellow graduate of Vienna, Johann Ehrlich.[73]

Karpov published in 1856 a *Systematic Exposition of Logic* after a number of years spent teaching the subject. The psychologism that was adumbrated in 1840 comes into clear focus now in the latter work. Karpov acknowledged that the mind works by laws that allow us to perform various functions. Our ability to communicate through language, for example, is possible owing to set grammatical laws in our mind. That we think everything in terms of space and time also accounts for the possibility of mathematics. Is logic too based on laws "in" the mind? If it is, then what is the nature of these laws? Logic governs how we think; therefore, its natural source is in our active faculty of thinking. For Karpov, there is an essential re-

---

damental principle of philosophy to be "not completely satisfactory." Nikitenko (1840), 721. Yet, Nikitenko was willing to be generous, writing "If, in some places, the reasoning behind the train of thought is too abstract and the language somewhat vague, readers should remember how difficult it is to avoid these deficiencies in a philosophical, and, moreover, systematic work, especially in our country, where philosophy is still so new." Nikitenko (1840), 721. Nikitenko, most likely, was also the author of the short summary mentioned above.

71 Belinskij (1840), 4.
72 Florovskij (2009), 271; Florovsky (1979), 248. Shpet characterized this and other restorations of Wolff's teachings as "running in place or, more precisely, moving around on a short chain tied to a pole. Each new step was not a step forward, but only in a new direction around one place – theistic spiritualism." Shpet (2008), 194.
73 Chistovich (1857), 293.

lationship between logic, i.e., the laws governing our mental processes, and psychology, i.e., the study of the human mind. Karpov drew from this the sharply psychologistic conclusion: "Being deeply convinced that the sciences of logic and psychology have an intrinsic mutual connection, I considered it necessary to base my logic on the principles of psychology."[74] Logic and psychology form a harmonious unity through the fact that they both rest on and reveal the human mind.

Karpov envisaged psychology to be the fundamental science or discipline that lays down the principles, factual principles, for a comprehensive investigation of all human mental activity including not only the activity involved in pursuing the natural sciences, but also our everyday awareness of the objects surrounding us. Thus, logic is subordinate to psychology in a complete philosophical scheme. The two are not the same: the subject matter of psychology is what *factually* lies in the mind, whereas the subject matter of logic is what *happens* in the mind. The psychologist as such can direct his/her attention to the mind's activity but takes this activity as factual without inquiring into the laws governing that activity.[75] Karpov's statements already provide a hint as to how he looked upon the laws of logic. If the laws that govern our thinking, and therefore of logic, are empirically derived, then the fact that we follow such laws would be a matter of habit. It also would not be the case that everyone would be aware of them or aware of their limitations, i.e., when those laws should and should not be applied. Moreover, if the laws of logic and of thought were objective, they could conceivably be replaced by others or simply rejected. If they were objective in this sense, their number would be arbitrary, depending on one's point of view. We would expect a divergence in their number and what they are from one philosophical system to another. "In all fairness, the laws of thought should be revered as the subjective laws of the understanding (*rassudok*), which form the basis of its activity. That activity would be impossible if it were restricted by external prescriptions."[76] And contrary to Kant, if the understanding were bound by subjective laws, this alone would not mean that autonomy must be ascribed to the understanding. Karpov acknowledged the *a priori* nature of logic and in general of rules of thinking. These, however, were not *a priori* in Kant's transcendental sense, but were understood quite well within the bounds of a realism, i.e., within a sphere of the psychological *a priori*.

---

74 Karpov (1856a), v.
75 Karpov (1856a), 8.
76 Karpov (1856a), 49.

Karpov's book received some notice but had little influence.[77] Yet, he also in 1856 published an article on the history of philosophy in which he argued for the essential connection between philosophy and religion.

> "Philosophy in the Christian world is more and more strikingly characterized by the fact that it could never develop apart from its relationship to the Christian faith. There apparently were times when philosophers distinguished the interests of philosophy from those of religion and even preached a doctrine that was incompatible with faith. However, the more they developed their theories and logically did so, the more obvious were the results that exposed their contradictions and delusions.[78]

He also extended this thesis by asserting that the various philosophical directions that have historically sprouted in the Christian world are intimately linked to the emergence of different types of Christianity. It is particularly this claim that he sought to develop in his article.

Karpov traced the relationship between philosophy and religion back to the Greeks, but he was particularly interested in medieval scholasticism and its divorce of the mind from the "heart." Such metaphorical language would become prominent among Russian religious thinkers in characterizing the difference between Orthodoxy and Western Christian denominations. Karpov held that scholasticism's activity was formulated in terms of a formal dialectic completely devoid of moral and religious significance. Its turn to Aristotle was at the expense of the inherent moral message in Platonic teaching. The Roman Catholic world forgot the great truth in Christianity, but which was preserved in Orthodoxy, namely that the Christian spirit requires both the mind and the heart.[79]

---

[77] Vladimir Solov'ëv in 1880 wrote a short review of Karpov's logic text finding that it "takes a Platonic view of human thought and cognition and develops this view with indubitable originality." Solov'ëv (1911), 237. Sadly, Solov'ëv's review was quite short and did not provide any critical remarks. In writing that Karpov's text "takes a Platonic view," did Solov'ëv see that as a compliment?
[78] Karpov (1856b), 171.
[79] The similarities between Karpov's philosophy of history and that of the Slavophiles, particularly of Kireevskij's, is great. Karpov, though, provided no references to their writings, leaving us to conjecture as to the source for his ideas. Both Karpov and Kireevskij rejected scholasticism on largely similar grounds. In general, the secular Slavophiles placed greater emphasis on the integral "spirit" of the Russian people, whereas Karpov, a cleric, located that integrity in Orthodox Christianity which was transmitted to the Russian people, who were amenable to such an infusion. A comparison of Karpov's views to those of Kireevskij can also be found in the late nineteenth century. One such was a P. M. Laskeev, who in 1898 relying almost exclusively on Karpov's *Introduction*, wrote that if we compare the respective projects of Kireevskij and Karpov, "one cannot help but notice that in many respects they are antipodes of each other. What for Karpov is the final result of a philosophical system is for Kireevskij its necessary principle. ... Karpov wants to present in his

Karpov continued insisting that the reformation initiated by Martin Luther did not fundamentally alter Western Christianity. A product of the Catholic school, he accepted the separation of knowledge and faith, which presumably is Karpov's alternate rendering of the mind versus heart dichotomy.[80] Lutheran philosophers may have freed philosophy from the shackles of scholasticism and with it a slavish deference to Aristotle, but they turned even more so away from tradition with their individualism and neglect of the importance of Christian tradition.

However odd it may sound, Karpov also characterized the Protestant Reformation as moving Christianity in a "pagan" direction through its reorientation of religious forms to independent, individual activity. Having turned religion inward, it was but a small step for philosophers to locate the basis for natural phenomena as well in oneself. Kant in the eighteenth century was the first, but not the last, to turn inward for the solution to philosophical problems. Many others followed Kant's example, placing the mind over all else and in doing so created "rationalistic" philosophy.[81] In asking how a synthetic cognition (*poznanie*) is possible, Kant sought the solution in the mind. However, for Karpov the answer is found in a direct appeal to theism. Kant forgot that we human beings in our entirety – and not just our minds – are nothing other than a synthesis of the Deity, of the "Creative Wisdom."[82] Consequently, the answer to be sought lies not in an analysis of our mental activity, but in our dependence on the Divine as it is given in faith. The ambiguity lurking here in Karpov's proposed reply to Kant would remain unclarified. But Karpov's idea that Kant adopted and transformed Lutheran philosophy would reverberate in the years ahead in classical Russian idealism and would subtly remain to this day.

For Karpov, Russian Orthodox Christianity took a different route oriented as it was toward a practical love of wisdom. The principles found in Orthodoxy together with a living sympathy for them and the entirety of the Christian faith passed from Byzantium – Karpov curiously did not explain how this happened – into the bosom of the Slavic peoples.[83] The love of wisdom reigned harmoniously together with

---

philosophical system a rational grounding for the veracity of Orthodoxy and the need to obey positive laws; Kireevskij advises to start first with the constructing of a philosophical system imbued not only with the truths of the Orthodox faith but with the works of the Church Fathers." Laskeev (1898), 748. There is much to be said for Laskeev's juxtaposition, but its closer examination would require a special study of its own.

80 Karpov (1856b), 183.
81 Karpov (1856b), 189.
82 Karpov (1856b), 192.
83 We should note that Karpov made no mention of, let alone account for, those Slavic tribes that did not share Orthodox Christianity, though he did write of the Slavic peoples in the plural. He certainly could not have been ignorant of the Poles, in particular.

their Christian faith within the Slavic tribes to form the general expression of their national life. This love of wisdom was responsible for the overthrow of the Mongol yoke in Russia, and it has reigned as the dominant philosophy over the centuries.[84] The Wolffian philosophy preached in the eighteenth-century theological schools could not find fertile Slavic soil in which to sprout. It left little lasting imprint in the Slavic soul and could be easily washed away, soon forgotten, and abandoned. "We will never commit to this rationalism, precisely because it cannot commit to our Orthodox faith."[85] Neither the heart nor the mind can be absorbed by the other, and the interests of one cannot be isolated from the other, as Western philosophies demand.

As mentioned, Karpov held German Idealism to be not just an idealism, but also a rationalism and a paganism. A clarification of Karpov's charge of paganism against the Idealists is in order. In one of a series of surviving archival sketches from 1855, he claimed that the subjective turn toward the "I" is not just tantamount, but actually the same as a rejection of religious faith, of worship of God, and of church institutions. The human individual is taken as an independent, self-legislative force, the source and adjudicator of moral actions.[86]

Karpov in 1858 began to teach a course entitled "History of Philosophy in the Post-Kantian Period," which required that he address German Idealism more directly than he had up to that time. This pedagogical activity led to a serialized work published in the house journal of the St. Petersburg Academy in 1860. Having traced to his satisfaction the origin of Russia's distinctive philosophical outlook back to Orthodoxy and a "volkish" natural predisposition to its message, Karpov set out to trace the origin of the individualistic and iconoclastic rationalism of German Idealism. He inquired how could such a philosophy, one that departs so sharply from the spirit of Christianity, arise in a supposedly Christian land. We must assume that the "pagan spirit" lay dormant in that society but was able to penetrate into its very heart. This spirit "ascribed to itself the right to judge and establish laws that would determine the sense of Christian dogmas, the inner dignity of Christian morality, the external form of the religious service, and the entire prac-

---

84 Karpov (1855), 102.
85 Karpov (1856b), 197.
86 Karpov (1855), 101. Many of the themes and even many words and phrases from this archival document found their way into Karpov's 1856b article. In the former, he already wrote of a love of wisdom and of a living sympathy for it that was brought from Byzantium into the bosom of the Slavic tribes along with the Orthodox Christian faith. For this reason, the Western scholasticism, taught in Latin throughout the Empire's schools in the eighteenth century, was unable to sink roots in Russian social life.

tical side of religious life."[87] The nation infected, so to speak, in this way was Germany, and its distorted form of Christianity was Protestantism.

In Karpov's telling, Kant became the leader of a new philosophical movement. He transformed the principle of Protestantism into a metaphysics, thereby creating a Protestant philosophy. What Luther accomplished in religion, Kant did in philosophy.[88] Just as Luther elevated the individual mind above all other authority, so too Kant made the individual the sole judge of morality. Since the German populace was already conditioned to this transformation through their religion, Kant's philosophical spirit entered easily and quickly into the thought of subsequent German thinkers. Hegel himself had proclaimed that Lutheranism, the best of all religions, served the development of free thought and of the sciences in general.[89]

Karpov, turning to Russian thought, saw it as being constantly tempted since Peter the Great by Western, particularly German, ideas even though these were fundamentally incompatible with Orthodoxy and the Russian way of life. Those who defended and promoted Kant did not realize that had these philosophical principles taken hold the existing social order would be in peril. Likewise, Hegel's thought, elevating the mind to serve as the oracle of unconditional truth, would lead to the dissolution of the sacred bonds holding societies together. It amounts to a moral disease. Religious faith and the moral convictions bound with that faith are the "glue" making a stable society possible. But German Idealism, if pervasive, would eliminate those beliefs and would undermine social cohesion. Thus, not only was German Idealism wrong as philosophy but it was wrong as a moral doctrine, wrong because no clear-minded person could abide the consequences of its acceptance.

Karpov continued to teach logic over the years, but in 1865 he was asked to present a course on psychology. This was not a foreign subject to him by any means. Already while at the Kyiv Academy he had lectured on it as well as philosophy. Karpov's explicit concern with psychological themes was most clearly shown in his essay "On Self-Knowledge" published in 1860. The title of Karpov's essay was surely occasioned by his interest in a popular eighteenth- century British tract by John Mason that at least in one of its many editions was entitled *Self-Knowledge*. It

---

87 Karpov (1860a), 132. How a "spirit" was able to do anything like the feats Karpov ascribed to it is left unsaid and certainly unexplained.
88 Karpov's linking of German Protestantism to Kant and German Idealism became a recurring conception in Russian philosophy. See, in particular Trubeckoj (1994), but the same sentiment was expressed shortly earlier than Karpov by the Slavophile Ivan Kireevskij in his 1856 "On the Necessity and Possibility of New Principles in Philosophy." See Kireevskij (1972).
89 Karpov (1860a), 136.

was published in Russian translation in three parts as early as 1783, but Karpov published a new translation in 1865 with his 1860 essay serving as an epilogue.[90]

Karpov's basic position held that self-knowledge, knowledge of our concrete, mundane self, was the proper starting point of the philosophical endeavor. Such self-knowledge will reveal our essential being. From it our activities and thinking flow. What we essentially are, what the human being is, cannot be entirely known by observation. It escapes natural science. What our inner self is can be discovered through introspection only if enlightened by faith. Although we may find Karpov's stance to be naïve, he believed that the human soul wishes for the good. Our active departures from it can be remedied through prayer and the various services of the Church. Again we find Karpov returning to a religious message, this time via psychological introspection.

Nevertheless, were we to think that Karpov's deliberations on self-knowledge concerned the human individual in isolation, we would be traveling down what he believed to be the same or a parallel road to that of German Idealism with its emphasis on human individuality. No, for Karpov the self-knowledge of which he wrote is just as much, if not more, the human race's self-knowledge.[91] Indeed, the discipline devoted to just such self-knowledge is psychology. Since its object, our own selves, is the one with which we should have the greatest familiarity, we might think that with the passing of the centuries our self-knowledge should have approached perfection. But our self-knowledge has not been cumulative and progressive. Karpov looked on psychology not as a natural science, but as an attitude at a time, i.e., how we as a species look upon ourselves. on the whole. Epochs of moral decline – he pointedly provides no examples – are routinely followed by a decline in self-knowledge and vice versa.[92]

Karpov recognized that as with every field of study, there can be errors and delusions. How are we, then, to distinguish between truth and falsity in psychology, in purported claims to self-knowledge? In looking through a telescope our view of heavenly bodies can be distorted and/or blurred by passing clouds fog, temperature inversions, etc. So too can our view of the human mind be distorted by an en-

---

[90] See Mejson (1783). This Russian edition was reprinted in 1786 and again in 1800, a testament to its popularity, or to an official belief that it should be popular. For Karpov's essay as epilogue, see Karpov (1865). There is no evidence that Karpov was aware of the eighteenth-century Russian edition. The "publisher," presumably Mikhail Katkov, in a short prefatory note to the 1865 edition noted without commentary that the translation was based on an 1818 English edition. Mejson (1865), ii.
[91] It must be said, though, that he often fails to distinguish individual self-knowledge from general human self-knowledge.
[92] Karpov (1860b), 265.

tire assortment of factors. The clearing away or dispersal of the "fog" that can impair the vision of even the most educated psychologist is possible only by religious means. Investigators of the human mind or soul must first try to illuminate their own soul so that consciousness can peer into it. Such illumination "is possible only by the power of a feeling of repentance, which would resonate deeply in the soul and with the warmth of prayer before God in the bosom of Christ's Church."[93] Here again, we find Karpov approaching genuine and serious questions only to retreat in the face of serious inquiry.

Karpov's thoughts on psychology resulted in a work specifically entitled "Opening Lecture on Psychology," though published only posthumously in 1868, a few months after his death. Karpov clearly thought of himself as an advocate of a moderate approach to issues arising on the border between philosophy and religion, reason and faith. Not at all hostile to the conception of innate ideas, he found the empiricist rejection as leading to a rejection of an inner sense of what is true and good. Morality would then be given purely from without. However, he also rejected Kant's supposed rationalism that totally discounted feelings – and thereby the "heart" – in favor of an abstract and cold sense of duty. For Karpov, these and similar psychological delusions arise from an inadequate knowledge of ourselves. Even more correctly, they arise from a deliberate ignoring of the clear evidence of inner experience in favor of some prejudiced conception.[94] The goal of psychology is not knowledge of the mind for its own sake, but for our own – understood again both individually and socially – moral perfection. This theme of morality would be one echoed again, albeit without this explicit psychological veneer, in the years ahead by a number of Russian Christian thinkers, particularly Vladimir Solov'ëv. This conception of perfection is quite vague, and one finds little clarification in modern philosophy. Where, then, must we turn for guidance concerning how to proceed, if philosophy cannot even provide a clear concept of what we lack? Karpov's answer was simple: the Christian religion. Psychology, as self-knowledge, cannot itself do more than illuminate facts of the mind. Karpov here stressed the role of education in preparing the mind to accept the road to moral improvement.

Karpov did essentially nothing to advance psychology, as we know that science today, in Russia. His reliance on introspection coupled with his insistence that the facts of our inner experience refer unquestionably to the "essence" of the mind was quite out of step, for better or worse, with later developments in the field. He displayed no knowledge of nor interest in the burgeoning "objective psycholo-

---

93 Karpov (1860b), 270.
94 Karpov (1868), 312.

gy" pioneered in Russia by Ivan Sechenov. As we shall see, though, Karpov would not be the only religious philosopher to cling to the efficacy of introspection.

Curriculum changes in the teaching of philosophy in the 1840s-early 1850s meant more specific courses were offered in addition to the general systematic ones. New courses in logic, psychology, and moral philosophy meant additional professors were needed. The general systematic philosophy course in 1843–1845 was taught by the St. Petersburg University professor Adam Fischer, then by Ilarion A. Chistovich, himself a graduate of the St. Petersburg Academy and who later wrote a history of the school and a biography of Prokopovich, for which he, Chistovich, was awarded the Demidov Prize in 1865. His textbook on empirical psychology from 1868 and reissued several times subsequently did not shy away from recognizing the limits of introspection. Still, efficacy of introspection would continue to be promoted and defended for decades. Although Karpov's psychologism would largely be abandoned by his students and successors, his resolution of philosophical issues through an appeal to religious faith would resonate in their own works. His concomitant sociologism, as seen in his linking of German Idealism to German Protestantism, though not unique to him, would echo into Russia's future, even into the present. As for Chistovich, we shall return to his psychology later, since it lies at the very edge of the pre-reform period.

Chapter 3
The Moscow Academy Under the First Charter

The Moscow Theological Academy opened in 1814, five years after that of the St. Petersburg Academy. This delay allowed the theological schools commission to evaluate the efficacy of the new charter and for the preparation of a set of instructors from the Petersburg Academy.[1] We must also not forget the disruption to the life of Moscow caused by the invasion of the Napoleonic forces.[2] The commission as well as the tsarist government was well aware of the shortage of qualified teachers to staff the higher educational institutions, the creation of which it had in mind. With the graduation of an entire class from Petersburg, Moscow was able to complete the necessary roster of instructors. Histories of the Academy like to stress that it was not a new institution, but merely a transformation of the long-existing Slavic-Greek-Latin Academy under a new charter. However we may view the case, the Moscow Academy upon its official opening had a first class consisting of 70 students, only 20 of whom were continuing their education from the Academy's former incarnation. The remainder were drawn from various seminaries in the surrounding educational district. This "new" Moscow Theological Academy opened with 12 instructors, three of whom were holdovers from the older school, one had been an instructor at a seminary, and eight were drawn from the first graduating class of the St. Petersburg Academy. Of these 12 one was selected to teach philosophy.

3.1 Philosophy's First Steps in Moscow – Kutnevich

Lectures in philosophy began at the Moscow Academy in late October 1814. The instructor was Ivan K. Nosov, one of the new graduates of the St. Petersburg Academy. He held the position for merely one year – until November 1815 – stepping down owing to some unspecified illness.[3] Nosov lectured in Latin until late Febru-

---

[1] Smirnov (1879), 1; Florovsky (1979), 179.
[2] The damage done in and to Moscow is often overlooked in histories. A counterexample, however, is Saltykov, who writes, "As a result of the events of 1812, the premises of the Academy were badly damaged. Nevertheless, every effort was made to resume classes as soon as possible, and already on March 31, 1813, Archbishop Augustine of Moscow solemnly opened the classes." Saltykov (1986), 84.
[3] Smirnov (1879), 389.

ary providing an introduction to philosophy and the history of philosophical systems. He also devoted some time to empirical psychology. Unlike the case of Fessler at the St. Petersburg Academy, Nosov's brief lectureship had no discernible impact on the future development of Russian thought.

Nosov's successor was Vasilij I. Kutnevich (1786–1865), who was also among the recent graduates of the St. Petersburg Academy. Kutnevich had already been lecturing in Latin at the Moscow Academy during the previous year on physics, mathematics, and the German language.[4] He would continue to lecture on general philosophy, logic, empirical psychology, and the history of philosophical systems for nine years, after which he left the Academy for a position as the chief priest administering to the Russian army and navy. His extensive library that included the works of many Western authors – Kant, Fichte, Schelling, and Jacobi – passed to the Moscow Academy's library.

Kutnevich left no writings by which we can determine for ourselves his philosophical stance, sympathies – if indeed he had any – or competence. However, in an autobiography one of Kutnevich's former students at the Moscow Academy recalled that his philosophy professor "was a very intelligent man, who was intimately familiar with the newest philosophies of the time. ... In the first year, he lectured on the history of philosophy. As he was ostensibly an eclectic, he lectured according to Brucker, Tennemann, and Buhle. ... In the second year, we listened to philosophy, or more precisely, to empirical psychology and logic, which were taught somehow in his own way, not at all from Karpe's textbook. Our professor loved idealism, but the Academy wanted us to be experimentalists. ... Excited by the clever lectures of the professor of philosophy, who respected mainly Plato, Plotinus, and all of the newest philosophers, excluding Hegel, who was not yet known in Russia, I zealously followed the development of the thinking faculty in the human race."[5]

Apart from personal accounts and testimonies, the lengthiest statement of Kutnevich's philosophical position is a record of his introductory lecture at the start of his philosophy course in 1818.[6] Kutnevich unremarkably proclaimed that in order

---

[4] The surviving record does not indicate in which language – he or the others at the Academy – taught the various languages. It certainly appears odd to us today that a Russian instructor would teach German to Russian students in Latin!

[5] Ismajlov (1860), 125–127. Filipp Ismajlov (1794–1863), a graduate of the Moscow Academy, became a secondary school teacher of physics, mathematics, and French.

[6] As we have no means to check the accuracy of the words or even of the ideas attributed to Kutnevich by an unnamed student, we must tread carefully. Moreover, Kutnevich delivered his lecture in Latin, but the record is in Russian. Thus, we are asked to accept at the outset that this student provided an accurate translation in addition to understanding the ideas expressed. Nonetheless, we can surmise that what has come down to us is at least indicative of the ideas in popular circulation at the time at the Moscow Academy.

to understand what philosophy is, one must turn to human nature, which is both corporeal and mental, i.e., "spiritual" in the terminology of the day. Inasmuch as philosophy is a product of human thought and is concerned with thought, we must concern ourselves with that aspect of our nature. An essential feature or quality of our thought is reason. We seek knowledge through the use of our reason, and we are impelled by reason to ask for answers to four questions: (1) What am I, i.e., the subjective world?; (2) What is the not-I, i.e., the objective world?; (3) What is the first cause of these two worlds?; and (4) What must I do? On this introductory level, Kutnevich proclaimed that of these four questions the first three deal with cognition and, thus, can be reduced to an inquiry concerning the possibility of knowledge. Much of this can, from a broad perspective, be seen within a basically Kantian-Fichtean framework. He remarked that "some" have posed – without indicating who have done so – an additional question: What can I hope? However, Kutnevich was rather dismissive of it, despite its important role in the third Kantian *Critique*, saying that its solution merely "follows from the essence and knowledge" of the other questions.[7] The four tasks mentioned above form the content of philosophy.

Had Kutnevich ended his "introductory lecture" at this point, we could excuse his posing of four tasks and their immediately subsequent "reduction" to two as a result of some conceptual legerdemain. But he persisted in furthering confusion by saying that the question concerning what can be known is contained in the first three tasks. This is truly odd given that the first two questions already stated that what was to be known is the subjective and the objective worlds respectively. Kutnevich did not appear to have a firm grasp of the distinction between the various subdisciplines of philosophy. Given the praise accorded him in student accounts, though, he did stimulate a number of young men to pursue philosophy further, regardless how confusing we may look on him today based on our extremely limited knowledge. When he left the teaching profession in 1824, Kutnevich already had his best student, his successor, assisting him.

3.2 Golubinskij – A Founder of Russian Religious Philosophy

Feodor A. Golubinskij (1797–1854), a graduate of the Kostroma Theological Seminary, entered the Moscow Academy with its opening in 1814.[8] Upon his completion of

---

7 Kutnevich (1864), 639.
8 Based on entries and mentions in the diary of Vasilij S. Arsen'ev, Golubinskij, as well as Kutnevich, at least flirted with masonry and possibly joined at this time. We should keep in mind that

the program there in 1818, he began teaching the history of philosophical systems for four years as an adjunct. In September 1822 he was assigned to teach metaphysics and moral philosophy. Golubinskij's elevation to Kutnevich's position meant that in 1824 he began teaching the introductory course in philosophy. The death of his wife[9] from illness in early 1841 left him with four young children, the oldest being his daughter Maria, who at the time was less than 13 years of age.[10] In January 1852 Golubinskij's eldest son Sergej, a student at the Academy, fell ill with tuberculosis and died at the end of the month. Within weeks another son Peter came down with scarlet fever and died one month after Sergej. These events impacted Golubinskij's health. He resigned his position at the Academy in 1854 to return to his native Kostroma province, where he contracted cholera and died later that year.[11]

Unfortunately, despite his many years of teaching at the Moscow Academy, Golubinskij himself published quite little in philosophy, "as if he suffered a writer's block."[12] His lectures were published only three decades after his death. Florovskij wisely advised us to be cautious with them, since they were based on unreliable and faulty student records.[13] They remain, however, the only significant source of his views even if we cannot be completely confident that they are a totally accurate reflection. Golubinskij's biographer Sergej Glagolev reminds us that, although the works bearing Golubinskij's name express his thoughts, they neither necessarily convey his actual words nor the manner and order in which he delivered them. The latter, in particular, is that of the students.[14]

Speranskij and Fessler were masons. For Arsen'ev's mentions of Golubinskij at masonic meetings, see Arsen'ev (2005), 273, 288. Conceivably, Fessler's influence had something to do with the attraction of masonry for Golubinskij and Kutnevich. Participation in masonry was not uncommon at the time in the highest rung of Russian society. Nonetheless, Golubinskij "remained faithful to the Church and retained his membership in the order so as to help prevent other freemasons from moving away from Orthodoxy." Kocjuba (2012), 36.

9 His wife Anna was Kutnevich's sister.

10 Later that decade Maria married a secondary school teacher, but she too succumbed to an early death at the age of 30, only four years after her father.

11 The biographical facts recounted here are drawn largely from Glagolev (1898).

12 Florovskij (2009), 307. Glagolev asserted that Golubinskij did not write out his Orthodox-religious system due to a lack of time to do so and his sense of humility. "We do not know which of these two reasons was the main one." Glagolev (1898), 28.

13 To say that the purported records of Golubinskij's lectures were faulty requires knowledge of the actual lectures. A later philosophy professor at the Moscow Academy Aleksej I. Vvedenskij, wrote that Golubinskij's words were rendered in the published texts "in a very imperfect way." Vvedenskij (1898), 1.

14 Glagolev (1898), 40.

A significant portion of the first volume of his works, a *General Introduction to Philosophy*, is likely drawn from his general course for first-year students of philosophy.[15] We have no information whether Golubinskij modified his course over the years and no firm information when the ideas expressed in this volume or in the other volumes were conveyed.[16] What comes clearly into focus virtually at the outset is the purely religious nature of Golubinskij's ideas and concerns. He claimed that the quest for wisdom, which lies at the heart of philosophy, is one for the Infinite, Golubinskij's obvious and continuous euphemism for God. Echoing his mentor Kutnevich, Golubinskij distinguished the I from the not-I and in doing so found the principle of philosophy. Everywhere one looks, one finds contingency and inconstancy. Thus, what surrounds us cannot be the principle of everything. We strive for the Infinite, evidence for which is in the mind. Without this aspiration, there would be no philosophy. Exactly what this evidence is remains unclear in this *Introduction*, but Golubinskij informed us that the basis of characterizing the Infinite as infinite is that everything grasped empirically is temporal and spatial. The form, then, of the Infinite must lack temporality and spatiality. And if we have a cognition (*poznanie*) of the Infinite, that cognition must be due to a higher mental power, a faith (*vera*) in the existence of the Infinite.[17] If we take such a statement at face value, we must conclude that faith is not merely a matter of the "heart," but can provide cognition as well.

Golubinskij in lectures presumably for his class on metaphysics – but from an unknown date – singled out metaphysics as the highest concern of all disciplines, for it concerns the affirmation of universal and necessary truths, such as God's existence and His perfections.[18] Although he charged philosophy with inquiring into what is essential in both the human spirit and in nature, these studies, thus, must

---

15 In view of the virtually unanimous panegyrics about Golubinskij in the scant secondary literature, we should turn to one of his students Nikolaj I. Nadezhdin, who remarked, "With particular interest, we all awaited the first lecture of the professor of philosophy, Feodor Golubinskij, whom we had heard about already in the seminary as a great philosopher. Therefore, when we awaited his lecture we listened with great attention. ... He spoke slowly and distinctly, but it is impossible to say that he was very clear. So at least it seemed to me. It was evident that he himself was well aware of what he was saying, but in my opinion he was inadequately developing his thoughts. To me – and probably for others, something seemed unspoken and remained not completely understandable." Nadezhdin (1914), 67, 69.
16 The published lectures are based largely on the manuscripts of Vladimir G. Nazarevskij (1819–1881), who started at the Moscow Academy in 1840 and finished with a *magister*'s degree in theology in 1844. Thus, we have at least fixed bounds for the earliest and latest possible dates for much of the published version of Golubinskij's lectures.
17 Golubinskij (1884a), 25.
18 Golubinskij (1884a), 75.

be of lesser importance than that of metaphysics. Whereas Golubinskij, surely, looked on philosophy as more than some abstract theology, it along with all other disciplines are subordinate to a metaphysical scheme. He left much to be clarified in this regard, but he attempted to explain himself – however inadequately – through a comparison with applied mathematics. The natural sciences obtain their rigor through their employment of mathematical laws. However, whether empirical objects correspond to our mathematical, more specifically geometrical, constructions would be impossible without metaphysics. Moreover, moral philosophy would be useless without metaphysics, "without knowledge in advance from psychology of the correct nature of the human being, of good and evil, and of the vocation of the human being, etc."[19] No doubt Golubinskij's students left the lecture room perplexed. One might wish to connect human psychology with ethics, but what connects ethics to *metaphysics* via psychology? On the face of it, a connection between ethics and psychology would appear to forestall any departure into metaphysics unless the human psyche has a means to "see" the non-sensible.

In his lectures on ontology, Golubinskij stressed that his objection to Kantianism lay in its repudiation of traditionally conceived metaphysics. Kant provided no path whatsoever to investigate the supersensible, viz., God and the properties or traits Christianity attributes to Him. Since a metaphysical ontology must be philosophically acceptable and Kantianism precludes such a possibility, the means by which Kant arrived at that preclusion must be incorrect. "Therefore, the ontology given by Wolff and Kant cannot serve as a guide for investigating metaphysical knowledge."[20] Intent on dismissing all forms of skepticism and seemingly oblivious to the Kantian distinction between empirical realism and transcendental realism, Golubinskij first wrote that our mental representations contain something which we immediately notice as being independent of our representations and, indeed, of us. Even the skeptic must realize this from the simple fact that he or she distinguishes one representation from another and representations of oneself from what is other. This, to Golubinskij, shows that solipsism is untenable, that our representations are not purely subjective products of the mind. Moreover, that our representations of objects are and can be distinguished shows also that the qualities found in our representations correspond precisely to qualities in the external objects.[21] Such at least is the concern of ontology. But Golubinskij's ultimate objec-

---

[19] Golubinskij (1884a), 79–80.
[20] Golubinskij (1884b), 5.
[21] Golubinskij believed this to be an argument against Fichte. The former wrote, "The variety of our sensible representations would be inexplicable if their origin were ascribed, as in Fichte, solely to our I, which is indivisible, invisible, and singular to the outer senses." Golubinskij (1884b), 30. Such a solipsistic reading of Fichte is quite questionable.

tion to skepticism of any sort was that it flies in the face of how we take the world in our everyday lives. "Is it possible that the Creator made us to be deceived, so that our very consciousness is an illusion? This is already the height of absurdity."[22]

However we may fault Golubinskij's technical mastery of Kantian transcendental idealism, it loomed over much of his thought. He shared Kant's view that the forms of space and time are original properties and conditions of our sensibility but withheld judgment on whether they also lie outside the cognizing mind. Whether they are or not remained a problem for philosophy to solve. This apparent agnosticism did not stop Golubinskij from defining space and time in metaphorical language. "The *form of space* is nothing other than a necessary *aspiration*, a *direction of our mind* (dush) *to seek objects situated next to one another.* Stated in this way, Golubinskij had hardly clarified what space is, since we must already know what "situated next to one another" means. Much the same criticism must be leveled against his definition of time, saying that it is a "direction of the mind by which it seeks one object after another." What is most startling here is not only the vain attempt to define space and time, but his portrayal of the mind as an active agent "seeking" something. On the contrary, we represent objects in space quite apart from whether we wish to do so or not. Time and space as forms are original, irreducible properties and laws of our sensibility. But is that all they are?

Golubinskij, as we see devoted considerable attention to space and time. He agreed with Kant that they are not independent objects, nor are they abstract concepts. They are also not properties of things. If they were, we would be unable to picture them as devoid of the objects of which they are properties. Arguably demonstrating his training in Leibnizian rationalism, he largely assented to viewing space and time as relations, an explanation that Kant did not accept but which "is close to the truth."[23] They are our means of relating one object to another; the means by which we limit one object in relation to another. Yet, despite his use of the grammatical active voice here, Golubinskij conceived space and time as laws governing the existence of things. If they were purely subjective, the sense manifold would initially be formless, without any lawful connection. We would, in effect, be the creators of nature, a position that Golubinskij treated as heretical. "If outside us there were no order and if it were the case that we

---

22 Golubinskij (1884b), 26.
23 Golubinskij (1884b), 39. Shpet correctly wrote, "As for his philosophical conviction, I dare to assert, contrary to the expressed opinions, that Golubinskij's teaching was above all as a Wolffian. Again, he gives the impression that he is committed to Wolffian rationalism, not because of a simple devotion to the academic tradition and conservatism, but because of a pure conviction." Shpet (2008), 203.

must imagine that order according to necessary laws of our cognitive power, then what would our representations be? They would be nothing but a lie, a deception, an empty mirage."[24] Golubinskij argued against the idea that space is infinite and time has no beginning. He does so – predictably enough – from a theological standpoint. If space were infinite, no understanding could "contain" it. Thus, even the Divine Mind could not grasp it in its entirety, and there would be in addition to God something that is unlimited, a claim that Golubinskij charged would be absurd. Likewise, if time had no beginning, God would not be able to "embrace" it. Thus, space and time must be finite, not as a result of the latest discoveries of physics, but because it would conflict with Golubinskij's preconceived conception of a Deity.

Many of his other remarks concerning space rested on his quasi-Leibnizian conception of it. If space were unlimited, this would mean that material objects too must be unlimited in number. On the other hand, if there were no sensible objects, there would be no space. Moreover, since space is relational, it adds nothing to reality. Golubinskij also made a curious remark upon recognizing that natural forces, such as that of gravity, are weaker as one moves away from the force's source. To account for this, Golubinskij attributed an active power to space in that it "externally limits" the action of the force. Were it not for space limiting it, a natural force would extend without limit.[25] Such, we must presume, was his answer to Newton's action at a distance.

Golubinskij clearly felt some influence from Kant, as his discussion of space and time demonstrates. He also recognized the importance of accounting for self-consciousness and for the conditions of its possibility, but, quite differently than Kant, he held that our empirical self-consciousness is possible due to our original consciousness of God. Just as God is the principle of all that exists, so a consciousness of God is the principle of all consciousness. Golubinskij was willing to concede that Kant's table of categories gave the correct order in enumerating the categorial forms. Kant correctly turned to judgments in order to obtain a complete enumeration of the *a priori* categories. The categories indeed express the need for unity in the sense manifold. However, Kant was incorrect in locating the categories in thought alone. They lie in nature itself.[26] Golubinskij provided, though, no argu-

---

24 Golubinskij (1884b), 44.
25 Golubinskij (1884b), 46. We hardly need to point out the problematic nature of such a claim. Even given Golubinskij's conception of space as a relation, it makes little sense.
26 Further on in the notes concerning ontology, Golubinskij stated – assuming these notes are an accurate reflection of his thought – "we cannot help but notice Kant's error in the derivation and disclosing of the categories." Golubinskij (1884c), 161. This presumably refers, in some unclarified manner, to Kant's restriction of the categories to the cognitive process. Golubinskij in this same

ment comparable to Kant's for his position. He wanted us again to accept it on faith, a faith stemming from his religious convictions. Golubinskij held that as a conscious and finite being we naturally seek the cause of all, the first cause, which itself cannot be finite. This claim, though apparently just psychological, cannot be confined to the human mind. Its primordiality in the mind means that it was given to us originally by the Creator. On the face of it, Golubinskij was aware of the need of a proof for his claims, but he acknowledged the difficulty, if not impossibility, of demonstrating what he takes as the initial thesis, a proposition that is immediately recognized as true. Such, above all, is the existence and the perfections of the Infinite, i.e., of God. That idea is the first and immediate principle of cognition in its entirety, though Golubinskij made no attempt to prove that it is such a principle or that without it there could be no cognition. Golubinskij in the fourth volume of his philosophy lectures, entitled *Speculative (Umozritel'noe) Theology*, said that properly speaking God's existence cannot be proven, since God is the principle of all else. Cognition of His existence is that from which all other cognitions derive their validity. "Thus, arguments for God's existence do not prove, but explain and confirm this truth, which must be known to all originally."[27] Our principal evidence for God's existence lies in our very idea of the Infinite Being. If the human mind did not have within it the idea of a necessary Infinite Being, it would be impossible to proceed from the contingent to the necessary, from the finite to the infinite.[28]

As with Kant, Golubinskij recognized three faculties in the human mind: that of cognizing, that of willing, and that of hoping. Predictably given what we have said, he held that the mind seeks to ascend from the finite to the infinite, to the first cause of all, viz., God. It cannot suffice to possess mere logical truths, i.e., an agreement of our representations with the represented objects. The mind seeks metaphysical truth, the agreement of its thoughts with the ideas of God.[29] To answer how the mind aspires to metaphysical truth, Golubinskij – again like Kant – disassembled our cognitive ability into three "branches": sensibility, under-

---

paragraph stated that the categories of modality should "more correctly" be called the categories of the being of things in general, since the three categories given by Kant refer to various types of being. "This is clear from the fact that even if there were not a single rational being who represents, there would still exist a being. ... In general, being with its various forms does not depend on our representations and can exist without them." Golubinskij (1884c), 161.

27 Golubinskij (1884d), 24.

28 Golubinskij assumed we do have an idea of infinity, which is by no means obvious. He also assumed that that infinity is equated in some undisclosed manner with necessity, that an infinite being – whatever that may mean – is a necessary being.

29 Golubinskij (1884b), 74.

standing, and reason. Sensibility alone cannot explain our aspiration for metaphysical truth. Similar to Kant, Golubinskij held that the understanding is responsible for bringing the sense manifold into a unity of consciousness. The understanding has categories, twelve of them, that both form and add to the manifold. However, these categories merely direct the activity of the understanding.[30] Taken alone, they have no direction, no uniting principle. A simple look at the categories reveals some opposition between them. Negation, contingency, and limitation, for example, refer to the finite world around us, whereas unity and reality properly belong to the Infinite. Thus, we must ask what directs, what lies behind, the categories themselves.

> The categories, of course, are the basic laws, but only for the operation of the understanding. They are not the sole source of our cognition, because they consist of two opposing sides. The categories of the understanding are correctly recognized as laws, which are based on an original law of the mind by which our spirit aspires for the Infinite. Consequently, we must seek another principle and cause of the categories.[31]

We must look into the mind for what we seek, and there we find within us, within the mind, the idea of the Infinite. The relation of the workings of the cognitive faculty with its categories and that of the real world was in Golubinskij's eyes quite simple: the categories Kant laid out are laws of the real world as well as of human cognition. There is an intrinsic connection between the two "worlds," the mental and the physical. The categories Kant discovered mediate our contingent and alterable world with the absolute and unalterable world of ideas. The categories are truly *a priori*, not just epistemically but also ontologically. They are as such not simply a construction of the cognitive faculty in any way.

Golubinskij followed essentially the same train of thought in ethics. We aspire in our actions to the moral good – the eternal good. An ultimate dissatisfaction with the enjoyment of finite objects and pleasures, with selfish sensibility, leads us to a recognition that there is something within us that is higher. The idea of the Infinite is essentially in the human spirit. It cannot be an idea acquired during human development, since such a process would have to be empirically discernible. No, it is a given in our nature by the Infinite. To the atheist's objection that he or she has no such idea, Golubinskij dismissively stated that the idea has been suppressed or drowned out by some other conception. In short, Golubinskij dogmati-

---

[30] Golubinskij (1884c), 60. Golubinskij raised what some may see as a significant omission: "Kant could not prove how one category relates to another, and why there are not more than that number." Golubinskij (1884c), 37.
[31] Golubinskij (1884b), 76.

cally offered no means by which he could be convinced of error. Since the existence of God and the moral good are essentially inherent in the human spirit, pagans, atheists, and amoralists who lived before Christ and the emergence of Christianity are responsible for their ignorance and will face the consequence of that neglect of the truth.[32] No philosophical proof relying on experience or reason alone can yield the existence of God as a conclusion. One cannot deduce the Infinite from the finite alone. Such a progression requires an intuition of what the Infinite is. The idea of the Infinite is naturally innate in our spirit, and it can only be seized intuitively.

Golubinskij was not one to applaud the priority of practical reason found in Kant's thought. Although Kant accorded faith a prominent role in his ethical theory, Golubinskij saw this as consequent upon the destruction of all true knowledge. This may seem favorable to defenders of Christianity, but he thought this Kantian maneuver, made out of epistemic agnosticism, had very little in common with the Christian religion. A faith that does not firmly believe its tenets correspond to what is true cannot itself be true. This Kantian faith asks us to believe in dreams and mirages. The faith of practical reason can be no more justified than the skepticism of theoretical reason.

More than one commentator has written of Golubinskij's debt not just to Wolffian rationalism, but also to Platonic idealism. The debt to Plato in fact is far more pronounced in Golubinskij than in Karpov. The Moscow theologian claimed that the invariable and essential laws of being were imprinted in us at the moment of our creation. God had determined these and other essences necessarily from the beginning of time. They exist in His mind from eternity before their realization.[33] To concede the opposite, that the essential laws governing and determining all of creation were formed or arose in time would mean that the mind of God changes and acquires in the course of time what was not present. This, to Golubinskij, is unacceptable. It would imply improvement, which is an unthinkable process in a perfect being. Golubinskij on this basis rejected any sense of evolution. There can be no transition from one species into another, since it would require the Deity's mind to be mutable. Golubinskij's universe is essentially static. All changes are superficial and cannot alter the fundamental nature and structure of God's eternal plan.

---

32 "Since every person, as experience shows, can come to an awareness in oneself of the idea of the Infinite Being, this idea is obviously universal." Golubinskij (1884b). 79.
33 Golubinskij (1884c), 125. Of course, such expressions make no sense, since for Golubinskij time had a beginning. To say that God had something from eternity would be to place time as an absolute alongside God, a position Golubinskij, as we saw, denied.

As for ourselves as philosophical investigators, we are to delve into the essences of finite things to reveal "their laws and ultimate goals, which are eternal and constantly abide."[34] True, Golubinskij was willing to allot empirical psychology a place within the sphere of philosophy. Although such psychology is guided by empirical cognitions and as such reveals nothing universal and necessary, it reveals properties of the human soul that we can always discern in all people, not just in particular individuals or nations. But Golubinskij's concern was not so much with empirical psychology – in fact he devoted very little attention to it – as with speculative or theoretical psychology, which he tells us is a part of metaphysics. It is the observation of our inner sense or of the acts of cognition that lead to ideas of the Infinite. In short, the goal of this theoretical psychology is to recognize the resemblance between the human spirit and God.[35] This similarity, this correlation between our spirit and God, serves as our connection with the Deity. Theoretical psychology examines this relationship not as a moral one, which is the concern of ethics, but from an ontological standpoint, detailing how we stand to the Infinite, which is the principal object of metaphysics as a whole. Golubinskij devoted considerable attention to such matters as the substantiality of the soul, its relation to the body, and where it lies within the body. These are matters for speculative theology, not philosophy, regardless of what Golubinskij may have thought. His conjectures were just that with neither empirical evidence nor rational argument. Whatever we may think of his thought today, that his dictated lectures notes were written down by students and published decades after his death itself alone testifies to the esteem his students held for him.

3.3 Kudrjavcev on the Concept of God and Evolution

Golubinskij's long tenure as the professor of philosophy at the Moscow Academy does not mean that he was the sole instructor of philosophy during this time – only the most committed. A number of individuals soon after their graduation became instructors, though how well they carried out their position is unknown. Most of these individuals produced no individual works in philosophy of their own and do not enter into a history of Russian philosophy even in the broadest sense. For example, Dmitrij P. Novskij taught logic and empirical psychology starting in 1824 but left the Academy in 1830. Mikhail E. Arkhidiakonskij, a graduate of the Petersburg Academy, taught a class on the history of philosophy in the fall of

---

34 Golubinskij (1884a), 39.
35 Golubinskij (1898), 3.

1828, and then in 1830 metaphysics and moral philosophy. The record is scant, but he appears to have left the Academy in 1835 for a position teaching literature in a secondary school.[36] Pavel I. Benevolenskij, a graduate of the Moscow Academy in 1826, lectured on logic and empirical psychology from 1830 but, entering the priesthood, left the Academy four years later serving at a church in Moscow. These individuals as well as a number of others lectured as they themselves were taught and thought little of contributing something original of their own.

Upon Golubinskij's retirement in 1854 he recommended as his successor Viktor D. Kudrjavcev, who had already from October 1852 been teaching Bible history and Greek at the Moscow Academy before his appointment to teach philosophy (at first, metaphysics and ancient philosophy) in 1854. He was promoted to a full professorship in 1858. Kudrjavcev, the son of a priest, received his secondary education in a theological seminary before enrolling at the Moscow Academy in 1848. There, he already attracted the attention of his superiors for his scholarly work, particularly for his earliest (1852) piece entitled "On the Unity of the Human Race," which sought to uphold the Biblical story of the genesis of humanity from a single couple.[37] In order to do so, Kudrjavcev invoked various contemporary sources – including scientific literature. He also attempted to show that all world languages originate from a single, common tongue.

Although he had already been teaching a course on the history of modern philosophy since 1856 at the Academy, Kudrjavcev continued in the immediately subsequent years to write on topics more intimately associated with Biblical apologetics than with philosophy. In fact, such apologetics, not philosophy in the modern sense, remained his central concern. In 1857 for example, he published an extended essay entitled "On Monotheism as the Original Religious Form of the Human Race," in which he argued against the view that the original religions of humanity were all polytheistic and that monotheism arose only in the course of time and

---

36 According again to Nadezhdin, Arkhidiakonskij was a real "chatterbox" [*bojkij govorun*], but not a philosopher. Nadezhdin (1914), 67. This Nadezhdin should not be confused with Fedor S. Nadezhin, whom we met in the previous chapter. Nikolaj I. Nadezhdin – note the letter "d" in his name – as editor of the journal *Teleskop* was instrumental in the publication of the first of Chaadaev's "Philosophical Letters." The Nadezhdin of *Teleskop* fame attended the Moscow Academy where he encountered Golubinskij. In 1830, he defended a dissertation *On the Origin, Nature, and Fate of So-Called Romantic Poetry.* He became a professor of the fine arts at Moscow University, but with his publication of Chaadaev's "Letter" he was declared insane and sent into "domestic exile." His contribution to our presentation here is the publication of a series of articles on Plato in 1830 in the journal *Vestnik Evropy*.

37 This work, for which Kudrjavcev received a *magister*'s degree, originally bore the title "On the Origin of All People from a Single Pair." See Kudrjavcev-Platonov (1893b), 11–12. The work itself was published serially between 1852–1854. See Kudrjavcev-Platonov (1894b), 1–195.

with education. Kudrjavcev, on the contrary, believed that in the earliest human social groups monotheism was predominant and an explicit belief therein. He asserted that over time, owing to external factors new superstitions, idols, and deities were added, and with this development the true foundations of religion were forgotten and distorted. Kudrjavcev believed that a look at the history of pagan religions will provide the inquirer with corroborating evidence for the Biblical teaching concerning the one God as the basic dogma common to all human religions.[38]

Kudrjavcev's essay "On Religious Indifferentism," published in 1861 was of more philosophical interest. One central topic of concern therein was to argue against those who believe that with the multitude of religions widespread in the world it is of little importance which is "best." As we surely must expect, Kudrjavcev could not countenance such an attitude. Only Christianity, he maintained, can completely satisfy our inner religious needs; only Christianity provides us with the abundant means for our moral perfection, which Kudrjavcev took for granted to be our human aspiration.[39] However, we must look at the issue of religion not solely from our perspective, but also from God's. Any true religion essentially must be a *revealed* religion, i.e., a religion based at least in part on God's message given directly to us. Since the revelations professed by all religions are not identical, not even compatible, they cannot all be God's word. "To think otherwise would be to assume that God revealed Himself at various times for different peoples in various ways, presented even various contradictory conceptions of Himself and of the

---

[38] See Kudrjavcev-Platonov (1892), 60–61; Kudrjavcev-Platonov (1857), 416. At this point an interesting biographical note concerning Kudrjavcev is in order. Among the many reforms introduced by Tsar Alexander II was the re-introduction of philosophy to the secular universities. The subject had been largely banned in the wake of the 1848 revolutions in Europe in the belief that the study of philosophy was the natural breeding ground of revolutionaries. The only qualified domestic source to fill the newly re-opened faculty positions was the theological academies. Already in 1860, Kudrjavcev was invited to the professorship at Moscow University, but politely rejected it out of love for the Academy. But his reputation had reached the ears of the highest echelons of the government leading to his appointment as a tutor in logic and the history of philosophy to the heir to the throne, Nicholas Alexandrovich, who regrettably died in 1865. Kudrjavcev spent the entire 1861 chronological year in Petersburg at the royal court, and in the course of that year he was offered the professorship at St. Petersburg University. This was a difficult offer to refuse, regardless of his own preferences. However, due to the intercession of Metropolitan Filaret, a high-placed Church official who wrote a gracious letter pleading to allow him to stay at the Moscow Academy, Kudrjavcev remained at his beloved school for the rest of his life. Smirnov (1879), 52; Kudrjavcev-Platonov (1893b), 44–45.

[39] We can safely assume that Kudrjavcev's assessment was dogmatic, made *without* having first undertaken a thorough study of all the world's religions, particularly with respect to humanity's "inner religious needs."

means to salvation."⁴⁰ Kudrjavcev saw this as a totally unacceptable position. The Truth is one and cannot be contradictory. Kudrjavcev provided no means by which one could ascertain independently which one of the religions contains the true revelation. Surely, we cannot ask God directly which religion has understood and conveyed the divine word correctly.

In his 1861 essay, Kudrjavcev raised an issue familiar to many, but odd to today's ears: Can an atheist or pagan be moral? Vladimir Solov'ëv, some three decades later, citing St. Paul, would remark that such persons can do good according to natural law "written in their hearts."⁴¹ For Solov'ëv, morality requires more than publicly condoned actions. It requires a moral will, the source of which is not limited to the inculcation of the moral dictates of revealed religion. One can listen to one's "heart" or dismiss these promptings.

Kudrjavcev wrote that before addressing the issue directly we must first clarify what the term "morality" encompasses. An ambiguity in our understanding of the term has resulted in the very posing of the issue. Some contend that morality is solely a matter of *actions* without taking into account the *intentions* that prompt behavior. In this limited, negative sense of morality, a good person is one who does no harm to others. If this is our understanding of morality, then a pagan or atheist can certainly be a morally good person, and objective criteria can be utilized in making such a determination. Kudrjavcev, however, was dissatisfied with this conception of morality, writing that "no one who truly respects morality and understands its essence is satisfied with such a one-sided and narrow conception of it."⁴² Were we to limit morality to the sphere of actions insofar as they directly and explicitly enhance or violate the rights of others, all sorts of vices and passions would be permitted as long as the rights of others are not intentionally violated. No, a more complete, or "truer," conception of morality must take into account whether the agent, of one's own free will, respects and seeks to fulfill the moral law without the inducement from any external conditions, including any perceived benefit for the agent. Thus, true morality is intimately linked to an agent's pure love of the moral good. Framed in these terms, Kudrjavcev's conception is one with which Kant would wholeheartedly agree.

In this article, Kudrjavcev was unconcerned with clarifying and defending human free will. He took for granted that we have, what Kant scholars call "prac-

---

40 Kudrjavcev-Platonov (1861), 81.
41 Solov'ëv in his *Justification of the Moral Good* quoted Paul. See Solov'ëv (2015), 4 and Romans 2: 14–15.
42 Kudrjavcev-Platonov (1861), 95.

tical freedom."⁴³ But Kudrjavcev was concerned with our sense of morality, what induces us to be moral, and what enhances our moral sense. He acknowledged that we have a natural inclination or predisposition for the moral good, but at the same time we also have in our nature evil and immoral instincts. If we are to reject pursuit of the latter and follow instead the arduous path of virtue, we must know and acknowledge virtue as worth the effort. It is not at all obvious that we should do this in light of the at times obscurity of the proper road and the opposition of our instincts. We must know why we should be good and why the virtuous path is worthy of respect. Only with answers to these questions will we always be prepared to be virtuous. Kant recognized the power of these issues and offered detailed but complex answers. Kudrjavcev, on the other hand, offered a simple answer: religion, and not just any religion, but only the true religion. "Only the true religion can lead to true morality. This is why the idea that a person can be good independently of religion or with just any religion is one of the most dangerous thoughts for the moral life."⁴⁴ Only by recognizing the connection of virtue to religion can we find virtue worthy of lasting respect. A person can be genuinely virtuous only with the assistance of a religious union with God. A Christian respects the moral law, seeing it as the prescriptions of the Divine. In presenting the connection between the moral impulse and religion in standard Christian terms, Kudrjavcev obviated, however simplistically, many of the complex quandaries of Kantian ethics.

The emergence of materialism in mid-nineteenth-century Germany found resonance rather quickly within Russia after the Crimean War. This materialism was not that of the "philosophical" variety ascribed to Feuerbach and Chernyshevskij, but of the "scientific" variety of Karl Vogt, Jacob Moleschott, and Ludwig Büchner.⁴⁵ Their works, owing to censorship, could not appear in translation before 1862, but this did not prevent their illegal import and illegal translation before then. These could be readily obtained at Moscow University. It is against this feverish background as an ominous threat to Christian beliefs that Kudrjavcev in early 1860 published a long essay entitled "On the Initial Origin on Earth of the Human Race." As the title indicates, it also belongs to Christian apologetics in its opposition not just

---

43 Likewise Kant wrote in his *Groundwork*, "We take ourselves as free in the order of efficient causes in order to think ourselves under moral laws in the order of ends." Kant (1996), 97 (Ak 4:450). References to Kant's works in German are to the standard edition published under the auspices of the Königlich Preussischen Akademie der Wissenschaften and cited throughout as "Ak.").
44 Kudrjavcev-Platonov (1861), 103.
45 As Scanlan noted, the writings of the three "began to enjoy great vogue—greater perhaps, than in their home country." Scanlan (1970), 69.

to spontaneous generation, but to the entire concept of organic life emerging from inorganic matter.

Kudrjavcev at the start informs the reader that his religious solution to the issue is set against the materialistic one in offering a simple reference to the direct action of the omnipotent God. Nothing speaks against this solution, although he admits there is something mysterious and incomprehensible in its conception. Nonetheless, the thinking person must accept it on pain of falling into the hopeless difficulties associated with pantheism. Unfortunately, Kudrjavcev failed to clarify in what way his conception of materialism evokes pantheism. Materialism appeals to the popular allure of being "scientific" in order to evade exposing its inherent weaknesses and the weaknesses of its practical applications. Kudrjavcev proposed demonstrating its inadequacies by looking at its explanation of: (1) the emergence of organic entities from inorganic matter, and (2) the "progressive development of organisms," i.e., evolutionary theory as it existed at the time of Kudrjavcev's writing.[46]

Since the materialists do not share his theistic beliefs, Kudrjavcev proposed initiating his inquiry from the common standpoint that the two parties shared, viz., the human being as an organic being. For Kudrjavcev, the question is whether organic life in general including human life can arise from inorganic substances. Can experience dispense with the assumption of Divine action in explaining the origin of life? Kudrjavcev was willing to concede the possibility that living organisms originally appeared in numerous and varied places on earth and that under particular chemical and physical conditions these organisms took on special characteristics. He contested, however, the materialists' conclusion that the origin of organisms was a result of inorganic agents of various types. All we can logically deduce from the facts is that similar plants and animals originally appeared in different places on earth, a conclusion that can easily be accommodated within a Judeo-Christian perspective.[47] We cannot be certain what timespan Kudrjavcev had in mind in his response to the materialists' areligious discussion of the genesis of life. He does not state when he believed the earth was created and what the conditions were in a reasonable time afterward, but he does give every indication that it did occur eons ago. He believed, however, that the facts warranted a quite different conclusion than that offered by the materialists. If inorganic material under a certain set of conditions produces living organisms, then at a different time but under the same conditions, the same organisms should appear. That this is not the case, that organisms do not emerge under the same conditions, means that

---

46 Kudrjavcev-Platonov (1860), 198.
47 Kudrjavcev-Platonov (1860), 202.

the materialists' picture is incorrect. Kudrjavcev viewed this negative result as establishing scientifically a universal and necessary natural law that "every organic being is derived from nothing but an organic being and that no organism can arise by itself from an inorganic mass."[48] In other words, a Biblical creationism is scientifically affirmed by our present inability to account for every step leading from the inorganic to the organic.

A number of evolutionary theories, of course, were propounded before Darwin's.[49] For Kudrjavcev, even if we should accept that higher species can arise from lower ones, this does not account for the origin of the first organisms. The evolutionary theories that Kudrjavcev sought to combat simply assumed the materialist account of the origin of the first life with the proviso that through a transformative process original, simple organisms evolved into more and more complex ones. None of them even seek to address the problem of the origin of life. Additionally, none of them address why the transformative process is consistently from the simple to the relatively more complex. Kudrjavcev, writing in apparent ignorance of the proposed mechanism of Darwinian natural selection, criticized the evolutionists and paleontologists he knew for assuming without proof not only that evolution proceeded exclusively in one direction, but also that higher forms of life could originate solely from a lower form. Their principal error in his eyes was that the empirical facts did not warrant the deductions they drew. Their conclusions always contained more than was given in the premises. Kudrjavcev concluded that once we are convinced that the origin of life on earth cannot be explained naturally, we will recognize the need for an independent creative spiritual princi-

---

48 Kudrjavcev-Platonov (1860), 211.

49 One distinguished scholar today writes, "Darwin's theory was first communicated to the Russian public in January 1860, when the *Journal of the Ministry of National Education* published a translation of Lyell's favorable comments about it before the British Association for the Advancement of Science. His ideas reached the broader reading public in 1864 with the publication of S. A. Rachinskii's translation of the *Origin* and the appearance of Pisarev's and Timiriazev's popular essays on the selection theory." Todes (1989), 23. Kudrjavcev understandably made no direct reference to *On the Origin of Species*, which after all appeared only at the end of November 1859, but he did mention Darwin once in a footnote, writing that Darwin "believed that water was the original element from which all living things arose through the gradual transformation of the simplest aquatic organisms, first into amphibians, then into land animals. According to this theory, man first existed in the form of an aquatic animal; then, after many centuries, he received some transitional form in the genus of an amphibian or a turtle, and then the real one." Kudrjavcev-Platonov (1860), 220–221f.

ple as well as a "chain of truths of infinite importance" for the conduct of a moral life.[50] All of this follows from faith in an eternal Creator of the world.

Kudrjavcev penned yet another piece belonging to Christian apologetics in 1864. In his "On the Source of Our Ideas of the Deity," he wrote that empirical evidence notwithstanding, we could not have a conception of God if beforehand it were not, however vaguely, already present in our mind. "No matter how menacing, the phenomena of nature could not form within us this concept [of God] if there were not already present an inducement to form it."[51] Likewise, every mental phantasy, whether it be incoherent or a highly artistic representation, is clearly recognized to be merely a subjective fiction. The same cannot be said of our idea of the Deity. Unlike our phantasies, we must conceive the object of that idea, viz., God, as really existing. Kudrjavcev claimed we cannot conceive God without recognizing the objective existence of the object of that conception. This alleged inability to conceive otherwise in contrast to other mental representations shows that the two have a quite different source. Indeed, our idea of the Deity has elements that cannot be obtained by any combination or exaggeration of those from other representations. "The boldest phantasy ... could not by itself conjure the absolute features that constitute the peculiarity of our conception of God if it were not guided by an idea of the infinite that lies already in our soul."[52] Kudrjavcev was willing to go even further with this train of thought, proclaiming that we would not have a conception of perfection, of a perfect state of affairs, were it not for that of the Deity *a priori* in our "soul." The universality and necessity of religion, an irresistible and ineradicable need for it, in all people testifies to the apriority of our conception of God. To think differently, to reject religion as an empty delusion on the part of the entire human race, amounts to accusing humanity of being afflicted with a chronic madness.

3.4 Kudrjavcev on Cognition and Comtean Positivism

The theological academies did not totally escape the reform spirit of the 1860s. A new charter received approval at the highest level in 1869 with its introduction first at the St. Petersburg and Kyiv Academies, followed the next year at the Moscow and Kazan Academies. One of the intents of the new charter was to broaden

---

50 Kudrjavcev-Platonov (1860), 247. We see here a time and again common argument used by Russian theologians/philosophers that since the science of their day cannot account for a particular natural phenomenon, a supernatural explanation is thereby vindicated.
51 Kudrjavcev-Platonov(1864), 7.
52 Kudrjavcev-Platonov (1864), 12.

the mission of the schools, a consequence of which was that not all courses taught were compulsory for all students.[53] The salaries for the teaching staff were increased in an attempt to compete with the universities for the best instructors.[54] The new charter also opened up the academies not just to seminarians, as previously, but also to other secondary school students. Interestingly, for the first time auditors were allowed to attend classes.[55] Other reforms included granting the academies the right to their own censorship and the introduction of several courses directly for the first time. Also implemented was a screening out process whereby after the third year of study those who did not receive higher than a particular score on a general test were dismissed from continuing their studies. The fourth year of study for those who proceeded was devoted to a few specialized subjects, as well as preparation for a *magister*'s degree thesis and examination. A requirement for the *magister*'s degree was the submission of a printed thesis and its public defense. This too was intended to dispel the generally held view that study at a theological academy was scholastically inferior to a university education. Public defenses of theses were considered a viable means of combating the popular prejudice.

For our purposes here, the most important change introduced by the 1869 Charter was the new requirement that full professors have a doctorate. Those professors on staff who did not have such a degree were required to obtain one within three years or face dismissal. The doctoral degree required the submission and defense of an appropriate dissertation. As one can imagine, this new demand sent many of the established professors at the academies into a veritable panic. They suddenly had to acquire that degree. The first such doctoral defense at the Moscow Academy took place in December 1871, but it was the fourth overall.

Kudrjavcev realizing what he had to do, quickly seized upon the opportunity and gathered his thoughts on a topic he had more than merely broached recently, as we have seen.[56] The large work, *Religion, its Essence and Origin*, published orig-

---

53 Florovskij (2009), 457–458. Florovskij wrote that as a consequence of this change "the integrity of the theological education was shattered."
54 Cvyk (2013), 47.
55 Saltykov (1986), 92. This is how Vladimir Solov'ëv was able to audit Kudrjavcev's classes at the Moscow Academy.
56 In his long biographical essay on Kudrjavcev prefacing the first volume of the collected works, Ivan Korsunskij (1849–1899) wrote that Kudrjavcev started work on what became his dissertation already in 1868. Korsunskij provided no evidence for his claim. Korsunskij (1893), 18. For us to accept Korsunskij's statement, we would have to assume Kudrjavcev had conceived writing what became his dissertation as a stand-alone volume. This is certainly possible, but the first installments of his work appeared only in the first half of 1870 in the house organ of the Academy where he

inally in installments in the house organ *Orthodox Review* [*Pravoslavnoe obozrenie*] formed his dissertation, which he would go on to defend in 1873 as his doctoral dissertation. In keeping with the style of a scholarly thesis, much of it is a summary of the attitudes and views of others, principally German philosophers such as Feuerbach, Kant, and Jacobi. Kudrjavcev himself conceived his work as belonging more to the philosophy of religion than to theology in a narrow sense, though submitting it for a theological degree.[57] The aim of the historical presentation was to present how religion was understood by various representatives of philosophy and thereby show its own intellectual evolution. Make no mistake, though, he wrote from a decidedly Christian standpoint affirming that his look at Feuerbach and the French *Encyclopédistes* was to show the "complete impossibility of explaining in any rationally satisfactory manner the universal presence of religion in human life without a recognition of the existence of a Supreme Being."[58] However, recognizing the veracity of the object of religious belief does not resolve the issue of its essence and origin within us.

Unlike his 1864 position that we have an original, albeit vague, conception of God, Kudrjavcev now in 1873 wrote that we have no such innate idea but only a *faculty* for supersensible cognition. That is, we have a natural aspiration for God and an ability to cognize the Divine. But this faculty would remain latent if it did not confront an object, if we were not presented with the actually existing Deity. That all of humanity has a religious sense of God shows that God exists. Thus, an explanation of religion with respect to its objective aspect requires us to grant the *continuous* action of God on us, on our natural faculty for such perception. "In order to explain the objective side of religion, we must assume not just a momentary, but a continuous action of the Deity on our spirit, on the faculty intended for perceiving the supersensible."[59] This Divine action is God's natural revelation in our spirit and is the sole possible explanation for the origin of our religious idea. It is distinct from His positive revelation to our five senses that we find, for example, in Bible stories. As he had written in previous essays, Kudr-

---

would have had no problem publishing a newly-finished work quickly. For the installments, see Kudrjavcev-Platonov (1870).

57 The theological academies were not permitted to offer degrees in philosophy *per se*. During the discussions over the proposed charter of 1869, the idea of awarding philosophy degrees was raised but rejected on the grounds that the religious schools should not compete with the secular universities in that regard. An additional consideration was that philosophy in the academies had been traditionally conceived as a secondary subject assisting theological aims and not as an independent line of inquiry that could conceivably take precedence over theology.

58 Kudrjavcev-Platonov (1898), 132.

59 Kudrjavcev-Platonov (1898), 290.

javcev affirmed that the universality of religion in humanity throughout the ages coupled with the power of its conviction within us demonstrates that its source cannot be a figment of our imagination or the product of our faculty of understanding (*rassudok*).

The Deity's relation to us in our everyday lives is not directly ascertainable through our five senses. Thus, His being is transcendent. Nonetheless, His transcendency as an external object for our supersensible cognition is analogous to other external objects for our sensible cognition except that the latter objects are known with a clarity that does not permit disagreement. On the other hand, God and the entire supersensible world are for the most part cognized only vaguely. As a result, we interpret our cognition of this supersensible world in various and often contradictory ways leading to the multitude of different religious beliefs. Continuing the analogy with our five senses, Kudrjavcev held that the acuity of our faculty for supersensible cognition can vary among people just as some have better eyesight or hearing.[60] The result of this deficiency in some is a lack of religious knowledge. If we, following Kant, term what the senses provide for discursive understanding "sensible intuition," then the parallel expression with regard to our supersensible faculty is "ideal intuition" or "ideal seeing." This intuition provides an immediate manifold of the supersensible.[61] Kudrjavcev urges us, however, not to call the result an "immediate cognition," since the affections are received not directly by the mind (or "soul"), but by this other, (super)sense organ. Moreover, just as we cognize the objects of our five senses only as they are given to the senses and within the bounds of those senses, not therefore as they are in themselves, so too God is not directly and fully revealed to us in Himself. We do not and cannot have a complete, totally accurate cognition of the Deity's nature. The nature and laws of all of our intuitive faculties are reflected in what we obtain through them. As a result, God's everyday activity must pass through the prism of our supersensible faculty and be-

---

[60] Kudrjavcev-Platonov (1898), 295. In a separately published piece "Theses of the Work *Religion, Its Essence and Origin*," Kudrjavcev, summarizing his dissertation. wrote, "The activity of this faculty in relation to the supersensible is perceptual, analogous in form to the activity of the outer senses in relation to the external world." Kudrjavcev-Platonov (1898), 319. One of the official opponents at Kudrjavcev's dissertation defense at the end of January 1873 was his colleague Vasilij N. Potapov, whom we shall see in some more detail later. At the defense, Potapov objected to the Golubinskij-Kudrjavcev position that our thought alone could not produce religion and the concept of an infinite Being. Potapov contended that through a denial of finitude, the human mind could produce the concept of infinity and with it of God. See Korsunskij (1890), 161–162. We also see from this incident that the stipulation in the new 1869 charter for dissertation defenses resulted in stimulating scholarship, but that stipulation also allowed for the airing of theological disputes and challenges to established doctrine for the first time in public.

[61] Kudrjavcev-Platonov (1898), 302.

comes tainted or corrupted, the intuition taking on features that it does not originally have. Our religious cognition, thus, contains an element, or elements, that are subjective in addition to those that are objective, but this process is entirely unavoidable, i.e., natural. Our religious conception can gradually develop or evolve along with our thinking. In other words, the forms of our religious thought will also undergo change along the way as we progressively move toward a greater and more accurate cognition of the objective Truth.

Kudrjavcev surely felt that the central contribution of his doctoral dissertation was his affirmation and defense of a supersensible cognitive faculty whereby we have direct contact with God's presence and activity in the world and on us. Kudrjavcev explicitly rejected what he took to be Kant's turn to practical reason and Schleiermacher's religious feeling as the original source of religion. For the Russian philosopher of religion, both morality and religious feeling acquire religious significance only with and through a preliminary knowledge of God, regardless of what form that knowledge may take.[62]

Continuing his slow turn from Christian apologetics to philosophy of religion and then to developing a general Christian philosophy, Kudrjavcev on 1 October 1874 gave a public talk on a topic that would appear anachronistic in light of his previous writings entitled "A Critical Analysis of Comte's Doctrine of the Three Methods of Philosophical Cognition." However, the influence and pervasiveness of Comtean positivism had been on the rise among the educated populace during the previous decade with the appearance of several works by various writers, such as Vladimir Miljutin, Nikolaj Serno-Solov'evich, and Dmitrij Pisarev. It did not take long for a reaction to emerge. In the third volume of his *Philosophical Lexicon* from 1866, Silvestr Gogockij (1813–1889), a philosophy professor at Kyiv University, rebuked Comte for his theoretical reliance on physical laws alone to explain not merely all empirical phenomena, but even moral ones as well. Whereas Gogockij approached Comte from a religio-philosophical standpoint, Vasilij Ja. Cinger[63] (1836–1907) a mathematician at Moscow University attacked from his specialty. In a public address "The Exact Sciences and Positivism" at Moscow University in

---

62 Kudrjavcev-Platonov (1898), 313. In the separately published "Theses," Kudrjavcev wrote, "The preference that Kant gives to practical reason over theoretical reason in grounding religious truths is quite unjustified. Practical religion with its moral proof of God's existence cannot explain the origin of religion, and it cannot explain the actual path by which religious truths arise in our mind. ... Limiting natural (rational) religion to morality alone leads not only to the destruction of religion, but also to the weakening of morality itself." Kudrjavcev-Platonov (1898), 317.
63 Cinger not only was a distinguished mathematician in Imperial Russia but also did considerable work on the taxonomy of plants. His grandfather had moved to Moscow from Germany in the late eighteenth century.

January 1874, Cinger sharply lambasted positivism, saying that it was undistinguished in terms of insight, and as a philosophical doctrine it offered nothing attractive.⁶⁴ The exponents of positivism had themselves propagandized its scientificity without demonstrating that this was the case. Cinger, on the other hand, challenged the scientific nature of the positivist creed, writing that its alleged scientificity was without merit. Unlike positivism's religious critics, who claimed it was blind to our spiritual nature, Cinger criticized Comte's understanding of mathematics. He charged Comte with not fully grasping so much as the first principles of science, let alone the recent literature that had disclosed so many new findings.⁶⁵

Even John Stuart Mill was not immune to Cinger's sallies. He accused Mill along with Comte of preaching a blind, one-sided empiricism, of ignoring all that philosophy had achieved, and of inconsistency.⁶⁶ Mill, in particular, was motivated not by conviction, but by following what he conceived to be the general attitude. In this, Mill was by nature a sophist.⁶⁷

Cinger's talk at the beginning of 1874 was but an opening salvo in what became a resurgent bulwark against Comtean positivism. Later that year on 1 October, Kudrjavcev gave a special yearly address at the Academy entitled "A Critical Review of A. Comte's Doctrine of the Three Methods of Philosophical Cognition."⁶⁸ Kudrjavcev started his talk asking whether religion and philosophy could cooperate, whether divine revelation and human reason must compete against each other. There have been many attempts, he continued, over time to destroy and even legitimize the antagonism between faith and reason. Hegel claimed that religion and philosophy were essentially identical but differed in form. Religion presented its content in representations, whereas philosophy presented the same in the form of concepts. Religion is, however, a lower transitional form of cognition that must

---

64 It remains unclear to this day whether Vladimir Solov'ëv attended this talk. S. M. Luk'janov, in his biography of the early Solov'ëv, wrote of a communication he received from a friend of the philosopher's early years. This friend stated that by his memory Solov'ëv, in his first year at the University, performed poorly on an analytic geometry examination with Cinger. Luk'janov adds that this is consistent with other information he had of Solov'ëv's mathematical misadventures. Luk'janov (1916), 209.
65 Cinger (1874), 52.
66 Cinger (1874), 59
67 Cinger (1874), 65.
68 Kudrjavcev's address was issued almost immediately as a separate brochure. It also appeared in a slightly expanded and reworked form in the house organ of the Academy in March 1875 and then much later, of course, in the collected edition of Kudrjavcev's works, bearing the title "Religion and Positive Philosophy." Owing to the easier accessibility of the latter, references to Kudrjavcev's address will be largely to it as found in the collected works.

disappear into the higher form of philosophical knowledge.[69] Auguste Comte is another figure, who although receiving little attention in strictly philosophical circles has gathered much in general society. He, similar to Hegel, considered all philosophical and religious systems dissimilar to his to be transitional, albeit necessary, movements of thought leading to the ultimate philosophy, his own. Kudrjavcev wrote, however, "What is important for us at present is not which philosophy, be it idealistic, positive, or some philosophy of the future should replace religion, but whether religion is really something replaceable, whether it is a lower passing moment that in the history of individual and general human development must be replaced by some higher form of knowledge."[70] Kudrjavcev objected to the understanding of religion taken for granted in the views of Hegel and Comte. The latter two have an unduly restricted notion of religion. It is neither a form of knowledge nor a cognitive method. Its boundaries extend into the sphere of feeling and activity. Nonetheless, Kudrjavcev wished to focus on the "theoretical" side of religion, on religion as a worldview and to what extent it is knowledge about God.

The laws and basic methods of cognizing remain the same at all stages of human cognitive development. The difference over time lies in our ability to apply those logical laws and principles to cognitive subjects. Kudrjavcev, in this regard, considered it strange that Comte found the three methods he detailed to be quite antagonistic and exclusive of each other. The methods are not incompatible as we can readily and factually see in multiple cases where a religious outlook or worldview is held by many who pursue scientific research. He also thought Comte's ordering of the three methods to be odd. Our mental development proceeds from the simpler to the more complex and abstract. Comte, on the other hand, portrayed human history as beginning with, from Kudrjavcev's viewpoint, the most abstract and difficult to fathom, viz., the concern of the theological method, and culminating in the simplest. However, if Comte were correct, he would, in effect, be acknowledging that religious knowledge is the most original, essential, and yet basic need of the human spirit.

Of the various cognitive methods, none is employed on the basis of a purely subjective whim. The method is chosen based on the object to be cognized. For example, we use a different method (*priem*) for cognizing an empirical object than when performing mathematical operations. This fact should have already showed Comte that the source of our worldviews does not lie in the mind, but outside it, that the religious, philosophical, and empirical worldviews are determined by the

---

69 Kudrjavcev-Platonov (1898), 324.
70 Kudrjavcev-Platonov (1898), 325.

cognitive object.⁷¹ Yet, as soon as we concede that external cognitive objects determine our worldview and we admit that one such worldview is the religious worldview, we concede the existence of a sphere of ideal objects that populate the supersensible world.⁷² That we routinely employ different cognitive techniques depending on the object shows, contrary to Comte's philosophy of history, that the three types of cognition are not mutually exclusive. Rather, the cognitive ideal is a harmonious combination of them, and only such a combination can provide a genuine reflection in our knowledge of what is.⁷³ Comte's view that the three worldviews are incompatible arises from his basic stance that the principles of each are radically different, a position Kudrjavcev rejected. The former denied the very possibility of cognition beyond the phenomenal sphere, which Kudrjavcev, as a religious thinker, simply could not abide. For him – but not for Comte – faith and revelation are sources of knowledge along with reason and empirical experience. Since the different methods correspond to different sets of existential objects, a discovery by one method, such as the scientific method, cannot refute or even undermine a religious tenet. A discovery in natural science could at most lend support to the standpoint that the object of the discovery does not belong within the religious sphere and thus cannot be viewed from that worldview. But no scientific discovery can refute a tenet from the religious sphere. Furthermore, Kudrjavcev disputed Comte's claim that religion and philosophy were historically transitional stages to the scientific worldview. Such a position would have to prove that each of these worldviews is in essence merely a temporary and fortuitous discovery of the mind. History, though, cannot be of help, for it informs us only of what was – or at most what is – but certainly not what can and should be. It would appear from this, then, that Kudrjavcev disavows any attempt at a speculative philosophy of history.⁷⁴

As we saw, Kudrjavcev was not the first Russian voice to rise up in alarm at the emerging influence of positivism among the educated populace. He would not be

---

71 Thus, we use a method employed in constructing a religious worldview when the object under consideration belongs to the supersensible world and an empirical method when dealing with physical objects. It is not the case that we can use a method drawn from, say, the religious worldview to study physical objects. Also there are no special sub-regions within a sphere populated with objects corresponding to those in another sphere. That is, as Kudrjavcev wrote, "There is no special religious or theological chemistry, astronomy, mathematics, or medicine." Kudrjavcev-Platonov (1874), 342.
72 Kudrjavcev-Platonov (1874), 329.
73 Kudrjavcev-Platonov (1874), 333. Kudrjavcev was willing to concede that due to the natural limitations of the individual it is impossible to have complete and universal knowledge.
74 Thus, judging from his *Crisis of Western Philosophy* Solov'ëv, unlike Kudrjavcev, but like Comte, was quite willing to engage in a speculative philosophy of history as early as January 1874.

the last. Within two months of his address, a young religious-minded but secular philosopher would begin his illustrious career with a thesis explicitly aimed at positivism.[75] His words would resound throughout the Russian intellectual community and transform the up-to-then moribund domestic philosophical scene. Whether Kudrjavcev himself altered his concerns is debatable. Whether he too felt an influence from the young Vladimir Solov'ëv can only be a matter of conjecture. What is clear is that in the years ahead, Kudrjavcev engaged not in Christian apologetics directly, but in developing a systematic Christian philosophy. We will turn to the specifics of his elaborations in the second part of this study when we return again to the Moscow Theological Academy in the years after the defense of Solov'ëv's *magister*'s thesis.

---

75 This is, at least, the conventional picture. I have sought to demonstrate its baseless nature in Nemeth (2016).

Chapter 4
The Kyiv and Kazan Academies Under the First Charter

In preparation for its transformation, the Kyiv-Mohyla Academy was closed in August 1817, and the Kyiv Theological Academy opened in late September 1819, five years after the Moscow Academy and ten years after the St. Petersburg Academy. From an administrative perspective, it stood at the summit of a religio-educational district that comprised 17 dioceses. The Academy's staff initially consisted of a rector, six professors and a number of teachers. The Academy's intent, as with the others in Imperial Russia, was to prepare higher-level Church administrators and teachers for the theological seminaries. During the first decade of the Kyiv Academy's existence, philosophy was taught in Latin, after which the language of instruction became Russian.[1]

4.1 Skvorcov's Philosophical Theology

The first instructor of philosophy at the new Kyiv Academy was Ivan M. Skvorcov (1795–1863), a graduate from the St. Petersburg Academy in 1817 with a *magister*'s degree, having placed first in his class.[2] In that year Skvorcov was appointed professor of philosophy, mathematics, and physics at the Kyiv Theological Seminary, which opened in late October 1817. When the Kyiv Academy officially opened in 1819, Skvorcov became the sole instructor of philosophy there. In 1824, he was named a full professor of philosophy, a position he held until 1849.[3] He was also made the librarian of the Academy in that same year, in which capacity he acquired for the library the works of such modern philosophers as Leibniz, Kant,

---

[1] "Although the Commission for Theological Schools, by a provision from 8 September 1819, left the choice between Latin and Russian for theology lectures to the rector, they were all read in Latin with the exception of lectures on the Holy Scriptures. The same was true of the philosophy class. The Russian language had not yet developed sufficiently for the transmission of the concepts that inevitably appear in philosophy lessons, particularly in logic." Askochenskij (1863), 72.

[2] Of course, each of us must determine for oneself the philosophical worth of Skvorcov's pronouncements. However, Shpet had no hesitation in writing that Skvorcov "was a philosopher of meager gifts, and as a teacher the content of his philosophical investigations was not very deep." Shpet (2008), 07.

[3] For a poignant account of his teaching method and what he required of his students, see the entry on Skvorcov in Ikonnikov (1884), 601–610.

and Fichte among others. Moreover, he held in addition a professorship at Kyiv University from 1834–1858, teaching theology, church history and church law.[4] In the years after he departed from the Academy, Skvorcov ceased his "philosophical" investigations.

On the occasion of the inauguration of the Kyiv Academy, Skvorcov delivered an address in Latin that much later in 1863 was published in a Russian-language translation made by the author himself at the request of the commission governing the theological schools. Skvorcov's talk entitled "On the Metaphysical Principle of Philosophy," represents the most complete statement of his own philosophical position. It began with the foundationalist assertion that every science must have a firm basis. Without such a basis, a discipline cannot be a science. The more important we claim a science to be, the more important it is that we ascertain this foundation. Philosophy, claiming to be the fundamental science, the science of science, must above all, furnish this first principle. The possibility of philosophy is directly dependent on the possibility of its chief principle.[5] Skvorcov did not mince his words. The principle he sought is not a logical one, but metaphysical. Through it, all questions concerning the possibility of things, their essence, and the true form of their being can be answered. Genuine knowledge of non-empirical objects must be deduced from this chief principle. The question, then, is whether such a principle is possible. As a Russian Orthodox cleric, Skvorcov had no doubt of its possibility and unequivocally affirmed that the "All-Perfect Mind," i.e., God, possessed perfect knowledge. This, to Skvorcov, meant that the chief principle is not just possible, but actually exists.

Since all knowledge ultimately follows from one principle, philosophy in Skvorcov's telling is a "harmonious system of truths" arrived at by the mind itself, though prompted by the idea of the Deity.[6] These truths form a harmony, because the universe itself is a simple whole, all parts of which are inextricably and harmoniously connected. If there were more than one principle, there, then, could be different truths and different probabilities of truth. Skvorcov utterly rejected such a conclusion. Additionally, he also rejected a dichotomy between theory and practice as though there were one truth in theory (or "theoretical philosophy") and another in human action ("practical philosophy" or ethics). Skvorcov could not accept the argument that the object of each sphere is fundamentally different. God's mind and God's will are one and the same. "Everything in the all-perfect mind is both true and good; all that God wants is both good and true."[7] Thus,

---

4 Kucenko (2002), 47.
5 Skvorcov (1863b), 49–50.
6 Skvorcov (1863b), 58.
7 Skvorcov (1863b), 63.

we, in and through our actions, are to fulfill God's will, not our own even if the effect of doing so would be beneficial to all of humanity.

Skvorcov had no quarrel with Kant concerning what the former called "the lower cognitive faculties," the activities of which were confined to experience. The understanding is naturally furnished with categories, and sensibility has its forms, viz., space and time. Skvorcov's argument made no appeal to any convoluted transcendental argument. We represent everything in space and yet it is nowhere in that we cannot assign a place to it, for it serves as a condition for any assignment. Likewise, time always exists in the sense that we cannot so much as imagine anything outside time, and yet it never is in that we cannot conceive assigning time to another time. The past already does not exist, and the future still does not exist. The present is only a fleeting mental boundary between the past and the future. Since God created everything including space and time, He cannot be "in" them nor must He represent things in them. Skvorcov concluded from this that space and time are, as Kant wrote, only forms of our representation.

However, are we, as human beings created in the image and likeness of God, limited to the empirical? Skvorcov held that we have yet another, a yet higher faculty than that which is employed in acquiring empirical knowledge, one that he calls the mind. The supreme object of this highest mental faculty is God, Who enters our mind neither as a form nor as a category, but as an idea even though the mind cannot fully embrace that idea. Skvorcov gave neither a proof for this claim nor did he present any argument in the hope of convincing the skeptic of his position. But he added that the mind has a practical aspect in addition to this cognitive one. There is in us a lower will based on self-love and a higher will governed by the pure moral law, the will of God, which instructs us to follow it out of love for God alone.

Given the nature and occasion of Skvorcov's address it is understandable that he did not venture into a further elucidation of his thoughts and, more importantly, specifics. He would, in any case, have found those specifics already at hand to all of us in the Church's teachings. Through all this, we see Skvorcov as a thoroughly committed religious thinker, not a philosopher in the contemporary sense. That we have the idea of an All-Perfect Being is enough to assure us that God exists, for our minds simply could not produce that idea. The mere idea of God within us assures us that God is the original being and is eternal, and the more we contemplate this idea, the more we tangibly feel God's presence. Skvorcov found no puzzle lurking in the traditional questions of philosophy and undoubtedly would have displayed no interest in those problems that hold the attention of analytic philosophers and phenomenologists. His ready answer to the skeptic was clear. A philosophy that rejects his understanding of Christian doctrine is blind, and "a wisdom that rejects

Revelation is insane."[8] For Christians, it is unforgivable to love a philosopher, whether it be Plato or Aristotle, more than the philosophy of Jesus.

Skvorcov's prolificity, such as it was, was largely confined to archival manuscripts, and the few works he did publish during his lifetime were largely analyses of the writings of others. We see this in particular in his apparently first published article stemming from 1835 and entitled "On the Philosophy of Plotinus." There can be no mistake that Skvorcov's essay manifestly dealt with the Neoplatonist, but it was, in effect, aimed as much at a critique of German *Naturphilosophie*, particularly the position of Schelling, which was gaining alarming recognition in Russia. Skvorcov saw in Plotinus a metaphysical scheme that served as a philosophical model for *Naturphilosophie*, but which could not be reconciled with Christian teachings. The doctrines of Plato and Pythagoras are confused with Eastern philosophy and pagan superstition. Whereas Plotinus, unmistakably, aspired for truth and virtue, there lingered in the shadows of his system an Egyptian superstition, an ethics distorted by fanaticism. What profundity lies in his expressions is distorted, and his physical concepts are taken for metaphysical ones. Clearly in evidence is the work of a feverish imagination.[9]

Skvorcov remarked that the "One" of Plotinus is quite unlike any concept in ancient philosophy. It is quite abstract and refined to such a degree that it is bereft of anything in Christianity. The God of the latter is love and is wise; the One of Plotinus is completely devoid of any heart or mind, despite his words to the contrary. Again, Skvorcov wished us to see Schelling lurking not far behind. "There is a striking similarity of the One of Plotinus, as the principle of everything possible, of existence, and even of God, to the *absolute of Schelling*, or his *Urgrund* and *Ungrund*."[10] Such a metaphysical conception as that offered by Plotinus can hardly serve as the basis for either religion or morality. An empty principle cannot yield anything. From nothing, nothing can come. Although Plotinus sets matter against spirit, he has matter emerging from the World Soul, which in turn ultimately springs from the One. Thus, either matter is spiritual or the One is material.[11] The metaphysical objection, aside, the question remains how can there be freedom (and concomitantly morality) if everything follows with necessity from something

---

8 Skvorcov (1863b), 66.
9 Skvorcov (1835), 58.
10 Skvorcov (1835), 59.
11 Skvorcov fails to see that these very charges against Plotinus may, possibly, apply just as much to the Judeo-Christian conception of God. How can such a God, without materiality, create matter? Vladimir Solov'ëv later in the nineteenth century would say that the material universe is to varying degrees spiritual, thereby partially dissolving the dichotomy. Of course, even such a claim does not explain how a pure spirit can create matter in the first place.

else.¹² This was and will remain a central concern and fear of Russian philosophical theology: A philosophical system must theoretically be wrong if it does not allow for morality and personal responsibility.

Skvorcov's next work, the one for which he is best known, insofar as he is known at all, is his lengthy 1838 "Critical Review of Kant's *Religion within the Bounds of Reason Alone.*" Skvorcov received a doctorate for this work, submitting it as his dissertation.¹³ Despite being sharply critical of Kant, Skvorcov opened his "review" by praising him for revealing three important philosophical truths: (1) that reason alone is insufficient to cognize the non-empirical; (2) that alleged moral principles based on the concepts of pleasure and happiness are themselves immoral; and (3) that human nature is corrupt or damaged. We know these truths through divine revelation, but Kant's service lies in having proved them through reason alone. Kant's error, however, was his contention that all other truths in divine revelation could be found through reason. Rather, "to the greater glory of Revelation, we see that all the best in Kant's *Religion* is borrowed from the Gospel, and all the worst belongs to Kantian philosophy proper."¹⁴ Kant's attempt to extract truth from Revelation and show that it is rational and in accordance with his philosophy, however, was bound to fail. No philosophy, as a product of the human mind, can possibly be adequate to express Divine truths completely. It is bound always to be incomplete.

Continuing to link morality with religion, the latter being necessary for the former, Skvorcov criticized Kant for transforming the most powerful of moral feeling into a non-religious feeling. One consequence of this is that Kant utterly omitted our immediate duties to God. He viewed morality strictly in terms of duties to others and to ourselves, but without a relation to God morality leads to egoism. If morality demands respect for our rational nature, which Kant emphatically and correctly recognizes, then by the same token morality demands the greatest possible respect for the highest rational nature, viz., for God.¹⁵ Skvorcov questioned whether Kant's replacement of virtue for God can rightly be called religion. Kant recognized no need for either Revelation or the supernatural. He also failed to recognize that owing to our corrupt nature we always stand in need of help from the Divine. Kant, in Skvorcov's opinion, ultimately presented us with a deism, which, instead of showing how we can approach God, would in practice only further distance us from Him. As a naturalism, Kant's "religion" cannot satisfy our essential, spiritual needs. It remains content with morality alone.

---

12 Skvorcov (1835), 64.
13 Kucenko (2008), 92.
14 Skvorcov (1838), 87.
15 Skvorcov (1838), 117–118.

Skvorcov demonstrated little, if any, interest in philosophical issues that bore no direct relation to theological matters. His mind was that of a theologian, not of a philosopher in the contemporary sense, and he accepted as a matter of faith that his Christianity was divinely revealed. He sought neither rational nor empirical proof for its provenance. Indeed, he affirmed over and over in his writings that the sphere of reason and that of the supernatural are distinct. Nevertheless, he stated that he understood that an individual could still love free philosophical thought while remaining true to one's Christian faith. Such a person, Skvorcov wrote, recognizes that boundaries exist, while in some instances they are blurred. There is philosophy that belongs to reason alone and philosophy that is contained in revelation.[16] Skvorcov saw this in the writings of the early Church Fathers, particularly in Gregory of Nyssa, whom Skvorcov considered to be an example and a model. Certainly, the objects or subject matters of faith transcend the powers of reason, and therefore reason cannot penetrate and disclose the ultimate foundations of the truths conveyed in revelation. Reason can, however, establish the connection between those truths and other truths that reason knows better. Gregory, in Skvorcov's opinion, followed precisely this course in order, for example, to help clarify the doctrines of the Trinity and the incarnation of Jesus, the Son of God.[17]

To follow Skvorcov's discussion of the Trinity would be a fruitless excursion into theology. A rational understanding of the Trinity is by official Christian teaching impossible. Skvorcov merely hoped to illuminate it with the help of working through Gregory's writings, and he thought that Gregory's procedure could be followed in handling other "philosophical" issues. We encounter the endeavor, in any case, again in Vladimir Solov'ëv, although whether he was aware of Skvorcov's appeal to Gregory of Nyssa is unknown.[18] Skvorcov, as we see, by no means defended philosophy as an independent discipline with its own concerns, as did, for example, Sidonskij. For the former, theological issues were paramount, and philosophy was of use as a handmaid, nothing more. In a 1843 letter to a former pupil and from 1830 rector of the Kyiv Academy Innokentij, Skvorcov wrote: "Philosophy with all of its might is needed in the Academy. This is a necessity of the age, and without it the Church teacher will have no influence on his students."[19] Skvorcov, needless to say, had his own conception of philosophy in mind. Whether it excited his students is a different matter.

---

16 Skvorcov (1863a), 34.
17 Skvorcov (1863a), 37.
18 See Soloviev (1889), 203–221.
19 Skvorcov (2014), 262.

4.2 Innokentij on Three Kinds of Knowledge

Although not a professor of philosophy and certainly not a philosopher in the credentialed sense, Archbishop Innokentij (1800–1857), whose secular name was Ivan A. Borisov, displayed some familiarity with German Idealism in his writings.[20] Innokentij placed first in his graduating class at the Kyiv Academy in 1823. In that year, he began teaching Church history and Greek at the St. Petersburg Academy and in the following year became an instructor of theology there. He was lured back to his Kyiv alma mater in 1830 with an appointment as rector and a professorship in theology. However, he relinquished his professorial position in 1839 in order to devote more attention to his administrative duties as rector.[21]

Not just as a professor of theology but as an archbishop, Innokentij surely had many opportunities to preach and do so at length both orally and in writing. Based on his voluminous works, he surely did so with considerable gusto. However, there are but a few instances in those writings where he ventured out of the purely theological sphere. We can hardly find this surprising given his administrative role, on the one hand, and his professorship in theology, on the other. Furthermore, in a set of prepared instructions outlining how he believed teaching ought to be conducted in the theological academies, he wrote, "It should be required of philosophy, for example, that it, leaving aside many unnecessary formalities, take up a thorough exposition of the theory (*uchenie*) of religion, of the inadequacies of a natural knowledge of God, the need for and the signs of Divine revelation, and of the worthlessness of false revelation, etc."[22] Continuing, Innokentij wrote that the

---

20 One might say that Innokentij has received a "bad press." Florovsky held that Innokentij "was not a thinker. He had a sharp and impressionistic mind, not a creative one. Nor was he a scholar. ... Only a brilliant delivery masked the persistent lack of creative independence. But it was always delivery and not erudition." Florovsky (1979), 233. In contrast, the normally highly caustic Shpet wrote of Innokentij that he was an outstanding professor and rector, and in the latter role Innokentij got the Academy "on its feet." His lectures on fundamental theology were "imbued with a serious philosophical tone and revealed his very broad acquaintance and understanding of philosophy, including also those of his day." Shpet (2008), 215.

21 There is apparently some disagreement as to just when Innokentij relinquished his duties as professor. One contemporary scholar writes that Innokentij did so in 1837. Kucenko (2008), 82. Another contemporary scholar writes, "In 1836, Innokentij was consecrated bishop of Chigirin [Chyhyryn], vicar of the Kyiv diocese, and relinquished his position as rector. True, in connection with being busy with the concerns of the diocesan administration, he, to his great regret, had to quit his position as professor of theology." Sukhova (2011b), 19. However, a possibly older and more reliable source placed Innokentij's resignation on 10 October 1839. Jastrebov (1900), 524.

22 Quoted in Sukhova (2010b), 60. Although the set of instructions is not dated, Sukhova ventures the educated guess that they date from 1837 or 1838. Her estimation of the date appears well taken. See Sukhova (2010b), 45.

Academy course in the history of philosophical systems should cease teaching the philosophical "ravings" of minor philosophical figures and concentrate on the philosophy of the Church Fathers and their successors, who successfully using reason in the religious sphere also ultimately show the paucity of those achievements in comparison to divine revelation. Even otherwise secular disciplines, such as physics, history, and literature, reveal their true meaning only when they are connected with theology, only when such subject matter is discussed and conducted in a spiritual direction, "which they have, properly speaking, by their very nature and without which they fade and die."[23] Considering the pace at which physics and the "secular" disciplines would develop in the immediate decades after Innokentij made his remark, it is hard to conceive how one could say they faded and died.

Yet despite his concerns regarding the study of philosophical systems divorced from religion, Innokentij employed his knowledge of "philosophical systems," such as it was, in service to religion during some, most likely early, period in his professorial career. In an undated text that has come down to us entitled "On Religion in General," Innokentij, however oddly, invoked the early Fichte. For both, self-consciousness is possible only if the self, or "I," is limited, or "checked," by something independent of its own strivings, which in Innokentij's view is the aggregate of everything other than the self. However, whereas in the early Fichte this non-self is simply externality, the independently existing reality other than myself, for Innokentij it is a "dark representation of God." Thus, for the latter, self-consciousness is possible only under the condition that God, "the beginning of everything," exists.[24] Innokentij, regrettably, did not defend his notion of externality being a representation of God, dark or otherwise, with the ineluctable consequence that he effectively championed pantheism.

Innokentij employed the inherent vagueness in his Fichtean-styled transcendental proof of God's existence to account for the diversity of existing religions. Human spiritual "forces" developed differently, resulting in the development of a variety of different beliefs. But Innokentij ultimately finds such a proof of God's existence, regardless of its utility, to be unsatisfactory. It and all other such rational proofs are merely *indicators* of one *path* leading to God. We, certainly however, cannot logically ascend from a lower state to a higher one with any assurance. But Innokentij affirms that human beings have three kinds of cognition, a claim that will resonate throughout the entirety of Russian philosophy, albeit with modifications. There is no dispute among philosophers that we can and do acquire knowledge through the senses. No one seriously denies that we obtain

---

23 Quoted in Sukhova (2010b), 59.
24 *Sbornik* (1869), 14.

some knowledge through concepts and inferences. God, though, being above all natural experience, cannot be determined by predicates of the understanding and therefore cannot be experienced in the same way we experience worldly things or processes. Indeed, although the essence of God is incomprehensible to us, we, being created in the image and likeness of God, can through the nature of our own mind and that of things partially at least glimpse the essence of God as it is reflected in our ideas.

Innokentij held that there is yet a third kind of knowledge, a knowledge "by means of ideas of the mind," which he also described as a "rational faith in objects that cannot be intellectually comprehended, a belief that is firmer and more certain than any [other] knowledge."[25] This third kind of knowledge is one that the metaphysical mind – in contrast to the rational understanding of the German philosophers – avails itself of in order to provide confidence in God's existence, an unconditional and necessary existence, and then proves on that basis the existence of things.[26] From the standpoint of the metaphysical mind, the existence of God requires no proof on the part of the logical understanding. The metaphysical mind sees God in everything. The understanding, on the other hand, unable to fathom "rational faith," views the acquisition of all knowledge by means of reasoning and has it confirmed by evidence. This is why it needs logical proofs for God. The Fichtean way, i.e., the way of understanding, sets everything against the self, and therefore relegates God purely to externality. This is wrong. God exists both within and without as well as in both the material and the spiritual world uniting both. Innokentij does not explicitly provide the basis for this claim, but in light of his silence we must presume it too is a conclusion from "rational faith."

In the end does theology, the "science" of religion, have the same validity as the other sciences? Innokentij, not surprisingly, held that it does, though the validity is of a unique sort. It is neither of the kind that we find attributed to the discipline of history nor of that in mathematics. No, the subject matter of the science of religion is acquired neither by logic, as in mathematics, nor by the corporeal senses. Knowledge of the subject matter of religion is acquired by an ideal intuition alone, whose validity is taken on faith. Despite the seeming subjectivity of such a claim, Innokentij is rather dismissive of such a criticism, writing that all knowledge is in the final instance based on faith, on faith in the validity of underlying premises. Where there is no faith, there is no knowledge.[27]

---

25 *Sbornik* (1869), 33.
26 *Sbornik* (1869), 27.
27 *Sbornik* (1869), 65–69.

Thus, the German Idealists (Kant, Fichte, Schelling – but oddly no mention of Hegel), performed a service to humanity through their ideas, but they remained crippled by their limitation to reason alone.[28] Their philosophies were unable to see that there was more to religion than abstract legislating on the part of the will. Their systems could not possibly amount to a religion. They appealed to the mind, but not to the heart. "Often with their wisdom they cast a shadow on the Christian religion rather than serve the good of humanity with it. From the practical side, their theories are extremely inadequate."[29] Kant rendered a service by clarifying the idea of morality. That idea, however, was already part and parcel of Christianity since its inception, and it was accompanied with the idea of compassion, unlike in the systems of the aforementioned German philosophers.

We see that despite his comments and adventures into philosophical speculation, Innokentij as a theology professor and then as an Academy rector was primarily concerned with theological instruction, which he found lacked adequate depth and breadth. One of his proposals was to transfer the teaching of divine revelation from the theology course to philosophy. Many of these would eventually be implemented but not immediately and certainly not within his lifetime.

Skvorcov's acknowledged successor teaching philosophy was Petr S. Avsenev, a graduate of the Kyiv Academy in 1833 with a *magister*'s degree in theology.[30] However, during the early 1830s others also, though for but a few years, taught philosophy at the Kyiv Academy. Orest M. Novickij (1806–1884), a graduate of the Academy in 1831, was retained to teach philosophy and the Polish language. With the opening of Kyiv University, Novickij taught philosophy there in a part-time capacity and was soon promoted, based on Innokentij's recommendation, to become the first professor of philosophy at the University.[31] He remained there until 1850,

---

[28] Innokentij's knowledge of Kant's ideas is questionable. He never refers specifically to Kant's texts, and his invocation of Kant's position in ethics is odd, to say the least. Innokentij would have Kant to be not a formulator of the categorical imperative, not as it has come down to us, but as an advocate of egoism. Innokentij's statement of Kant's ethical principle runs: "Act so that all others can act by your example." *Sbornik* (1869), 233. True, this can be interpreted so that it is in accord with Kant's imperative, but why introduce "your example"? Mere mentions of Hegel's name are rare indeed in Innokentij's writings.
[29] *Sbornik* (1869), 83.
[30] Askochenskij (1863), 232.
[31] The charter for Kyiv University was approved in late 1833, and the school was officially opened in July 1834 with just the liberal arts faculty. The law faculty was added in 1835 and the medical in 1841. Students of all faculties were required during their first two years of study to attend lectures in logic and psychology. Students in the liberal arts and law were required during their final two years to take the class on the history of philosophy and moral philosophy, which included instruction in natural law. Khomenko (2012), 182.

when, apart from logic and psychology, instruction in philosophy was prohibited on the grounds that it promoted revolutionary thinking. Novickij then served as a censor. While he taught at the Theological Academy, Novickij penned no philosophical texts. Another instructor in philosophy for several years was Iosif G. Mikhnevich (1809–1885), who assumed Karpov's position, who the reader will recall, moved to St. Petersburg. Mikhnevich taught at the Kyiv Academy until 1839, when he accepted an offer as professor of philosophy at a lyceum for children of the aristocracy and wealthy merchants in Odessa. Mikhnevich did publish a number of philosophical works, but as they stemmed from his years at the lyceum they all, like those of Novickij, fall outside our purview.

4.3 Avsenev on Three Approaches to God

Petr S. Avsenev (1810–1852), a graduate of the Kyiv Academy in 1833, who took the monastic name Feofan, was appointed immediately upon the conclusion of his studies to a lectureship in German by Innokentij. Teaching German literature gave Avsenev the opportunity to become acquainted with German Idealism, so much so that the mandatory Christian Platonism of Orthodox officialdom was further mystified under the influence of the later Schelling and his disciples, particularly of the now virtually forgotten Gotthilf Heinrich von Schubert (1780–1860).[32] With Novickij's departure for the secular Kyiv University, Avsenev began as an instructor in philosophy in 1836 and then in 1839 as "extraordinary professor" upon Mikhnevich's departure. In 1845, he was promoted to "ordinary professor." He also taught logic and the history of modern philosophy from 1839 to 1844 as an adjunct at Kyiv University.[33]

During his lifetime, Avsenev published only a few works, none of which were remarkable. Those that give insight into his thought remained as manuscripts, published only after his death. Although these remain largely neglected, many of the ideas presented in them found receptive ground in successive generations of students. This is particularly true with regard to his course in psychology, which remained the one constant throughout his pedagogical career and his favorite sub-

---

[32] Askochenskij 1863: (271), D. P. (1869), VIII. Shpet writes, "In the form in which Avsenev's *Notes* have come down to us, Schubert's influence is nonetheless visible – and not only with regard to special issues, but general ones as well." Shpet (2008), 216.
[33] Avsenev twice attempted to secure the professorship in philosophy at Moscow University without success. Resolute opposition from Count Sergej Stroganov, the head of the Moscow Education District and one who could not abide German philosophy, doomed Avsenev's chances. Mozgovaja (2016), 9.

ject. Avsenev's book-length "From Notes on Psychology" begins with an introductory section that seeks to establish the pivotal role of psychology for philosophy. The psychology that Avsenev had in mind, however, was one that bore great similarity, if not identity, with that of the German romantics of the time and also with, of course, patristic theology and the mystical thought of Boehme.

Through introspection, we see what constitutes our uniqueness in creation, the human essence, as against all of lower nature, which includes our bodies and all of nature, as well as against what is higher than us, viz., the Divine, whose presence we experience within ourselves. Another term for this human essence is the soul (*dusha*). Thus, the soul is what distinguishes us from all else in creation, rendering as unnecessary the qualification the *human* soul. No others have souls. Psychology is the discipline, or science, that seeks to explain the soul's structure and activity so that we can fulfill the ancient Greek maxim "Know thyself."[34] Of course, each of us as human individuals is more than this essence. We have particular habits and desires. Just as there are many individuals, there are many habits and desires. Nevertheless, there is one general *human* character, a universal type, that over time in the grouping called a nation acquires dominance over these particularities. Avsenev called the complete realization of this essence at the expense of individual habits and desires the "eternal," the "divine person" (*bogochelovek*).[35]

Avsenev held that there are three means for acquiring knowledge of the soul: (1) observation; (2) speculation; and (3) revelation. Predictably enough, observation is the instrument used in empirical psychology. This "observation" is not that of careful laboratory work, which would make its entrance later in the century, but the observation of oneself, introspection, and allied with it of analogies to ascribe psychological states to others. Avsenev discussed the second means, speculation, in vaguer terms. He stated that speculative cognition of the soul is a kind of intuition or inner vision (*sozercanie*) by means of pure thought of the complete image of the soul.[36] If we associate observation of ourselves with introspection, then how we are to understand this supposed second means of acquiring knowledge of the soul becomes difficult, if not impossible, particularly as Avsenev also

---

34 Avsenev (1869), 2; Avsenev (2016), 37.
35 Avsenev, regrettably, did not expand significantly here on either this conception of historical development or on the concept of the "divine person." Both would later become central to the thought of Vladimir Solov'ëv. However, Avsenev's use of the expression "divine person" should be contrasted with the certainly more Christian use of it in his "On Religion in General" to refer to Jesus of Nazareth. See *Sbornik* (1869), 87. Skvorcov also used it to refer to Jesus in his "Notes on Moral Philosophy." See *Sbornik* (1869), 21.
36 Avsenev (1869), 5; Avsenev (2016), 39.

characterized it as bereft of all deficiencies and limitations.³⁷ Our third source for knowledge of the soul is – predictably enough – Biblical revelation, where God informs us of its God-like nature and structure. Avsenev conceded that these scriptural revelations are scattered explanations, but theology has collected them into a single harmonious doctrine.

Given the assumption that the human soul aspires toward God, the psychologist's method as a scientific discipline is to proceed from the temporal to the eternal, from the specific to the general. The first task of psychology is to describe the image of the soul, which reflects the image of God, and the goal of such a conception of psychology is to provide us with the fortitude to fulfill our duties to God, to our neighbors, and to ourselves.³⁸ However, it must be said that Avsenev expressed little interest in ethical concerns in these notes. Of more interest to him was the delineation of the distinction between levels of existence. An inorganic body, for example, is distinguished from an organic one by the former's inactivity. A living body, on the other hand, reveals internal movement. This movement presupposes the presence within it of a special principle responsible for its activity, whereas in an inorganic body there is no such principle that dominates over its substantiality. The elements of the inorganic body strive merely to form a unitary mass and seek to remain in that state. There, Avsenev found a total absence of its own formative principle. It is the object of an external, infinitely superior creative force. In other words, in the inorganic world the kingdom of the Divine law rules supreme and without compromise.

Turning to the organic world, Avsenev unsurprisingly found three kingdoms: the vegetable, the animal, and the human kingdoms. We need not here dwell on Avsenev's empirical distinctions between these kingdoms, most of which are commonplace. He ascribed these distinctions to the presence or relative absence of a spiritual principle in each. The human being shares material or "earthly" inclinations and abilities, such as movement, with animals, but what elevates humans above animals is the possession of a genuine spirit. Whereas animals do not know God and do not have any notion of worshiping the Creator in His likeness, they do have a certain dark divination of Him.³⁹ Humans, of course, worship God,

---

37 As would again later be the case with Solov'ëv, Avsenev was led in his quest by an unflinching intent to find triadic schemes wherever possible at the expense of evidence and precision.

38 Note again the triadic scheme. Of course, in this particular case such a triad may not appear contrived, but that we have duties to ourselves is by no means universally accepted by ethicists. Again, Solov'ëv was one who later would affirm that we have such duties.

39 Avsenev (1869), 35; Avsenev (2016), 62. Avsenev provides no evidence for this claim. That is, he does not adduce the basis for either the claim that animals have some divination of God nor, assuming a "divination" of some sort, that it is of God and not of some other entity. As in virtually all

but with our spirit we also strive toward Him. Invoking a triad that would be repeated in generations of Russian philosophers, Avsenev wrote that our reason, which he associated with the human spirit in cognitive matters, strives to *know* God; the heart seeks emotional *fulfillment* in God; and the human will *wants* to approach ever closer to Him.[40] However, God can never be completely reached in any of these respective perfections. These three strivings of our worldly endeavors have as their respective goal: truth, beauty, and the good. That is, the cognition of God's manifest, empirical essence is *truth*; the manifest display of His perfections in the world is *beauty*; and the realization of His goals in the world is the *moral good*.[41] We see in this that God had to have manifested Himself, His essence, partially in the world in order for us, as creatures created in His likeness, to know the truth, to enjoy beauty, and to do the moral good. In the quest for truth, beauty, and goodness we share in a living union with our Creator. Additionally, in this quest we human beings act as an intermediary between creatures of a lower nature than ourselves and the Divine. This intermediary role represents the human essence, i.e., what it is to be a human being.

While none of this may have startled Avsenev's administrative superiors, his further contention that the entire world in general "is essentially nothing more than an idea, i.e., God's thought" may have given them pause. To be sure, he may have mollified some potential criticism by immediately adding that God's word posited, "so to speak," infinitely different forms of being outside Himself.[42] Avsenev added his own touch of Schellingianism in claiming that each worldly creature represents a particular idea and seeks to place itself in God's overall scheme.

Avsenev also launched a foray, most unbecoming for a philosopher even though Kant himself did so, into anthropology. His characterizations of the African peoples are along lines that were not uncommon given his time and place. Of

---

such reported instances, the criteria employed in establishing the identity of the alleged object is not specified.

40 The editors of these "Notes on Psychology" from 1869 wrote that Avsenev's main task was the elaboration of a systematically harmonious classification of human abilities and actions, the guide in this being Schubert with his conception of the parallelism of the mental faculties and the corporeal organs with their functions. See Avsenev (1869), 67; Avsenev (2016), 83.

41 Solov'ëv, in his "Philosophical Principles of Integral Knowledge," wrote, "Of course, the fundamental forms of general human life must have their source in principles that determine human nature itself. Human nature as such presents three fundamental forms of being: feeling, thinking, and the active will. ... Feeling has as its object *objective beauty*; thinking has as its object *objective truth* (consequently, cognizing thought or knowledge), and the will has as its object the *objective good*." Solov'ëv (2000b), 190.

42 Avsenev (1869), 74; Avsenev (2016), 88.

course, he had high praise for the general Russian character, which displayed the best of Asiatic and European qualities, rendering it as "universal."[43] He recognized that the Russian people had not yet made an original contribution to philosophy, but when it would eventually happen it would be of a fundamentally religious nature. Russians are by nature a religious people. He resolutely expected religious philosophy to arise in his nation, since its faith did not shy away from reflection. "Even the simplest people among us have never shied away from reflecting on our faith."[44] Unlike in the western church – presumably an allusion to Catholicism – which seeks to keep the mind enslaved, Orthodoxy is devoid of despotism, and people are free to read the Bible.[45]

Secondary studies of Avsenev's thought have, correctly, pointed to his discussions of sleep, dreams, and sleepwalking for evidence of his intellectual debt to Schubert. Avsenev clearly sympathized with Schubert's efforts to see dreams as symbolic and as a state in which the mind is particularly sensitive to divine promptings. However odd, if not bizarre, his musings – all produced without the slightest evidential substantiation – appear to us today, they would hardly arouse the ire of theologians. However, Avsenev also turned to the question of the origin of the soul, which he believed could not necessarily be handled as easily as that of the material world. He rejected the idea that a particular individual's soul existed from eternity. My consciousness had a beginning. That is, if the soul had always existed, why do I not remember anything from this time period before my corporeal birth? Moreover, where did it reside before being joined to the body, and why was it inactive before that union?[46]

Avsenev was also dismissive of the idea that the human soul was created at the time of birth. That conjecture would be to assume that the Deity is perpetually involved in a supernatural creation in the natural order. It also makes inexplicable the origin of evil. If we believe in original sin, as the Bible says, this hypothesis would require God to create constantly a damaged product, viz., the soul carrying that sin. There must be a way to account for the corrupt moral character of the soul. Avsenev's solution was to present the soul as passing from parents to children. Experience testifies to a direct connection between children and parents. This can be accounted for by allowing the transference of something in the soul from parents to child.

---

[43] Avsenev (1869), 138; Avsenev (2016), 132.
[44] Avsenev (1869), 139; Avsenev (2016), 133.
[45] Given the widespread illiteracy of Russians at the time of Avsenev's writing, this statement must be taken with a grain of salt. Moreover, the Bible did not appear in a one-volume Russian (as opposed to Slavonic) translation until 1876, long after Avsenev gave his lectures on psychology.
[46] Avsenev (1869), 210; Avsenev (2016), 184.

Avsenev's elaborations remained largely unknown both during and after his Academic career. But aspects of his thought were carried forward by his successor and then into Russian secular philosophy. As for Avsenev himself, he left the Academy in 1850 at his own request due to deteriorating health, moving from Kyiv to St. Petersburg, where he remained during the long winter due to illness. Assigned to the embassy church in Rome, he arrived there in the summer of 1851. Although he initially felt better, his illness returned, and he died in Rome at the end of March 1852.

4.4 Jurkevich as Conduit from the Academy to the University

Judged in terms of subsequent influence, Pamfil Jurkevich (1826–1874) was undoubtedly the most significant philosopher to teach at the Kyiv Academy under the first charter. Born near Poltava in Ukraine, Jurkevich received schooling in a theological seminary and initially hoped to study medicine. His father had planned for the young boy to attend the Kyiv Academy. In the battle of wills, the father won. Soon after the commencement of his studies in 1847, Jurkevich earned a reputation as one of the school's best students, and he turned with enthusiasm to philosophy. Completing his Academic studies in June 1851 and given Avsenev's resignation, he was retained at his alma mater to teach philosophy. The following year he received a *magister*'s degree and in 1858 was promoted to extraordinary professor. Jurkevich published soon afterward several articles, but it was his 1860 philosophical reply to Chernyshevskij encased in a resolute and multifaceted rejection of materialism that opened the door for his ideas to enter secular Russia. Published in the Academy's house organ, the lengthy article happened to catch the attention of Mikhail Katkov, a prominent and "well-connected" conservative who arranged to have extensive extracts of the piece reprinted in his own far-more notable journal *Russkij vestnik* in 1861. The resumption of instruction in philosophy banned since 1850 at Russian secular universities at this time created an opening at Moscow University. Katkov and Konstantin N. Leont'ev, a fellow conservative and staunch monarchist, were instrumental in acquiring Jurkevich for the University.[47] Although Jurkevich leaves our story with his move from Kyiv to Moscow, he more than any other single figure served as a bridge from the highly religiously-oriented philoso-

---

47 Katkov and Leont'ev hoped that Jurkevich's appointment would stem the growing radicalism and materialism of young university students. Officialdom came by this time to the conclusion that the absence of philosophy only contributed to the rise of ideologies that they feared.

phy of the Academies to the largely metaphysical and ostensibly secular philosophies that came to dominate the last years of Imperial Russia.

Jurkevich's first publication, a lengthy two-part article simply entitled "The Idea," already in 1859 set forth his fundamental philosophical orientation toward Platonic idealism, as mandated by his church but which he fully endorsed and, indeed, further elaborated.[48] The ancient Greeks, in general, discerned a harmonious order in nature. Plato explicitly indicated the possibility of seeing this order by ascending from an intuition of the sensible world to a cognition of the supersensible, a realm of forms where regularity, harmony, and unity reigned. The mind intuits ideas just as the eyes intuit the appearance of sensible objects. We say we have a representation of a thing when we have a subjective sensation of it. Such a representation has a quite accidental character. When we say, however, that we have a concept of it, we exclude subjective arbitrariness from it. There is in our consciousness a necessary correlation between the various parts and facets of the thing's appearance as deemed by my original sensible intuition of the thing. We move to an idea when the correlation is objectively necessary. An idea is a cognition of the thing's essence. Jurkevich expressed this as a coincidence of thought and being. Although we may interpret his statements as implying that ideas are ontologically objective entities, Jurkevich clarified that they are the bases, the laws, and norms of appearance.[49] They are, in other words, the bases for the cognition of truth.

> When we say this appearance, this state of affairs, does not correspond to its idea, ... then in these common expressions an idea is posited as an objective concept, which the object itself does not determine, but on the contrary which determines the object. The idea is thought of as the object's law and the condition of its correct formation.[50]

Assuming a decidedly ontological realist attitude, Jurkevich held that if psychology could show that the world in our consciousness is one of appearances, a mental state, that world is, nevertheless, a system of ordered entities subject to law prior to our abstractions.

Ideas serve as the basis of the harmonization of thought and being. Without them, science is unthinkable. This does not mean that the active scientist must be preoccupied with the necessary presuppositions for engaging in his/her activity. Quite the contrary, Jurkevich, like Hegel before him, maintained that "in order to

---

[48] Despite the fundamental significance of Jurkevich's article for an understanding of his later works, it remained unknown to Solov'ëv. See Solov'ëv (2000a), 157; Solov'ev (2019), 178.
[49] Jurkevich (1990), 12.
[50] Jurkevich (1990), 13.

know, it is unnecessary to have knowledge of knowledge itself."[51] A person may know how to play a musical instrument exquisitely without knowing the underlying physics of sound vibrations. Our knowledge would be illusory or at least a bundle of contradictions if the ideal order, the world of forms as law, did not enter into our world of cognition, making it possible. Without presupposing the objectivity of these forms, we could not draw necessary conclusions about experience; we could not consistently distinguish true from false representations, normal phenomena from abnormal ones.

The empirical properties of things around us that we sense are inessential. True reality is what is rational and divine. Jurkevich believed that it follows from this that the true essence of an object is known not in seeing it, but in the object's idea. Thus, the essence itself is ideal. Jurkevich saw his opponents here in 1859 as proponents of what he called a "mechanical worldview."[52] Yet, even they see that the world presents regularity, so much so, in fact, that they cannot help but speak of eternal and unalterable laws. In doing so, they admit what they wished to deny. However, without the slightest hesitation Jurkevich ascribes the source of these laws to God.

> True, genuine reality belongs to the divine and rational as a spiritual entity that acts as the source of being and of our knowledge of it. Just as the sun is the cause of what we see and of the fact that things are visible, so the *Good* makes the truth cognizable and gives the ability to know to the cognizer.[53]

The divine and the rational are homogeneous, and what is divine and rational in the universe is ideal. We see the true nature of things in their idea. Thus, ideas have a unique sort of being different from the contingent beings that surround us. They are not substantial, but conceivable. Jurkevich, unfortunately, did not probe into how we obtain knowledge of ideas. He was content with stating that consciousness does not invent the laws of knowledge, but finds them in actually existing objects and in the spirit that really exists. Wrapping his fundamental Platonism in a religious blanket, he criticized a number of modern philosophers, including particularly Kant, for their subjectivism and for not realizing that the spirit is more than our individual consciousness. Jurkevich would have it that the spirit is more than cognizing activities; it is a real substance. Thus, the human consciousness "finds" laws or ideas of the spirit just as it "finds" laws or ideas in nature.

---

51 Jurkevich (1990), 17.
52 Jurkevich (1990), 23.
53 Jurkevich (1990), 25.

During the following year, 1860, Jurkevich shifted his critical attention to the raging concern at the time with eliminative materialism.[54] Many of Jurkevich's criticisms of materialism were based on a practical application of the ideas presented in his previous article. As such and because they were taken for granted independently of Jurkevich's presentation by the secular philosophers of classical Russian idealism, we need not linger long on them.[55] Against materialism, Jurkevich held that only through an interaction between the material and the spiritual does experience arise. He had no wish to dismiss the results of natural science and physiological investigations, in particular, for the light they throw on psychological phenomena. He believed that careful study would reveal the mutual dependence of internal and external factors on experience. However, the intentional object of a psychological investigation is given only in introspection. "The physiologist will observe the most complex movement of the nerves. But since these movements exist for external experience, i.e., they are spatial movements that arise between material elements, they are not transformed into sensation, representation, and thought."[56] We do not know from physiological investigations that the external stimulation of certain nerves transforms into psychological affects, since the physiologist has never directly seen such transformation. There would have to be a necessary law governing this change, a law that cannot be explained as material.

Materialism forgets the role of the spectator of the phenomena it seeks to explain. Quantity and quality are distinct, and one cannot be simply transformed into the other without reservation, i.e., into a generalization. The plucking of a taut string remains a plucking, not a sound. For particular frequencies of electromagnetic radiation to be transformed into light requires a sensing being in whom the transformation of a physical phenomenon into the quality of a color is accomplished. In the absence of such a being, the electromagnetic radiation remains just that. A sound is not a property of a vibrating body, but of the interaction between that body and the cognizing "spirit." Thus, the key to the transformation lies in the relation of the object to the sensing subject.[57]

---

54 Jurkevich's long article "From the Science of the Human Spirit" was prompted by Chernyshevskij's "The Anthropological Principle in Philosophy," which appeared earlier in 1860 and which argued that mental phenomena could be totally explained in terms of changes from within and as effects from externality.
55 We find this irreductionism running throughout Russian idealism from Solov'ëv's early writings ("Philosophical Principles of Integral Knowledge" and *Critique of Abstract Principles*) to Shpet's *History as a Problem of Logic*.
56 Jurkevich (1990), 115.
57 Jurkevich (1990), 129. The relation of the object to the sensing subject was for Gustav Shpet the key element in his understanding and acceptance of Husserl's phenomenological reduction. For

The materialism that Jurkevich combated sought to eliminate a fundamental role for "spiritual" phenomena. Such an elimination would require the complete reduction of these phenomena by explaining them in terms of purely physiological processes. Jurkevich's opposition to materialism did not entail for him an opposition to natural science in general. The physiologist acts quite scientifically in seeking the causal connection between two sets of data without seeking to reduce one to another, without introducing any metaphysical assumptions. "The physiologist does not talk about matter in general or in the abstract, but about this visible and tangible nerve, which in no way possesses an abstract being in our conception. He asks: Do the movements, changes, and states of this nerve completely and adequately serve as the causal basis or as the source of this mental phenomenon?"[58] If the physiologist in this particular case can demonstrate with scientific reliability, i.e., with mathematical certainty, a complete dependence of certain mental phenomena on physiological ones, he can become a metaphysician with scientific dignity. However, he would not thereby have the right to construct an eliminative materialism in which matter or some empirically-based abstraction is the single fundamental concept for explaining all phenomena.

Whereas much of the substance of Jurkevich's articles examined thus far can be read and understood by today's readership, not all of his writings were that way despite the influence they have exerted either directly or indirectly on later Russian idealism. In particular, another lengthy piece published at the start of 1860 in the new house organ of the Kyiv Academy tempts our patience to hold back from dismissing the article outright. The work entitled "The Heart and Its Significance in Human Spiritual Life according to the Doctrine of God's Word" opens with a discussion of the understanding of the heart, taken not only metaphorically, but also as the corporeal organ mentioned in the Bible. Jurkevich informed us that in the Holy Scriptures the heart is seen as the focus of the entirety of our corporeal and spiritual life. Whereas physiologists tell us that the seat of thought lies in the brain, thought does not exhaust the entirety of our spiritual life. Our own inner experience testifies to this truth. The great philosophers and great poets throughout time recognized that the heart is the seat of our deep ideas. Thought merely adds clarity and certainty to these ideas. Indeed, the heart precedes reason in cognizing truth and feeling beauty. Often in everyday experience and particularly in times of great stress and bewilderment, when there is no time for logical syllogisms, we turn to our heart to render a judgment. Unfortunately, Jurkevich pro-

---

Shpet, phenomenology in its investigations always takes the object in its intentional relationship to consciousness, whereas other disciplines do not. See Nemeth (2018), 272.
58 Jurkevich (1990), 201.

vides neither independent criteria nor any indication that there are any against which the veracity of the heart's judgments can be determined.

Jurkevich's particular concern here in this article from 1860, however, is not with epistemology, but morality. "The heart is the focus of a person's moral life."[59] He sought to connect Biblical teaching about the heart and its role in human life with the Christian conception of morality. The heart can tell us much that reason cannot; the former serves as the fuel for the mind. Without it, the mind's reason runs dry, and in a not-so-veiled criticism of Kantian morality, Jurkevich held that without the feelings of the heart our moral ideas slowly extinguish until they finally disappear. And in another such criticism, he wrote that when we commit an immoral act our conscience reproaches us for doing so, not because we have contradicted our mind's legislative dictates. No, it says to us that we have done something unworthy of a human being. Jurkevich saw the connection with Christianity in its message of love for one's neighbor expressed as compassion, generosity, feeling other's pain in oneself, etc. All of these moral qualities stem not from the abstract, rational mind, but from the heart.[60]

During the two years prior to his move to Moscow and its secular university, Jurkevich remarkably published several other long articles, one dealing with the first of the eventual four-volume *Philosophical Lexicon* by Sil'vestr S. Gogockij, himself a graduate of the Kyiv Academy and a former professor of philosophy at Kyiv University until the ban on teaching philosophy at secular schools went into effect.[61] Jurkevich's criticism of Gogockij can be traced to the latter's broad sympathy with Hegel, whereas Jurkevich was trying to reconcile Platonism and Kant's alleged subjective idealism. He also published over three issues of the Academy's house organ in 1861 yet another long piece on "Proofs of God's Existence," which was largely devoted to presenting an appreciative but highly critical view of Kant's analysis of the concept of existence and of Kant's treatment of the classical proofs. In summary, Jurkevich found the "Transcendental Dialectic" to be "one of the most artificial and imperfect parts of the *Critique of Pure Reason*, wherein the most profound observations and ideas are quite often confused with strange positions."[62]

Jurkevich's first lecture at Moscow University took place in January 1862. His recent spate of extended publications quickly came to an end. Although his literary activity did not cease, his output by no means matched his work at the Academy, and there is no reason to think his philosophical position fundamentally changed.

---

59 Jurkevich (1990), 71.
60 Jurkevich (1990), 102.
61 After a short time working as a censor, Gogockij received an appointment in the University's department of pedagogy.
62 Jurkevich (1861), 340.

That his influence continued to be felt over the entire period of classical Russian idealism is clear from Solov'ëv's touching essay from late 1899 "Three Testimonials" and Shpet's 1914 extended summary of Jurkevich's *oeuvre*.[63]

4.5 The Seemingly Tortuous Start of the Kazan Academy

The last of the four theological academies to be established in Imperial Russia was the Kazan Academy, founded in 1842. Actually, the school traces its establishment much earlier to the Kazan Slavic-Latin School founded in 1723 with the intention of training literate priests for the Kazan diocese. The school became the Kazan Theological Seminary in 1732, and during the reign of Paul I the Seminary became an academy. The planned reform of theological education under Alexander I found that the academies and the one in Kazan in particular rested on unstable foundations that could not support an academy in Kazan conceived according to the plan. "Due to the lack of capable personnel and in order to avoid huge material costs, the transformation of the theological schools was to be carried out gradually in the educational districts with St. Petersburg coming first."[64] The consequence was that in 1818 when it would have been the turn of the Kazan Academy to undergo the transformation it reverted back to a seminary.

The long postponed opening of the Kazan Theological Academy finally came on 25 May 1842 with the express intention to follow the same educational procedures as at the other theological academies. The number of teachers, according to the accepted plan, was to be fourteen, six being professors and eight instructors. However, owing to circumstances the Academy opened with four professors and four instructors. Also at its opening the history of philosophy was designated as a separate course from the general course in philosophy. Upon its opening and thereafter, the Kazan Academy had two teachers in philosophy, one at the level of professor and one instructor. As a further illustration of the precarious position of the Kazan Academy, in August 1854 the governing board decided to eliminate outright the teaching of the natural sciences and mathematics, since they were taught in the seminaries and had no close relationship to the Academy's goal of further spiritual education. The proposal also called for the history of philosophy to be taught only briefly and in the established context of the general philosophy course.[65] This recommendation remained in effect for only a few years.

---

63 See Solov'ëv (1913), 391–397 and Shpet (1914).
64 Znamenskij (1891), 3.
65 Znamenskij (1892), 11–12.

The first professor of philosophy at the Kazan Academy was Ivan A. Smirnov (1818–1860), who, like Kudrjavcev, legally affixed the designation "Platonov" to his surname as a recipient of an annual scholarship established by a church official, Platon, who set aside funds for this purpose. Smirnov, the son of a priest, had completed his studies under Golubinskij at the Moscow Academy with a *magister*'s degree in 1840. He was retained there as a history instructor until the appointment came from Kazan. However well-intentioned his lectures and care for the education of his students, Smirnov clearly felt some dissatisfaction with Kazan, either as a location or his own situation – perhaps both. In any case, after a mere few years, Smirnov went on vacation to Moscow in 1847 and never returned to Kazan, officially resigning from his professorship in November of that year. The following year he was assigned to a parish in Moscow and then later served as a rector in St. Petersburg, where he died. He left no lasting imprint on Russian philosophy.

Occupying the instructorship in philosophy was another graduate of the Moscow Academy, Nafanail P. Sokolov (1818–1881), who, unlike Smirnov, appeared quite content with life in Kazan, never leaving the town and remaining a lifelong bachelor. Despite being recognized wherever he went, in part owing to his great height, he never entertained visitors except on business, and his personal idiosyncrasies became a subject of jokes and student mocks. With Smirnov's resignation, Sokolov was promoted, first to extraordinary professor and then in 1850 to ordinary professor. He relished purely routine bureaucratic work for the Academy and its own publications, particularly the Academy's journal *Orthodox Interlocutor* [*Pravoslavnyj sobesednik*], at the expense of probing scholarship.[66]

Sokolov's sole published piece in philosophy was an article appearing in the Academy's journal in 1861 entitled "A View of Hegel's Philosophy." Sokolov remained highly critical of Hegel's objective idealism, it being replete in his eyes with all manner of errors. Hegel concluded that there is but one kind of being, viz., ideas, which are the essence of all that is objective as well as subjective.[67] For Sokolov, Hegel's system retains no place for God, at least not in his understanding of the Deity as the Being who has a perfect awareness of Himself and His actions. Admittedly, Hegel's system does designate his conception of the "Idea" as God, but his "God" is not the being that precedes all others, but a product, i.e., the result of a process. This "God" has completeness only after understanding Him-

---

[66] Znamenskij (1892), 23. Znamenskij has hardly a good word to say about Sokolov's personality, which makes us wish to "second guess" Znamenskij's impartiality and the accuracy of his portrayal. For an account of the founding and early years of the *Orthodox Interlocutor* see Znamenskij (1892), 531–555.

[67] Sokolov (1861), 307.

self. Hegel denies not only the soul's immortality, but also its personal existence. Unlike the systems of Fichte and Schelling, both of which, in their own way, respected the universal laws of reason despite the huge contradictions those systems contained, Hegel's search for contradiction was his main method. The result was that Hegel's philosophy is not only the most pantheistic of all pantheisms, but is actually quite atheistic. Rather than an absolute idealism, it should be called an "absolute atheism."[68] Such a brief summary already shows the depth of Sokolov's reading of Hegel's works.

Sokolov's career as a philosophy professor came to an abrupt end in mid-1858, at which time after sixteen years he was shifted to teaching church history. There were, of course, several other instructors of philosophy during Sokolov's professorship, but none were particularly interested in philosophy. Their interests were elsewhere, but owing to their academic performance they stood out as capable of fulfilling a pedagogical role. It hardly need be said that they contributed nothing to the development of Russian philosophy. The teaching of philosophy was divided in two. Psychology and metaphysics was assigned to Aleksandr I. Lilov, while logic, moral philosophy, and the history of philosophy was given to Petr G. Rublevskij. Lilov, the son of a priest, was a graduate of the Kazan Academy in 1856, and was retained as an instructor in Greek and paleography. Whether dissatisfied with being assigned to teach subjects in which he previously had little interest or for some other unknown reason, Lilov left the Academy abruptly just after presenting the material on psychology and a few introductory lectures on metaphysics in 1859. His subsequent career was notable, but had nothing to do with philosophy. He died of tuberculosis in 1890.

Rublevskij, also a graduate of the Kazan Academy but from the following year, 1857, took over Lilov's metaphysics class with Lilov's resignation. Fortunately for all concerned, the assignment posed no scheduling issue for him. However, he too relatively soon left the Academy (June 1860) for a position teaching theology at the Kyiv Academy, where he remained for five years before taking a job with the ministry of education.

As we see, the Kazan Academy had some difficulty retaining philosophy instructors during these early years of its existence. Another instructor who took over philosophy classes at the Academy was Mikhail I. Mitropol'skij (1834–1894), a graduate of the St. Petersburg Academy in 1859. His tenure at the Academy was unsteady almost from the start. In addition to his dry and dense lectures, he ran into considerable resistance from his superiors. In 1867, he apparently suffered a nervous breakdown, for which he went to St. Petersburg for treatment and

---

68 Sokolov (1861), 332.

then to his original home in Tver. He was dismissed from the Academy the following year, after which he eventually was able to obtain a position at the Tver seminary teaching physics and mathematics.

However depressing the fate of the Kazan Academy may look to us up to this time, it surely would dramatically change in the coming years with the approval of a new charter for the theological academies in the Russian Empire and with the appointment of Veniamin A. Snegirev, Petr A. Miloslavskij, et al. Nonetheless, there were indications of a "philosophico-historical" approach to philosophy at Kazan already during the years of our concern, albeit not among the philosophy instructors, but in theology.[69] The first article on philosophy to appear in the Kazan house organ was in 1860 entitled "A View of the Opinion of the Latest Rationalists on the Essence of Religion." The author Bishop Khrisanf (Vladimir N. Retivcev) (1832–1883) studied at the Moscow Academy and upon completing his studies there taught at the Kostroma Seminary. In 1858, he was appointed instructor in theology at the Kazan Academy. He was promoted to extraordinary professor in April 1865, but already in August of that year he transferred to the St. Petersburg Academy.

Khrisanf in his 1860 article presented a stinging indictment of German Idealism but nevertheless remained more nuanced than did Sokolov, even though the latter's piece appeared later and undoubtedly, given his managing role with the journal, with knowledge of the former. If we take Khrisanf's opening lines literally, he wished to place strict limitations on philosophical investigations of religion. Unrestricted rationally-conducted studies lead either to false conceptions or to by no means complete ones. Those by the German Idealists are a case in point. Their investigations were biased, and their ultimate conclusions were hostile to the true conception of religion, which, after all, in Khrisanf's eyes, is the chief and fundamental phenomenon in human life.[70]

What immediately strikes the eye of the contemporary Western reader is Khrisanf's succinct and unvarnished characterization of entire peoples based on popular conceptions of them. Seeking to summarily dismiss the French Enlightenment thinkers, particularly Voltaire, Khrisanf wrote of the French:

> This nation, in comparison with others in Europe, is less capable of serious and deep thought, and its country remains a country of fashion and frivolity. Out of it came the sage of Ferney,

---

69 Znamenskij (1892), 259.
70 Needless to say, the good bishop provides no proof or argument that his conception is "true." Presumably, then, that religion plays such a fundamental role in our lives means it is "true."

who rejected all sacred truths for humanity, not by the power of the mind, not by a serious study of humanity, ... but only with witticisms and petty childish ridicule.[71]

In a comparatively short time, however, German philosophers overtook, albeit from the opposite direction, the French Enlightenment's superficial religious views.

Khrisanf traced the basic German Idealist attitude toward religion to the Protestant Reformation with its rejection of external authority.[72] Luther and Calvin focused on one's inner life, but as the newly emerging Protestant philosophy developed it ever more downplayed the role of reason and of the human spirit as distinct from the infinite Spirit. This trend led to an adoration of the self and ultimately to an identification of the human spirit with the Infinite. But with Hegel, the development continued by becoming increasingly abstract and fantastical, though with the same result. His system would have all that exists be transformed into an empty, abstract concept. In contrast, Khrisanf held that the true conception of religion is a living union of God with the human being, which German Idealism has lost. This union becomes vacuous in German philosophy, since the human being assumes the place of God in it.[73] God, for Kant, lies outside the world but does not currently impact it. What is important is not whether He actually exists but only that we believe in His existence for the sake of morality. For Fichte, there is no distinct God existing separate from the physical world including human beings. Instead of God, there is only the human individual. However, the final word in German Idealism is Hegel's system, wherein God is merely an abstract concept or idea.[74] Hegel conceived the entire world with all of history as the development of thought. Thus, to study the laws of thought is to study the essence of being, which is the same as God Himself.

However mistaken and crude we may view Khrisanf's depictions of German Idealism, his motivation for discrediting it was what he perceived as its implications for human morality. If there were no God, in the Christian conception, no

---

71 Khrisanf (1860), 167.
72 Znamenskij wrote that Khrisanf "took each religion and religio-philosophical doctrine, above all, as a historical phenomenon and studied its origin and development on the historical basis of the culture contemporary to it and the nationality that gave birth to it." Znamenskij (1892), 261. Whether Khrisanf actually employed such a method, as an early and rudimentary form of sociology of knowledge is, at least as seen in his 1860 article, doubtful. Had Khrisanf actually done so, we would expect him to trace the rise of Christianity itself to Jewish culture during the Roman Empire. He did not do so.
73 Khrisanf (1860), 171.
74 Khrisanf identifies "concept" with "idea." See Khrisanf (1860), 188.

Divine Revelation coupled with the giving of moral law, what becomes of morality? "Without religion there is no morality; without true religion there is no true morality."[75] The religious person is a moral person principally owing to the knowledge that the Creator placed the moral law within each of us as individuals. Reiterating a metaphor we saw in Jurkevich, Khrisanf wrote that such knowledge springs not from the mind, but from the heart. The religious person believes in this heart-felt truth as a direct revelation from God and not that it is an invention of the mind. Khrisanf in this way links – even though without acknowledgment – Kazan with Kyiv.

Bishop Khrisanf received a promotion to an extraordinary professorship at the Kazan Academy in April 1865, but he did not stay long afterward there. In August of that year, he transferred to the St. Petersburg Academy, where he remained. Unfortunately, he suffered two strokes at the beginning of 1879 that left his right side paralyzed. He spent his last years in a Moscow monastery, where he died as a result of a third stroke in 1883.

4.6 The Teaching of Logic in the 1850s

We already saw that logic had been taught in the seventeenth-century educational institutions, albeit of course in its Aristotelian form. The popularity of rationalistic treatments in the eighteenth century found expression in the publication of Baumeister's *Logik* in a Russian edition as early as 1760, followed by a second edition in 1787. And Wolff's *Vernünftige Gedanken von den Kräften des menschlichen Verstandes* appeared in 1765 in a Russian translation. The tradition of teaching logic continued with the refashioning of the higher educational system at the start of the nineteenth century. With the establishment of four secular universities, the need for suitable logic textbooks that could be used at all levels of instruction became palpable. In 1806, Petr I. Bogdanov (1776–1816), a teacher at the boarding school attached to Moscow University published a *Brief Logic* text for use at the school. Even earlier, Aleksandr S. Nikol'skij (1755–1834), a translator and government official, had an earlier work of his on rhetoric republished without his consent in 1803 under the title *Short Logic and Rhetoric for Students in Russian Theological Schools*. The work received several reprintings in subsequent years. Although only published in 1807, Aleksandr S. Lubkin's *Outline of Logic* was written years earlier while he taught at the St. Petersburg Army Seminary, a recently created institution to train clergy for the military but with which he was no longer

---

75 Khrisanf (1860), 465.

associated, having taken a position at the Petersburg Pedagogical Institute. Lubkin's text scarcely resembles logic texts today, combining remarks more closely associated with epistemology than logic and classifying the types of judgments, concepts, syllogisms, etc. In short, the number of logic texts began to sprout rapidly during these years, a complete list being tediously long.

Although philosophical education in Russia's secular universities was severely hampered after the Decembrist Uprising at the end of 1825, classes in the subject continued. However, with the revolutionary events of 1848, Russian officialdom became obsessed with the thought that the aborted events from almost a quarter century earlier might happen again, this time more effectively. Fearing the spread of critical thinking, the government took the step in September 1850 that it had earlier deemed unnecessarily extreme – the elimination of instruction in philosophy in the secular universities with the exception of logic and psychology but with the proviso that they be taught by theology professors. The Holy Synod commissioned all the Academies at the time to develop a program in logic for the Russian universities.[76] The syllabus compiled by the Moscow Academy was approved by the Holy Synod and sent to the universities. This syllabus largely corresponded with that used in the logic courses before the ban on philosophy instruction and which did not substantially differ from logic courses taught in the Academies. We should note that the ban on philosophy did not extend to the theological schools. They all continued with their own programs without any recognizable break over the years.

The syllabus drawn up in 1850 included such topics as the forms of thinking in general, empirical thought, and speculative thought. An introductory section discussed the relationship of logic to psychology, but, most importantly, that all thought stemmed from God. This is certainly not surprising, but it should be pointed out in order to contrast the understanding of logic then with logic today. Included in the program is the tenet that the idea of God is innate and must be recognized as the "root principle of thinking." The paucity of what is contained in pure self-consciousness prevents it from serving as a first principle – presumably an attack on Cartesianism. But that very paucity also serves in the theologians' eyes to prevent human hubris and makes us subordinate to divine revelation.[77]

The program recommended several textbooks, all of which amazingly were by German authors. F. Bachman's logic textbook, which was already available in Russian translation, was included in the list, but so was F. Trendelenburg's text, which had not yet been translated. None of the textbooks by Russian authors was recom-

---

[76] Khomenko (2012), 183.
[77] Bazhanov (2012b),15.

mended.⁷⁸ Which texts were actually used in the academies is hard to determine. At the St. Petersburg Academy, Andrej I. Rajkovskij (1802–1860) taught the approved subjects of logic and psychology, publishing in 1857 his text, which presumably were his lecture notes, entitled *Logic, describing the mechanism of our thought, its forms and laws on the basis of common sense guided by Christianity*.

Skvorcov was chosen in 1850 to teach the approved course in logic at Kyiv University. He did so only that one year. Who succeeded him in that particular case is unclear. However, since in 1859 Nazarij A. Favorov (1820–1897), who taught theology at the Kyiv Academy was promoted to a professorship at the University, where his duties included teaching logic, it is quite possible he had already been teaching logic there for some time.⁷⁹ He published nothing, however, in the field. Logic would remain deeply mired in the Aristotelian categories with no hint of the advances that would refashion our understanding of it in a few short decades.

---

78 Bazhanov (2012a), 148. Bazhanov comments in this regard, "apparently, the compilers of the program did not consider them quite perfect."
79 Khomenko (2012), 183.

Part II: **Under the 1869 Charter**

In the face of Russia's humiliating performance in the Crimean War (1853–1856), the newly installed Tsar Alexander II cautiously recognized a widespread assessment of the country's shortcomings and comparatively backward state. His introduction of a series of measures, collectively termed the "Great Reforms," included freeing the serfs, earning Alexander the sobriquet "The Tsar-Liberator," and the reintroduction of philosophy into the secular universities. The reform mood, however short-lived, was infectious, leading even to a reconsideration of the established rules and principles governing the theological academies. For many at these institutions, the time had long come for changes to the original charter. One pedagogic challenge that needed to be addressed was the mounting of an appropriate theological response to the religious skepticism arising from the recent and rapid scientific advances, particularly in geology and psychology. At issue was the modernization of the curriculum that could be accomplished only by theological research, which the current procedures effectively hindered, if not made practically impossible in most cases, within the walls of the academies. The secular authorities at the time also sensed a need to raise the prestige accorded the Orthodox clergy in the vast empire, a prestige that had suffered owing to its isolation from society at large and its outmoded thinking and general poor education.

As we have seen, the teaching staff up to this time seldom chose their assignments on the basis of some specialization if they even had any. The faculty were shifted around as necessary from one department to another with little regard for their qualification to teach a particular subject matter. Officials largely reacted with outright indifference to original research by the teaching staff, and there was minimal contact with secular scholars and no participation in secular scholarly societies. Even among the staff of the theological academies, there were no such societies. Given these facts, it should hardly come as a surprise that although the academies had reasonably good libraries with both domestic and foreign publications the professors did not themselves contribute anything to scholarly research.[1]

The precise means by which to ameliorate the above deficiencies were not clear to everyone. Could the problems be addressed locally, or would sweeping changes across the four academies be necessary? Another fundamental issue on which there was no immediate consensus concerned the retention of the existing restrictions limiting the theological academies only to those from the first estate. The individual academies had their own interests at stake, but eventually the decision was made to pursue an entirely new charter. A special committee for the

---

1 Sukhova (2009a), 24.

preparation of one was formed in 1867, and decided upon in two years.² The charter was to be implemented initially in that year, 1869, in St. Petersburg and Kyiv and in the following year in Moscow and Kazan.³

The chief purpose of the new charter was to encourage research in theology by the teaching faculty and advanced students. The way to do this in the eyes of those who wrote the charter was through specialization. Professors were to focus solely on the disciplines that they taught, and students too were to concentrate within a chosen department. The only requirement for all students was Biblical Scripture of the Old and New Testaments, basic theology, and a group of philosophy courses. In addition to logic and psychology, a course in pedagogy and one in metaphysics were introduced into the teaching curriculum. Thus, philosophy was to be taught during all four years of study, despite the fact that the theological academies were not permitted to issue degrees in philosophy. Under the new charter, all professors were permitted to create their own syllabi and to choose their own textbooks for class use.⁴ The academies were now allowed to conduct their own censorship, to organize scholarly societies, and to hold public lectures. Admission was also no longer to be restricted to those from the first estate, and graduates of secular educational institutions were permitted to attend classes in accordance with rules established locally.⁵ Amazingly, according to the terms of the charter, salaries were substantially increased. Full professors, who previously received 858 rubles/year were now to receive 3000! The "catch," if the term is appropriate, is that those without a doctoral degree had to present dissertations or suitable scholarly works in their respective field to obtain such a degree within three years.⁶ Needless to say, those without doctorates rushed to write dissertations, leading to an upsurge in research publications as the charter had intended. Not all full professors succeeded in writing dissertations and defending them in the time stipulated. For example, only three at the St. Petersburg Academy managed to complete the degree requirements. The Moscow Academy witnessed a similar situation. It

---

2 As one can well imagine, there were sharp disagreements among the committee members concerning what changes were desirable, let alone necessary. The details of the discussions need not be recounted here, but see Chistovich (1889), 109–113, and for further details see the various references Chistovich provides there.
3 Chistovich (1889), 118–119.
4 Sukhova (2017), 405.
5 Ship (2010), 113. We see that it was under this provision in the 1869 Charter that Vladimir Solov'ëv could attend classes at the Moscow Academy within a few years. This would not have been permitted previously. We can easily imagine then that his attendance there in 1873 was still a novelty, perhaps even unheard of among his circle of friends. Given that this opportunity had existed for only three years, their astonishment is understandable.
6 Chistovich (1889), 119.

had seven ordinary (full) professors without doctorates in 1869, but only four were able to defend dissertations within the stipulated time period.⁷ Some nearing the tenure limit set by the Charter of 35 years of service at the academy simply chose to retire rather than prepare and defend a dissertation.⁸ Additionally, unlike previously, dissertation defenses were now to be public events. In a short time, these became important proceedings in the life of the academies, sometimes drawing large audiences for what many hoped would be intellectual fireworks. The unintended consequence was that some religious and theological topics that had earlier been dogmatically resolved or passed over in silence were now revealed to be controversial and disputable. Since the new charter permitted the academies to subscribe to scholarly works without censorship, dissertations could provide information concerning banned items, thus bringing them – and the possibly heretical positions contained therein – to the attention of the public.

---

7 Sukhova (2010a), 29. The situation was little different at the Kazan Academy. Only three of the five full professors managed to defend doctoral dissertations within the allotted time.
8 Such was the case, for example, of Vasilij I. Dolockij (1814–1885), who was teaching in the theology department at the time but who had taught many different courses and held many positions over his career. He simply retired from the St. Petersburg Academy in 1873, at which time he had completed 35 years of service. Another professor there left in 1874. Chistovich (1889), 121. At the Moscow Academy, Professor Filaret Sergievskij left to take up the position of rector of a seminary where a *magister*'s degree was sufficient.

Chapter 5
The St. Petersburg Academy Under the Second Charter

The terms of the 1869 charter surely came as a surprise to many and a shock to some among the teaching staff of the theological academies who, as we saw, had to be concerned now with preparing dissertations and publications. Still, the reforms meant that the academies would more greatly resemble the secular universities, which was one of the aims of the reforms in the first place. Indeed, the Russian university reforms of 1835 and 1863 influenced the shaping of the 1869 charter as did, though undoubtedly discretely and without explicit acknowledgment, the German Humboldtian model of higher education.[1] The primary authors of the charter hoped that the emphasis on specialization and research would lead the teaching staff to incorporate that research into their lessons, making the instruction more interesting from the students' perspective and prompt the students in time to pursue further research themselves.

5.1 Chistovich's Psychology

One of the three ordinary professors at the Petersburg Academy who successfully submitted and defended a dissertation within the time-limit stipulated by the 1869 Charter was Illarion A. Chistovich (1828–1893), best known today for his history of the Academy and not for his writings in psychology, philosophy, or theology. He taught psychology and the history of philosophy before Kant from 1859–1864 and the entire history of philosophy from 1864. Although he defended a dissertation in 1871, he left the Academy and teaching in general in 1873 having secured prominent positions within the civil service.[2]

---

[1] Sukhova (2013a), 59.
[2] Advances in Chistovich's professional career may have been facilitated by his marriage to the daughter of the Imperial family's personal confessor-priest. This "connection" may also have been behind the fact that he was granted access to archival material not open to others for use in his writings. See Kadosov (2016), 63. Unfortunately, Chistovich's wife died in 1876 at the age of 36. A second wife, Elizaveta, whom he married in April 1882, died in childbirth in January 1884 at the age of 40. He remained a widower, then, until his own death. Although Chistovich had one daughter from this second marriage and nine children from the first, several suffered from mental illness. For further information on Chistovich's family tree, see Kadosov (2019).

Chistovich began to teach psychology already with the start of his appointment at the St. Petersburg Academy in 1853. His additional part-time employment, starting in 1866, at a highly exclusive school for boys in the capital, the Imperial School of Jurisprudence, teaching logic, psychology and the history of philosophy prompted Chistovich to write a psychology textbook that went through a number of editions. As a text it strove for clarity and succinctness, but for that same reason it presented its content, even on contentious issues, as though it were uncontentious and simple. His positions were neither very original nor influential, but they are illustrative of surely an officially acceptable approach to psychology.

Chistovich, as with so many at the time and even into the following century, hailed introspection as the proper means of acquiring psychological knowledge. But he realized that reflection on one's own mental states and activities can no more reveal all possible psychological states and activities than can my own experience of the world reveal everything about the world "in itself," so to speak. It is impossible to study the life of the mind by observing just one person, even if it be my own mind. Without the slightest hesitation, Chistovich, held that each of us has privileged access to one's own mental states, but not to those of others. The mental life of others is revealed only inferentially, i.e., through corporeal movements or through verbal descriptions. But all such phenomena would indicate nothing about the inner states of others if (1) the assumption that my corporeal behavior is intimately associated with my inner states were not true, or (2) if the other's corporeal behavior were not intimately associated with the other's mental states in just the same way as it is in me.[3] Of course, Chistovich did not so much as point out these assumptions, let alone prove them. Furthermore, implicit in his discussion is a Cartesian dichotomy between the mind and the body, whereby the dichotomy is factually based, but not necessary. That is, corporeal behavior logically might not stand in a one-to-one association with our inner states.

Indeed, Chistovich acknowledged his acceptance of a Cartesian dichotomy between the mind and the body writing: "To the self-conscious mind, the body is an external object, but at the same time the mind understands the body as a means, as an organ of its own activity by means of which it establishes an active connection with the external world."[4] The world appears at first to the self-conscious "spirit" as fragmentary and disconnected. It, then, appears in some manner that Chistovich did not explain to be in an ordered system of forms and relations.[5]

---

[3] See Chistovich (1876), 3. The reader will surely recall that these matters played a large role in twentieth-century Anglophone philosophy.

[4] Chistovich (1876), 13.

[5] The basis, if any, of Chistovich's claim is unstated. Since it is presented in a psychological text, we must assume that the statement was factual, not logical.

Nevertheless, the objects we perceive as populating the world actually exist as they appear to us together with their relationships. There is no Kantian thing in itself. We can create in our minds ideal images of objects from parts or elements taken from our actual perceptions of those objects. Such an ideal image is the concept of space, which we form in our understanding on the basis of sensibly given spatial limitations. Whereas space is a concept, spatial extension as an intuition is logically prior to space. The latter is immediately given in viewing externality. Time likewise is a concept formed from abstraction on observed changes in things or in their relation to other things.[6]

We find, in short, that Chistovich treated many epistemological issues from a decidedly empiricist standpoint. He criticized Kant's table of categories for allegedly including in it many empirical concepts. The three categories of modality (possibility, existence, and necessity), for example, are empirical concepts formed by abstraction on sense intuitions, and are not *a priori*. Existence "is revealed to us by means of experience and not by means of thought. It is impossible to deduce analytically a thing's existence from its concept."[7] Even mathematical cognition has in his eyes an empirical foundation, but mathematical constructions and formulas, being mental abstractions, are not subject to empirical verification. This accounts for their universality and necessity.

Chistovich's understanding of philosophy is that its concern is with acquiring metaphysical knowledge. Such knowledge, being non-empirical, is not contingent, and therefore, like mathematics is universal and necessary. Philosophy as an enterprise seeks knowledge of the origin, goals, and highest laws governing the universe. The subject matter of philosophy is ultimately everything as falling under the idea of the infinite as well as the ideas of truth, goodness, and beauty, which are based on it. In a quite obscure manner, Chistovich proclaimed that the mentioned qualities of mathematics are based on the same qualities that the foundations of philosophical knowledge possess. These foundations are innate, i.e., "inherent in the mind of every human being by our very nature."[8] Chistovich, unfortunately, failed to enumerate them, but the idea of God was certainly one of them. He argued that since we do not obtain these ideas by means of either internal or external intuitions they could not possibly be considered factual. They also could not be the result of the imagination or of discursive thought, since nei-

---

6 Chistovich (1876), 74.
7 Chistovich (1876), 77. A proper Kantian reply to Chistovich would require a lengthy discussion that would be tangential to our concern here. However, in short we can note that Kant denied that existence is an empirical concept, while in agreement with Chistovich that existence of something cannot be deduced *analytically* from its concept.
8 Chistovich (1876), 82.

ther is capable of creating anything original. Both can merely generalize and develop what is given from another source. Through all of our mental activity, we find a desire for the infinite, which forces us to seek the source for this desire beyond the bounds of experience. Chistovich, without further ado, believed that this desire and our innate ideas are intimately related and that therefore our innate ideas have a non-empirical origin. "Ideas are innate within us, not as finished concepts of cognized objects, but as invested in the mind by the Highest Being, its Creator."[9] In an unelaborated manner, Chistovich held that these innate ideas pass into conceptual forms in the understanding. This process also holds for other spheres of the mind. For example, the mind strives for higher ideal, unbounded forms of the spiritual life and for rationality constituting not just the forms of truth, but also of morality and aesthetics.

Chistovich sought to combine a general empiricism in epistemology with the officially prescribed Christian Platonism, but he did not attend to the difficulties doing so entailed. In any case, his efforts, such as they were, failed to stir either the succeeding generation of students or any contemporary readers. His direct influence appears marginal at best, but his treatment of the Kantian categories was representative of an approach to them among Academy philosophers. His contribution in this was his explicitness, a quality not always found in the writings of other Academicians. Chistovich was an eminently practical man, who knew how to advance his career without sacrificing his well-honed scholarly skills.

5.2 Svetilin's Logic and the Question of Psychologism

Karpov's death in 1867 initiated a search for his replacement at the St. Petersburg Academy. Although not the sole applicant for the position, Aleksandr E. Svetilin (1842–1887), a teacher of logic and psychology at the St. Petersburg Seminary and a former student of Karpov's, received the appointment. Svetilin comparatively quickly composed a *Textbook of Formal Logic* (*Uchebnik formal'noj logiki*) that went through fourteen editions to 1916, the first edition appearing in 1871.[10] As the title indicates, it was intended for classroom use, not for specialists. To what extent we can ascribe the positions espoused in this textbook to Svetilin himself is unclear. He himself in the 1871 text as well as in the 1880 revision stated that it was composed on the basis of what he considered to be the best German text

---

9 Chistovich (1876), 89.
10 By the time of the fifth edition of 1880, the title had changed simply to *Textbook of Logic*.

at the time, Adolf Lindner's *Lehrbuch der formalen Logik*.[11] Its value for our story is that it, unlike Karpov's works, clearly distanced logic from psychology. The text, whether an expression of Svetilin's considered opinions or not, stressed from the outset that our thinking must follow prescriptive laws in order to obtain correct results. Logic as a field of study is concerned with indicating what these laws are and how they are to be used. Psychology, on the other hand, "is concerned with the investigation of natural laws of thought,"[12] i.e., not with how we should think, but with how we actually do think. Psychology, thus, examines thinking as it is, whereas logic is concerned with how thinking should take place. A logically correct train of thought is by no means assured of a correspondence to reality, though the logically unthinkable must be objectively impossible.[13]

Another laudable discussion in Svetilin's textbook was his recognition, in effect, of the intentionality of consciousness, although he did not use the expression. He remarked that when we think, we think of "something." If there were no object of a thought, there would be no thinking. Svetilin did not proceed further, unfortunately, into topics that have riveted some inquiries in twentieth-century philosophy of mind, such as intentional inexistence. Although in successive editions, Svetilin claimed he made many changes to his text, including introducing a "psychological element" into it, his position in the matters just mentioned did not change.[14]

By the late 1870s, the issue of materialism and the need to confront and combat it directly had largely become a thing of the past. In the eyes of the theologians, the war was over and had been decisively won with the assistance of psychology over the previous two decades. A summary of the decisive battles and their outcome would now be sufficient. Svetilin summed up the popular stand among theologians that materialism is not a scientific doctrine, but a metaphysical one that sets moral and social goals for itself. It cannot be the result of applying the scientific method, for the external world presents us not with the essence of things, their substance. That method's concern is only with the action of various natural forces and properties. These are what we can know, but we cannot think of phenomena and of the properties of things without representing things to which

---

[11] Svetilin (1871), vi; Svetilin (1880), i. Already in the first edition, Svetilin, stated that his text had incorporated formulations that differed from Lindner. See Svetilin (1871), vii.
[12] Svetilin (1871), 1.
[13] Svetilin (1871), 4. Svetilin expounded on this distinction between psychology and logic in a lengthy review of Vladislavlev's 1872 logic textbook. He also criticized Vladislavlev for overlooking a number of recent German philosophers and for simplifying logical concepts to the point of presenting them superficially and inaccurately. See Svetilin (1874).
[14] Svetilin (1880), i.

those phenomena and properties belong. However, we do not and cannot know what these things "essentially" are.[15]

Svetilin held that psychology can study mental phenomena, but only the phenomena. It does not and cannot study of what they are phenomena, i.e., what lies "behind" the manifestations. We know as little about the "I" as about an external thing. However, introspection does present our thoughts and feelings immediately as they really are in themselves, whereas our external senses present us merely with signs, or symbols, of external facts.[16] This demonstrates the complete dichotomy between psychology and physiology, which relies on external observations. Svetilin did not rule out some correlation between psychological and physiological phenomena. Indeed, he held that to be one of the principal tasks awaiting further study. However, this dichotomy shows that our understanding of physical things and events involves an recognition of them and is a significant step along the path to idealism. Svetilin interpreted this dichotomy as affirming the independence of the mind from the body. The "moderate materialist" does not want to dismiss mental phenomena – rejecting thereby that they can be fully explained in physical terms – and views mental and physical processes as occurring in parallel, as two sides or aspects of something ultimately unknowable. The Christian, though, sees the mind as distinct from the corporeal. To be sure, Christian writers have made seemingly confusing assertions, such as that the mind is the body, but what they meant was that "the mind exists just as indubitably as does the body."[17]

Svetilin's influence at the St. Petersburg Academy and on the development of philosophy in the setting of a theological academy, like that of Chistovich, was brief and apparently on only a few students. He published little during his relatively brief tenure at the Academy. In particular, his lectures on psychology remained unpublished. However, one former student offered a quite different understanding of Svetilin's positions from those expressed in his logic text, an understanding based presumably on classroom lectures and his own psychologistic construal. In a short speech on the anniversary of Svetilin's death, the future Archbishop Antonij, whom we shall turn to shortly, said that for Svetilin the laws and techniques of thought and cognition arise from a positive principle of spiritual life, a principle that the human will points out. There is no independent source through which we obtain the laws of logic. They are, rather, developed from mental powers more basic than those laws. Psychology precedes logic, content before form.[18] Certainly, there are grounds for thinking that Antonij projected his own views onto his teach-

---

15 Svetilin (1878), 563.
16 Svetilin (1878), 583.
17 Svetilin (1878), 567.
18 Antonij(1900), 274–276.

er. There is no argument in Svetilin's scant publications that would lead us to think he advanced the human will over thought as there is in Antonij. But of course the mere fact that Svetilin admitted he had introduced psychological elements into his logic text leaves open the possibility that he introduced "unwritten doctrines" to his students in the classroom.

In February 1884, suffering from some severe mental ailment he had to resign from teaching.

5.3 Debol'skij's Theistic Phenomenalism from Kant to Hegel

Unlike Chistovich and Svetilin, neither of whom authored much in philosophy, Nikolaj G. Debol'skij (1842–1918) wrote a number of works, both books and articles, including the first Russian translation of Hegel's *Science of Logic*. Almost alone in the history of Russian philosophy, he was self-educated in philosophy and wrote his principal works while not a university or academy professor.[19] He testified to his autodidacticism in the preface, dated 1878, to his later *Philosophy of the Future*, published in 1882: "The entire course of my philosophical development took place quite independently, without the help of a prior education, without the influence from any scientific or philosophical circle, and without the slightest help from scientific or literary criticism."[20] Indeed, Debol'skij, though the son of a priest, was a graduate of the natural sciences faculty at St. Petersburg University in 1865. As he recalled in the above preface, he, like a majority of the youth at the time who studied the natural sciences, held to a worldview that combined materialism and empiricism.[21] He did not cling to this stand for long. He soon realized the inconsistency in combining the anti-metaphysical stance of empiricism with a materialism, understood as a metaphysical doctrine, a realization that led him to reject the latter in favor of the former. Ever the restless youth, Debol'skij's study of Kant, most likely through the interpretation of Kuno Fischer, as well as unnamed others, propelled him onward yet again.

---

[19] Chizhevskij called Debol'skij: "One of the most solitary figures in the history of Russian thought." Chizhevskij (2007), 338.
[20] Debol'skij (1882), i. Of course, the critic of Debol'skij's elaborations can point to his lack of proper philosophical training as responsible for his many failures and oversights.
[21] The reader may recall that Vladimir Solov'ëv too was enrolled in the natural sciences faculty at Moscow University in 1870, though he rather quickly chafed at having to deal with microscopes and test tubes, a concern that was far removed from his essentially religious and aesthetic sensibilities. See Nemeth (2014), 1–2.

Debol'skij's first of many teaching assignments began in 1868 at the First St. Petersburg Military Gymnasium, where he was employed while writing his first philosophical tract, *Introduction to the Theory of Cognition*, which appeared in 1870. In the 1878 preface mentioned above, Debol'skij stated that his chief goal in that earlier work was "to show, contrary to empiricism, that metaphysical or ontological cognition is possible, i.e., that in addition to a theory of appearances, cognition of what exists in itself, a theory of things in themselves is possible."[22] Contrary to empiricism, which ascribes existence to phenomena alone, there must be something causing these phenomena. But a more important reason driving Debol'skij onward was empiricism's inability to account for the unity of the manifold of cognition. There is a unifying principle, a form, connecting the content of sensation in even the most elementary cognitive act. Moreover, along with this unifying form, which does not stem from sensation, there is a unity of the conscious subject in every instance of cognition, a unity constantly given along with the form.

To be sure, much of Debol'skij's retrospective account of his philosophical position as it was in 1870 depicts that position like a much-simplified Kantianism. He himself would later call it the first stage in his philosophical development.[23] However, a second stage quickly followed upon realizing that the unifying principle must also be a universal principle. In this interpretation, all that exists, exists only as an object of consciousness. There can be no existing things or states apart from a consciousness, but Debol'skij left open the possibility that the consciousness in question is not merely that of an individual, but of a universal consciousness. Rather than realizing the similarity of his new position to that of Berkeley, Debol'skij wrote that he could not fully subscribe to Hegelianism owing to his adamant insistence that the content of cognition cannot be deduced *a priori* from reason. He continued to maintain that the form and the content of cognition are irreducible to one or the other. It is also wrong to consider the universe anthropomorphically as though it were a universal consciousness with all states of nature being comparable to the individual human consciousness with all of its states. Whether he viewed Hegel as holding that position is unclear, but Debol'skij did specifically part with Hegel – or at least his understanding of Hegel – in rejecting the need for the dialectical method in developing a philosophical system. Debol'skij could not accept the use of the dialectical method as providing a reproduction of the logical order of the universe.

---

22 Debol'skij (1882), xvi. This entire quotation in the original is italicized, thereby indicating that Debol'skij attached great importance to it for an understanding of his earlier work.
23 Debol'skij (1882), vii-viii.

Debol'skij's 1872 tract *On the Dialectical Method* was announced as the first part of a planned larger work. A second part never appeared, Debol'skij giving as the reason that he was not able at the time to resolve the difficulties mentioned immediately above. In retrospect, he attributed this inability to his adherence to a principle, which seemed obviously correct to him, but that did not allow for the further development of a method that to him also seemed correct. Having to choose between a principle and a method, Debol'skij opted to choose a new principle, and this adoption initiated a third stage in his philosophical development. Whereas previously consciousness, however that may be understood, had forms that unified the content, or manifold, of sensations, now he saw sensations in this third stage as already formed or united – two terms that he took to be synonymous – when presented to consciousness. In order to account for this, Debol'skij believed he had to accept the possibility of a super-conscious reason that was responsible for the uniting of sensations. The consciousness of the human individual, then, does not impose a unity onto the manifold, but intuits the pre-unified manifold given in perception. This represents for Debol'skij a definitive break with Kant and move in the direction of Hegel. It also meant to him, though, that there was no need to understand "consciousness" pantheistically, as a universal world consciousness.[24] The move toward a theistic conception is clear. The imposition of form onto content is a manifestation of reason that Debol'skij understood as a religious act and which he interpreted as an idealism inasmuch as it meant we can intelligibly speak of the idea of the universe.

Debol'skij's career at the St. Petersburg Academy was relatively brief, a mere five years (1882–1887) after which he was employed at the Ministry of National Education, where he rose to a high bureaucratic position.[25] Already before the start of his teaching at the Academy, Debol'skij had published a number of works, and after his departure he published many more. In what follows, we keep for the most part to the publications from his time at the Academy, even though by doing so we must unfortunately leave aside the full maturation of his philosophical thought.

---

[24] Debol'skij (1882), xiii. However bizarre we may find Debol'skij's suggestion that consciousness might be understood in this ambiguous manner, he clearly did not find it so and never explained what sense we could or should attribute to talk of a universal world consciousness.

[25] Debol'skij's previous employment as a teacher at all levels of the educational system surely stood him in good stead at the education ministry, since from his experience he could understand practical issues and difficulties. Walicki mentions that Debol'skij taught at the St. Petersburg Academy but mentions neither the fact that his tenure there was relatively brief nor his bureaucratic career, which was considerably longer, thus quite possibly giving the incorrect impression that Debol'skij spent his career at the St. Petersburg Academy. Walicki (2015), 638.

In the already mentioned *Philosophy of the Future*, which was published just as he started teaching at the St. Petersburg Academy, Debol'skij focused on developing both a metaphysics, through grappling with the cognizability of the thing in itself, as well as an epistemology, investigating whether there are *a priori* forms of cognition. He stressed in 1882 that his philosophical aim remained the same as earlier, namely, to show that the cognition of things in themselves is possible. However, before engaging in a full exposition of his own views, Debol'skij sought to clarify his terminology, finding that operative terms have been understood over the years in different senses, thereby obstructing engagements between apparently conflicting viewpoints. Empiricists are those who maintain that the only cognition we have is that of sensible appearances. On that basis, they reject all of metaphysics. An analysis of their position, though, shows their own confusion. Certainly, no one can dispute that we know the world around us only as it appears to us, for example, under particular lighting conditions. How those same things are "in themselves" apart from us human observers we cannot ever know. Nevertheless, we do know that the brilliant flower bed even in dim light remains a flower bed. The failure to recognize this distinction lies behind the "extreme empiricist" position to reject metaphysics *in toto* as well as behind those who see the world as an attribute of some "Will" or "Reason." If all that exists is an appearance, then there can be no connection between appearances and, thus, no explanation for their regularity.[26]

Debol'skij acknowledged that his philosophical outlook bore a striking similarity at first to the "moderate empiricism" of Herbert Spencer in allowing for the existence of an unknown basis of appearances. Nonetheless, no identification of the viewpoints is possible. Ontology, taken as a doctrine (*uchenie*) of the general form of the thing in itself, is possible based on a special sort of knowledge, an ontological knowledge. This knowledge is independent and distinct from the knowledge we have of the properties of things. It informs us of the fundamental causes of appearances, namely the things in themselves. We know by means of ontological knowledge that things in themselves exist, that they are responsible as well for the changes we empirically sense in appearances.

Debol'skij focused on three concepts: existence, change, and causality. All three are always given together with experience and are not of subjective origin. To claim otherwise, of course, would result in solipsism. Since they are *always* given along with and at the outset of experience, they are, in contrast to Chistovich's view,[27] not of empirical origin, and are therefore of super-empirical origin,

---

26 Debol'skij (1882), 15–23.
27 The contrast is ours. Debol'skij never mentioned Chistovich.

invariably entering into the structure of experience. Whereas Kant had written that concepts that are a necessary condition of experience are *a priori* concepts of the understanding, i.e., of the cognitive faculty and as such are strictly limited to experiential employment, Debol'skij, based on similar reasoning, comes to a quite dissimilar conclusion. He wrote:

> Let us assume that these concepts are necessarily applied *to something given in experience* along with its properties. Then, since the thing in itself is always *given* along with appearances, these concepts are also applicable to the thing in itself. Therefore, assuming that the thing in itself is quite distinct from the appearances, we must admit that it has in common with appearances the determinations of existence, change, and causality.[28]

We have here, in effect, Debol'skij's reply to the table of categories offered by Kant. There are not twelve fundamental concepts, but only three.[29] Kant held that these concepts have legitimate employment only with respect to appearances, whereas Debol'skij held that their proper employment extended to things in themselves.

In order for us to perceive the given manifold of a perception as a single perception we must be able to distinguish within that manifold the different elements: (1) as given, (2) as distinct from each other, but (3) also as comprising the unity of a single perception. Debol'skij stated that we thus have determined the three forms found in any basic perceptual act: (1) position, (2) distinction, and (3) unity. These are elementary in the sense that they cannot be derived from other forms or from each other. These three forms understood temporally become the three fundamental concepts we have seen: The assertion of a position of a given element is the concept of existence, a distinguishing of states in time is change, and their unity over time is causality.[30] Debol'skij cautioned us that even though we have, thus, generated the fundamental concepts, or categories, from a temporal understanding of sensible features, we must not conclude that the concept of time has a legitimate employment outside the experiential sphere. He wrote that we are prevented from considering time as a property of the thing in itself by its clearly conditional character.[31] Debol'skij, of course, also denied the employment of space to things in themselves. Time and space, he argued, could apply to things in themselves only

---

[28] Debol'skij (1882), 40–41.
[29] Regrettably, Debol'skij made no reference to Chistovich's treatment of the categories, in particular that of existence. In fact, the standpoints of the two Academy professors stand in sharp contrast even though from the Kantian position they both upheld a transcendental realism.
[30] Debol'skij (1882), 71.
[31] Debol'skij's quite bare statement, taken as an argument for the strictly phenomenal employment of time, is specious. On the same grounds, we should restrict our usage of his supposedly three fundamental concepts to phenomena, not to things in themselves.

if they were properties of the three fundamental concepts. Time, however, though a determination of these concepts, is not a property of them, but merely their phenomenal feature.[32] The very possibility that we have those concepts is dependent on our perceptions being given in the sensible forms of position, distinction, and unity.

In a move reminiscent of Kant despite major differences, Debol'skij distinguished sensibility from reason (*razum*). The properties of the objects of the former are relative, relative to us. In other words, they appear as things for us. In contrast, the properties of things in themselves are not relative. In an odd move, for which Debol'skij provided no explanation – indeed none can be given – he claims that the non-relativity of the properties of things in themselves means that they have no relations whatsoever. That is, they are independent of being, causality, and change.[33] Whatever Debol'skij may have thought of his reasoning at this point, he has left the sphere of rational discourse. He tells us that form and content are united in the sphere of the in-itself. Yet, although the form of the thing in itself is uncognizable as such, we can understand it by analogy with the form of our own reason, but he utterly failed to explain what he took to be a "form of reason." The content of the thing in itself too is uncognizable, but, unlike the form, we cannot understand it even by analogy "since it has no analogy with our sense content."[34] One point Debol'skij wished to draw from this is that human reason cannot reveal the rational character of our sense manifold, and we cannot rationally be expected to show the properties of things in themselves.

We have seen that in the opening pages of his *Philosophy of the Future* Debol'skij wrestled with a philosophical problem reminiscent of topics in Kant and German Idealism in general. However, as we advance in the book an unmistakable departure emerges into a metaphysics that, although the terminology is retained, makes conceptual leaps bearing scant traces of logical argument and coherence. Most alarming is Debol'skij's introduction of the euphemism "Supreme Reason" without establishing any basis for doing so.[35] Debol'skij contended that this Reason

---

[32] In so arguing, Debol'skij presupposed what he intended to demonstrate, namely that time is limited to the phenomenal realm.

[33] As we shall see this train of thought is important for the conclusion that Debol'skij drew. Nonetheless, stating that the properties of things in themselves are not relative means only that they are not relative to us, not that they totally lack properties.

[34] Debol'skij (1882), 81. He did not explain why content is not analogous to the sense manifold of our intuitions. Moreover, if the form and the content in the sphere of the in-itself are identical and an analogy applies to the form, why does it not apply as well to the content? ((a = b) and (a → c)) → (b → c).

[35] Debol'skij criticized Hegel for construing God as a form. As we saw at the Moscow Academy in discussing Sokolov, Debol'skij charged Hegel with atheism, a formalistic atheism, rejecting the "Su-

"individualizes" itself in a "multitude of limited intelligences."[36] Since a characteristic of consciousness is the sensing of a flow of time, the "Supreme Reason" cannot possibly possess consciousness. Indeed, It "transcends" all determinations, such as time, space, and quantity, but Debol'skij provided no argument whatever for his claim. Curiously, then, he explicitly identifies the sphere of things in themselves with this "Reason."[37]

Earlier in his 1882 work, Debol'skij asserted that experience alone can serve as the means to obtain concepts for cognition. "Without experience, there can be no cognition. Consequently, concepts concerning the super-experiential, if they exist, can be obtained only through experience."[38] If there are no such concepts, then the fundamental concepts of causality, alteration, and existence are inapplicable to experience. He proceeded, however, with the claim that there are such concepts and that they are always found in experience, but are not produced by experience. Thus, in his eyes they must have a super-experiential origin. But unlike others at the time he rejected constructing a metaphysical system on the basis of a mystical experience, which he feared led to pantheism and determinism. Surely, one can uphold a metaphysical realism that views things in themselves as causal agents of the phenomenal features of our surrounding world, but Debol'skij proceeded considerably beyond such a bare statement. Certainly, in his later works, he further developed his fundamentally theistic position. Still, the outlines and more were presented here in 1882 and were found officially acceptable even if they did not conform to the letter of Church teaching.

5.4 Debol'skij's Right Hegelianism and Nationalism

Debol'skij's concerns upon beginning his relatively brief academic career were not limited to "theoretical philosophy" nor would they remain so during his years in the Russian civil service. Indeed, he turned often to "practical philosophy" or morality stemming from his work first as a pedagogue and then as an administrator with an interest in educational theory. Debol'skij, not unlike many at the time, held morality to be impossible without religion, but morality was the broader concept of the two. God has placed within each of us a distinction between good and bad, but not knowledge of what exactly is good and bad. Relying on reason alone,

---

preme Divine Being." Religion, in Hegel's thought, "became simply a construction of the human spirit and not a relation to the Supreme Power independent of us." Debol'skij (1882), 144.
36 Debol'skij (1882), 83.
37 Debol'skij (1882), 90, 142.
38 Debol'skij (1882), 32.

we could not know specifically how we should proceed in a moral situation. Debol'skij's critique of Kantian ethics stemmed from his approach, viz., what he saw as its ambiguity. There is no single set of specific moral principles to which everyone at all times must adhere. Debol'skij reiterated this now familiar point that the sheer universality of the Kantian categorical imperative makes its application in a specific instance indeterminate.[39] "Should not a person always and everywhere be moral, i.e., honest, truthful, virtuous, hard-working, etc.? The fact is, though, that these qualities by themselves are only general schemes of moral activity. They do not indicate any positive direction, i.e., no thoroughly guiding idea."[40] Morality, being concerned not with what is but with what ought to be, posits goals, but taken in their concrete form they are set not by God, but by us ourselves.

Debol'skij found utilitarianism, taken as an ethical theory with a norm for social activity, to be adequate as a guide within the bounds of a firmly delimited group. Its principle, the greatest happiness for the greatest number, can provide guidance for specific groups of people at a specific time. For Debol'skij, however, this idea of a restriction to a certain number of people is not derived from the utilitarian principle itself. That principle cannot itself explain why its applicability must be restricted and specifically to whom. "If, in making other beings the object of our concern, we must limit ourselves only to certain beings, then surely there must be a basis, the consequence of which is that we prefer certain beings over all others."[41] This delimitation must be based on another, a "higher" principle, one that takes into account the group's time-line, i.e., its history, which utilitarianism omits from consideration. A few years later he would remark that the highest good was a "harmonious combination of all sorts of goal-conforming activity."[42] In order to avoid a lapse into sheer hedonism, the utilitarian principle must also take into account the nature of those involved in the calculation. Given his background in teaching, we cannot be surprised that Debol'skij saw the moral concern for happiness not in the achievement of a momentary state, but as a long-term goal. He interpreted the "nature" of moral objects not as what nature is at the moment, but as what it can and should become upon its development. The true determination of a person's nature is that person's goal or vocation. A moral concern or care

---

[39] "The complete inadequacy of Kant's formalism is seen in the fact that his principle does not provide any specific practical guidance." Debol'skij (1880), 73.
[40] Debol'skij (1880), 112.
[41] Debol'skij (1880), 65.
[42] Debol'skij (1886), 105.

for a person is caring for that person's own vocation, actively caring that the person, through one's own efforts, fulfills that vocation.[43]

The temporal development of the moral object that Debol'skij had in mind has no final goal, but extends without end. He conceived this infinite telos as an idea and for this reason termed his conception an idealism. There is more than one such idea, and these can be ranked with some higher than others. Debol'skij provided no criteria for establishing this ranking, but clearly believed humanity has a "higher idea" than others in the animal kingdom. Thus, a concern for the welfare of humanity ranks higher in the moral order than a concern for animals, since the former calls for the realization of a higher idea.

To be sure, most of us do acknowledge a higher moral concern for our own species above others. For example, in a choice between saving a person – even though he or she may be a total stranger – and a dog from a burning building, our immediate as well as considered reaction is for the safety of the former. However, Debol'skij also wished to distinguish between groups within humanity itself. Some are, he believes, more capable than others of an all-round endless development of their natural gifts. Some groups, in other words, present a more favorable field for the realization of their idea and, therefore, have more right to a moral concern from others. It is not a matter of how many human individuals constitute this group or part of humanity, but of their ideal. "That is, the right of certain beings to moral concern is acquired not on the basis of their number, but on the basis of their ideal tendencies."[44] Now totally abandoning utilitarianism, Debol'skij stated that the goal of his moral idealism is not human happiness, but the realization of the human idea. Thus, if a particular country or people is undoubtedly the highest representative of the highest human idea in comparison with the majority of humanity, then the "elevation" – Debol'skij did not clarify this term – of that country or people represents a progressive step forward for humanity even if it be at the expense of the happiness of humanity on the whole.

Who the moral agent is has up to this point been left unsaid. Whom did Debol'skij see as the one who assesses that some group is progressive in terms of advancing the people's idea? Debol'skij's answer is simple: you and I, viz., the individual human being. "If I am convinced that my country can favorably serve the independent development of the universal idea, then I am obliged to direct my con-

---

[43] We see already from the discussion thus far that Debol'skij is not interested in pursuing the traditional model of what a human individual should do in a particular situation, especially in one where moral obligations conflict. No, his interest is in large groups.

[44] Debol'skij (1880), 68. This disturbing, indeed scary, idea needs no commentary in light of the history of the twentieth century. Debol'skij, if we may be charitable, lived in an era that could not conceive to what end his conception would lead.

cern to this development without the least questioning about the rest of humanity as a collective unit."⁴⁵ On the basis of this conclusion, Debol'skij drew his own version of the categorical imperative, although he merely termed it "a quite specific principle," namely: "Act when, where, and *on whom* you expect the best result for the realization of an idea."⁴⁶ He, then, goes on to write that, for example, the goal of medicine is not a matter of the individual human being, but of the ideal improvement of the human organism. The individual human being is merely a means to this end. Such was Debol'skij's unusual interpretation of the Hippocratic Oath.

Debol'skij elaborated on his reference above to one's country, after briefly summarizing his position. The first concern of moral activity is the development of social life, the basic forms of which are family, society, the state, and property. The correct or proper participation in the development of these forms assumes not only knowledge of them as they are presently manifested but also a basic knowledge of the "normal" course of their development. Debol'skij simply stated this without argument, but he acknowledged that these forms as well as their development are not uniform across all human societies. He called the set of features that distinguish one society from another its tribal type.⁴⁷ The various tribal types across societies also undergo a developmental process, which can be known from their history, and it is conscious participation in this process, the goal of which is the idea, that forms a proper task of moral activity. The realization of the tribal type is the highest moral task to which all else is subordinate. The history of humanity is populated with national products: the Greeks of antiquity gave pure science; the Germans gave us the Reformation; the English parliamentarism. All great achievements that propelled humanity ahead were the result not of humanity in general, but of particular nations.⁴⁸

The legitimacy of a political nation-state depends on whether that state can be traced or deduced from a tribal type. Those that cannot will not survive long in the absence of compulsion. A key factor in the tribal type is language, which is an expression of the tribe's culture. Liberalism formally seeks the improvement of social forms, but in a clash with national goals and demands, liberal goals must cede any alleged priority. The principle and source of a state's unity is its configuration around one tribe. Such is the ground of nationalism. Not every tribe can rise to become a nationality, only one that has sufficient intrinsic power to rise above others and in doing so realize itself as the basis of the unity of the state. Debol'skij

---

45 Debol'skij (1880), 69.
46 Debol'skij (1880), 70.
47 Debol'skij (1880), 108.
48 Debol'skij (1880), 114.

gave as an example the success of Russia in the Russo-Turkish War of 1877–1878, which stemmed in his eyes from the comparative strength of the Russian sense of itself as a single Russian nation over the lack of the same in the disunited multi-tribal Turkish state. Whereas liberalism plots the future of a nation on the basis of a particular preconceived, abstract principle, independent of the nation's history, a nation guided by the principle of nationality not only takes that history into account, but recognizes the pivotal role played by and which must be played by the actual course of the nation's development.[49] Whether our concern is the human individual or the individual nation, the moral course of action is dictated by the nation's historical duty, dictated by its peculiar destiny. Clearly with the Russian Empire as it existed in his lifetime in mind, Debol'skij allowed the political state to have more than one tribe within it as long as there is a spiritual unity, a cultural hegemony – though he did not use that expression – of the most powerful tribe over the others. In the absence of such hegemony, the state will not last long.

Debol'skij himself viewed his conception of "nationality" as idiosyncratic, although it likely conjures in our minds its usage during the already long-gone era of Tsar Nicholas I, the government ideology of whose reign came to be known by historians starting in the late nineteenth century as "Official Nationality."[50] Just like Uvarov, the minister of education in 1833, who proclaimed the three pillars of the imperial regime to be Orthodoxy, autocracy and nationality, without clarification, Debol'skij never managed to give a precise definition of the concept of "nationality." Both usages would remain obscure. But there is no reason for us to think that Debol'skij longed for either the reactionary policies of Nicholas or the right-wing fanaticism of the Black Hundreds. There is no evidence either that Debol'skij supported the latter or that he associated his conception of nationality in an inti-

---

49 Debol'skij (1880), 112. In his own example, though, Debol'skij demonstrated how little he understood his own depiction of liberalism. He wrote that liberals question the attempt to liberate the Slavic people in the Ottoman Empire, thinking that it would be "better" for Russia to concentrate on internal affairs. In contrast, if, on the basis of the "national principle," a war, such as the Russo-Turkish War, is "a legitimate product of Russia's historic vocation, i.e., if it consistently follows from the tasks bequeathed to Russia by its history, then the war was thereby justified." Debol'skij (1880), 113. Thus, if one reads a nation's history as ever expansive, then it is morally justified to seize the lands of others. "The only question is whether today's historic epoch appears mature enough for Russia's historical tasks to be fulfilled to the desired extent, not how legitimate these tasks are in themselves." Debol'skij (1880), 113.
50 Riasanovsky (1969), 73.

mate linkage with Orthodoxy and autocracy. As mightily as he tried, he characterized "nationality" more in what it is not than in what it is.[51]

We should add almost parenthetically, as it were, that Debol'skij was succeeded at the Academy by Mikhail I. Smolenskij (1847–1881), who, like Debol'skij, taught for only five years (1876–1881). Smolenskij's tenure was cut short prematurely by his early death. A graduate of the St. Petersburg Academy, he apparently had little lasting influence either through his pedagogical activity or writings, of which there were very few. The resulting vacancy was left open for almost one and a half years.

5.5 Karinskij on the History of Modern Philosophy

Arguably the most philosophically talented figure, in the Western sense, of all the academy instructors in the imperial Russian era was Mikhail I. Karinskij (1840–1917). Coming from the clerical estate, he entered the Moscow Theological Seminary in 1852 and the Moscow Academy in 1858. He finished his course of studies there in 1862, earning a *magister*'s degree in theology with a thesis entitled "Egyptian Jews under the Ptolemies." In 1865, he began teaching logic, psychology, and Latin at the Moscow Seminary. With Karpov's death in late 1867, Karinskij applied for the vacancy at the Academy. The position, unfortunately for Karinskij, went to Svetilin, but the committee was so suitably impressed with the material Karinskij had submitted in support of his application that in June 1868 they issued a resolution that he would be invited to take a position in metaphysics when such an opening would arise. He did not have to wait long. With the adoption of the 1869 Charter, Karinskij was appointed assistant professor in metaphysics. Already the following year, the Academic council filed a petition with the Holy Synod to grant Karinskij permission and finances for additional study in Germany, primarily Göttingen and Jena, for a period of one year in order to acquaint him with the current state of philosophy as taught there.[52] During his stay between April 1871 and April 1872 in Germany, Karinskij attended lectures not only in the universities of the two mentioned cities but also in Heidelberg. In 1872, another opening in the theology department arose, this time an associate professorship. The candidates were Svetilin and Karinskij. At a general meeting of the Academic council Karinskij received 12 votes to Svetilin's 11. As a result, the former was appointed to the asso-

---

51 For his final treatment of the subject, written while the Russian Empire was at war, see Debol'skij (1916). Much earlier he tried to distinguish his conception of "nationality" from that of Solov'ëv. See Debol'skij (1886).
52 Chistovich (1889), 134.

ciate professorship in September 1873, and with Chistovich's departure from the Academy Karinskij assumed the teaching of the history of philosophy in May 1874.

Karinskij wrote and published an extensive and thorough report on the current general state of philosophy in Germany upon his return to Russia. In his 1873 "Critical Survey of the Recent Period in German Philosophy," Karinskij depicted the development of nineteenth-century German thought from Fichte to Eduard von Hartmann as stemming from Kant, attempting to resolve issues the respective parties saw in it.[53] But all of them, all of the post-Kantian philosophical movements in Germany, sought to retain what each considered the chief results of Kant's thought while finding a philosophically justified way to achieve objective knowledge. To accomplish this task, those who immediately followed Kant pursued a "speculative" direction in philosophy and sought to remove the contradiction between a tenet they saw in Kant's philosophy and the conclusions it had hailed. For Karinskij, Kant's contention that the cognitive faculty had pure intuitions and pure categories was the starting point of all subsequent German philosophy. However, Kant's admission of the concept of the thing in itself, being unjustified, is a dogmatic element, a kind of axiom, and the only way to avoid this non-Critical admission without contradicting the general thrust of Kant's epistemology was simply to reject the thing in itself, to deny it any role in the cognitive process. Such was Fichte's train of thought. In Karinskij's telling, Fichte realized that the realm of the in-itself was the final factor in the Critical analysis of cognition that was not seen as a subjective condition. Fichte took the step of freeing the sense manifold of its dependence on an existence standing outside thought, i.e., apart from consciousness.[54] Here in this pithy observation, we find Karinskij foreshadowing the later Husserlian thesis of the essential capability of an existing thing to be perceived.[55] Karinskij again reiterated his position.

> It is impossible for us to think of the thing in itself as being independent of any faculty of representation. Whenever we think of a thing, we necessarily add an intelligence trying to cog-

---

[53] Karinskij (1873a), 71–72. Unfortunately, given the sheer size of Karinskij's book-length report we cannot do full justice to its contents. On the other hand, much of it is of a historical nature with criticisms now well-known to the student of the history of German philosophy, criticisms lodged by other Germans at the time. For a brief treatment of Karinskij's view of Kant, see Nemeth (2017), 172–175.

[54] Karinskij (1873a), 83.

[55] "We see *that the sort of being which belongs to the mental process is such that the latter is essentially capable of being perceived in reflection*. The physical thing is also essentially *capable of being perceived*, and it is seized upon in perception as a physical thing belonging to my surrounding world." Husserl (1982), 99 (§45).

nize it. The result from this position should be that a thing can be conceived only as an object of thought.[56]

The thing in itself, as Kant conceived it, became for this speculative direction pointless. It served no function with the expansion of the functioning of the cognitive faculties starting already in Fichte.

Although Karinskij noted the later-Schelling's criticisms of Hegel's system, he, like the early Solov'ëv, gave short shrift to the role of the romantic philosopher's place in the German Idealist movement. Schelling's contribution was to show nature's gradual rise to the level of spirit. Hegel added to what his predecessors had done by revealing the absolute principle grounding the historical and the logical process. His was, in Karinskij's eyes the fullest and most consistent representative of the speculative direction stemming from Kant. Hegel's system, however, spawned other systems, one of which was the left-Hegelian materialism of Feuerbach, which was a consistent derivation from Hegelian philosophy. To be sure, Hegel's elevation of categories to the true essence of being gave them objective significance and thereby closed the abyss between being and thought. But was this move, by its identification of being and thought the only means of escape from Kantian subjectivism?

Two possibilities fairly soon arose in answer to the above question. Would it be impossible, without identifying being and thought, to recognize the categories as forms equally of both? Also, "why would it be impossible to attribute immediate objective significance to the cognitive process, taking it as an actual event within the mind, regardless of whether the result corresponds to external reality?"[57] Two German philosophers attempted to develop the respective approaches posed by the questions above. The first question was taken up by Trendelenburg and the second by Lotze. We need not here enter into an extended discussion of either philosophers' views. Trendelenburg is perhaps best known today for rejecting the Kantian *exclusive* subjectivity of space and time. He maintained that Kant did not show that they could not also be objective forms, and much the same can be said of the Kantian categories.[58] Karinskij recognized that Lotze too rejected the sharp opposition of being to knowledge that Kant had established. Lotze, like Hegel, ascribed objective significance to cognition, presenting it even as a higher "event [*byva-*

---

56 Karinskij (1873a), 86.
57 Karinskij (1873b), 526.
58 For Karinskij's discussion of Trendelenburg's treatment of space and time, see Karinskij (1873c), 658–660.

nie] toward which being necessarily strives."⁵⁹ Karinskij singled out as the particular merit of Lotze's system its view of the cognitive process not as a disinterested quest on the part of subjectivity for objectivity, but as a process serving the good. In this, we see both Karinskij's own fundamental religiosity, on the one hand, and Lotze's early inspiration from Fichte.

What, according to Karinskij, all German philosophers after Kant did not fully realize but which would doom their own efforts was Kant's problem, asking how *a priori* synthetic judgments are possible. Kant assumed without philosophical justification that there are necessary and universal judgments and thereby introduced an error into his investigation at the outset, before it got underway. Karinskij would ask of Kant what are the logical bases for this conviction that certain judgments are universally and necessarily valid. Kant simply assumed that there could be no justification that we could understand. Karinskij thought this amounted to a contradiction, and from a contradiction we cannot be surprised that other contradictions logically follow.⁶⁰

Karinskij in his "Critical Survey" examined a number of additional nineteenth-century German philosophers including Herbart, Schopenhauer, and even von Hartmann, whom Solov'ëv saw as the last representative of Western philosophy. In doing so, Karinskij covered much the same ground as did Solov'ëv in his *magister*'s thesis only in Karinskij's case in much greater depth and completeness. However, whereas Solov'ëv found *all* of modern Western philosophy from Descartes onward as culminating in von Hartmann, having with his philosophy exhausted all its options for further development, Karinskij's scope was narrower. None of the numerous German philosophies after Kant denied the essential results of his Critical philosophy, but none is above "powerful objections."⁶¹ Karinskij concluded from this, unlike Solov'ëv, merely that all avenues for the further development of *Kantian philosophy* had been exhausted, and that therefore either we return to it with its rejection of the possibility of objective knowledge – and implicitly therefore in his eyes a form of skepticism – or we recognize the need for a new theory of knowledge. Karinskij certainly did not here in 1873 propose an alternative epistemology of his own; he expressed it only as a desideratum in contrast

---

59 Karinskij (1873c), 689. I take Karinskij's word *byvanie* as his Russian translation of Lotze's term *Gestalten*.
60 Karinskij (1873d), 257–258. Karinskij is notably evasive in clearly spelling out just where the contradiction lies. His argument is that Kantianism promotes a vicious circle: given a particular thesis, we surely can find some means to justify it if we are not provided with the means to verify the conclusions independently. A vicious circle, no matter how clever the argument, is, nevertheless, no contradiction.
61 Karinskij (1873d), 248.

to Solov'ëv, who at this time wanted an ontology of "that which truly exists."[62] He, again unlike Solov'ëv, did not even so much as hint at specifics apart from writing that the fundamental error of post-Kantian German philosophy lies "in its excessive belittling of real, living thought."[63] Karinskij was silent on just where this "real, living thought" that would also presumably count as an epistemology could be found; Solov'ëv in this was far more explicit, viz., in "the great theological teachers of the East."[64] Karinskij, however, would be far more detailed in his treatment of German thought than Solov'ëv.

In early October 1874, the sole professor of philosophy at Moscow University, Pamfil Jurkevich suddenly and unexpectedly died. His colleagues, consequently, were unprepared for the news, but the search for a replacement had to begin in earnest quickly. Karinskij's name was one of two raised for consideration, but in view of the lack of familiarity with Karinskij or Troickij – the other name mentioned – the issue was tabled for eight weeks to allow the faculty time to consider the writings of each and their respective candidacies. When the meeting was reconvened on 9 December, those present recognized that Karinskij did not possess a doctoral degree, but a *magister*'s, and moreover one in theology, not philosophy. According to the secular university statute a professor had to have a doctorate in one's particular field, which Karinskij, as a faculty member at a theological academy, could not possibly have, the academies being permitted to bestow degrees only in theology, not philosophy. This doomed Karinskij's chances for a professorship. Nonetheless, Karinskij's early work on current German philosophy had in the meantime been brought to the attention of the Moscow faculty members.

The defense of Vladimir Solov'ëv's *magister*'s thesis took place in St. Petersburg on 24 November, thus prior to the faculty meeting in Moscow mentioned above. Karinskij, undoubtedly owing to his position at the St. Petersburg Academy teaching the history of philosophy, served as one of the opponents at the thesis defense. Karinskij's specific remarks went unrecorded, but Solov'ëv's early biographer Sergej M. Luk'janov reported that Karinskij "responded in a rather unflattering tone" to Solov'ëv's remarks, and another attendee at the defense, Nikolaj N. Strakhov, wrote that Karinskij "said some words about the fact that the disputant [i.e., Solov'ëv] paid no attention to the epistemological side of positivism and consequently did not refute its strongest support."[65] Based on the various reports afterward, Karinskij was not pleased with Solov'ëv's account of what positivism is

---

62 See Solovyov (1996), 146.
63 Karinskij (1873d), 253.
64 Solovyov (1996), 149.
65 Luk'janov (1916), 418, 428.

and of the role of epistemology within it. Such would be the primary concern of Karinskij's next publication the following year.

Whether or not spurred on by Solov'ëv's *Crisis* text or by the published version (March 1875) of Kudrjavcev's October 1874 talk at the Moscow Academy on "Religion and Positive Philosophy," Karinskij in October 1875 published an article entitled "On the Problem of Positivism." He opened his piece with a puzzling statement, writing "The so-called positive philosophy has already existed for several decades; not once has it been subjected to a critical analysis."[66] Inasmuch as he could not have been unaware of Solov'ëv's *Crisis* and in all likelihood would have known of Kudrjavcev's talk, Karinskij was either simply lying or by "critical analysis" he meant a treatment of positivism quite different than that given by his predecessors. Under the circumstances, the former is unlikely; the difference between Karinskij's treatment of positivism and those of Solov'ëv and Kudrjavcev is striking. Unlike the latter, Karinskij's concern was from a secular viewpoint, and unlike Solov'ëv, Karinskij emphasized the epistemological position of positivism.[67]

To be sure, Karinskij only occasionally showed his personal position. His critique of positivism moved on a historical plane. That is, he looked on it as a historically situated manifestation. He did not use his "critique" of positivism as a mere platform to develop his own views and as such we need not linger long on it. For Karinskij, the positivism of his era was above all the philosophy espoused by Comte, and it was essentially a theory of cognition. In this, positivism was another modern philosophy, and as such was characterized by seeking the conditions, limits, and validity of human cognition. In short, Comtean positivism was erected around epistemological empiricism, more specifically on Humean empiricism, and any struggle against positivism must, in order to be decisive, be directed against just such empiricism.[68] Karinskij saw empiricism as a modern form of ancient skepticism and as an expression of the time's popular indifference to genuine philosophical thought.[69] Natural science, in his eyes, aims at laws connecting appearances, but not at the underlying causes producing those appearances. In this way, modern science is permeated with a certain skeptical attitude even more than it may appear at first sight.

---

66 Karinskij (1875), 345.
67 Just how Solov'ëv viewed Comte's positivism in 1874 is unclear, despite his work's subtitle. Positivism is almost an afterthought in this treatment of modern philosophy. Solov'ëv actually devoted little attention to positivism in his thesis. See Nemeth (2016).
68 "Rationalism is just a consistent execution of empiricism in the form that Hume gave to it." Karinskij (1875), 366.
69 Husserl in his *Ideas I* also saw empiricism as a skepticism. See Husserl (1982), 37–39 (§20).

Karinskij remarked that whereas empiricism leaves the unconditional universality and necessity of some part of our knowledge a mystery, rationalism provides a satisfactory explanation of knowledge and thus retains a certain value even if its results turn out to be inconsistent. Hume had grounds for excepting mathematics from his theory of knowledge, even though doing so introduced an inconsistency into his philosophy. Hume recognized the inapplicability of empiricism to account for mathematical knowledge.[70]

As others have pointed out, Karinskij's writings are particularly notable for their parsimonious and clumsy style.[71] We need to add to this list his evasive style, which hinted at what troubled him in the views of others without specifying where precisely those authors faltered. Karinskij wrote that empiricism attempted to solve a "very serious scientific problem," but what that problem precisely is remains undisclosed.[72] Nevertheless, there are, as mentioned, undeveloped positive hints in his works that alone make Karinskij stand out from contemporaries. One such conception that he would develop gradually, particularly after leaving the Academy, is that behind all philosophical systems there are axioms, self-evident truths, that cannot themselves be proved, but are essential to the system.[73] Another was his explicit view of the pivotal role of epistemology in philosophy which, taken alone, sets him apart from so many other Russian idealist philosophers who held ontology or ethics as the pivotal sub-discipline. With his according primacy to epistemology, we find at least a hint of his anti-psychologism. "One must be careful not to confuse psychological explanations of faith with logical explanations of the foundations of faith."[74] Karinskij's anti-psychologism again would be reaffirmed and amplified in the years ahead.

5.6 Karinskij's Proto-Phenomenological Inquiries

In May 1880, Karinskij defended a dissertation for a doctorate not in theology, but in philosophy, not at one of the theological academies, but at the secular St. Petersburg University, where Vladislavlev and Matvej M. Troickij, the professor of philosophy at Moscow University, were his opponents.[75] *The Classification of Inferences* is

---

70 Karinskij (1875), 374.
71 Zenkovsky (1953), 584; Lossky (1951), 149.
72 Karinskij (1875), 374.
73 "Axioms form the ultimate premises of knowledge." Karinskij (1875), 370.
74 Karinskij (1875), 373.
75 The reader should keep in mind that the academies were legally permitted to award degrees only in theology. Karinskij, believing his dissertation and "calling" were more in line with philos-

a lengthy treatment of simple logical inferences, critically dealing with logical works principally from earlier in the century, such as Mill's. Written totally from a pre-Fregean perspective, of course, it remains at most of historical value, lacking the mathematical machinery routinely found today in texts on logic.[76] Not surprisingly, even in Russia today it has received scant attention.

Of greater interest for our theme here is Karinskij's 1878 article "Appearance and Reality" ["Javlenie i dejstvitel'nost'"]. Karinskij opened his work with the claim that for a thousand years philosophy has tried unsuccessfully to establish itself on a firm foundation that would dispel skeptical counterattacks on its right to exist, to uncover truth. Such is the natural consequence, Karinskij charged, of proceeding with the deepest and most complex problems without adequate preparation in advance. Yes, such fields as mathematics and psychology have had noticeable successes, but we have witnessed scant progress in a precise analysis of their methods of proof. Additionally, they have totally failed in the discovery of truth.[77] The metaphysical constructions of recent philosophy, presumably of German Idealism, may have ended as futile attempts, but the general consensus, rather than saying that skepticism is also inconclusive, disregards philosophy altogether. Instead of reinvigorating philosophy, a widespread view is that science shows that appearances alone are cognizable and that philosophy wants to cognize the transcendentally real. "There is nothing apart from appearances, in their opinion, and cannot be. Therefore, the tasks of philosophical knowledge are not just insoluble, but also meaningless."[78] These "objects" of philosophy must remain quite unfathomable.

Karinskij, as we see, viewed philosophy, as a discipline, to be a quest for uncovering truth, ultimate truth, and not for the mere dispelling of linguistic confusion or for pragmatic utility. He looked on Kantianism as a phenomenalism and thus as a form of skepticism, since it would forever doom us from ever obtaining

---

ophy, certainly believed it more appropriate to seek a degree specifically in philosophy and that entailed doing so at a secular university. We should also not forget the possibility that Karinskij may have found out that he was summarily passed over for the professorship at Moscow University because he did not have a philosophy degree. By securing one, he made sure that such an incident could not happen again.

76 Ernest L. Radlov, who had done graduate work in Germany and worked at the St. Petersburg Public Library, wrote that Karinskij's published dissertation was "the sole fully original work on logic in the Russian language." Radlov (1895), 423.

77 Karinskij (1878), 660. It is difficult to be certain of interpretation here, since Karinskij provides no definitions or conceptual clarifications. Nevertheless, we can assume he was arguing from, in Kantian terms, a "transcendental realist" position. But even if that assumption is correct, it is difficult to know why he avers that psychology and other "social sciences" have failed in the quest for truth.

78 Karinskij (1878), 661.

knowledge of things in themselves, things as they truly are. As would other critics of phenomenalism, Karinskij asked how, if my perceptions are mine and your perceptions are yours, "how could there be one and the same object in the perception of two individual people?"[79] More enigmatic was his view that whereas the prevailing distinction between the objects of external perception and those of inner perception rested on a correct thought, that distinction was obviously mistaken. The hegemonic opinion was that external objects are accessible to all, but inner objects are perceptible only to the individual perceiver. Regrettably, Karinskij never clearly informs us just where the mistake lies or even what he meant in writing of the problem's development. He tells us at the start of his article that "philosophy" – thereby treating a discipline as an individual agent – has constructed its systems without first preparing the foundations. "It started not at the beginning, but with the end."[80] The beginning should consist not of speculative, metaphysical propositions, but with self-evident or obvious truths that refer to the immediate world around us. Karinskij, however, merely hinted at this; it would feature more prominently in a later exposition from 1893, *On Self-Evident Truths*.[81]

Karinskij here in this 1878 article also dealt with consciousness and its object upon self-reflection, viz., the "I." At any particular moment, the "I" has only the content given at that moment. If we were able to abstract or remove that content there would be no sign of it. All that would result would be the empty idea of a subject experiencing a certain state.[82] We represent the "I" as having content only as a result of conceiving it as possessing the sum-total of our previous experiences, namely in our memory. For Karinskij, like Gustav Shpet much later, a misunderstanding as a result of an ambiguity of what we mean by the term "I" has caused much damage in philosophy.

> The "I" that appears in consciousness is not at all the actual subject of consciousness, but a represented subject, i.e., the representation of the subject of itself. In this sense, it is just as much an object as something from the external world. There is, of course, the essential difference that in the one case the individual represents reality external to oneself. In the case of the "I," however, the individual represents the being that underlies one's inner states.[83]

---

79 Karinskij (1878), 665.
80 Karinskij (1878), 659.
81 For a short summary of Karinskij's 1893 work, see Nemeth (2017), 246–253.
82 Karinskij (1878), 672. Karinskij's remarks in this regard have drawn the attention recently of some with a background in Husserlian phenomenology. Chubarov writes that Karinskij's stand "is, in part, close to Husserl's project of a pure logic (the first edition of the *Logical Investigations*) with its rejection of the 'pure I' and a recognition of the autonomous reality of conscious experiences." Chubarov (1997), 24–25.
83 Karinskij (1878), 674.

The "I" given in an act of self-consciousness is not the entity experiencing conscious states.

At the start of modern philosophy, Descartes and Spinoza hoped to achieve an obviously impossible task, namely the logical deduction of all forms of reality from our ideas of the Deity. Karinskij held that this failure was not entirely abandoned, but rather transformed through the idea of historical development taken up by Hegel. The German philosopher, like his rationalist forebears, sought to establish reality and its multiple forms not through painstaking investigations, but through demonstrating the supposed rational necessity of the absolute idea's development. Karinskij saw philosophy's approach to reality as progressing in the reverse direction. The simple truth of reality is that it appears directly before us. We confront not just appearances *of* what is real, but "living reality which we experience ourselves immediately and which therefore is beyond doubt." [84] Every science, properly speaking, starts with what is directly given to consciousness. Our knowledge, thus, proceeds, not as the speculative philosophers would have it, but from the given, passing to its conditions and from facts to the laws governing those facts, from particulars to the whole. All natural sciences, despite their different concerns have in common objects in external reality. From this, Karinskij concluded that the methods used in those sciences are inapplicable to the study of consciousness, which is not found in externality. We cannot legitimately even use scientific methods to establish the very existence of consciousness.

Karinskij, not unusual for his time, hailed the analogical argument as the means by which we become convinced that others have an inner life, i.e., mental processes, essentially like my own. From observations of the behavior of others and our knowledge of a correlation between our own corporeal movements and our psychic processes, we infer that another person has the same mental processes as I do when I behave in some particular manner. Karinskij, as is his typical manner of philosophizing, did not dwell on details, but he conceded that we infer animals as well have mental states comparable to my own on the basis of their behavior.[85]

We see from all of the above positions that Karinskij was deeply indebted to Humean empiricism, all the while recognizing the importance of Kantian philosophy in orienting philosophy in an epistemological direction. Karinskij recognized that an adamant adherence to Hume's approach raises problems that cannot be satisfactorily resolved within that framework. Humean doubt about regularity in nature deprives such investigations of a firm ground and with it of any assurance

---

84 Karinskij (1878), 677.
85 Karinskij (1878), 691.

we have any knowledge at all. But the Kantian approach, dismissing at the start the immediate givenness of reality to the cognizer is also unsatisfactory, excluding us from ever attaining genuine knowledge of reality.

Karinskij came to few positive conclusions of his own and certainly no all-encompassing system. His efforts were largely forays into the history of modern philosophy, finding fault with those who sought to reject or at least neglect self-evident truths. To be sure, he sought to distinguish logic from psychology; a confusion of the two he felt would surely lead to error. Implicit in his argument against skepticism is its confusion of the content of perception with the perceptual act, with the result being, for example, Berkeley's immaterialism. These aspects of Karinskij's thought found scant notice among the ostensibly secular Russian philosophers. Had Karinskij received the professorship at Moscow University which he along with Solov'ëv had sought Russian philosophy may have taken a more epistemological "turn" than it did. It was not to be. Karinskij taught the history of philosophy at the St. Petersburg Academy until 1894, but he remained engaged in philosophy until the end, including a protracted discussion with Aleksandr Vvedenskij, the philosophy professor at St. Petersburg University, on the correct interpretation of Kant. As we shall see later, he actively upheld in these later years his view of self-evident truths.[86] To what extent he was heard is another matter.

---

[86] Apart from his already mentioned 1893 work on self-evident truths, he published a large study of recent empiricism (Mill and Spencer) in 1914, *Disagreement within the Schools of Modern Empiricism on the Question of Self-Evident Truths*, that had been previously serialized in the *Journal of the Ministry of National Education*.

Chapter 6
Philosophy at the Moscow Academy Under the Second Charter

The Moscow Academy enjoyed a relatively stable professorial staff in philosophy during the period of the second charter. Of most interest from a "popular" perspective was, as mentioned, the introduction of public dissertation defenses, which previously simply did not take place. These public displays of academic riposte acted as a new form of entertainment for the privileged who were able to attend and understand, at least to some degree, the topic under discussion.[1] These included local officials, society figures, and those whom we would today call "public intellectuals." Of course, the teaching staff attended these defenses, but they were often accompanied, at least at the Moscow Academy, by their respective families! Students at the academy often attended, particularly after the new charter was adopted in order to witness how their own teachers fared when pitted against their colleagues. Student memoirs write of the strong impression these events made on them, which, after all, was one of the purposes for the introduction of the new charter. The defenses provided a topic for lively discussion among the students, who in turn would take up and discuss the points made.[2] The public dissertation defenses, in effect, served as a public-relations event, intended to promote a vivid intellectual environment at the academies. It may come as no surprise, then, that the number of students at the Moscow Academy grew rapidly in the years immediately after the adoption of the second charter.

6.1 Potapov's Understanding of Gravitational Attraction

Vasilij N. Potapov (1836–1890), whom we saw briefly in Chapter 3, taught the history of philosophy at the Moscow Academy and died at the age of 54. Schooled first at home, he entered the Moscow Theological Seminary at the age of 12, receiving special permission from Church authorities to do so given his age. He then began studies in 1854 at the Moscow Academy, graduating first in his class four

---

[1] The first defense of a doctoral dissertation at the Moscow Academy took place in early 1872 and was the fourth overall. The applicant was Archimandrite Mikhail Luzin (1830–1887), who submitted as his dissertation a work he had already published in 1870 on Renan's *Life of Jesus*.
[2] Sokolov (1916), 24. Sokolov himself went on to become a history professor at the Moscow Academy, teaching there from 1874–1904.

years later. He immediately received an appointment at the Academy to lecture on logic and the history of medieval and modern philosophy. With the introduction of the new charter in 1870, Potapov stopped teaching logic. Precisely when he displayed symptoms of his illness is unrecorded, but debilitating sickness clearly affected his teaching. An anonymous student recalls in his memoirs that Potapov "was a half-dead, sick man suffering from asthma. His lectures were so boring and inexpressive that those in attendance could take nothing away of use for scholarship. By prior arrangement, two or three people would attend his lectures fearing that otherwise no one would go."[3] Potapov submitted his resignation to the Academy in 1883, citing the state of his health.

Potapov published little in philosophy, most of his scholarly work being in the field of biblical studies. However, in an early article "Is the method of the natural sciences enough for philosophy?" published in 1864 in an obscure collection of essays, Potapov attacked British empiricism. Like many Academy philosophers who found empiricism to be a particularly favorable target, Potapov maintained it leads to skepticism and materialism. He held that sense experience is but one source of knowledge, and it cannot account for a number of irrefutable elements of knowledge that are *a priori*, i.e., given to us independently of externality. This, however, did not amount, in his eyes, to an endorsement of Kantianism, the consistent consequence of which would lead us, he feared, along the path of German Idealism from Fichte to Hegel.[4] Based on the few available secondary sources, which are consistent among themselves and with other accessible pieces by Potapov, he did defend his position even if not in writing.

Of greater importance for us here and more indicative of his frame of mind is his talk – later published – delivered in October 1879 at the Moscow Academy on "spooky" action at a distance, a topic we may be surprised to learn was still at the time very much in the air, as it had been for centuries since Newton.[5] Potapov decided to weigh in on this issue, albeit gingerly. The concept of action between two physical bodies with no apparent medium between them appeared puzzling to Leibniz among others. Potapov too wrote that he found gravitation difficult to ex-

---

[3] Student (1914), 184. Judging from his performance during and shortly after the dissertation defense of Kudrjavcev mentioned earlier, Potapov had a feisty character. Acting as an official opponent at that defense, Potapov did not hesitate to voice his opposition to one of Kudrjavcev's central theses. Shortly afterward, an account in the local Moscow newspaper of the dispute stated that the objections of the official opponents were "insignificant." Potapov found this to be insulting, demanding a public rebuttal that was published in the February 1873 issue of the Academy's journal *Pravoslavnoe obozrenie*. See Korsunskij (1890), 161.
[4] Korsunskij (1890), 157.
[5] For a classic account of the history, see Hesse (2005).

plain from a philosophical standpoint. How can a physical body act where it is not located? Having the gravitational attraction between the Sun and the Earth in mind, "it is unclear," he wrote, "by what means one body can attract another to itself."[6] Leibniz recognized the issue, but he rejected the view of the occasionalists, who would resolve the issue through invoking constant interaction by the Deity. Potapov wished to solve the problem relying on what he took to be the general features of Leibniz's view of nature, but it must be said that his view was quite devoid of the philosophical sophistication of the German rationalist's perspective. Potapov proposed that bodies do not move one another in a causal sequence, but that each is composed of atoms having internal movements. Each atom of a body moves itself in such a fashion that no movement is forcibly communicated from one body to another! The atoms of a body in this scheme act in concert, and all movements are independent of the others. Here we find an adaptation of the Aristotelian idea that the cause of motion lies in the thing moved. Potapov solved one problem, action at a distance, by introducing a host of others. To explain a particular movement, such as a falling body, Potapov again appealed to the Aristotelian idea of a "proper place" for each thing.[7] He wrote, "Instead of saying, for example, that the Earth attracts a falling body to itself, it would be more correct to say that that body aspires [*stremitsja*] to the Earth."[8]

Nevertheless, Potapov remained open to other possible interpretations and solutions. One such possibility was to maintain that a body may approach so close to another that the first produces a change in the state of the atoms of the second body, a consequence of which is that this second body then moves itself by its own inner force. Potapov did not elaborate how one body can bring about a change in the inner state of another and how that would differ from action at a distance, but he thought it would at least offer an explanation.[9] Indeed, in his eyes, there was no need to assume action at a distance in the proper sense ever takes place. On the contrary, "the laws of the propagation of light and heat force us to accept that the space between world bodies is not empty, but filled with a special kind of matter, which is called aether."[10] With this assumption, an action could, then, be seen as impacting another body much like a sound is conveyed through the air. Potapov recognized that such an explanation may be all well and good when speaking of a ray of light, but it runs into a problem when our concern is explaining gravitational attraction. The difficulty with introducing the con-

---

6 Potapov (1880), 137.
7 For a discussion of Aristotle on motion, see Hesse (2005), 63–67.
8 Potapov (1880), 142.
9 Potapov (1880), 145.
10 Potapov (1880), 145.

cept of "aspiration" is that it leaves unexplained how a body can sense the presence at a distance of the other body to which it is supposed to be attracted. Potapov tentatively conjectured that a body can disperse through its movement the aether around itself, thus making itself "felt" at a distance, even a significant one. Potapov added that he was merely seeking an explanation and did not claim it to be absolutely true.[11] But only an explanation that appeals to the inner states of bodies can make progress in the understanding of physical phenomena. Without it, we must confine ourselves to analyzing what we see.

Potapov is to be applauded for inquiring into a puzzling problem in physics and doing so without invoking an "occult quality" as some had done when the issue came to the fore. In fact, his proposal was by no means odd or out of sync with the time. Although there are many differences between his conjecture and those of, for example, Euler in the previous century and Maxwell in his own, the most obvious one is Potapov's total omission not just of their views but – and arguably more importantly – of any mathematization of the problem. Given his interest in the philosophical understanding of physics, that he was able to make only a brief foray into it stands as a significant loss for Academic philosophy.

6.2 Kudrjavcev on the Nature of Philosophy

As mentioned in Chapter 3, Kudrjavcev continued teaching at the Moscow Academy after the adoption of the 1869 Charter, after Vladimir Solov'ëv's appearance on the Russian philosophical stage, and even through the 1880s. But before turning to Kudrjavcev's systematic writings from his last decade, let us at least recognize that he was not the sole teacher of philosophy over the long years while he was employed at the Moscow Academy. We have just looked at Potapov, but during that one year of 1861 when Kudrjavcev was in St. Petersburg tutoring at the royal court, the teaching of metaphysics and the history of philosophy was the concern of Petr M. Khupockij (1837–1890). The son of a priest in the Rjazan province, Khupockij entered the Moscow Academy in 1856, having just graduated from the Rjazan Seminary. He finished the course of studies in Moscow in 1860, graduating first in the class, and consequently, following a common practice at the time, he was retained to teach psychology and ethics. While Kudrjavcev was in the capital tutoring the tsarevich, Khupockij taught the former's courses as well. With the death of his father, Khupockij as an older child wished to help support his family, but the salary at the Academy being quite low, Khupockij realized his compensa-

---

11 Potapov (1880), 146.

tion was inadequate for him to contribute. He resigned from the Academy and from the clerical estate, accepting a position at the Ministry of Public Education, thus passing outside the scope of the present study.[12] In any case, he left no philosophical writings of consequence.

Kudrjavcev in the 1880s penned a number of articles published in the house organ of the Kharkov Theological Seminary, namely, *Vera i Razum*, and in the journal of the Moscow Academy, *Pravoslavnoe obozrenie*. These presented a systematic account of his own philosophy and were largely given originally in lectures at the Academy. In addition, he wrote two textbooks for use in teaching at the theological seminaries. The articles after his death were arranged thematically and published as a set under the collective title *Works of V. D. Kudrjavcev.* The obviously hasty publication did not allow for *any* editing and, thus, although there is a great deal of similarity between the respective texts in the *Works* and the textbooks, they were not taken over word for word. The journal articles understandably are considerably more complete, with more technical language and contain far more scholarly references to figures in the history of philosophy. The fundamental ideas conveyed are the same, albeit as we shall see not without contradictions or at least ambiguities. We must note, however, that Kudrjavcev's textbooks were all written in a clear and easily-read style, which may not have been entirely beneficial for pedagogical purposes.[13] He developed already in his youth the religious and philosophical views that he would hold throughout his life. As one commentator expressed the matter, "the character of Kudrjavcev's thinking is striking in its monumentally static character."[14]

Kudrjavcev was aware of the spectacular advances of the natural sciences in his day and of the emergence of psychology as a discipline, competing with philos-

---

[12] Clearly impressing his superiors in the Ministry, Khupockij was sent to Germany for two years (1865–1867) by the Ministry, not by a university, for study. He never completed a doctoral dissertation, though the Ministry itself encouraged him to do so by pointing out two vacant positions in Kyiv and Kharkov. He failed to act, instead settling for teaching at the secondary-school level. Later in 1887, he exhibited signs of mental illness. He was admitted to a psychiatric hospital in Moscow the following year. Whatever the specifics may have been, Khupockij died in a mental hospital in Kyiv in 1890.

[13] One of Kudrjavcev's students from the early 1870s remarked: "Despite all of their indubitable merits, Kudrjavcev's lectures did not make the possibly expected impression on most of the audience. The reason for this was their manner of delivery. His readings, though clear and distinct, were at the same time so smooth, dispassionate, and monotonal that they exhausted in some manner his listeners' attention and did not convey any idea of enthusiasm." Sokolov (1916), 267.

[14] Ivanov (1986), 143.

ophy for recognition as fundamental.[15] As with many other philosophers and philosophically-inclined scientists of the time, he too posed the issue of what was the proper subject-matter of philosophy. "Do the positive sciences actually exhaust the entire content of human knowledge, so that at the present time there remains nothing as the subject matter of philosophy, as an independent and special discipline?"[16] Kudrjavcev proposed that in order to answer this question we turn to the most important "content" of scientific knowledge looking to see whether we find in it all questions resolved or could be so within the bounds of the individual sciences and with the assistance of empirical methods. However, Kudrjavcev had already determined to his satisfaction that in each of the natural sciences there are: (1) fundamental concepts that are accepted without examination, i.e., on faith, and (2) questions important for life and knowledge but for which science either does not have an answer or gives only a one-sided and therefore incorrect answer.[17]

Kudrjavcev held that the natural sciences are concerned merely with facts and their manifest connections. But the supreme goal of science is the understanding of the meaning of these facts, their inner principle, and a clarification of the relationship between that principle and those facts. This goal is unattainable by natural science, which is restricted to empirical methods. For example, in dealing with the concept of matter science investigates its structure, the laws of its combination, and how given material things are formed. But by denying the legitimacy and very possibility of other means of knowing nature besides the empirical, science, as empirical science, never turns to just what matter in itself is. When science does turn to more fundamental questions, it becomes philosophy, since those questions cannot be resolved by empirical observation. Science as such cannot explain the conditions that make the world possible. Science has no means of accounting for space, time, and the laws of nature, for example. Kudrjavcev had no doubt that they can be explained, that there is an inner law and goal. Indeed, humanity on the whole has always pondered these matters and has never accepted an exclusively empirical approach to the study of nature.

Kudrjavcev, relying on what he takes to be a universal and timeless *psychological* need for an integrated understanding of the universe, concluded that this need must correspond to an *ontologically* independent and objectively existing some-

---

15 We must add, though, that his writings never addressed technical matters and displayed no awareness at all of the growing mathematization of physics.
16 Kudrjavcev (1908), 8.
17 Such a determination, of course, presupposes one has already determined what a completely correct answer would be.

thing, a Supreme Reason.[18] Yet, Kudrjavcev did not wish to race ahead too quickly, favoring instead to say merely that this train of thought, which concerns the needs of the human mind, does not belong to empirical science, but to philosophy. In this way, philosophy is concerned with God, the universe as a whole, and with the human essence, i.e., our inner principle that cannot be externally observed but that philosophy can elucidate. "Thus, philosophy by its general content can be defined as the science of the essence, ultimate foundation, and goal of what exists."[19] We should note, however, that in his far more comprehensive 1893 textbook, *The First Foundations of Philosophy*, Kudrjavcev remarked that these are merely the chief object of philosophy.[20] Unlike the sciences, which investigate particular objects, the concern of philosophy is with the general structure of being. Whereas the natural sciences employ empirical means, philosophy clearly is distinguished from them not just in terms of its concerns, but also by its investigative means, which must be non-empirical. Philosophy seeks to present a complete and integral worldview, not give, as do the sciences, merely particular information about a delimited group of objects. The fulfillment of this quest requires that we survey all that exists from the lowest to the highest, starting with firmly grounded principles and ascending to a single worldview with a harmonized connection between all the parts.[21] Philosophy, then, is the supreme science in that it encompasses all that exists and all knowledge. It unifies all the sciences, showing the place of each in the totality and "serves as the thread connecting each special investigation with the general system of scientific knowledge as it is at a given time."[22]

However, taking a cue, most likely from Kant, Kudrjavcev advanced the thesis that the sciences take for granted that knowledge is possible and do not even ask under what, if any, conditions it is possible. If the natural sciences, taken together, are to be rigorously grounded knowledge, there must be a "science," a discipline, that investigates the assumptions underlying them. "This science is the science of knowledge in general, its laws, conditions, and validity."[23] Since this science does not have an empirical object, it cannot be conducted by empirical means.[24]

---

18 Many secular philosophers today would surely question the blatant psychologism – the failure to distinguish the noetic moments of consciousness from its noematic moments – of Kudrjavcev's reasoning here. He himself would retort, as did Solov'ëv, that the human mind is part of the integral whole of the universe.
19 Kudrjavcev (1908), 22.
20 Kudrjavcev (1893a), 1.
21 Kudrjavcev (1908), 36.
22 Kudrjavcev (1908), 54.
23 Kudrjavcev (1908), 17.
24 Kudrjavcev has, in effect, given us an account of the place of epistemology. What he has not provided is where epistemology fits into his overall scheme. He defined "philosophy," as we just

But these laws are necessary, universal and, therefore, universally obligatory. Kudrjavcev does not tell us why they must be so. However, if we assume he did have a conceptual debt to Kant, although one not fully acknowledged, much becomes intelligible. Kudrjavcev wrote that a theory of cognition based on an analytic investigation of our cognitive organ, namely, our reason, must precede the positive construction of a philosophical system. If we take Kudrjavcev's use of "reason" (*razum*) as corresponding to Kant's term "*Verstand*," then we see the former's debt to the latter when writing, "the investigation of our very reason is philosophy's first and essential concern."[25] Not only do the intrinsic concerns of philosophy demand such an investigation, but the history of philosophy also demonstrates that we must undertake such an investigation.

To complicate his understanding of just what philosophy is, Kudrjavcev claimed that the concerns of philosophy can be divided into three groups:
1. The basic sub-disciplines of logic, empirical psychology, and the history of philosophy. These sub-disciplines all make use of an analytic method.
2. Metaphysics, ethics, and aesthetics. These sub-disciplines use predominantly a synthetic method.
3. The applied sub-disciplines, such as the philosophy of history, the philosophy of religion, etc. These use analysis and synthesis equally.

Whatever specific faults we may find in Kudrjavcev's delineation of philosophy's task, it appears neither striking nor sectarian. However, he, then, asserts that of all disciplines the subject matter of religion is closest to that of philosophy. "With regard to content, the most important parts and tasks of theology and philosophy coincide."[26] Of course, we could ask of Kudrjavcev what is his reasoning for

---

saw, as concerned with what exists insofar as the investigation employs non-empirical means. In short, he identified "philosophy" with metaphysical ontology. But epistemology is clearly not a part of such ontology. "The chief task of philosophy lies in answering the question of the essence, the ultimate foundation, and the goal of being. According to the demand of the scientific-philosophical method, the resolution of this task is possible only after a preliminary investigation of the problem of cognition. ... After such an investigation, philosophy must pass to a theory of being." Kudrjavcev (1893a), 147. Epistemology cannot, then, be a sub-discipline within philosophy. It is the investigation of whether and under what conditions "philosophy" is possible. Therefore, we must consider it part of "meta-philosophy," or a prolegomena to philosophy.

25 Kudrjavcev (1908), 33.
26 Kudrjavcev (1908), 43. Solov'ëv, in the "Introduction" to his *Justification of the Moral Good*, would write that moral philosophy, but not all of philosophy, is essentially closest to religion. Solov'ëv (2015), 3. In his text originally from 1884 "What is Philosophy?," Kudrjavcev was more specific, writing "In terms of content, theology and philosophy in their most important aspects and tasks obviously coincide. Both equally tell us about the supreme principle of being, viz., God

this blanket statement, and where is the evidence for his claim? Why would it be wrong to say that philosophy is closest to physics? Nevertheless, Kudrjavcev did recognize the fundamental difference between philosophy and religion. The former seeks rational and "scientific" knowledge, whereas religion is based on faith and a trust in authority.[27] Of course, as we saw earlier, Kudrjavcev was critical of positivism for dismissing truly fundamental questions, but he was also critical of those who saw philosophy as useless in confronting revealed religion. Our divinely-given reason plays a natural and legitimate role in the clarification of the questions of knowledge and of life. "The independent participation of our reason is as necessary for knowledge of the truth as is the activity of our eyes for seeing external objects."[28]

Reason, for Kudrjavcev as for Kant, is a faculty of the mind that works as if it were an independent entity. Reason, he tells us, is uncomfortable with simply recognizing the veracity of religious tenets, "truths,"[29] but seeks a systematic expression of these religious truths and confirms them with appropriate proofs, presumably logical ones. By doing so, religious faith passes from a faith of the heart to a faith of the mind, the latter, presumably, being a deductive system in which the initial premises are presupposed as true but are not alone self-evidently true, hence taken on faith.

Where, then, should philosophy as a systematic discipline start? Should it begin with a critique of our cognitive faculty, as Kudrjavcev suggested, or should it begin with a survey of everything starting with the lowest existent, as he at another time suggested? "How can philosophy achieve the goal it seeks, viz., the knowledge of the ideal side of what exists; what is the best and most reliable way to solve its problems?"[30]

---

and other higher questions of knowledge and life." Kudrjavcev (1893b), 10. Since not all would agree with Kudrjavcev that these are the concerns of philosophy, he should have written that philosophy *should* be – and not *is* – closest to religion.

27 In reply to Kudrjavcev, we could say that philosophy seeks "scientific," i.e., systematic, knowledge by means of reason, whereas physics seeks such knowledge by empirical means in contrast to religion's employment of faith.

28 Kudrjavcev (1908), 48.

29 Kudrjavcev failed to explain how reason could possibly take these tenets as truths, since they are given only in another mental faculty of the mind, viz., faith, which apparently can operate independently of the other mental faculties. If faith, as such a faculty of the mind, has the ability to distinguish truth from falsehood – and it must in order to say that Christian dogma is true but that of Islam is not – then surely a critique of pure faith would appear to be in order before or at least independently of a critique of reason.

30 Kudrjavcev (1893a), 195.

6.3 Kudrjavcev on Philosophical Method

Despite what he wrote, Kudrjavcev started neither with a reflection on the conditions and possibility of natural science nor with reflection, for that matter, on the possibility of religion. He also rejected proceeding from the lowest to the highest sphere of being. But there is a caveat. Our reasoning proceeds by firm rules, which we know from studying cognition. In order for philosophy to become a science, not only must it have content worthy of a rational examination, but it must conduct itself in the proper, i.e., the scientific, manner. A general consensus concerning philosophy is that its method should be deductive and rational. The natural sciences are concerned with a study of facts, whereas philosophy is concerned with ideas attained by reason. It is not surprising that philosophy's detractors are among those who have always impugned the ability of reason to grapple with fundamental questions. However, deductive reasoning must have a given starting point. This initial principle cannot be deduced from something else, for that something would then be the initial principle. Therefore, there can be no fundamental proof of it. This, Kudrjavcev claimed, is why any attempt to prove God's existence must be unsuccessful.[31]

Contradicting, as we see, that we begin with the lowest existent, Kudrjavcev maintained that philosophy must present a harmonious system of ideas, starting with the highest idea of the absolute and descend in steps to the concrete. It must proceed from the general to the particular. "The integrity and completeness of a philosophical worldview is possible only when we survey all that exists, starting with the highest principle, with the idea of the truly existent and original."[32] Such a method, the "synthetic method," is a natural characteristic of philosophical knowledge. What, then, for Kudrjavcev, is this highest principle?

We know that what truly exists for Descartes is the "I" that thinks. Kudrjavcev found Descartes' approach to be essentially inadequate. Descartes questioned the veracity of all our cognition in general without first inquiring whether his methodology might have a legitimate application only within certain spheres. In other words, Descartes doubted what he need not have doubted. What he did not realize is that the concept of truth is broader than the concept of rationally provable truth. "Certain positions are true and can be taken as true by our consciousness independently of whether or not they are rationally proven. The truths of divinely revealed religion, above all, are of such a sort."[33] And with this one statement we see

---

[31] Kudrjavcev (1893a), 13.
[32] Kudrjavcev (1893b), 199.
[33] Kudrjavcev (1893a), 23.

the nucleus of Kudrjavcev's thought. He took religious revelations – Christian revelations, not Islamic, not Hindu, etc. – as true and that they lie outside the scope of rational debate. Reason can support or aid revelation, but it cannot question, let alone refute, those truths. Reason cannot judge in a sphere foreign to it. Thus, the practice of philosophizing cannot legitimately extend into the religious sphere, but only to where rational proofs are applicable.[34]

Kudrjavcev saw one of the central roles, perhaps the central role, of philosophy not in resolving metaphysical questions by rational means, but in raising our immediate convictions, such as a belief in God's existence, to a rational level by rationally grounding the concepts involved in our convictions. He wrote that if immediate certainty in given truths were sufficient, if such certainty could stand as knowledge, philosophy would not exist. One of the chief tasks of philosophy is "the examination of the very foundations of knowledge and of the basic truths of consciousness, despite the fact that for ordinary thought they seem immediately clear and convincing."[35] In much the same way as the Marburg School of neo-Kantianism made philosophy a handmaiden to mathematical physics by accepting it as the paradigm of scientific knowledge, so too Kudrjavcev made philosophy a handmaiden to religion by accepting religious tenets without reservation or criticism.

We saw briefly in Chapter 3 that Kudrjavcev held our unaided thought could not produce the concept of an infinite Being. This is a, if not the, central point around which he constructed all of his philosophy, and as we shall see it is pivotal in his dismissal of the traditional proofs of God's existence. Indeed, not just the concept of a divine being, but also those of absolute truth and perfect goodness do not originate from sense experience. They are neither objects of sense intuition nor are they abstracted from sensible objects. This, to Kudrjavcev, is clear from the fact that empirical objects have only empirical characteristics. "Empirical cognition does not point to them and therefore cannot abstract them from representations."[36] Nevertheless, we have such ideas in our cognition, and since they are neither deduced from experience nor obtained from reflection we must have a special faculty that has these ideas, a faculty distinct from the understanding. "The real effect of the Deity on our spirit assumes that there is in us a special faculty for

---

[34] With this understanding of philosophy and of religion, the common expression "philosophy of religion" borders on being an oxymoron. Philosophy can only be a rational inquiry, but religion, in its essence, is extra-rational. Can one speak of a rational inquiry of what is extra-rational?
[35] Kudrjavcev (1893a), 196.
[36] Kudrjavcev (1893a), 116. Cf. Kudrjavcev (1894a), 175.

the perception of this effect."[37] Kudrjavcev called this faculty "reason" (*razum*) or "mind" (*um*).[38]

Certainly, some philosophers have turned their attention to our empirical cognition, claiming that all of our knowledge is ultimately of empirical origin, whereas others see rational cognition as the principle source of "genuine" knowledge. Kudrjavcev disparaged *both* in favor of what he, idiosyncratically, called "ideal cognition," which for him is distinct from empirical and rational cognition. The chief and most important object of ideal cognition for investigation is the most general and the most fundamental idea. It serves as the principle uniting all other representations having ideal qualities and existential perfections. Of course, for Kudrjavcev, this idea is that of God, Who is the absolute, perfect Being.[39]

Kudrjavcev cautioned us not to take his account of ideal cognition as an explicit endorsement of mysticism, although to be sure it does correctly recognize that the idea of God within us is an effect on our "soul" of His presence. Mysticism errs, however, in rejecting any participation of reason in the cognition of God. Our reason sees in most of its concepts, however inadequate they may be, not an empty play of subjective views, but at least a gradual approach to an understanding of absolute truth. Were we to agree with the mystics that all of our rational aspirations to know God are impossible, it would be, in effect, a rejection of thousands of years of religious thought. But such aspirations as well as our efforts for moral perfection show that we have more than an intuition of the supersensible; we have representations and concepts of it. Mysticism is correct, though, in recognizing the need to explain the source of our conception of God.

Kudrjavcev did not dispute that there are *a priori* forms of cognition, proposed by Kant, such as space, time, and categories.[40] The former, however, did not acknowledge their limited justified application within the bounds of sense. For Kudrjavcev, space and time are not merely forms of our sensible cognition, but have

---

[37] Kudrjavcev (1893a), 141.

[38] Kudrjavcev (1893a), 117; Kudrjavcev (1894a), 178. Elsewhere in his text, Kudrjavcev stated merely that since the idea of God cannot be produced by the imagination nor obtained empirically, its origin must lie in God Himself. Kudrjavcev (1893a), 125. We mentioned above that Kudrjavcev's use of "reason" could be compared to Kant's "*Verstand*" in that for both an investigation of the respective faculties is the first concern of philosophy. Although Kudrjavcev expressed a wish for such an investigation, he, by no means, actually set out to investigate the limits of "reason." Quite the contrary, he took for granted that "reason" with its conception of God provides absolute truth.

[39] Readers will be disappointed if they expect Kudrjavcev to then provide an elaboration of how the idea of God unites all other ideal qualities and perfections of being, in the manner, say, of Spinoza in his *Ethics*.

[40] Having dealt with Kudrjavcev's position vis-à-vis Kant elsewhere, I will not linger long on it. See Nemeth (2017), 184–189.

also an objective, i.e., transcendent, significance. They exist in reality itself, not merely in our cognition. "Space and time form essential and inseparable characteristics not only of real things, but also of things thought by us, of *all* beings."[41] Space and time, therefore, are not independent entities; they are properties of things.

Kudrjavcev also rejected what he considered the *pure* subjectivity of Kant's treatment of the categories. Were Kant correct, there would be no explanation for why we invoke categorical determinations in one instance but not in others. As with other historical critics of Kant's transcendental idealism, Kudrjavcev saw the alleged pure subjectivity of the categories as dooming the very possibility of objective cognition. Kant was wrong, he thought, to think that the subjectivity of the categories prevented their separation from the objectivity of cognition. In short, Kudrjavcev simply could not fathom Kant's distinction between the transcendent and the transcendental.

Along with categories of the understanding, Kudrjavcev proposed that there are distinct *a priori* ideal concepts of "reason." These include God, truth, the moral good, the infinite, etc. Unlike Kant, he did not offer a complete table of them nor did he propose to trace them, as did Kant, to logical functions of the cognitive faculty. Kudrjavcev held that we can immediately recognize that ideal concepts, unlike the Kantian categories, are, above all, perfections of being. Kudrjavcev maintained that there is another distinctive difference between these "ideal concepts" and the Kantian categories of the understanding. The universality and necessity of the former are ideal and not, as with the latter, empirical and categorical. That is, the necessity of the ideal concepts is ideal in that, for example, *every* object *should* correspond to the concept of truth and *all* behavior *should* correspond or accord with the concept of the moral good whether or not it in reality does so or not.[42] The universality of the ideal concepts is here markedly different from the universality of the categories of the understanding. The aspiration for perfection, whether it be of our cognition or of our behavior would be inconceivable and impossible if we lacked certainty in the real existence of such perfections, that truth and goodness, actually exist. In order to strive for something we must be certain that the object is attainable, that that object actually exists. Kudrjavcev found in this another distinction between the "ideal concepts" of reason and the categories of the understanding. The "ideal concepts" are perfections, and thus, based on what we just saw, there must be an actually *existing* perfection corresponding to the *idea* of perfection. "The single and fundamental idea of which we spoke is the idea not only of an abstract, absolute perfection, but of an absolutely perfect

---

41 Kudrjavcev (1893a), 84.
42 Kudrjavcev (1894a), 177.

being."[43] Just as the idea of truth finds its realization in science and that of the moral good in moral and social life, the idea of the absolutely perfect being finds its expression in religion. A continuation of this line of thinking would have us pass from philosophy into theology, but having seen his ultimate conclusion let us turn to his critique of the traditional proofs for God's existence.

6.4 Kudrjavcev on the Traditional Proofs for God's Existence

One common formulation of the cosmological argument for God's existence is to infer from the impossibility of an infinite series of causes in the empirical world to a first cause. Kant found the argument specious in that the principle of causality has a justified employment only within the bounds of the sensible world. The argument, though, attempts to establish something beyond those bounds.[44] Kudrjavcev, unsurprisingly given his unequivocal rejection of Kant's transcendental, saw no restraints in applying the principle of causality. He believed that on the basis of the principle of sufficient reason we must seek the first cause of empirical phenomena until we find a sufficient reason that explains the phenomena. We would directly violate the principle of sufficient reason if we were to postulate an infinite chain of conditioned causes. On the other hand, if the positing of a supreme being can explain the aggregate of worldly phenomena, then reason must be quite satisfied that the principle of sufficient reason has been satisfied. This is Kudrjavcev's preferred choice. He expressed his argument in terms of a necessary being.

> If none of the entities in the world necessarily exist, then clearly the entire aggregate of these entities, viz., the whole world, cannot necessarily exist. Thus, we must accept that neither outside the world nor in the world itself is there a necessary cause of being. But this is impossible. ... Thus, we must accept the existence of a first cause, an unchanging and independent Being.[45]

Even Kudrjavcev, however, recognized that the cosmological argument as stated cannot justify that the sufficient reason is an *independent* Being. Taken alone, it leads at most to a pantheistic Absolute.

Kudrjavcev next turned to the teleological proof – the argument from design. That the world exhibits a rigorously rational construction scheme cannot be ex-

---

43 Kudrjavcev (1894a), 181.
44 Kant (1997). 572 (A609-A610/B637-B638).
45 Kudrjavcev (1893a), 155.

plained if it arose by blind chance. The order and purpose of the universe must have first been planned in the thought of a rational entity. On the basis of this train of thought, the teleological argument concludes that there exists a supreme rational being as the cause of the world and, therefore, existing apart from the world. Kudrjavcev readily admitted that the conclusion to the existence of a supreme rational cause of the world is merely probable and not indubitable, though he believed that the probability is quite high verging on indubitability.

Another criticism of the teleological argument is that even if it were valid, it does not provide a "true" concept of God. Certainly, there is an analogy in it to artistic works of the human mind, but our artistry is upon already present material. The artist imparts merely form. The teleological argument says nothing about the creator of both form *and* matter. This omission of accounting for the creation of the "stuff" of the universe represents the weak side of the argument.[46]

Kudrjavcev accorded greater value to the ontological argument, which proceeds from the idea that existence is a perfection. By this reasoning, a conceived being that exists only in my mind but that lacks the quality of actual existence would not, despite its other perfections, be all-perfect.[47] Therefore, the conceived all-perfect being, viz., God, must exist. Kudrjavcev rejected the criticism that the argument establishes only the conception of God as actually existing, not His actual existence apart from us and the world.[48] In other words, the argument concludes only to a subjective necessity, but there is no logical justification to pass from a concept to an actual being. Kudrjavcev, rejecting this criticism, believed it to be effective only from the standpoint of subjective idealism, which rejects the possibility of objective cognition. If, as Kant thought, our basic concepts, categories, and ideas are merely subjective forms of the cognitive faculty, to which nothing corresponds in reality, then, yes, the ontological argument completely fails. But Kudrjavcev denied the veracity of such a view of cognition. "A close analysis of our cognition shows us that, contrary to subjective idealism, reality outside our reason must cor-

---

[46] Kudrjavcev (1893a), 164.
[47] Kudrjavcev's formulation of the ontological argument can be faulted on many levels. But one that he overlooked lies in his belief that we cannot conceive the infinite. Since he did not provide a listing of all possible perfections, we can reasonably assume there are an infinite number of them. But, then, how can we know that our conception of an all-perfect being does contain all possible perfections? No correspondence is possible that would allow me to conclude I have properly conceived an all-perfect being without begging the issue in the first place.
[48] Tsvyk, seeking to clarify Kudrjavcev's thinking here, writes that he "believed (more along the lines of Aristotle than Plato) that the idea of a thing was inseparable from the thing, that the idea is contained in the thing as its ideal aspect, as its permanent and immutable essence. The idea is constant, immutable and consequently constitutes something primal with regard to the changing phenomena." Tsvyk (2010), 151.

respond to the necessary and logically formed concepts of our reason. For otherwise, we would have to reject the possibility and validity of our cognition."[49] As soon as we have established that a representation is neither contingent nor imagined but is a necessary concept or idea in our reason, we have a right to conclude to its corresponding objective, independent existence. A concept's necessity is indubitably such if it is *a priori* and universal. Of course, Kudrjavcev merely claimed that the concept of God is *a priori* and universal, but he certainly did not show that to be the case.

The final argument for God's existence is the moral argument, which states that the presence of the moral law within us and that our highest aspiration is to be morally perfect proves God's existence and that God is the author of these facts.

> That there exists within us a moral law, unconditionally demanding us to do good and avoid evil, is an indubitable fact. ... The law's very content tells us that it cannot be of empirical origin as the result of a simple generalization of impressions or from the influence of our environment.[50]

The external world can arouse in us pleasant and unpleasant feelings, but such feelings have nothing to do with morality. It and the moral law stem from and speak of our higher, spiritual nature. The question remains how to account for the moral law. That it is rational and universally applicable to all human beings does not answer whether it is the product of human reason, as Kant thought, or given to us by a higher rational being. Against the former possibility, Kudrjavcev argued that there is no "hallelujah moment" in our lives when we discover the moral law within and decide to obligate our will in accordance with it. On the contrary, at the start of our conscious life we find it within ourselves, not as our product, but as complete and given. Kudrjavcev also charged that if we produced the moral law ourselves, it would correspond to our present condition, not to an infinitely perfect ideal. Yet, we have an idea of absolute perfection, including absolute moral perfection. Therefore, there must be an author of this idea other than ourselves. This author can only be an absolutely perfect entity, viz., God.

Having examined the major philosophical proofs for God's existence, Kudrjavcev sought to situate their importance within a theistic framework. He asserted that the original source for our knowledge of God is the idea of Him within us, within our "spirit." This idea provides us with an immediate certainty and serves as a more reliable basis for our conviction than any philosophical proof, including

---

49 Kudrjavcev (1893a), 168–169.
50 Kudrjavcev (1893a), 184.

those just discussed. We have seen that the traditional, rational proofs have met with criticism, some of it justifiably so by Kudrjavcev's own admission. For this reason, whereas the philosophical proofs can prove a useful supplement to faith, Kudrjavcev feared that excessive reliance on these "proofs" can weaken one's faith as a result of their deficiencies.

Kudrjavcev originally presented his analyses of the proofs for God's existence during the 1880s in *Pravoslavnoe obozrenie*. As well as the traditional proofs we have discussed above, he also did the same for what he labeled the epistemological, the psychological, and the historical proofs. Finally, in 1890 he reflected on the significance of the rational proofs, if taken as an ensemble, writing, "Although each of the proofs has deficiencies, taken as a whole and consistently developed, in mutually complementing each other, they can be considered quite sufficient for a rational substantiation of the truth of God's existence as the supremely perfect Being and as independent of the world."[51] Kudrjavcev held that the principal concern of philosophy is the substantiation of the basic and original truths given *a priori* to us. If the original truths were sufficient to satisfy us, there would have been and still would be no need for philosophy. Among these truths is the existence of God. Therefore, the attempt to prove God's existence rationally is simply philosophy doing what it should do, viz., frame our immediate convictions rationally. This is done by rationally substantiating them.[52]

6.5 Kudrjavcev on Modern Science

Kudrjavcev's antagonism toward materialism is understandable given his comprehensive religious outlook, which holds that in addition to matter there exists a spiritual realm. In his eyes, materialism leads to the rejection of truth and morality. If all that there is material and therefore contingent, the search for the timeless, which is a characteristic of *the* truth, is doomed. Kudrjavcev extended this train of thought, collapsing a distinction between different understandings of "exis-

---

51 Kudrjavcev (1890), 3.
52 Kudrjavcev (1890), 25; Kudrjavcev (1893a), 196. Of course, Kudrjavcev has simply defined philosophy in such a manner that the attempt to prove God's existence is part and parcel of philosophy's concerns. That Kudrjavcev paid so much attention to these traditional proofs is itself somewhat amazing for someone with his background and position. He certainly could not have been trying to convince the atheist. There were no nonbelievers in the theological academies. However, as I believe Collins in general has correctly indicated, efforts such as that of Kudrjavcev were attempts to create "a turf for pure intellectual activity within the institutional space of the religious schools" Collins (2002), 391.

tence" he himself had observed when discussing the ontological proof. If everything is material, then everything is contingent. Therefore, everything, even values and verities, are contingent. "All our thoughts must be a product of nature, and all equally 'true'. The distinction between true and false has no objective significance."[53] However, he was also critical of both subjective and objective idealism. In his eyes, idealism "reduced" matter to ideas, but it also verged on pantheism, seeing no need for a supreme spiritual being separate and independent of both matter and ideas, but which unifies both. Kudrjavcev called his position "transcendental monism" in that it refused to separate the three realms of matter, ideas, and the Absolute.[54]

In Kudrjavcev's day, the existence of atoms was still debatable. Since atoms were inaccessible to empirical observation what utility could their postulation serve except as a metaphysical explanation? Neither natural science nor philosophy convinced Kudrjavcev that atomism was correct. On the contrary, "the indisputable and unavoidable demand of our intellect is that everything spatial and material can be infinitely divisible."[55] Another inadequacy of atomism as he understood it was its inability to explain how material bodies could interact. Being separate particles, we have to presume that between atoms there is complete emptiness, i.e., nothing, which Kudrjavcev claimed is inconceivable. Here lay his difficulty with conceiving atoms as individual, discrete units. Space, for Kudrjavcev, is always space or the extension *of* something. "Without things filling space, space is a purely abstract concept, which cannot serve as a medium for the action of presumably real objects on each other."[56]

Kudrjavcev was also a determined opponent of the dynamic theory of matter, one of the most well-known advocates of which in history was Kant. Kudrjavcev believed the dynamic theory contradicted the commonly held stand that distinguishes a force from its substrate and that on which the force acts. Arguing in a surprisingly positivistic manner, he averred that forces cannot exist independently of some substrate and cannot act if there is no object on which they act. Of course, Kudrjavcev's reasoning was a product of his age. But it is disconcerting that he, like so many others who commented on the physical sciences from the clerical estate, made pronouncements on how the world must be based on present scientific inabilities and inadequacies. They simply could not imagine that scientific and technological progress may necessitate a changed scientific paradigm or that new discoveries would upset their "common-sensical" conclusions. Kudrjavcev held that

---

53 Kudrjavcev (1893a), 46.
54 Kudrjavcev (1893a), 71–72.
55 Kudrjavcev (1893a), 258.
56 Kudrjavcev (1893a), 261 f.

the dynamic theory of matter is one-sided in that it cannot explain the various properties matter exhibits and the phenomena that it engenders. The dynamic theory cannot explain the chemical properties of substances.

Nonetheless, although atomism fails as a satisfying theory of matter's essence, it can prove useful in science as a working hypothesis to explain certain phenomena. Therefore, we can distinguish metaphysical atomism from scientific or methodological atomism.

Of more interest to us and more illustrative of his general attitude toward natural science was Kudrjavcev's reception of Darwinian evolutionary theory. An overall picture of the reception of Darwin's thought within Russia is much too varied and complex even to survey here and would take us far beyond the bounds of the present work. Fortunately, excellent secondary studies already exist.[57] Unlike some who would dismiss evolutionary theory out of hand, Kudrjavcev merely tried to point out its assumptions and its failures to account for them. He saw evolutionary theory as proposing that transformations proceed from simple forms of life to ever more complex ones and that historically, then, the earliest organisms were the simplest in comparison with those that exist today. Kudrjavcev found this to be questionable based on the scientific findings of his day. He also found no evidence to support Darwin's idea that the essential features or characteristics of a plant or animal breeds can mutate. Based on scientific observations of plant and animal life of several thousand years ago, we find no such transformations. That time period – five, even six thousand years – is rather long, and yet we see no such phenomena. Kudrjavcev asked what does a temporal lapse have to do with a change of the inner essence of a species, which, after all, is timeless.[58] Darwin held that in the struggle for survival those features that are useful are retained over time whereas those that are distinctively not useful recede, but Kudrjavcev claimed that observations show this is not the case. Obviously useful characteristics for life do not develop from nothing.

Kudrjavcev was willing to follow Darwin to a degree. In discussing changes within a species, Kudrjavcev conceded the scientific value of evolutionary theory, but it loses that value when it turns to the formation of species. There, it contradicts the observed facts and is entirely unproven. But evolutionary theory is just as much a philosophical theory as it is a scientific one owing to the conclusions defenders of materialism have sought to extract from it for their own purposes. They have used it to support their atheistic outlook and to reduce everything to the action of necessary natural laws of nature. But by itself the theory of evolution

---

57 See, for example, Vucinich (1988).
58 Kudrjavcev (1893a), 312.

does not have such a sense. "It does not extend in general to the origin of the original organic species."⁵⁹ In Kudrjavcev's reading, the theory of evolution by no means espouses a materialism. Darwin himself, in this reading, accepted the act of creation at the start and then allots broad scope to natural development. Kudrjavcev's interest in the theory of evolution, in summary, was not to determine its scientific value as such, but to enlist it as a cudgel in a religious war against atheistic materialism.⁶⁰

6.6 Kudrjavcev on Morality

Kudrjavcev devoted little attention to ethical issues and none to the means of resolving conflicting moral duties. Why this is so is by no means clear, but his general moral position is obvious from his religious commitment. That morality required human free will was unquestionable. It made possible our aspiration for moral development and perfection. Unlike Kant, however, Kudrjavcev did not see it as a postulate of pure practical reason, but as a fact of transcendent reality. This cannot surprise us given his rejection of the Kantian distinction between the transcendent and the merely phenomenal. But in other respects, there is a similarity with Kant. Since there is no break between the phenomenal and the transcendent, what is true of the phenomenal world is true in the transcendent. Phenomenally, we feel that we freely decide our actions.

> The chief proof of our free will lies in our self-consciousness. In each of our free actions, we clearly are aware that we ourselves determine it, that it depends on us, that whatever may be our motives to act in a certain way, that action would not take place if we did not decide to do it.⁶¹

Without a free will, there can be no meaningful sense of responsibility. Moral life and all that is connected with it would be undermined, if not eliminated. To charge that our sense of freedom is merely an illusion, that *all* of our actions are subject to the law of causality and as such cannot be "free," i.e., initiated by an autonomous

---

59 Kudrjavcev (1898), 186.
60 Vucinich was correct in writing, "Kudriavtsev-Platonov thought that creationism and Darwinism were not natural enemies. He contended that it was possible to reconcile the two theories. He expected Darwin's theory, however, to make all the concessions." Vucinich (1988), 248. The theory of evolution should recognize the divine creation of all species, reject any pretension to explain how species can transform, and deny natural selection's place as the primary factor in evolution.
61 Kudrjavcev (1893a), 405.

legislative will is to confuse mechanical causality with a causality operative in the spiritual world. Although human actions are not caused in the same way as are physical phenomena, this does not mean that they are completely uncaused, and in this Kudrjavcev sees himself as making common cause with Kant. Our free will is determined by its own, inherent causes. "These causes lie in the ideas and concepts of reason, which indicate the object and the goal of the will's desire and which serve as the foundation why in each given case the will acts in this or that way."[62] If there were no such cause, a rational cause, the entire process would be senseless and arbitrary. That our free will is legislative is, again, proved by our inner experience.

Kudrjavcev was dismissive of such moral doctrines as hedonism, eudaimonism, and utilitarianism. The principle in none of these, in his eyes, is universal and obligatory. A morality must in principle be binding for all people in all cases, a position for which he offered no argument. All moral actors must be able clearly to see the goal of their behavior and of the means to that goal. But what is that goal? All of the three mentioned moral theories find it in earthly pleasure and satisfaction. Even some moral theories that appeal to reason do so in order to seek rational means for earthly well-being. Kudrjavcev saw in human beings not just a material side with senses, but as having also a spiritual side, which informs us of our moral obligations and provides us with a moral conscience and consciousness. Our moral free will wishes us to be morally perfect. The highest principle of moral activity is the aspiration for moral perfection. It, unlike the principles underlying the mentioned moral theories, is clear, universal, and unconditional.[63] However incredible to us today, Kudrjavcev maintained that even the most immoral person could not avert the torment of a guilty conscience arising from not acting as one should. This alleged fact, he held, shows that we have planted, so to speak, within us from the start an unconditional moral law. If the moral law – and note Kudrjavcev never spells out clearly what that law is, nor how it unambiguously prescribes what to do in concrete cases, nor how to resolve apparently conflicting duties – were of subjective origin, it could make no claim to unconditional obligation. He also leveled the same charge of subjectivism against Kant's conception of the autonomous will despite its claim to universality. Conceived as a product of human limitations, it cannot possibly have the qualities it purports to have. The genuine source of the moral law must lie outside us in a being that can prescribe universal and necessary laws, viz. God.

---

62 Kudrjavcev (1893a), 411–412.
63 Kudrjavcev (1893a), 430.

Unlike his one-time student Vladimir Solov'ëv, Kudrjavcev obviously devoted little attention to the details of his ethical theory. We find not a single extended treatment of moral issues in his posthumously purported *Works*. His interest was primarily in combating modern secular epistemological views, which, in brief, he saw as stemming from a human-centered standpoint. Seeking to reaffirm Orthodox philosophy's orientation toward ontology and metaphysical realism, he recognized the competition for intellectual allegiance stemming from Western thought, both scientific and philosophical. Fearing any concession to subjectivity doomed that realism and opened the door to relativism – both epistemological and ethical – Kudrjavcev held that all manner of conceptions ranging from the idea of the infinite to the obligatory character of morality had to be sourced from without, a source that could not itself be contingent and finite. He labeled this source to be God, of course without demonstrating how that source could be identified with the specifically Christian conception.[64] We already mentioned, albeit in passing, that not all, even among his colleagues, agreed with his means of circumventing subjectivism. Potapov was one, but he unfortunately was unable to work out the details of his position.[65] This is where Kudrjavcev excelled. The multi-volume exposition of his thought broke little new ground in theology and certainly none in philosophy. In simply positing God as the source of so much coupled with his obfuscation in treating the ontological argument, he may have consolidated a traditional religious outlook, but he surely contributed nothing of note to it.

6.7 Roman Levickij on the Morality of Christianity

Roman I. Levickij (1855/56 – 1886) taught theology at the Moscow Academy. A graduate of the Academy in 1879 and having finished first in his class, Levickij, following the custom, was appointed *privat-docent* there. He married in February 1880, but his wife died later that same year. Whether for that reason or some other,

---

[64] Kudrjavcev's successor at the Moscow Academy would write, "The basic guiding threat of Kudrjavcev's entire religious philosophy was the idea or, more precisely, an indication of the fact that we have a certain original and immediate awareness, a sensation, as it were, a vision of the Deity." Vvedenskij (1893a), 53.

[65] Solov'ëv's early biographer, Sergej Luk'janov, wrote, "Potapov was not very sympathetic (*sočuvstvenno*). Concerning his colleague [Kudrjavcev], Potapov put it this way: Here is a philosopher, who has not read a single philosophy." Luk'janov (1916), 341 f. Assuming Luk'janov has correctly quoted Potapov, the statement, if taken literally, is demonstrably incorrect. Kudrjavcev's articles published in the 1880s, unlike his textbooks, contain a wealth of references to modern philosophical texts as well as to the literature of his day. Nevertheless, Potapov may have meant something entirely different, viz., not just with reading, but reading with understanding.

he suffered a nervous breakdown and resigned the next year, citing his health. Given the short time available to him, he was unable either to publish much or leave a lasting influence at the Academy. More than Kudrjavcev, Levickij saw faith as needing a rational, objective guarantee. Faith and reason are not in opposition, and although we cannot expect the tenets of religious faith to be proved with mathematical rigor, the value of rational arguments lies in their support of such faith.

Levickij's ascription of a positive role to reason-based argument already, at least in principle, sets him apart from Kudrjavcev. Whether he was consistent in this respect is another matter. Nonetheless, in his 1880 article "On the Moral Teaching of Christianity," he made a most promising start, proclaiming that the veracity or falsity of a particular doctrine is best established by its practical consequences, by the results of its application in experience. Thus, if Christianity as a body of beliefs is held to be not just true, but to be a body of divinely revealed truth, it must show that it cannot have proceeded from the human mind. The Christian moral doctrine, as the practical application of Christian beliefs, must, in turn, also be the demonstrably most perfect moral theory.[66] Such a demonstration would be a proof of the divine inspiration of Christianity as a whole, and we could accord a primacy to it over theoretical arguments in support of the veracity of Christianity. In this, we can see Levickij favored an appeal to Christian morality, as he conceived it, over "theoretical proofs," over revelation, and over blind faith.[67]

A proof that Christian morality is not just superior to others, but the perfect moral theory must have both a logical element, or aspect, and an element that appeals to the human heart, to our feelings. Both of these elements must exhibit the highest possible perfection. In order to show that the logical or philosophical element of Christian morality is perfect, we must show that it could not be a fabrication of the human mind. Demonstrating its superiority over other moral systems, be they religious or not, will not be sufficient. It would amount only to a comparative superiority, but not to perfection. "If the morality found in the Gospels is actually the Divine Word and not that of the human mind, it must be not simply true and perfect, but the absolutely true, absolutely perfect morality (of course, for humans)."[68] A morality that cannot possibly be the work of the human mind must exhibit properties that distinguish it as of divine origin. Levickij claimed that the means to do this was to point out that Christian morality demonstrated a harmonious, all-encompassing completeness, i.e., an absence of any one-sided exclusivity,

---

66 L[evickij] (1880), 13.
67 Solov'ëv, at least with regard to "theoretical philosophy," was in sympathy with Levickij's position. Practical philosophy has primacy over theoretical philosophy.
68 Levickij (1880), 17.

which is an essential attribute of all human-created philosophical and religious outlooks. This inadequacy is an unavoidable limitation of any creation of the human mind.

Levickij held that not only is the human mind necessarily limited in scope, it is always entwined in contradictions when it seeks to formulate a coherent worldview. Owing to its finitude, it is fundamentally unable to find a highest encompassing unity of these contradictions, such as between the ideal and the real, between freedom and determinism. The mind seeks a universal all-unity (*vseedinstvo*), an expression we find repeatedly in Solov'ëv and in the works of others associated with the theological academies. This all-unity, however, is inaccessible to our finite intuition, though Levickij provided no evidence for this purported fact or even a clarification of what would be involved in having such an intuition. Nevertheless, if this all-unity, which he also labeled the absolute, could be cognized, it would be something existing in the world and consequently grasped by our finite understanding. The fact that we cannot understand the absolute established to Levickij's satisfaction that it is distinct and independent from the world. Philosophical analysis reveals a border separating our finite thought from the absolute. This border cannot be transgressed in the hope of overcoming the dualism of the contradictory principles and thereby arrive at a universal all-unity from which the contradictory principles could be deduced. "The all-unity to which our reason aspires is something necessarily presupposed, but is quite unfathomable, something sought but not at all acquired. It lies beyond the bounds of our finite understanding, and this is why we can only point to it, but not grasp, not fathom it."[69] Having thus aroused the reader's anticipation for a previously unknown moral theory that would appeal to the intellect for its sheer rationality, to the heart for its gentleness and compassion, and to tradition for its origin in the Gospel narrative, it only turns out to be a disappointment when Levickij wrote, "only the morality of the Gospels is absolutely foreign to any one-sidedness."[70] Levickij presented no demonstration that the Christian Gospels preached a moral doctrine bereft of all one-sidedness. He offered no argument that the moral teaching found in the Gospels – which one(s)? – is intrinsically perfect. He gave no evidence that that moral teaching appeals to the heart more than does utilitarianism, let alone completely and perfect-

---

[69] Levickij (1880), 19. Of course, Levickij presupposed much here, none of which he pointed out, let alone proved. Merely in saying that there is an absolute beyond the bounds of human consciousness, Levickij made, in effect, the same claim as critics of the Kantian thing in itself charged against that conception, namely, positing the existence of something beyond the legitimate bounds of our finitude. Moreover, Levickij provided no evidence that would allow him to characterize what lies beyond the bounds of human consciousness as absolute.

[70] Levickij (1880), 22.

ly. Levickij asserted, but does not show, that Christian morality unites the divine and the human. He maintained, but did not show, that the principle in Christian morality penetrates into the mind and the heart more profoundly than any other to a depth that is beyond the power of any finite thought. Again the issue remains how could one know that unless one has independently penetrated to that depth and ascertained that one could go no deeper. Levickij produced an essay in theology, not philosophy.

Philosophy at the Moscow Theological Academy under the 1869 Charter prevailed with little innovation, contrary to the Charter's intent. In terms of outlook, the philosophical "research" of Kudrjavcev remained attached to tradition, hardly confronting the issues posed by developments in the natural sciences, even though a few at the Academy were aware of some developments. Kudrjavcev continued to teach philosophy until his death in 1891 well after the second charter had run its course. In his hands, an Orthodox philosophy became systematized and codified, as it were, making any divergence suspect.

Chapter 7
Philosophy at the Kyiv and Kazan Academies Under the Second Charter

In the second half of the nineteenth century, general interest in the heritage of the Church Fathers increased, and professors at the theological academies responded, producing translations and offering courses on the theology of the first Christian apologists. This, in large part, was in response to a desire to set the Orthodox Church apart from the West with its alleged corrupt papacy and to expunge as much as possible the lingering influence, as they saw it, of Catholic scholasticism. Whether they were at all successful in this is another matter.[1] At no time, however, did the Church Fathers, so revered by the nineteenth-century Russian Orthodox theologians, reject a role for philosophy, "philosophy" of course being understood as a rational inquiry, but one which neither shirked metaphysics nor was intended to be a Husserlian "rigorous science." We find an example of his increasing interest in the Church Fathers and in their attitude toward philosophy in Konstantin I. Skvorcov's 1868 *Philosophy of the Church Fathers and Teachers.* Skvorcov, the son of Ivan Skvorcov, whom we saw in Chapter Four, was himself a graduate of the Kyiv Academy and became a professor of patristics in 1857 at his *alma mater* having previously taught German there for many years. He tells us in this 1868 work that by "philosophy" he meant the employment of rational principles to explain and to defend the true teachings of revelation, the objects of Christian faith.[2] As Skvorcov saw the matter, the pagan philosophers who confronted the Christianity of the Church Fathers presented only vain attempts to create the ideal moral and practical life. They could not rise above a purely national point of view on morality; they did not have a criterion for judging how things truly are and for distinguishing the truly good from evil.[3] Writing some six years later, a young would-be philosopher in Moscow too would be attracted to the teachings of the Christian Church Fathers largely at the expense of modern philosophy.

---

[1] The first comprehensive presentation in Russian of the teachings of the Church Fathers was Archbishop Filaret's 1859 three volume *Historical Teachings of the Church Fathers.* Filaret, whose secular name was Dmitrij G. Gumilevskij (1805–1866), was at the time Archbishop of Kharkov and a graduate in 1830 of the Moscow Academy. Filaret's work includes as "Church Fathers" many more individuals than is typical in the West.
[2] Skvorcov (1869), I.
[3] Skvorcov (1869), VIII.

If he was familiar with Skvorcov's work, Vladimir Solov'ëv gave not a hint. But he updated the essential claim in it, holding that Western philosophy's development had concluded with an affirmation of the same truths as those the Church Fathers had advanced, namely that Western philosophy, like pagan philosophy of old, had failed owing to its one-sided perspective.[4]

7.1 Olesnickij's "Protestant"-Oriented Ethics

Dmitrij V. Pospekhov (1821–1899) entered the Kyiv Theological Academy in 1841 and completed the course of study four years later, when he, owing to his excellent academic record, was retained by the Academy and began teaching there. Among his own professors were Ivan Skvorcov, Avsenev, and Gogockij. During his long professorial career, he had among his students Jurkevich and M. M. Troickij, a future philosophy professor at Moscow University. Although Pospekhov did much editorial work and many translations, he exhibited no interest in producing original philosophical or psychological work. As mentioned previously, the Charter of 1869 required full professors to have a doctorate and those who did not had to obtain one in several years or be dismissed. Pospekhov, having been appointed to a full professorship already in 1853 hurriedly had to prepare, submit, and defend a dissertation, which he did with a large work published in 1873 entitled *The Wisdom of Solomon, Its Origin and Relation to Judeo-Alexandrian Philosophy*. The book in six chapters paints an overall picture of Judeo-Hellenistic philosophy with particular reference to Platonic and Stoic philosophy.[5]

Pospekhov gave his students – or at least one of them – the impression of maintaining an acquaintance with current literature in psychology, but he made no overt effort to introduce what he knew to his students despite his obvious enthusiasm for psychology.[6] He was yet another figure who largely failed to make a distinctive mark in the history of Russian thought. At the time of his death, he was the oldest teacher of philosophy in Imperial Russia.

---

[4] Solovyov (1996), 149. In the eyes of a secular audience Solov'ëv's claim may have seemed startling, but not to those at the theological academies acquainted with the resurgence of interest in early Christianity.

[5] In a piece in the journal *Orthodox Review* after the dissertation defense and publication, the editor wrote that Pospekhov viewed *The Wisdom of Solomon* "not as an original work of the religious spirit, but as a product of reflective thought." Raznyja izvestija (1874), 162.

[6] Kudrjavcev (1899), 799.

Another figure worthy of some note was Markellin A. Olesnickij (1848–1905).[7] Although not particularly prolific compared to some others, his work in ethics demonstrates a depth of scholarship wholly lacking, for example, in Solov'ëv's publications. Olesnickij, as we can expect, came from a clerical background. He studied at the Kyiv Academy, from which he graduated in 1873 with a *magister*'s degree with a thesis entitled "The Book of Ecclesiastes." Unlike many others we have discussed thus far, Olesnickij's primary – if not sole – interest was ethics, understood broadly to include the history of moral systems, the role of morality, particularly that of the individual, in society, and the essence and development of Christian ethics. Olesnickij's positions on "moral theology" did not meet with the approval of his superiors which forced him in 1895 to cease teaching that subject and switch to teaching psychology, which he did until his death.[8]

Olesnickij in 1882 published a large and quite erudite work entitled *A History of Morality and of Moral Doctrines*. Throughout its expanse the author drew from a most impressive number of works by an equally impressive number of nineteenth-century authors, many if not most of whom were German Protestant moral theologians and philosophers, a fact that cannot have escaped the attention of his superiors and colleagues. Olesnickij's apparent intellectual debt to non-Orthodox sources surely left a lasting impression on readers even before a reading of the first lines of any of his later writings.

Another clear feature of Olesnickij's work, both in 1882 as well as subsequently, was his turn to and reliance on human psychology, as we shall see, when examining central issues in moral theology. It is this feature of his thought, coupled with his explicit negative opinion of the state of Russian ethical philosophy, that cost him his professorship in that department. For Olesnickij, Russian ethics had made progress since its inception, but any additional forward movement required reform in the understanding of ethical theory. Olesnickij believed that ethics in Russia was not a systematically constructed discipline, a "science," and this had led many, both in the general population and among its educated sector, to disparage it. What the available manuals provided, Olesnickij saw as incomplete. Certainly, the progress that had been made had up to that time been necessary, but that was all. He believed that although morality in the nineteenth century had sought to

---

[7] Olesnickij is not so much as even mentioned in the histories of Zenkovsky, Lossky, and Shpet. Jakovenko did *mention* him for his work on the history of morality and of moral theories, but oddly placed Olesnickij at the Kharkov Academy. Jakovenko (2003), 302. Shpet's silence is understandable, since his history did not cover the late nineteenth century. Zenkovsky and Lossky wished to stress the monolithic and symbiotic character of Russian philosophy and the Orthodox Church. In this way, their silence too is understandable even if regrettable.
[8] Kudrjavcev (1905), 677.

advance the moral aspect of Christian teachings, it remained noticeably inferior compared to other aspects of theology.[9] What must have particularly incensed Olesnickij's compatriots was his recommendation that they follow developments in Western moral theory. If this were done and if Russian translations of the best Western ethical manuals were available, the "scientific" level of ethical theory in Russia would rise much faster than it was doing at present.

If we are to advance in making ethics a "science," we must first determine its proper concerns. Does it even have its own subject matter apart from other "sciences"? If it should have its own distinct sphere of interest, is that sphere large enough to warrant allotting to it special attention and discussion? Surely, ethics deals with human behavior, but psychology does so as well. If psychology can explain our conduct, at least theoretically, what remains for ethics? "Will not ethics, then, only repeat what psychology has said?"[10] Without much scrutiny and undoubtedly realizing its implications, Olesnickij drew back from pursuing this question further. Psychology has no right to make "scientific" pronouncements concerning the human will insofar as it concerns ethics. But the entire matter does show a close affinity between the sciences, all of which – not just psychology and ethics – form a single whole. Olesnickij conceded, though, that ethics is a special part of psychology, the part that deals with purposeful human activity and that its erection into a science must be based on a systematic psychological study of the human will, taken independently of the external consequences of its employment.

Ethics is a peripheral part of psychology not just in that it addresses the human will, but also in that we have a deep and irresistible psychological need for moral ideals, a need rooted in our nature. Olesnickij was fully aware that all worldly phenomena, including those within the moral sphere, are governed by causal laws, but the objective relations in and on which the human will is active is selected by the eternal absolute being, viz., God. The norm for our purposeful actions is formed from observations of the human social order. The recognition of this norm leads our thought "upward" to an imperative, which we see as a demand from God.

Having placed so much weight on human psychology in ethical theory, it is surprising how little Olesnickij invoked psychology and psychological considerations as his lengthy introductory section progressed. In discussing free will, he acknowledged that there is something "mysterious and incomprehensible about it, and this is why freedom of the will cannot be proved mathematically."[11] It is also for this

---

9 Olesnickij (1882), 36.
10 Olesnickij (1882), 21.
11 Olesnickij (1882), 54.

reason that we cannot represent it as clearly as we can sensible objects. Unfortunately, Olesnickij provided no further elaboration of this mystery, no appeal to psychological determinism or even a mention of it.

As with virtually all Russian philosophically-minded theologians, Olesnickij held that there is a parallelism between the structure of the cognitive faculty and the structure of the world. Kant too had noticed this, but he erred in Olesnickij's opinion by not realizing that the structure of the world existed before us, before our cognition.[12] Such a tenet alone by no means would have raised suspicions among other Orthodox theologians, but, coupled with his general debt to German Protestant thinkers, a reference to Pietistic Kant did not serve to lessen his colleagues' misgivings about Olesnickij's commitment to Orthodoxy. As with Potapov at the Moscow Academy, Olesnickij championed the position that there can be no cognition without both *a priori* and *a posteriori* elements. "If we do not combine real and ideal moments harmoniously, but follow one path predominantly or even exclusively, the result will be skepticism."[13] This warning applies as much to the German Idealists as it does to the empiricists.

The reader of Olesnickij's treatise will particularly notice the absence in it of direct moral prescriptions and imperatives. Indeed, in his eyes Russian theological ethics at the time was guided largely by talk of duties and obligations as against the recognition of the role of social factors in moral deliberations and evaluations. Insofar as the social factor enters the picture, it is with respect to the Russian Church. One significant flaw – presumably Olesnickij found there to be others – in Russian theological ethics was a deficiency of rational arguments and deductions drawn from facts and observations. Instead, it remained preoccupied with collecting Biblical texts and the works of the Church Fathers and their systematic presentation. The result was that "for a long time our theology and, in particular, our theological ethics, kept spinning its head as in a fog enveloped by medieval scholasticism."[14] Owing to this, Olesnickij concluded that theology had to go out and catch a breath of fresh air. Drawing back ever so slightly from this highly critical comment, he offered his opinion that the construction of morality as a discipline must take into account religion, albeit in a broad sense. But since the divine is best spoken of in the Bible – Old and New Testaments – Christian ethics must turn to it as one of its sources and its doctrinal norms. Olesnickij had nothing to say about non-Christian theological ethics, assuming he would concede that such a doctrine is not oxymoronic.

---

12 Olesnickij (1882), 67.
13 Olesnickij (1882), 97.
14 Olesnickij (1882), 125.

Olesnickij's salient hostility to traditional theological ethics with its reliance on authority led him ultimately to an individualistic stand. One's self, the "I," being the organ of all knowledge, is also the organ of theological knowledge. With the truths of ethics being closer to universal human concerns and interests, ethics as a discipline must appeal less frequently to the Bible than dogmatics. What, then, is the difference – assuming there is one – between theological and philosophical (i.e., secular) ethics? For Olesnickij, the difference lies not in their respective objects of investigation nor in their methods. The difference stems from their starting points. Theology presupposes the possession of truth, the truth of revelation, as its *terminus a quo*, whereas truth is the *terminus ad quem* of philosophy. "Theology and philosophy proceed in two opposite directions. Philosophy goes from the unknown to the known. ... Theology goes from the known to the unknown."[15] Olesnickij concluded that there is, nonetheless, no difference between theology and philosophy. Ethics, as a sub-discipline in both, has a single object of investigation.

Those who sought to uphold the purity of Orthodox moral theology were aghast at Olesnickij's deviation from its canon and his conceptual turn toward German Protestantism. His silence both on philosophical arguments intended to uphold traditional values and on norms and practical prescriptions for guiding human conduct could be interpreted as a tilt toward ethical nihilism, something that the Church could not abide. To be fair, Olesnickij saw the attempt to subjugate human desires and actions to general laws to be fraught with difficulty.[16] On the other hand, the traditionalists among his colleagues and superiors saw this hesitancy and resignation as itself a form of skepticism. Human beings need determined, practical guidelines, something that Olesnickij denied as possible.[17]

The discomfort Olesnickij's superiors felt toward his views was first manifested by some disapproval from his Academic superiors in his choice of readings for his course on moral theology. The published records provide no indication of hesitancy with the serial publication of his work on "The Morality of the Semitic Peoples" that appeared over the course of 1883–1884 in the *Trudy Kievskoj dukhovnoj akademii*, but his essay on "Moral Progress" in December 1884 did encounter objections from the archbishop, who, resolutely objecting to Olesnickij's understanding of moral theology, demanded corrections and abridgments of the paper before its publication.[18]

---

15 Olesnickij (1882), 143–144.
16 Olesnickij (1882), 11.
17 Kozlovs'kij (2007), 113.
18 Kudrjavcev (1905), 677. In his article, Olesnickij sought the cause of what he took to be the pessimism of his age. The overcoming of undue pessimism and also optimism can be achieved by moral perfection and the realization of the moral ideal, though this cannot take place in earthly

Later in 1897, Olesnickij submitted as a doctoral dissertation a work "From the System of Christian Moral Teaching" to the Kyiv Academy, but it was rejected. One colleague of Olesnickij's faulted him for veering away from the traditional formulation of Russian moral theology.[19] Another of Olesnickij's own colleagues, reiterating the familiar objections, wrote that the dissertation failed to provide the fundamental and general concepts of the subject matter. The critic also remarked that Olesnickij's dissertation specified neither the task and the sources of the methodology employed in moral theology nor did it "review the works that already exist in this country on the topic."[20] Olesnickij had not properly delineated Christian morality from other moral systems. Thus, the proposed dissertation lacked the specificity of just what is the basic principle of Christian morality. Just as egregious was Olesnickij's distancing of morality from religion:

> The author, placing universal principles as the basis of morality, in the spirit of Protestantism, distinguishes morality therefore from positive religious beliefs. Religion and morality, according to the author, are two separate spheres. Instead of talking about a false understanding of religion and morality, the author talks about religion without morality and about morality without religion. He does, however, recognize that religion is the root of morality.[21]

The critic, Petr Linickij, to whom we will turn next, saw all of Olesnickij's faults as stemming from the influence of Protestant moral systems.

Not accepting defeat, Olesnickij next submitted his dissertation to the Moscow Theological Academy, where Nikolai G. Gorodenskij, who, at the time was teaching moral theology, and Sergej S. Glagolev, who taught theology, also rejected his work. Finally, in 1904 it was accepted, though with assistance, at the St. Petersburg Academy a few months before Olesnickij's death.

7.2 Linickij's Ambiguous Conception of Philosophy

Given his sheer prolificity, it is puzzling that Petr I. Linickij (1839–1906) was completely passed over in such traditional histories of Russian philosophy as those by Zenkovsky and Lossky. Indeed, his philosophical works were arguably not particularly original. Nevertheless, given his long tenure at the Kyiv Academy, the sheer paucity of secondary treatments of his thought serves as testimony to a self-im-

---

life dominated by "the law of dualism. It must be realized in another sphere and in another life." Olesnickij (1884), 486.
19 Jastrebov (1897), 371.
20 Linickij (1898), 304.
21 Linickij (1898), 316.

posed isolation of the secular and clerical realms from each other in Imperial Russia.

Linickij received his education at the Kharkov Theological Seminary and then at the Kyiv Theological Academy, where he obtained a *magister*'s degree in theology in 1865 with a thesis on "The Various Directions of German Philosophy After Hegel in Relation to Religion."[22] As with other outstanding students, Linickij was retained by the Academy after his graduation to teach philosophy. He received a promotion after two years and became a docent after another two years with the adoption of the new charter. In yet another two years, he was promoted again, this time to an extraordinary professorship. For his 1876 dissertation on "Plato's Theory of the Deity," he received a doctorate in theology – which as we saw the new charter required.[23]

Linickij had already distinguished himself with one of his earliest works, his *Survey of Philosophical Doctrines*, from 1874, it being officially recommended for use in the history of philosophy course taught at the theological seminaries. In this work, the author covered the main epochs in the history of philosophy as well as presented what the author considered to be the principal philosophical problems involved in cognition, existence, and practical principles. However, being in effect an introductory text Linickij sought at the start to delimit the concept of philosophy from other disciplines and thereby engage in a currently raging topic in Western thought. Linickij recognized that philosophy, both in terms of sophistication and even in its very conception, had changed over the years. Human curiosity had not remained static throughout history. As a result, any definition of philosophy would have to be general and preliminary. If philosophy is a reflection of the mind unto itself, an expression of self-consciousness, it is understandable that the emergence of philosophy would require a level of maturity, conceived both phylogenetically and ontogenetically. Doubt and questioning are the original manifestations of philosophical consciousness. But doubt need not lead to Cartesianism, let alone skepticism. Such would be a misunderstanding of the proper nature of doubt. Rather, doubt is the consequence of the demand for invariable and absolute truth. We seek what is rationally necessary in existence and certainty in cognition.[24] Consequently, the motive arousing the philosophical quest is the opposite of the skeptic's conclusion. The philosopher does not seek to doubt for its own

---

[22] This work was published with modifications in 1887, albeit under the pseudonym "I. Petrov," in the journal of the Kharkov Theological Academy *Vera i razum* [*Faith and Reason*], a favorite organ for Linickij's writings. The reason for the pseudonym is unclear.
[23] It is just a bit ironic that Olesnickij, whom Linickij later, as we saw, faulted for "Protestantism," served as one of the "official" opponents at Linickij's dissertation defense.
[24] Linickij (1874), 5.

sake or to dismiss all truths, but wishes to account for our confidence in our accepted truths. We see from this that philosophy has no special object; this is its distinctive trait and shows its special significance. As a discipline, it seeks to provide a general worldview.

Nonetheless, Linickij apparently backtracked on his own assertion regarding the non-specificity of the object of philosophy. He quickly informs us that philosophy strives for knowledge of the essence of being, for "an understanding of the intrinsic bases that establish the unity and connection of all that exists."[25] Certainly, he did not limit philosophy's quest for this essence to a rather sharply delimited sphere as, say, biology does to the sphere of organic, living beings. But in writing that philosophy seeks the essence of being, he set it against what the individual sciences provide, and whatever that may be it is not such an essence. Linickij remarked that the simple combination of scientific conclusions does not satisfy the philosophical aspiration. Even the internal connections between the individual parts of a systematic natural-scientific system would not be sufficient. To be sure, philosophy includes the results of the individual sciences, but it refers to them much like any single science refers to the conclusions of another. Just what, then, did Linickij have in mind when writing that philosophy provides a general worldview?

Without providing examples, Linickij held that philosophical problems have changed over the course of human intellectual history. To the extent that the same problems have emerged in successive systems merely testifies to their "richness." Every philosophical system is an expression of its time insofar as it meets the educational needs of that time. What precisely Linickij had in mind is difficult to determine. It certainly could be understood as an expression of a weak historicism. But however we may interpret this assertion as well as his pronouncement concerning philosophy as a worldview, he stated that we stand in a three-fold relation to God, nature, and humanity given to us before philosophical reflection and these form the possible objects of philosophical inquiry. Why they should be such objects is left unsaid, as well as what remains outside the three mentioned spheres and that, thus, are not, properly speaking, objects of inquiry. In other words, it is unclear what is *not*, for Linickij, an object of philosophy.

Finally dispensing with his ambiguous understanding of philosophy and its concerns, Linickij informs us that at least one, if not the primary, question of philosophy is that of being. We come to it from a comparison of the different forms of existence presented to us. Based on these very differences, we "inevitably" assume that there must be something singular and original from which all of the varieties

---

25 Linickij (1874), 8.

we see arise and interact. Unfortunately, Linickij provided neither the reason why we *must* make this assumption nor did he raise the logical possibility that even if the assumption is one we must make, it cannot be a psychological necessity, a result of how the human mind operates. He made no effort to clarify why we must conclude from an "inevitable" assumption that something objectively exists. Nonetheless, that "we" must assume the existence of something singular brings "us" to the philosophical question of the essence of all being.[26]

Having, in effect, shed the pretense that philosophical questions change over time, Linickij again tells us that another important question is that of how God is the cause of being, a question that demands an inquiry into the true concept of God and the Deity's relation to the world. The means by which we are to answer these questions is left unsaid, but they lead us to new questions concerning cognition, which, in turn, lead finally to the study of human nature. Our quest for fundamental ontology can only be resolved through a turn to epistemology. In other words, before we can obtain ontological certainty, we must know whether and how cognition of the essence of being is attainable.[27]

7.3 Linickij on Cognition

Linickij's 1874 *Survey* was not intended to be a contribution to philosophy as such, but an introductory text, and in this role it succeeded, despite some notable shortcomings. In the immediate years that followed, he wrote in addition to his doctoral dissertation a series of articles that attempted to provide a thorough examination of the 1879 book *Science and Religion* by Boris Chicherin, a prominent figure in Russian jurisprudence and politics.[28] Linickij's articles were published in the house organ of the Kyiv Academy in 1880–1881 and upon their completion collected into book form. The respective positions of Chicherin and Linickij were actually close despite the differences that Linickij sought to point out. Both singled out positivism and the positivistic spirit for rebuke. However, whereas Chicherin held the Hegelian dialectic in high regard, Linickij drew more inspiration from Kantian epistemology, albeit without an acceptance of transcendental idealism.

In the context of a discussion of the "basic law of thought," which he called the law of identity, Linickij found the concept of essence. Over time and with changes

---

[26] Linickij (1874), 9.
[27] Linickij (1874), 147.
[28] Chicherin in his later years turned to philosophy including the publication of two lengthy and stinging critiques of Vladimir Solov'ëv's forays.

in an object, that we can recognize the object as the same throughout, that "it remains this thing and not some other thing despite all possible changes," means that we have grasped the object's essence.[29] Linickij recognized that the logical law of identity is more abstract than seeing it exemplified in the recognition of essences, but he wished to demonstrate the link between our thought with its laws and objective reality. The concept of essence, being dependent on the fundamental law of identity, is, he claimed, a necessary form of thought. For Linickij, that we can grasp the essence of things is already a major blow to both Kantianism and positivism, for both, he claimed, deny the cognizability of the essence of things. Implicit in this criticism, of course, is Linickij's view of Kant's theory of cognition as a subjectivism for which human cognition does not grasp a thing's essence, but only its phenomenal representation. Linickij took it for granted that what he considered to be the "essence" of a perceived object is what Kant understood as the thing in itself, this without textual support from Kant's own writings.

Linickij also held that if we cannot grasp essences, which is what all subjectivisms profess, then we also cannot attain truths. For truths concerning an object or state of affairs cannot vary over time. Just as essences cannot change, so too truths cannot change. Truths must be based on the cognitions of the essences of things.[30] Linickij provided no extended treatment of his idea and no examples. The danger, however, is his apparent failure to distinguish the cognitive act, with its sense, from its referent, and thereby tempts a lapse into psychologism. He made no effort to distinguish the cognitive grasping of truth from the grasped object. For one thing, Linickij attempted to ground even the most basic laws of logic on the contingency of the world, a connection that consistently developed would surely lead either to a relativism or to a misunderstanding of the sense of the world. Yet from the bare assertion that essences and truths are singular, i.e., cannot change, Linickij remarked that a third law of thinking follows, namely, that all of our judgments have a sufficient reason.[31] This third law, in turn, is the law of causality, i.e., that everything has a cause, and, therefore, causality is not some category of the human cognitive faculty, of the understanding, as in Kant, but an expression of a law of logic.

Having accused Linickij of an implicit psychologism, we must face, however, a counter-argument. He was by no means consistent in this matter, perhaps because

---

29 Linickij (1881), 9.
30 Linickij (1881), 21.
31 Linickij did not specify precisely what the first two laws are, but he did mention the law of identity, which "inevitably" leads to the concept of essence, and that "the essence of each thing is singular and identical. Therefore, truth whatever be its object, can only be one in relation to this object." See Linickij (1881), 9, 15.

he simply did not proceed to analyze his position to its foundation. He admitted the possibility of another world that operated in accordance with different contingent laws than ours does. There is no dispute in this matter. He went on, though, to write that rational truths cannot become untrue. For that would require reason itself to change. "The possibility of another reason that would essentially be different from ours is quite inconceivable."[32] As we shall see, Linickij, surely, did not fully realize the incompatibility of the inalterability of reason, on the one hand, with his monistic treatment of the cognitive process.

Of course, Linickij forcefully rejected empiricism, for he recognized that were we to ground the principles of cognition on the contingency of worldly facts only other contingencies would follow. But in recognition of what he considered the variability of human mental habits with the consequence that in time different theories, different views will arise, how do we avoid empiricism, which allows for no absolutes? Linickij answered that we "correctly assume and conclude that the order of things serves as the source of our present mental habits."[33] However, with this are we not in effect back again to empiricism? Linickij did not see it that way. Whereas it would be wrong for us to conclude that the laws of reality can be derived from *a priori* thought, there are necessary and invariable laws governing our thinking.

To be sure, there is much confusion in Linickij's treatment of the cognitive process when he ventured to provide his own opinions in wishing to buttress his firm Orthodox faith. However, when he turned to an analysis of historical figures in philosophy he was on firmer ground. Although the use of the term "speculation" is more often employed historically in connection with the excesses of post-Kantian German Idealism, Linickij saw it as the very method by which Kant proceeded. Thought can cognize its own activity and can cognize the very laws and forms inherent in its activity.[34] Speculation reveals the concepts that are "so necessary for us that they enter into every worldview as essential, fundamental elements of it."[35] Nonetheless, Linickij wished to distinguish speculation, which he associated with self-consciousness, from self-observation. The former is the subject of the thinking process with laws and forms as its object. These laws are the general forms and means by which we think, and we ascribe to them uni-

---

32 Linickij (1881), 119.
33 Linickij (1881), 293.
34 Linickij (1881), 58, 292. Likewise, Chicherin wrote, "it is impossible to deduce an unconditionally general law from experience. On the contrary, speculation fully explains to us its properties and its origin. The law of causality, like that of identity and contradiction, is nothing other than a certain operative mode of reason, which cognizes reason." Chicherin (1999), 46–47.
35 Linickij (1881), 291.

versal applicability. Linickij provided scant elaboration for this claim, but he added, again without argument, that the cognitions that result from speculation have an objective significance. He took it for granted that, unlike Kant, these general laws do not prevent our cognition of things as they are in themselves. The only objects of speculation are the activities of the mind. Linickij thought that herein lies the fundamental error of post-Kantian idealism. It wished to extend speculation to all cognizable reality, to employ it universally. Unfortunately, Linickij's failure to recognize Kant's conception of the transcendental is one factor that drew him close to perilous conclusions.

Self-observation, however, just as with external observation but unlike speculation, gives us knowledge only of individual facts, not of laws. If our reflection on mental activity were limited solely to self-observation, we would have no more than an aggregate of data found in consciousness.

For Linickij, since the mind is our only means, our only instrument, of probing both reality and the cognitive process itself, he understood that there must be some analogy between the discovery of our mental operations and the laws of externality. We cannot seek a reason for employing reason. It is itself its own supreme justification for its use. Thus, we must look on externality as rational. "There is in our thinking a necessary and inherent conviction that the order of things in the world must agree with the laws of reason."[36] This inevitably assumed rational order leads us inevitably to the thought of its Creator. This conclusion alone shows us that Linickij has moved outside the orbit of Kantianism. But most disturbing is his characterization of logic which he sees as studying the laws and forms of thought. Of course, this statement in isolation is ambiguous, but one interpretation would have logic be merely abstractions of our proper thought processes, thus reducing logic to psychology. Unfortunately, Linickij did not elaborate, but he did remark that mathematics, as well, is known through the speculative method. Moreover, expressly in agreement with Chicherin, he viewed the matter of the physical world, with its particulars, and the thoughts of the spiritual world, with its abstractions and generalities, are necessary for the other's existence.[37] One cannot be without the other. But is the simplest of truths of, say, arithmetic, such as $2 + 2 = 4$, dependent on the existence of a physical

---

36 Linickij (1881), 65.
37 Chicherin wrote, "What we called the simplest elements of the physical and spiritual world, simple matter and pure thought, constitute two opposite extremes, from which the entire universe is composed. The first represents a particular element, the second an abstract general element. One prevails in the physical world, the other in the spiritual world. But just as the particular cannot exist without the general, so the general cannot exist without the particular." Chicherin (1999), 37.

world? The relativistic implication of such a view is one that follows from any monistic reductionism of the ideal to the contingency of the physical.

One glaring difference, as Linickij himself saw it, with Chicherin concerned their respective views of space. Chicherin did indeed hold that our representations of spatial connections are the result of conscious acts, the only possible explanation of which is one based on an innate property of the mind. "The representation of space is a general form, by which the cognizing mind connects the manifold of impressions. If this form were not innate (*pripozhdena*), if there were no connecting principle in the mind itself, then impressions would forever remain incoherent."[38] Linickij agreed with the substance of Chicherin's argument, but not its conclusion that our representation of space is innate. For the former, the representation of space is applicable only to externality. It is a form of sensibility, but not a form of the understanding. Space can be given only in sense intuition, but for Linickij, contrary to Kant and to Chicherin, it is not itself an *a priori* intuition. For both Chicherin and Kant, our *a priori* intuition of space grounds the basic tenets of geometry. Chicherin alleged that there is no necessary appeal to empirical sense experience in either geometry or arithmetic. Geometry can speak of one-dimensional lines and zero-dimensional points, neither of which is given in experience. "The first assumption of geometry, without which science cannot take a single step, is that any two points in space can be connected by lines, which, of course, we are not able to produce in experience."[39] To this, Linickij was willing to concede that geometry was a speculative science, i.e., one based on some sort of cognitive reflection upon mental activities, and not an empirical science. However, unwilling to sever a tight connection to experience, he added that geometry is an abstract application of the laws of cognition to our sense intuition, the most general of these applications. Geometrical objects, though not given as such in experience, are the general form of intuited empirical objects, or they are the aggregate of the possible spatial relations that we can derive *a priori* from the representation of space. For what it is worth, Linickij found his disagreement with Chicherin on the nature of geometry to be of little practical interest.

Linickij argued, above all, against positions that many in Russia had thought had been disposed of a decade earlier and which remained in circulation only among a small number of political revolutionaries, but certainly not professional philosophers. Although seeking to combat empiricism and positivism, his *bêtes*

---

38 Chicherin (1999), 62. Our principal concern here is not with Chicherin, but if he understood the term "innateness" (*prirozhdennost'*) in some naturalistic manner, his conclusion would not follow from the thesis. That there has to be a connecting principle in cognition for the sense manifold to be coherent is an epistemological, not an ontological, claim.
39 Chicherin (1999), 65.

noires, he yet rejected Kant's supposed phenomenalism, seeing it as maintaining that our representations of things are illusory. If, he asked, our representations are illusions, what are they illusions of? Are they of the senses or of the mind? These are the only two instruments of cognition that we have. If we cannot in principle reach the essence of independently existing things, we thereby deprive ourselves of any chance of knowing whether what we take for knowledge is true, whether our cognitions correspond to existence. Linickij, disliking, nay fearing, the consequences of that position, dismissed it, holding that "both speculation and experience incline us to a belief in the objective significance of our representations."[40] He showed us with this that he had no real understanding of Kant's distinction between transcendental idealism and empirical realism, a distinction that he in no way attempted to refute or show as being unfounded. Tempted again to lapse into psychologism, he concluded his epistemological inquiry holding that being and cognition are merely two aspects of one reality, aspects that are irreducible to one another. Such, he claimed, is the "sole possible solution to the relation between cognition and being,"[41] but in writing this he solved no problems. He merely opened himself up to even more questions and problems. If the laws of being agree with the laws of reason, is this a contingent agreement or a necessary one? If it is the former, Linickij averts a dualism but at the cost of relativism.[42] If it is the latter, he averts relativism, but at the cost of his monism.

To be sure, we have discussed in this and the previous section only a few works from Linickij's total literary output, most of which date from the 1890s. Yet even those we have seen are verbose, repetitious, and superficial. On the other hand, his writings on the history of philosophy, more than his own views, demonstrate his pedagogical skills that his students at the Academy surely valued more than any sense of originality. Linickij concluded his work with a summary that hardly clarified his own position. He charged Chicherin with not understanding what speculation is, its usage, and its limitations. These faults, Linickij believed, he had overcome with his own book.

---

40 Linickij (1881), 126.
41 Linickij (1881), 154.
42 Mozgavaja writes that Linickij "defends a dualism by erecting a firm border between the spirit and the body." Mozgavaja (2012), 37. But, as we saw, this dualism is an epistemological dualism, not an ontological one.

7.4 Snegirev and Miloslavskij Confront Psychology

The journal of the Kazan Academy *Pravoslavnij sobesednik* [*Orthodox Interlocutor*] began publication in 1855. As with virtually all journals, its mission changed over the years and the circulation waxed and waned. The reputation of the journal began to improve under the rector Archimandrite Nikanor, a major figure whom we shall see in depth later. Under his rectorship, the number of articles on philosophical themes in the journal increased.[43] As already mentioned in Chapter 4, Bishop Khrisanf's 1860 article was the first to appear and took what the author considered to be a philosophico-historical approach to the subject matter, even though he found that the German Idealists had taken a "one-sided" view of religion and that their "final conclusions were hostile to the true conception of religion."[44]

Nafanail Sokolov became rector of the Academy in 1864, and until the adoption of the new charter no new articles on philosophy appeared in the journal. In 1869, Aleksandr A. Nekrasov (1839–1905), who taught Greek at the Kazan Academy, published an article in *Pravoslavnij sobesednik* entitled "The Word and Human Nature," in which he noted that in light of the many physiological similarities between the human being and the monkey, there are essential differences not discernible to physical analysis. Among these is our ability to communicate verbally.[45]

In 1870, Veniamin A. Snegirev (1842–1889) published his *magister*'s thesis, entitled "On the Person of Our Lord Jesus Christ in the First Three Centuries of Christianity," as an appendix to the journal *Pravoslavnij sobesednik*. Snegirev followed up the following year with a serialized work "Spiritualism as a Philosophical and Religious Doctrine" in the same journal. Snegirev had entered the Kazan Academy in 1864 and remained there after finishing the necessary course work in four years. At this time, since he ranked first in his graduating class and following common practice, he began teaching logic and psychology, and with the awarding of a *magister*'s degree he became an assistant professor. Additionally, he lectured on psychology and logic at the secular Kazan University until mid-1885. Snegirev died from esophageal cancer but introduced many students at the Kazan Academy to his view of the importance of the scope of philosophy.

---

[43] Solov'ev (2017), 274.
[44] Khrisanf (Retivcev) (1860), 164.
[45] Solov'ev (2017), 283.

Snegirev's predominant interest was in psychology, which led him to investigate dreams and mental activity during sleep.[46] He displayed amazing erudition on the treatment of those topics by ancient writers but little interest for recent and contemporary literature. Snegirev summarily rejected the entire notion of the unconscious, writing that there can be no such sphere "within" the mind, since the latter, being pure energy, has no spatial dimensions. Thus, there cannot be anything "within" it. For a similar reason, it made no sense to him to speak of a sphere of latent ideas buried deep within the mind that can be brought forth in some manner to consciousness. "Each idea, having ceased to be conscious, ceases to live and breaks down into its component parts, because consciousness is its life, its sole form of being."[47] Yet, despite this denial Snegirev still found the soul to be a substantial entity, the existence of which grounded the phenomena of one's inner life. The soul's existence was one of the necessary truths that once understood becomes obvious and indubitable without needing any logical proof. The soul is an inner reality.

Snegirev held that there are three sources of human knowledge: experience, divine revelation, and an intuition of the whole. All knowledge and all ideas, though, are ultimately subjective phenomena. Holding psychology to be the preeminent science, owing to its concern for the subjective, led Snegirev to see it as central to any study of the human individual.[48] Psychology, in his conception, describes all phenomena common to our spiritual life included in the spheres of thinking, feeling, and desiring. He conceived it as free of speculation and as an independent, empirical discipline, but one which chiefly, though not exclusively relied on introspection. He was willing to accord a limited role to the just emerging use of laboratory work in psychology. But he still saw it as part of philosophy. Indeed, the first task of the philosopher, wishing to understand the world as a whole, "is to explain internal subjective processes, to conduct a psychological analysis, and to show how and from what our representation of the world is built."[49] Thus, the first task of philosophy is a psychological one, in effect to study our mental life. Our inner phenomena are subject to immutable laws just like all other phenomena. We, as philosophers, must first explain our internal subjective processes by which our representations of the world are constructed. Having determined the nature of these processes, we then turn to determine the representations that all people

---

46 For his 1886 work *Uchenie o sne i snovidenijakh* [*Theory of Sleep and Dreams*] Snegirev was awarded the annual Makariev Academic Prize, which was established in 1884 by the terms of the will of Metropolitan Makarij for an outstanding work in history and theology.
47 Snegirev (1875), 224.
48 Snegirev (1876a), 88–89.
49 Snegirev (1876b), 448.

hold in common. These representations introduce harmony and uniformity into our view of the world. Psychology and logic are independent and are empirical sciences. Yet, they belong to the discipline of philosophy, since "they serve as the sole starting point and support for any philosophical speculation claiming to be scientific."[50] In the end, Snegirev provided no unequivocal statement that logic can in principle be seen as reducible to psychology. However, in claiming that it, as well as psychology, are empirical "sciences" together with numerous assertions throughout his writings, he tempts the reader to conclude he was committed to a psychologism. In his article "The Sciences of the Human Being," he placed both psychology and logic among the human sciences.[51]

Snegirev's primary appeal in his philosophical articles to the writings of the ancient Greeks and the Church Fathers stemmed from a view not uncommon at the time among those in Russian theological circles and even to Solov'ëv. In Snegirev's eyes, the Church Fathers had, as he put it, "combined the entire sum of rational knowledge of their day and harmonized it with the true faith, taking what is given in revelation and only what in human knowledge does not contradict revealed truth."[52] Human reason can acquire nothing more perfect than the truths contained in Christian revelation. Snegirev welcomed scientific progress but saw it as needing the approach he believed the Church Fathers had taken, namely, to view the latest scientific developments through the lens of Church teachings.

Another figure at the Kazan Academy during much of the second-charter period was Petr A. Miloslavskij (1846–1884), who finished his studies there in 1872 and in 1874 submitted and defended a *magister*'s thesis "The Ancient Pagan Doctrine of the Wanderings and Transmigrations of Souls and Its Traces in the First Centuries of Christianity." Snegirev acted as the official opponent at the thesis defense. Miloslavskij, then, following the standard practice of the time, went for further study to Germany, more specifically to become familiar with the position of metaphysics in contemporary German university philosophy. Snegirev composed

---

50 Snegirev (1876b), 451.
51 A successor and student of Snegirev's, V. I. Nesmelov, whom we shall see later, wrote that for Snegirev "the ideas of subject and object, of matter and spirit, of space and time, cause, and absolute can all be reduced psychologically, and if not decisively resolved by psychological analysis, then at least significantly prepared for such a resolution by its means." Nesmelov (1889), 151. Such a position, of course, would place Snegirev among the most resolute proponents of psychologism.
52 Snegirev (1871), 30.

the official program Miloslavskij was to follow while at the universities in Berlin, Heidelberg, Halle, and Marburg.[53]

Miloslavskij's thesis – as we can surmise from the title – was hardly a philosophical treatise. The concern was to establish the unique nature of the Christian doctrine of the immortality of the soul in human history up to that time. Although we can find the idea in earlier societies, it was associated with fantastical visions and lacked definition. Miloslavskij connected the primitive conception of the soul with that of reincarnation. Recognizing the transient nature of all individual things, ancient peoples sought permanency particularly in human life.

Miloslavskij followed up his thesis with an article in 1875 that revealed his interpretation at the time of the history of philosophy. In his "Contemporary Theory of Substances," published in the Kazan Academy's house organ, Miloslavskij held that the concept of substance was the starting point of humanity's entire scientific and philosophical development.[54] He distinguished modern philosophy from all previous philosophy by their completely different understandings of substance. Whereas modern philosophy viewed substance in general as a dubitable and incomprehensible concept or representation, earlier thought viewed it as the obvious and valid *fundamentum* of everything. For this reason ontology held priority over epistemological considerations in ancient thought. Modern philosophy, however, has placed cognition in the foreground and created a strict dichotomy that has hampered the development of philosophy. But Miloslavskij concluded, not unlike the early Solov'ëv, that the modern viewpoint will sooner or later come to an end by exhausting the options it has evoked around this prejudice.

Miloslavskij composed a lengthy report on the status of metaphysics in German universities upon his return to Kazan. The report was first serialized in 1876 over three years in the journal *Pravoslavnyj sobesednik*, and then published in book form in 1878. Its contents, which contain a history of metaphysical thought in modern philosophy, particularly in recent German thought, can be compared with Solov'ëv's 1875 *Crisis of Western Philosophy*, much at the expense of the latter. This is not to say that Miloslavskij's book is impeccably impartial, which it is not, nor is it exhaustive, which, again, it is not. Unlike Solov'ëv, Miloslavskij did not view the "pessimistic" philosophies of Schopenhauer and von Hartmann, as the culmination of Western philosophy, but he did provide a lengthy presentation of their views as well as that of others such as Eugen Dühring and Friedrich Lange, the latter being an instrumental figure in the early German neo-Kantian

---

53 His stays at each of these universities had to have been quite short, since the record shows him abroad only during the period 1874–1875. See Solov'ev (2021a), 276–278.
54 Miloslavskij (1875), 402.

movement, which Solov'ëv entirely overlooked. Like Solov'ëv, Miloslavskij had an agenda, a fundamentally religious one, and again like Solov'ëv, Miloslavskij hoped to show the failures of German Idealism in general and Kant, who spearheaded that movement, in particular. Miloslavskij covered considerable ground and made many points, only a few of which we could possibly mention here. He, certainly, was not terribly original.[55] Many of this criticisms are ones we have already seen. Although the title of his work leads us to think his sole focus would be the German philosophical thought of his day, Miloslavskij devoted considerable attention to Comtean positivism and its errors. In this, he shared a concern with secular Russian philosophy. Clearly, there was something about positivism that Russian philosophers especially feared.

As in his thesis, Miloslavskij hailed Kant as having reoriented German philosophy toward epistemology rather than ontology. In the former's sketch of the history of philosophy, the fundamental problem after Kant became how to account for human cognition and its relation to existence. The medieval scholastic tradition, however, would not be broken unequivocally and so quickly with the appearance of the first *Critique*. Kant's three major successors Fichte, Schelling, and Hegel, each with his own respective form of idealism still intimately tied thought to being. The consistent development of idealism finally ended with Hegel's system. Miloslavskij, like Solov'ëv in this respect, could not see it proceeding further. After the formulation of absolute idealism, Herbart's realism came to the fore only in time to pass into an absolute realism.[56]

Nonetheless, Miloslavskij saw Kant still influencing the posing of philosophical questions despite the fact that different solutions were offered than the ones he gave. Miloslavskij saw the originality of recent German philosophy, with the possible exception of Schopenhauer, as limited to interpretation and critique of "old or incomprehensible mixtures and variations of earlier philosophical views, colored in the majority of cases by the tendencies of natural science."[57] The most recent German philosophers, sensing a confusion in their ideas, turned to natural science,

---

55 Miloslavskij followed what was by this time the standard critique of Kant within theological circles. Space and time are not subjective forms, which would make them relative. They are not appearances, but the independent, unconditional property of pure reason. "Pure reason," of course, is also not to be understood here as a subjective human faculty. That German philosophy understood it along subjective lines was "the first false premise that directed all of its further development." Miloslavskij (1878), 265.
56 Miloslavskij (1878), 116.
57 Miloslavskij (1878), 29. Schopenhauer clearly was influenced by a turn toward Buddhism. Miloslavskij saw the "charm" and significance of Schopenhauer and the philosophers of pessimism in their amassing of facts for investigation that testify to the presence in the world of physical and moral evil. Miloslavskij (1878), 161.

which had witnessed many notable successes in their day, and back to Kant. The most gifted exponent of a return to Kant and of a restructuring of philosophy in conformity with the results of natural science was Lange. Many others, however, found solutions to traditional inquiries, such as questions about causality and freedom, about being and appearance, about categories and substances, from conceptual analysis alone and only later in some cases attempted to buttress their opinions by reference to facts and scientific data. Miloslavskij's own example is that the existence or non-existence of atoms is "proved" solely on the basis of the concept of an atom. "In this reasoning, scientific data are allowed only on the condition of a slavish subordination to *a priori* principles. Clearly, such metaphysics can hardly arouse our sympathy and generate an interest in philosophy."[58]

Miloslavskij authored a number of additional works published in both the Kazan journal as well as in that of the Moscow Academy. But his 1879 article "Origin and Significance of Philosophy" and a subsequent work from 1883 are particularly important for the theme of the present treatise. Miloslavskij argued that philosophical inquiry was part of human nature. More specifically, opposing the positivist belief that the natural sciences can and will eventually entirely replace philosophical inquiry, Miloslavskij affirmed that we naturally seek to move beyond what the sciences with their reliance on empirical data can provide. If our knowledge were limited to what the senses can provide, the differences between things and between appearances would be limited to what sensations and feelings can provide.

> No matter how hard we may try to fit the differences and oppositions that exist in nature and which are accessible to human knowledge into the body of the natural and human sciences, without philosophy we would be left without a place for these differences and oppositions. They are found in knowledge itself, indeed in the very sciences, and throughout the entirety of human history up to the present.[59]

Were positivism to be correct, human knowledge would remain static. "Without a preliminary philosophical attitude toward existing knowledge, without doubts and critique, knowledge would not take a step further."[60] Miloslavskij then stated that what humanity needs is the development of philosophy as a science. The fact that presently existing philosophical theories are inadequate for the formation of philosophy as a science explains why even a higher intellectual development does not protect a person from an egregious moral outlook.[61] We would be mistaken if we

---

58 Miloslavskij (1878), 33.
59 Miloslavskij (1879b), 251.
60 Miloslavskij (1879b), 252.
61 Miloslavskij (1879b), 259.

imagined that humanity's quest for greater knowledge and an ever better life was confined within the bounds of science and pure philosophy. To make up for our deficiencies humanity has turned since antiquity to religious doctrines.

The spread of Christianity rendered the entirety of ancient theoretical and practical wisdom obsolete. Christian doctrine laid down the principle of a new civilization, but it did not provide the sole guidebook for our worldly life. We remain earthly creatures with earthly interests, and we must again turn to science and philosophy, which form part of a Christian education. The fact remains, though, that many reject philosophy and even science, displaying little interest in it. Why is this so? Why did philosophy fall from its natural summit of human knowledge, and why has its progress lagged behind that of the natural sciences? For Miloslavskij, the answer to these questions "must be sought in the historical destinies of philosophy."[62] It is with this claim that he ends his article.

Miloslavskij planned to continue his work on the nature of philosophy but succeeded in completing only the first volume. The task he set was to establish philosophy as an independent, or "special," science. We again find lurking in this quest the wish to combat and forestall the spread of Comtean positivism, which predicted the dissolution of philosophy into the various natural sciences. Miloslavskij did hold that the history of philosophy was replete with metaphysical adventures and that in order to overcome positivism a proper philosophical method and subject matter would need to be elaborated. Philosophy in Miloslavskij's mind concerned itself above all with investigating the phenomena or manifestations that make up human knowledge, as well as the causal connections and laws between these manifestations.

Psychology and logic have traditionally been conceived as parts of philosophy, but the sphere of philosophy is larger than even the two together. Whereas psychology studies cognition as a factual possession of the individual human mind, as a subjective phenomenon in connection with our physiological processes, philosophy studies universal phenomena across all individuals and all times. Thus, despite the traditional placement of psychology within philosophy, the former is a separate branch of knowledge, and one cannot replace the other.[63]

Miloslavskij's 1883 work, to be sure, was largely an expanded and systematized version of ideas he had previously set out in his journal articles. Again, he reproached modern philosophers for viewing the entire world as projections of their own concepts, feelings, and desires.

---

62 Miloslavskij (1879b), 266,
63 Miloslavskij (1883), 407.

7.4 Snegirev and Miloslavskij Confront Psychology — 197

> In the extended and thinking substance of Descartes, in Spinoza's substance, in Fichte's 'I', in Hegel's absolute idea, in Schopenhauer's will and representation, in von Hartmann's unconscious, in the energy or force of the materialists, despite the philosophical abstraction of these philosophical principles, it is not difficult to discern philosophical portraits, copies of man himself, taken abstractly, apart from the living, real world, outside the biological and socio-historical conditions.[64]

Miloslavskij sought to carve out a special province for philosophy that would be immune to any encroachments from the sciences, including psychology. Whether he succeeded in this is highly doubtful. Miloslavskij failed to address particular issues and failed as well to make his case for his conception of either ancient or modern philosophy. He evidently knew the texts in question but failed to marshal his knowledge in a pointed argument, being content with apparently dogmatic claims.

Miloslavskij, though, did make a somewhat ambiguous excursion of sorts into epistemology, the basic idea of which would play a central role in Imperial Russian philosophy, both secular and non-secular. Under the influence of both German (Helmholtz, Dühring) and Russian (Nikanor, whom we shall see shortly) thinkers, Miloslavskij introduced the notion of "conceptual sensations," sensations that "are not always the result of external stimulations."[65] These sensations occur when, for no apparent external reason, something comes to mind. These are cases of self-observation, of reflection. Had Miloslavskij left his discussion with this mere indication, we could dismiss it immediately as a psychological matter with no philosophical consequences. However, without pause he conjectured that "conceptual sensations" are related to the fact that "philosophers have long insisted on the existence of some special way of knowing, in addition to the generally known types of sensations, and directly place this means of knowing on an equal footing with experience."[66] Miloslavskij contended that this special way of knowing is what Plato meant by the term "anamnesis" and Schelling by "intellectual intuition." Terming it now a method and a philosophical principle, its utilization ends the hegemony in philosophy of logical categories and conceptual systematization in favor of living, real representations. We find the most illustrious and instructive examples of the use made of "conceptual sensations" in the creations of poets and artists, of mystics and dreamers. But Miloslavskij added that its use lies behind even the hypotheses proposed by scientists that have the force of evidence. It ultimately remains hard for us to fathom how Miloslavskij could have

---

64 Miloslavskij (1883), 165.
65 Miloslavskij (1883), 287.
66 Miloslavskij (1883), 288.

thought others failed to recognize the viability of this nebulous conception or how it resolved perplexing problems.

Miloslavskij contracted tuberculosis during his study period in Germany in the mid-1870s. He fought it valiantly for years, but the disease eventually won the war. Miloslavskij retired from teaching at the Academy at the end of 1883 and died the following March at the age of 36, leaving his wife, who would give birth to their second child a week later. In April, just two weeks later, she too died.[67]

As we have seen throughout our study, there was more than a single philosophy instructor at each of the academies at one time. Many would teach the subject, be it the history of philosophy, psychology, logic, or general philosophy, for only a brief time. The instructors in many instances were surprisingly underqualified by our standards today for their assignments, itself an indication of the depth of the lessons taught. At the Kazan Academy, for example, Vasilij G. Rozhdestvenskij (1839–1917), a graduate of the St. Petersburg Academy in 1865, taught the history of philosophy for only one and a half years, lecturing on the basis of Friedrich Überweg's recently published *Grundriss der Geschichte der Philosophie*. At his own request, he was transferred to the St. Petersburg Theological Seminary and then a few years later to the Academy there. But importantly his principal interest was theology, authoring a number of works on the New Testament. His successor in Kazan was Vasilij K. Volkov (1844–1902), who published several undistinguished expository works on contemporary pessimistic philosophy.[68] Setting it against Mill – a favorite target at the Kazan Academy – whose positivistic response to pessimism is replete with contradictions and therefore "clearly absurd," Volkov declared that for the inquiring mind the mystery of God's will is more satisfying. Christian faith also provides additional benefits that he left unspecified.

7.5 Archbishop Nikanor and His Positive Philosophy

The most illustrious name associated with the Kazan Academy was one we have mentioned but only in passing. He served as rector for just three years, 1868–1871, but while in that office he began the three-volume work for which he is best known *Positive Philosophy and Supersensory Being*. In it, he introduced the "method," the "positive philosophical method" – not to be confused with Comtean positivism – that was intended to be a development of Jurkevich's own "positive philosophy."

---

67 Solov'ev (2021a), 277.
68 Znamenskij (1892), 51. For an example of his treatment of pessimism, see Volkov (1884).

7.5 Archbishop Nikanor and His Positive Philosophy

Aleksandr I. Brovkovich (1826–1890), best known by his chosen monastic name Nikanor and by which he will be referred to here, began studies at the St. Petersburg Academy in 1847 and completed them in 1851. Placing first in his graduating class, Nikanor, following custom, was asked to remain at the Academy to teach theology. In April 1856, he was appointed rector of the Riga Theological Seminary. He returned to St. Petersburg for a short time in the following decade and then was appointed rector of yet another theological seminary. His apparent administrative skills came to the attention of his superiors, and once again he was transferred, this time to the Kazan Academy in 1868 to prepare for the restructuring called for in the 1869 charter. While in his role as rector, Nikanor also taught the required fundamental course in theology. Not all of the authorities were entirely pleased with his performance, but in 1871 he was appointed to a bishopric. During these years, he continued the work he had begun on his *Positive Philosophy* while at the Kazan Academy. Despite the significance of this large book in Imperial Russian philosophy and the discussions concerning it and his views, the second and third volumes fall outside the scope of the present study. An adequate discussion of their contents and Nikanor's overall role in Russian philosophy, in any case, would properly demand a separate study.[69]

The first volume of the *Positive Philosophy* was published in 1875 with the second and third volumes following in 1876 and 1888 respectively. The actual writing of the second volume can be dated to early 1873, and that of the third volume to much later.[70] The first volume, however, was clearly started while Nikanor taught at the Kazan Academy, and our attention here will be focused on it. The writing of the *Positive Philosophy* was prompted by a question Nikanor posed to students in his basic theology course, a question on which he was clearly fixated. How the students responded is not recorded, but in 1871 Nikanor published an article entitled "Can the Positive Philosophical Method Prove the Existence of Something Super-Sensible – God, the Spiritual Immortal Soul, Etc.?" in the Academy's journal.[71]

---

[69] The third volume of Nikanor's work was entitled *A Critique of Kant's Critique of Pure Reason*, indicating thereby the volume's central concern. For a short summary of its contents, see Nemeth (2017), 189–194. Nikanor intended to contribute an essay "On Free Will From the Christian Point of View" to the secular journal *Voprosy filosofii i psikhologii*, which under the auspices of the Moscow Psychological Society, encouraged at the time the submission of such pieces. The ongoing polemic on the topic drew responses from such figures as N. Ja. Grot and L. M. Lopatin in 1889. Nikanor's intended contribution, in which he wished to show the Orthodox Christian viewpoint, remained unfinished owing to illness.

[70] Solov'ev (2015), 84.

[71] In a footnote to the journal article's title, Nikanor wrote that it "is a collection of critical remarks in connection with essays written by students on the given theme." Nikanor (1871), 41.

This article formed the first five chapters and most of the sixth chapter of Part I of the *Positive Philosophy*.[72]

The opening of Nikanor's first volume would not strike the reader as particularly innovative, perhaps even pointless.

> Positive philosophy accepts only *real, objective knowledge to be true knowledge*. It takes as possible true cognition only what is either immediately based on experience – the evidence of our senses – or what is logically correct, what by the rigorously positive method – the inductive or deductive method – follows from immediate experience, observation and the evidence of the senses.[73]

The words could just as well have been written by a Comtean positivist if one were to overlook the fact that Nikanor's understanding of certain terms, such as "experience," may be considerably broader than that of the empiricist or the positivist. Contrasting subjective to objective knowledge, Nikanor claimed that the former is knowledge that conforms merely to cognitive laws without relating to the existence of external objects. He thereby, of course, avoided the thorny question of how to distinguish externality from internality. Nonetheless, he had at least an inkling of the problem in maintaining that any division of the senses into internal and external ones is precarious. For all five "external" senses present to the perceiving subject something internally. The red color and fragrant smell of a rose are my subjective impressions, representations, or experiences of it, of an objective object. Few will argue that some information provided by the senses is subjective. Nikanor, however, wished to extend the argument further saying that all of our concepts or representations of objects are subjective; that between the object itself and our minds there is the mediation of our senses. To a decisive extent, what is objective is a matter of a social consensus. Although I can never be sure that what you and others see as red is exactly the same representation that I have, that we all consistently agree that the rose is red when presented with it is evidence that the rose is objectively red. There is no other objective standard by which we can affirm the objectivity of something or some property.[74]

Whereas we can doubt whether the rose is "truly" red, we cannot doubt that an internal physiological feeling is true. I cannot doubt that the pain from my toothache, for example, is actually a pain, but I can doubt that the cause is a cavity. My physiological sensations are, to be sure, more subjective than the evidence of

---

[72] Although Nikanor writes at the end of the journal article that there would be a continuation, I have found no indication that he continued it in the form of a journal article. See Nikanor (1871), 100.
[73] Nikanor (1871), 41; Nikanor (1875), i.
[74] Nikanor (1871), 53–54; Nikanor (1875), 12.

the external senses, but we can be absolutely certain of them unlike the evidence of our externally oriented senses. This much may be considered true, but trivial. However, Nikanor's next step is not. The veracity of our feelings of hunger and thirst reveal to us that there are objects that are capable of satiating our hunger and thirst. Contrary to Nikanor's statement, this is far from clear. Certainly when someone feels hungry or thirsty, they truly are so. But that mere feeling by itself does not reveal what objects or liquids are capable of revealing what is edible or potable – some may indeed be poisonous – or even whether there are any that are consumable. The issue here is that Nikanor's language at times suggests *not* simply that there are objects in general capable of satiating our hunger or thirst, but that the feeling tells us what *specifically* can do so. Nikanor wrote,

> We maintain that *the indications of these feelings are the most objective.* This is clear from the fact that it is impossible by rational abstraction to doubt that the properties these feelings reveal belong to the objects. On the contrary, more than anything, it is impossible to doubt that the feelings the properties reveal to the senses belong to the objects.[75]

Nikanor extended this reasoning to all matters of aesthetics, ethics, and, yes, cognition. Thus, our aesthetic taste seeks out the beauty in objects, albeit that this beauty can take on various forms. That we have such a feeling of beauty means that there must be something that satisfies that feeling. Likewise, that we have a sense of moral goodness means that there must be something that can be sensed as morally good; the sense seeks out and reveals what is moral. Finally, our cognition seeks the "true," i.e., the really existent (*dejstvitel'no sushchee*) just as our will seeks the good. This "true," Nikanor tells us, must exclude all objective inconsistencies. It is the absolute.[76]

Fortunately, Nikanor did realize at least the *logical* possibility that a "mental feeling" (*dushevnoe chuvstvo*) may not have an objective correlate. He did expressly raise the possibility that our feelings or sensations of beauty, goodness and truth were entirely subjective. The principal question is not whether objects have the properties corresponding to those "feelings," but whether there are external objects that arouse in us such sensations that make us think them as being beautiful, morally good, or cognitively true. Nikanor's answer was hardly compelling.

> Humanity has already answered the question whether there are such objects. Outside me, in externality, and in human society there are objects that arouse sensations in me corresponding to the idea of beauty, the good, and the true.[77]

---

75 Nikanor (1871), 56; Nikanor (1875), 14.
76 Nikanor (1871), 63; Nikanor (1875), 20.
77 Nikanor (1871), 64; Nikanor (1875), 21.

To put the best gloss on Nikanor's statement, we would say it is a contingent fact of human nature that our feelings indicate the objective existence of objects that give rise to those feelings or that can satiate them.

Humanity has affirmed generally recognized ideals of beauty. Thus, for Nikanor, this means that beauty does objectively exist. We by nature and not by habit know beauty and learn to value it. Additionally, there are generally recognized moral standards as evidenced by human conscience. There is a striking similarity of moral foundations and moral legislation across the centuries and among all "civilized" people. As with beauty, we by nature know that there is goodness and learn to value the good itself, not rebel or act contrary to it. In short, the moral good objectively exists. Turning to the sphere of cognition, we can ask whether there is, first, anything absolutely true without qualification, and, second, anything generally recognized by humanity as true in all three spheres, i.e., one existent that is the embodiment of truth, goodness, and beauty.

Animals instinctually, i.e., innately, know how to survive; they know what to eat and drink and avoid what is harmful. The human being's mind innately bears the laws and forms of thinking that if applied correctly coincide with the laws of nature. In addition to those laws and forms, the categories of the understanding and the higher fundamental ideas of reason – Nikanor does not state what precisely the latter are – are likewise innate. Not only are these forms, laws, ideas, and categories innate in all people, but so also is the fact that we should adhere to them in our thinking. They are the same as the laws, forms, etc. of objective reality. Just as the moral law is inscribed in our heart, so too are these laws, forms, etc. inscribed in our consciousness. We hear the voice of God in the voice of our conscience, and we see the real, objective world in the vision, or mental feeling, of our consciousness.[78] "We are convinced that an inner mental feeling can reveal objective properties of objects beyond the doubt of any rational analysis."[79] The basis of Nikanor's conviction remains unclear, but he certainly takes this "inner mental feeling" to be analogous to our external vision. Indeed, this inner feeling has an advantage over our other externally-oriented feelings in that the former has the immediacy of a contact of the subject with the object sensed.

Nikanor expanded on these thoughts and this broadening of sensory cognition to include within it a virtually mystical union of the human consciousness with objectively existing objects. It allowed him to construct what others have referred to as an ontological epistemology, with a clear emphasis on the word "ontological,"

---

[78] Nikanor (1871), 83; Nikanor (1875), 36.
[79] Nikanor (1871), 88; Nikanor (1875), 40.

since the mechanism by which one knows what exists remained unelucidated. Already while at the Kazan Academy, Nikanor distinguished, as we see, between "external feelings," i.e., the five senses the majority of humans possess, and "inner feelings" that inform us of such properties as beauty, morality, and truth, which consciousness provides as long as it adheres to its innate laws and forms. Just as we can be mistaken in ascertaining aesthetic and moral matters, so too can we be mistaken in determining veracity.

To what extent Nikanor's positions influenced Solov'ëv in the development of his philosophical thinking, we can never be certain. But that he, Solov'ëv, had some familiarity with them, we can be sure. In one of the few notices in the Russian press of the appearance of Nikanor's first volume of the *Positive Philosophy*, Solov'ëv wrote that only rarely is there in Russian theological literature an independent philosophical investigation. He found in Nikanor's treatment "inadequacies in both form and content," but he recognized and surely valued Nikanor's trichotomization of cognition into external feeling, inner organic feeling, and – most importantly – a higher, inner mental feeling.[80] Nikanor developed and elaborated his overall position in the coming years with the second and third volumes of the *Positive Philosophy*. His stance would have an impact on secular Russian philosophy also through his exchanges with such figures as N. Ja. Grot, who went on to teach at Moscow University. In any case, these show that the split between secular and clerical philosophy in Imperial Russia was not as rigid as one might believe.[81]

---

[80] Solov'ëv's exceedingly short notice originally appeared in 1876 in the journal of the Moscow Academy *Pravoslavnoe obozrenie*. Solov'ëv (2000a), 213. Solov'ëv published in 1877 a more substantive review of the second volume of Nikanor's *Positive Philosophy* again in *Pravoslavnoe obozrenie*. Since this second volume was composed in 1873 and thus after Nikanor had left the Academy, it falls outside the scope of the present work. Solov'ev (2013), 97. Vladimir Solov'ëv's review shows his continued interest in Nikanor's work despite his reservations concerning it. Solov'ëv wrote, "Above all, we must say that the author does not directly and fully consciously pose his synthetic task. Nowhere does he give a precise specification of the normal relationships between theology, philosophy, and positive science. This inadequacy in the formulation of his task is reflected in its execution." Solov'ëv (2000a), 221. We see that Solov'ëv continued to hold a high opinion of Nikanor's work even later. In his 1884 essay "Judaism and the Christian Question," Solov'ëv remarked that Nikanor was "the author of a remarkable and still little-valued work on religious philosophy." Solov'ëv (1914), 138–139.

[81] Miloslavskij in 1879 wrote that in Russia who wrote a book largely determines how it is received. "A book is considered 'spiritual' not only by its content, but simply by the author's position (*zvanie*). Everything published by a priest or bishop, everything published in theological journals is, for that very reason, 'theological' literature. ... There is a very popular belief that between 'theological' and secular scholars there is nothing in common. Only secular scholars can be its genuine representatives; clerical ones are just so-so." Miloslavskij (1879a), 266–267.

Part III: **Under the 1884 Charter**

In early March 1881, Tsar Alexander II was killed by a terrorist bomb. His successor and son, Alexander III, frightened and by nature no liberal, reacted by enacting repressive measures and halted other much needed reforms. Nevertheless, even before this event winds of reaction could be felt. Student demonstrations were increasing over the previous decade, leading to demands for greater government control of the secular universities, both in terms of overall administration and in teaching. The government in 1879 instituted a system of external inspectors to supervise student discipline. Dmitrij Tolstoy, the minister of the interior in late-1882 drafted a new charter for the secular universities that in 1884 was adopted. Under its provisions, power shifted from locally controlled faculty councils to the Ministry. University rectors were no longer to be elected, as stipulated by the previous charter, but appointed by the government. The department heads were to be named by a representative of the minister, who himself controlled faculty appointments. An inspector was now to be in charge of the disbursement of scholarships, and these were to be awarded based largely on political reliability. Although a number of the Tsar's advisors objected to provisions in this new charter, Alexander approved it in late-August 1884.[1]

Whereas the government did not initially have the same unease that unrest and disturbances would emanate from within the walls of the theological academies, there was a concern about the lack of focus on their fundamental *raison d'être*. The newly installed chief procurator of the Holy Synod, Konstantin Pobedonoscev (1827–1907), a former law professor at Moscow University, had no sympathy for the reforms introduced with the 1869 Charter. If those in charge of the theological academies did not recognize problems associated with the implementation of the 1869 Charter early on, they certainly did so by the early 1880s. Students under the Charter could specialize in some particular area of theology quite soon after beginning their education at the academies, resulting in a narrow education, which was easily discernible in the theses that students submitted. But neither the academies themselves nor the entire structure of the Orthodox Church in Imperial Russia was prepared for the radical innovations that the 1869 Charter introduced. Given the low level of education in the general populace, administrators began to query what need was there for such a number of intellectually specialized personnel. What was needed was clergy who could relate to the broad masses in a still largely agrarian society, not academics with a passion for research at the expense of basic knowledge of the liturgy and the needs of parishioners.

---

1 Kassow (1989), 28.

In 1880, the rectors of the theological academies were asked to discuss and consider necessary and useful modifications to the existing charter.² As one might expect, there was no unanimity concerning what changes were needed. At both the St. Petersburg and the Kyiv Academies, there were even internal disagreements. A commission was established late in 1881 under the auspices of the Holy Synod. Drafts of the amended charter and statutes were prepared and sent out with remarks reviewed by senior figures in the Church. The changes and amendments requested of the existing charter were so extensive that a new charter would be required. The completion of the draft was time-consuming, difficult, and contentious. Finally, after a year and a half of deliberations the final version of the charter was completed, albeit in strict secrecy and apparently in the office of the chief procurator, i.e., the head of the Holy Synod, and officially approved by the Holy Synod with extreme haste and without discussion in April 1884.³ The new charter, which received the Tsar's approval, was introduced at the beginning of the 1884–1885 academic year.

This new charter eliminated many of the innovations of the previous one. In many ways, it represented a reactionary turn to the administrative measures of the first charter. In addition to canceling the department specialization of the students, there were no longer to be public defenses of doctoral dissertations. The degrees were to be awarded based solely on the assessment by two reviewers of the student's work with the Holy Synod appointing an additional reviewer, who had to give his approval.⁴ This clearly meant that public discussions of theological and related matters were eliminated, being replaced by closed meetings in which politics in a broad sense could come into play. The final essays of all students completing the four-year course of studies were to be on theological matters.⁵ These could, in principle, serve as *magister*'s theses, but only after the works' publication and defense. Classes at the academies were to be taught along pre-determined lines, and an emphasis was now placed on religious life and pastoral training instead of scholarly research. Many courses were again mandatory, including philosophy, which consisted of logic, psychology, metaphysics, and the history of philosophy.

---

2 Sukhova (2013a), 61.
3 Florovskij (2009), 527.
4 Sukhova (2009b), 105. The Synod-appointed reviewer was often not a permanent member of that body, but a bishop who was summoned for this purpose. The danger of this system, pointed out already in 1897 by a theology professor at the St. Petersburg Academy Nikolaj N. Glubokovskij, was that it inhibited criticism of an approved thesis. Since a work had been officially approved, any criticism could be understood as an implicit criticism of the process and of the attending bishop.
5 Pavlov (2017), 167.

Of course, as happened at the beginning of the century instructors and professors managed to incorporate into lessons what they believed was most important in terms of recent scholarship, this despite repeated requests from the Holy Synod to adhere strictly to the approved lesson-plans.[6] The charter wished to make it clear to all that the academies were not universities with multiple faculties, but single-minded institutions devoted to theological education with pastoral and administrative functions ever in mind. Nonetheless, the idea of the theological academy as a research institution had taken hold, and as we shall see in the pages that follow the genie could not readily be placed back in the bottle. Actually, professorial specialization and the encouragement of scholarly research did receive a boost in the new charter despite the emphasis on producing graduates who could meet the Church's basic needs.

The abrupt introduction of the 1884 Charter was not met with universal elation. Students who were in their last year of study had to meet its stipulated requirements. In other words, they now had to demonstrate mastery of all the disciplines specified in the newly approved document. Even professors found this to be a slight of their own specialization.[7]

Students, as mentioned, were required under the Charter to study philosophy, but the purpose of this study was not to enlighten. The historian of the Petersburg Academy Ilarion Chistovich best summed up the intent, writing:

> Changes in systems and guidelines did not change the direction and main goal behind the teaching of philosophy in theological educational institutions. The goal remains to inquire about the weakness and impotence of the human mind, of the impossibility of discovering the truth by one's own means without the higher light of Revelation.[8]

Although his words pertained to the position of philosophy under the first Charter, they could and did apply just as well to academic life under the third. Philosophy was seen as but a handmaiden to theology.

Whether by the hand of Pobedonoscev, who is often characterized as the chief ideologist of the Tsar's counter-reforms, or by his instigation, the "Rules for the Consideration of Works Submitted for the Awarding of Scholarly Theological Degrees" went into effect in 1889. Theses were to have a definitive and settled standpoint. The main task was the prevention of heretical doctrine in accordance with the spirit, letter, and dignity of the Orthodox Church, and examiners were to have these features in mind, not just scholarship. Such works were neither to be con-

---

6 Sukhova (2017), 407.
7 Sukhova (2013a), 63.
8 Chistovich (1857), 294–295.

cerned with heretical doctrines or movements nor were they to trace unorthodox ideas to some source. Theses could not be accepted that questioned the authenticity of events that church tradition and national beliefs had taken as factual even if supported by otherwise sound scholarship.[9]

---

[9] Florovskij (2009), 531. Sukhova points out that Archbishop Makarij (Bulgakov) on a visit to the academies in 1874–1875 already indicated the inadmissibility of awarding theological degrees on the basis of dissertations on secular topics with no clear connection to theology. Sukhova (2006), 9.

Chapter 8
Philosophy at the St. Petersburg Academy Under the Third Charter

The winds of official reaction that blew with the accession of Tsar Alexander III and the appointment of Pobedonoscev as Chief Procurator of the Holy Synod were barely felt – at least at first – at the Petersburg Academy. The Metropolitan of St. Petersburg Isidor (Jakov S. Nikolskij) (1799–1892) handled the Academy within his jurisdiction calmly with no major incidents, and in the eyes of the teaching staff there were no reprisals for alleged liberalism. Isidor evidenced no urgency to implement Pobedonoscev's outlook. His successor Metropolitan Palladij (Pavel I. Raev) (1827–1898), like Isidor, was reluctant to carry out Pobedonoscev's counter-reforms and stood in direct opposition to them. Although no scholar himself, he respected the scholarship emanating from the theological academies. Unlike the relative stability in the office of the metropolitan, there were five rectors at the Petersburg Academy between 1884–1896. In contrast, there had been just one during the previous seventeen years.

The political security that both the Orthodox Church and the government felt in the theological academies at mid-century began to wane by the 1880s. A concern slowly grew that the radicalism among university students just might spread even to Orthodoxy's educational institutions. At first, this unease was dismissed by those in charge of those establishments even when the worries of the teaching staff were brought to their attention. One incident in particular, though, was sure to raise consternation and fear that the revolutionary impulse might seize some in the student body. Mikhail V. Novorusskij (1861–1925) graduated at the top of his class in 1886 writing a *kandidat*'s thesis entitled "Foundations of Morality in Empirical Philosophy." As a result, he was even asked to remain at the Academy and awarded a professorial fellowship. His future certainly looked bright from the Academy's perspective. What was unknown to his professors was that Novorusskij was an active participant in the terrorist group "People's Will" [*Narodnaja Volja*] which at that very time was preparing an attempt to assassinate the Tsar. Novorusskij was arrested in March 1887, two days after the failed attempt and sentenced to death. His sentence was commuted in May to life imprisonment and was finally released in 1906. A theology professor at the Petersburg Academy, Aleksandr L. Katanskij (1836–1919), remarked in his memoirs that before the final exam in a course he was teaching Novorusskij asked to take the exam for his course with Katanskij the day prior to its scheduled date. Although unusual, the rector's permission was granted, and Novorusskij answered all the questions correctly. Only after the exam did it become clear why the student was in a hurry – he had to assist in preparing for the attempted assassination.[1]

The lines within Russian society between revolution and reaction were being drawn ever more sharply and definitively as the years passed with no segment of society – not even the Church – being spared.

8.1 Karinskij on Kant

The light that shined so bright and vigorous while Mikhail Karinskij taught philosophy at the St. Petersburg Academy grew dim indeed with his retirement in September 1894. During the final decade of his professorial career when the Academy operated under its third charter he had engaged with others on issues related to logic and epistemology. He remained an active participant in Russian philosophical discussions, particularly in those that took place in the capital. The problem of self-evident truths remained until the end the focus of his philosophical concern. He began the systematic elaboration of his position concerning such truths in the final year of his tenure at the Academy, but its publication marked only the beginning of an engaging discussion with others, particularly with the most prominent Russian defender of Kantian epistemology, Aleksandr I. Vvedenskij, who taught at St. Petersburg University. The discussion would continue for several years after Karinskij had left the Academy.

Karinskij serialized his work *On Self-Evident Truths* first in the *Journal of the Ministry of Higher Education* in 1893 and then had it published as a book that same year.[2] The work starts with the seemingly innocuous assertion that the proof of any claim, seen from a logical viewpoint, is a deduction from other claims taken as true. Obviously, the claim to be proved must logically follow from others that pertain to it and is not arbitrarily or randomly chosen. These other claims, or premises, are, for the purposes of the proof, assumed to be true. In other words, every proof rests on unproven premises. The veracity of those premises, in turn, depend on still other premises that are taken as true. This cycle of thought cannot go on forever. To generalize our findings, in a proof, we must "clarify what kinds of truth need to be recognized as unprovable, but are nevertheless valid, and wherein

---

[1] Katanskij (2010), 354.
[2] That Karinskij's work drew the attention of Vvedenskij demonstrates that at least at this comparatively late date the clerical and the secular spheres were not completely isolated from each other. Karinskij's work also prompted a response from Vitalij S. Serebrenikov, who taught psychology at the Petersburg Academy and whom we shall see later in this chapter.

lies their right to validity."³ In short, there must be a starting point in premises that we take to be self-evidently true.

Karinskij's book proceeded from the above conception of a proof, but it amounted, in effect, to a detailed commentary on Kant's epistemology – a rarity in Russian philosophy. Karinskij wished to show that Kant's argument took much for granted. For example, in his attempt to establish the *a priori* conditions of certain judgments, he appealed to their universality and necessity as a fact not needing further substantiation. This, in Karinskij's opinion, was a mistake that could not be ignored. Of course, it, in turn, would be a mistake on our part were we to blame Kant for this omission. "Before Kant, not one serious thinker expressed doubts about the unconditional character of the validity that was attributed to, at least, mathematical axioms."⁴ Consequently, Kant had no reason to question their universality and necessity.

Karinskij was not a skeptic. He assumed that objectivity was given in cognition and charged Kant with unnecessarily complicating the cognitive process by introducing unnecessary concepts that form, in effect, a secondary layer of reality. The epistemological task he set for himself was to explain our cognition of this fabricated layer instead of reality itself. Kant, proceeding from Hume, axiomatically understood the universality and necessity of a judgment as an indication of its independence of reality without first showing that we cannot find those features in objectivity. Kant's dogmatism lies herein. Kant also failed to demonstrate the connection between the alleged *a priori* character of space and time and the pure apriority of geometry and arithmetic. His argument should have proceeded from first establishing that mathematical judgments cannot be grounded by empirical experience and then showed that their apparent validity can only be explained by grounding them on the apriority of space and time. "To assert that present mathematical knowledge is rational (*umozritel'noe*) knowledge solely on the basis that it concerns constructions given in an *a priori* intuition would be to assume that rational knowledge is only possible from constructions of such a sort and empirical knowledge is quite impossible."⁵ Yet, for Karinskij each geometric theorem can be proved in a purely practical way by means of measurement and comparison with spatial figures given in external experience.

---

3 Karinskij (1893), 3.
4 Karinskij (1893), 8.
5 Karinskij (1893), 19. The translation of Karinskij's word "*umozritel'noe*" into English as "rational" needs a brief explanation. Quoting Kant from the first *Critique* at A713/B741, Karinskij translated Kant's "*Vernunfterkenntnis*" as "*umozritel'noe poznanie.*" See Karinskij (1893), 22. We should also recognize that Karinskij translated Kant's term *Anschauung* as "*sozercanie.*"

Another assumption Kant made in Karinskij's estimation concerned the connection between the concepts in a judgment. In universal and necessary judgments, i.e., *a priori* ones, the intuition binding the concepts must itself be *a priori*, for an empirical intuition, again, cannot provide universality and necessity. If mathematics as a body of knowledge consists of *a priori* judgments, it must, therefore, rest on *a priori* intuitions. Kant assumed, again, without proof, that the intuition of space employed in geometric constructions is the same space that we intuit as the form of outer appearances. Karinskij contested this assumption, arguing that the consistency of non-Euclidean geometries demonstrates that the intuited space of geometers is different from the space we intuit in everyday experience.

> In order to retain the validity of our geometric axioms and theorems, we would have to speak not about space, but about our space, and not about a triangle in general, but about a triangle as it is given in our space, etc. The possibility of another space with other laws cannot simply be rejected as an empty impossibility in a scientific investigation, as a completely abstract assumption. It needs scientific confirmation.[6]

Again, Kant overlooked this possibility.

As had so many commentators on the "Transcendental Analytic" in Kant's first *Critique*, Karinskij remarked that Kant had not provided a convincing derivation of the *a priori* categories from the table of judgments. Kant conceived the understanding to be the faculty for cognizing by means of concepts. He derived an exhaustive accounting of the *a priori* categories from the judgmental forms that determine the understanding's natural activity, but Kant made no attempt to justify the derivation from the content and structure of the judgmental activity itself. Had he tried to do so, he would have realized the futility of his endeavor, for it simply is an impossibility. "From the simple determination that the faculty of judging unites representations, it is impossible to derive the various forms of its functioning. In the absence of any other clearly stated criterion, this isolation of the forms of the understanding can present in its favor only an inexplicable and automatic conviction in its validity."[7] Karinskij, to be sure, does not wish to blame Kant for this oversight, but merely point it out. The latter simply relied on what he took to be the definitive authority of traditional logic.

Karinskij was quite willing to concede that the creation of an objective order in the mind necessarily presupposes a mental activity that does not begin with the emergence of reflection. This mental activity is inextricably intertwined with passive processes that are also necessary for our immediate conscious sense of objec-

---

6 Karinskij (1893), 35.
7 Karinskij (1893), 51.

tivity. But Kant misinterpreted these processes and the epistemological meaning of the assumptions owing, in Karinskij's view, on the one hand, to his completely faulty psychological analysis and, on the other hand, to his prejudicial tendency to describe these processes so as to obtain a demonstration of the presupposed fundamental relations.

Karinskij, like so many others, was particularly interested in the Kantian categories of relation. The first of these categories, that of community or interaction, is quickly dismissed. Kant derived it from the disjunctive judgment, but Kant's argument for community is forced. The disjunctive judgment has nothing to do with the real interactions between objects of cognition. This is just one example of Karinskij's general charge that Kant assumed a connection between the functions of a judgment and the judgment's object or subject matter, the object, of a judgment. Kant cannot appeal to some authoritative tradition for support here.

> In the functions of judgment, he seeks assumptions about being, which are the object of judgment. Logic has never assumed this. ... But if we turn to the categories of relation, which were to give the most important synthetic foundations of thought, we will see that Kant does not act as a critical philosopher, but as a dogmatist who approaches his investigation with a preconceived view.[8]

Although Karinskij found Kant's derivation of the relational categories of causality and substance to be more understandable, he charged Kant with adjusting his logical schemes to match his view of the categories. Additionally, he did not see why Kant excluded simultaneity and succession from the table of categories, since they are employed in judgments when distinguishing a necessary connection as against mere contingency.[9] Karinskij held that Kant did not even attempt to prove that his table of twelve categories was exhaustive.

Karinskij contested Kant's account of both causality and substance. In the case of a change in a certain state of affairs, Kant provided no means to distinguish between an objective change in the thing itself as against a change in our perception. In the absence of such a means of distinguishing between an objective change and an illusory one, his proof of the law of causality could amount merely to a psychological claim about changes in empirical consciousness with no pretension to objectivity. "Are we saying that establishing a connection between a certain change and a preceding one accords objectivity not only to it, but also to the preceding

---

8 Karinskij (1893), 52.
9 From a Kantian viewpoint, Karinskij's suggestion demonstrates a misunderstanding of the categories, which are concepts of the understanding. Simultaneity and succession involve time, which, of course, is an *a priori* form of intuition, a faculty distinct from the understanding.

one in a single stroke, so that consciousness needs no other grounds for recognizing the objectivity of the latter?"[10] The necessity of causality becomes a mere law of mental events. But no one would claim that such psychological necessity underlies natural science. Kant, in speaking in general of the significance of causality and interaction in establishing objective succession and simultaneity, takes examples directly from our observable mental activity. But we, then, face the question whether there are any bases for his view. Karinskij believes there are objective bases for ascribing causality to cases that make no appeal to transcendental functions of the mind.

The starting point for the revolution in Kant's thought was Hume's own skepticism with its questioning of what can be given in empirical perceptions. Kant's treatment of causality was dependent on the precarious character of the concept of objectivity. The influence of Hume's treatment made it possible for Kant to forget the connection between perceptions and objectivity, to disengage the two so that the former does not present direct evidence of reality.[11] Karinskij concluded his extended treatment, writing:

> It is clear from all of this that dogmatism permeates the *Critique of Pure Reason* not just in the formulation of the question of self-evident truths, but the entire investigation and its solution. In my opinion, the solution to the problem of the ultimate premises of knowledge as presented in the so-called Critical Philosophy belongs neither to the present nor to the future of philosophy, but to its past.[12]

The importance of Karinskij's commentary on Kantian epistemology for our study of philosophy within the Russian Empire's academies lies in its sophisticated criticisms from a standpoint common to virtually all philosophers within those walls, a type of epistemological realism.[13] Karinskij largely took his position for granted and sought to examine philosophies critically from this standpoint. In this way, he helped clarify unexamined assumptions those philosophies made. Given his largely secular handling of the problems, his contribution would have been easier for those outside the religious academies to recognize had the secular sphere not already adopted many of the concerns and the attitude prevalent in the academies. Unfortunately, few who came later would build on Karinskij's example, being con-

---

10 Karinskij (1893), 95–96.
11 Karinskij (1893), 110.
12 Karinskij (1893), 196.
13 Karinskij, in a lengthy and harsh review of Petr Linickij's 1888 *Idealism and Realism*, showed the difficulty in simply characterizing as idealist or realist any philosophical attitude worthy of consideration. See Karinskij (1892).

tent instead with philosophical issues drawn from a quite noticeable religious perspective and treated in a religious context.

8.2 Akvilonov on Proving God's Existence

The dimming light of recognizable philosophical inquiry at the Petersburg Academy with the approach of a new century and under Pobedonoscev's reign at the Holy Synod can be shown through many examples, but one of the clearest is that of Evgenij P. Akvilonov (1861–1911). To be sure, Akvilonov taught theology, not philosophy, at the Academy, but in other respects his thought and academic career are vivid illustrations of points previously made in this chapter's introductory remarks about life at the Petersburg Academy under the 1884 Charter.

Akvilonov was, not surprisingly, born into a clerical family. He was a graduate of the Petersburg Academy in 1886 and became a docent there in theology in 1891. He submitted a purely theological thesis for the *magister*'s degree during the following year and defended it as required. However, despite its satisfactory evaluation by the Academy, the Holy Synod opposed awarding the degree to Akvilonov, seeing in the thesis a view of the Christian Church that was innovative – and therefore potentially disruptive and dangerous.[14] Not one to suffer a setback easily, Akvilonov offered a second *magister*'s thesis in 1896 – actually a significant revision of his previous submission – and successfully defended it in 1899, this time without the opposition of the Holy Synod. Akvilonov was appointed during the following year to a professorship at the Petersburg Academy.

During the decade between the writing of his *magister*'s thesis and his doctoral dissertation, Akvilonov wrote exclusively on theological themes with, as we would expect, little regard for philosophy. His 1905 dissertation, though, was on a topic philosophers have debated virtually from the start of such inquiries, viz.,

---

[14] The thesis was written under Katanskij's supervision. He wrote, "Unfortunately, the critics of the thesis did not notice the quite valuable thoughts worked out in it, but paid attention exclusively to its actually numerous shortcomings, which I also recognized, but I relied on the gifted author's mental caste, which was more of a brilliant orator and lively pamphleteer than a rigorous scholar. ... Several times, I forced him to revise the manuscript and yet the work ultimately turned out to be not to my taste." Katanskij (2010), 362f. The critics Katanskij mentions were based in Moscow and published in the journal *Brotherly Word* [*Bratskoe slovo*], whose editor Nikolaj Subbotin, was a close friend of Pobedonoscev's. A telegram from Crimea, where Pobedonoscev was staying at the time, arrived before the degree could be awarded to Akvilonov. Metropolitan Palladij interpreted Pobedonoscev's intervention as a rebuke aimed more at himself than at Akvilonov. Regardless of whether that was entirely the case, there was undoubtedly some truth to it. See Katanskij (2010), 348.

philosophical proofs for God's existence. Before turning to it, a short discussion of another popular essay he wrote that same year would not be out of order. As, above all, a Christian theologian, Akvilonov sought to defend the possibility of human sinning, which in his eyes required a defense of free will and of a soft determinism. He, unlike many others, distinguished freedom from arbitrariness, marshaling common sense in support of his position. To find freedom in outbursts of anger, frenzied acts of passion, or the wild behavior of an inebriated individual is not an expression of freedom, but of slavery to the passions and the lowest excesses of human nature. Such is not to be considered the "freedom granted by our Sovereign Lord to His subjects."[15] However, Akvilonov extended his argument to the feverish political atmosphere at the time in Petersburg. He held that some understood freedom in terms of independence from moral obligation, a disregard of the Ten Commandments. Some go even further to understand freedom as permissibility to disregard any and all authority. Akvilonov, deeply committed to monarchism, found the true sense of freedom to be manifested in subordination to law.[16]

Of more interest to us here is Akvilonov's dissertation, "On the Physico-Teleological Proof of God's Existence," which covered substantially more ground than merely the physico-teleological proof of God's existence. Akvilonov attempted to defend that proof as well as the ontological proof, relying on principles that others had questioned but which were becoming a staple of much of Russian idealism. Kant, he held, sought to combat the abuses of one-sided empiricism, retaining the objectivity of a supersensible being, but his view that we cannot know the essence of things resulted in the introduction of considerable conceptual confusion.[17] Kant recognized, on the one hand, that much of nature exhibited an inner purposiveness, but, on the other hand, he thought the concept of a goal was only a subjective mental form, a mere regulative principle. Such an outlook necessarily leads to skepticism.

As with virtually all the philosophically-minded academicians in Imperial Russia, Akvilonov rejected transcendental idealism. He found purposiveness objectively present in the world. But at least at the start of his work, Akvilonov explicitly affirmed that the intention of philosophical proofs is not to create in us a recognition of God's existence if none is already present.[18] They merely wish to assist in

---

15 Akvilonov (1905a), 4.
16 Akvilonov (1905a), 6.
17 Akvilonov did not elaborate what he meant in writing that Kant upheld "the objective significance of a supersensible being." Akvilonov (1905b), 32.
18 Akvilonov here, without referring explicitly to Kant's treatment of the teleological argument, agrees that it, taken alone, cannot *prove* God's existence. Kant continued that only the ontological proof could establish the existence of a highest being, the teleological argument serving as an in-

the transition from an indefinite and vague affirmation to a clear and definite recognition of His existence.[19] This is done through raising that vague awareness to clarity through a reflective examination on everything in our environment and on everything that we are. Akvilonov is himself quite vague on the process by which we come to such clarity. He wrote that it proceeds along a parallel track to the development of human thought, thereby leaving us to think that humanity should be more religious, not less, with time. This surely could be hotly contested.

In any case, Akvilonov recognized that the teleological proof dated from the emergence of humanity. Just as we, as rational beings, actively pursue definite goals, so too nature aims at particular goals. Reason tells us that every action must have a cause, a sufficient reason, for each action. For there to be regularity in the universe, there must be a rational will seeking goals. However, "since nature by itself is endowed with neither reason nor a free will, a Being must rise over it, a Being Who uses natural forces as the means to attain its goals."[20] Akvilonov understood Kant's presentation of the teleological argument to be based on an analogous inference from human actions to God. This, Akvilonov believed, was Kant's fundamental mistake. The teleological argument is similar to the cosmological argument in that both invoke the law of causality as it applied to empirically-observed nature. But unlike causality as used in the cosmological argument, we do not observe conformity to an established law, i.e., regularity, on which the teleological depends, everywhere in everything. Why, then, he asked, do we see conformity to a law everywhere in nature even when there is no such conformity? If it indubitably lies almost everywhere in nature, the idea we have of it must have objective – and not just subjective – significance.[21]

Akvilonov, similar to Chistovich at the Petersburg Academy and others, held that we have in our minds the idea of the infinite, an innate idea. It "can have arisen in us only under the influence of the infinite itself on us. For there is no way of passing from the finite to the infinite. No matter how many times we combine the finite with the finite the sum will never be infinite."[22] Yet, however odd, Akvilonov maintained that the idea of finitude can only be formed under the influence of the infinite! We can eliminate or exclude spatial and temporal conditions from the absolute to arrive at the idea of a finite thing. From this highly questionable presup-

---

troduction to the ontological. Kant (1997), 580 (A625/B653). Akvilonov himself would devote considerable attention in his book to the ontological proof.

19 Akvilonov (1905b), 8–9.
20 Akvilonov (1905b), 17.
21 There is, of course, much here in this abrupt conclusion that Kant, for one, would contest, but Akvilonov's presuppositions should be quite apparent whether one agrees with him or not.
22 Akvilonov (1905b), 412.

position, Akvilonov concluded that we have our innate idea of infinity given from the Infinite itself, viz., God, Who must, therefore, exist not only as an idea in consciousness, but also objectively. We can hardly be surprised that Akvilonov held that what Kant labeled regulative ideas, such as that of God and of the soul, would be seen by him as necessary conditions for rational thought and that God and the soul exist both as ideas in the mind as well as objectively. To maintain the opposite would be to succumb to skepticism. "The idea of God, which is found in our mind, and its regulative significance shows that this idea is not only a *ens rationis ratiocinantis*, but also a governing force in rational thinking, which is essentially innate in our organism."[23] Nevertheless, Akvilonov applauded Kant for having shown as a result of his investigations into the cognitive mechanism that our reason necessarily forms the idea of God.

Akvilonov dealt with many other philosophical issues in his dissertation, all of which for the sake of brevity we must forego here. He defended, for example, an extreme idealist stance not dissimilar from Plotinus that the human being can better be described not as a body that has reason, but as reason that has a body, which accounts for the dominance of the spirit over the body. Likewise, contrary to the materialists, the human brain does not generate consciousness.[24] Rather, consciousness uses the brain as a tool, the former existing before the latter.

In the years subsequent to his dissertation, Akvilonov held various positions within the Orthodox Church, but he also drew close to monarchist political organizations that apart from their reactionary political stands preached a virulent anti-Semitism.[25] He died from a throat cancer at the relatively youthful age of 50.

8.3 Khrapovickij and Gribanovskij: A Turn to Self-Consciousness

Akvilonov was surely not the only prominent Church figure to engage in political activity as social unrest spread in the early twentieth century. Aleksej P. Khrapovickij (1863–1936) came from the nobility and received a secular secondary education (*gymnasium*) in St. Petersburg. He was, however, attracted to the priesthood very early in life, and against his father's wishes he enrolled at the Petersburg

---

[23] Akvilonov (1905b), 418. The expression *ens rationis ratiocinantis* can be found also in Kant (1997), 605 (A670/B698).
[24] Akvilonov (1905b), 141–142.
[25] He himself penned a slim tract in 1907 in which he concluded that if Russia awarded full rights to Jews, it would thereby "voluntarily surrender to their power and expose all of Russia to the dangerous risk of a gradual transformation into a lifeless corpse." Akvilonov (1907), 44.

Theological Academy in 1881. He graduated four years later and took monastic vows assuming the name Antonij, by which he henceforth signed his writings.[26] He too was retained by the Academy on a professorial fellowship and was appointed docent there, teaching the Old Testament. His only book and only work on philosophy was his published 1888 *magister*'s thesis *Psychological Data in Favor of Freedom of the Will and Moral Responsibility*. However, his teaching career at the Petersburg Academy was short-lived. In 1890, he was appointed rector of the seminary in the capital and then rector the following year of the Moscow Academy. Due to disagreements at the time with the metropolitan of Moscow, he was reassigned to the Kazan Academy in 1895.

Antonij's brief excursion into philosophy and tenure at the Petersburg Academy virtually precluded him from having a significant influence on Russian philosophy, but it does show that Russian academic philosophy was not entirely uniform, unoriginal, and unequivocally hostile to Kant's subjectivism. Although his thesis combines ideas from disparate sources, his positive references to Kant to buttress his ultimately realist and religious position are noteworthy.

We cannot here even hope to summarize all of the claims Antonij made in his thesis. Indeed, many of them are quite contentious. He sought to connect a subjectivism in the theory of cognition to a defense of free will. His subjectivism was definitely not of the Kantian transcendental variety, but stemmed from Svetilin's psychological approach.[27] His understanding of free will was, most assuredly, metaphysical. Although highly critical of Kant, Antonij's debt to Kant is, nevertheless, apparent throughout his thesis.[28] Antonij wished to start with the "I," but unlike Kant, this "I" is the empirical individual, endowed with a consciousness that freely guides actions and is aware of itself in the form of self-consciousness. Without much argument apart from this bare statement, Antonij maintained the primacy of the practical moral aspect of mental activity over its theoretical cognitive activity. That we possess a free will is clear from our universal awareness that it is so. Theoretical arguments that tie willful decisions to one's psychological make-up are simply incorrect.

Antonij understood and accepted Kant's claim that all representations have a necessary relation to a possible empirical consciousness. In representing an external object as external, I am implicitly aware that that object is not identical with me and that I am representing it. The very act of representing contains in itself an

---

26 This is the Archbishop Antonij mentioned in Chapter 5 when discussing Svetilin's psychologism.
27 Svetilin proposed to Antonij the topic for his *kandidat*'s thesis, "Free Will and Determinism from a Religio-Moral Viewpoint," which he then further developed into his *magister*'s thesis.
28 For a summary of Antonij's critique of Kant, see Nemeth (2017), 196–199.

indication that the representation is only in my I. "Therefore, the thought of my I enters directly into every state of mind. Without this I, all of my thoughts, feelings, and desires would not be mine. They would completely merge with their objects."[29] Thus, the implicit presence of self-consciousness – Antonij, unlike Kant, made no distinction between an empirical and a transcendental one – is a necessary condition of separate states of consciousness, i.e., of cognition. Antonij explicitly acknowledged that this idea can be found in all the principal figures of recent German philosophy starting with Kant.

Antonij took Kant's insistence on the unity of self-consciousness as a necessary condition for the synthesis required of all cognition as having practical significance. The logical independence of self-consciousness from the sensory manifold also means that the subject is independent of the mechanism of representing and is independent of other determinations. The I does not amount to nothing, as determinism would have us believe. The I, or self, of self-consciousness is free and independent of other factors. In the absence of self-consciousness, I would be completely dependent on the consciousness of another. I would be only an appearance in the cognition of another.

Antonij is also respectful of Kant's invocation of *a priori* categorical forms. Not only does he hold that at least some of the categories specified by Kant are principles of empirical cognition, but if their presence in human reason can be shown to be due to the activity of the human individual's self-consciousness, then the importance of self-consciousness in discursive thought gains even more strength. Whereas this conclusion, given the premises, may possibly appear to be trivial, Antonij takes it, on the one hand, as a further affirmation in the practical sphere of the individual's free will and, on the other hand, as an argument for the role of self-consciousness, a rejection of which leads to skepticism. "The presented explanation of the processes of knowledge shows us that the free will in no way stands apart from other aspects of the human spirit, that the independence of the subject on the part of its will fully corresponds to its cognitive activity."[30] A corollary of this is that we can speak of discursive cognition only if we are free, self-conscious beings.

Antonij's point was not just to affirm the linkage between the theoretical and the practical spheres, but also to link free will with the possibility of cognition in general. The unity of consciousness of which Kant wrote is not a logical unity, but a personal, dynamic unity. Another consequence of this linkage coupled with a rejec-

---

[29] Antonij (1888), 35.
[30] Antonij (1888), 52. He acknowledged a debt here to the psychologistic view of logic of his teacher Svetilin.

tion of Kantian transcendentalism was a view of at least some of the Kantian categories as generalizations of psychological experience. Antonij was willing to expand the scope of the will's activity to include a process of self-objectification. We are aware of externality, of things outside us, not by theoretical, but by practical reason. Thus, "all cognition is in its essence, at its core, practical cognition."[31] To establish philosophy on theoretical grounds will always remain a futile endeavor.

As mentioned above, his 1888 thesis was Antonij's sole substantial foray into philosophy. He went on to a bishopric in 1897 and in 1906 was elevated to archbishop. He received a doctorate in theology from the Kazan Academy in 1911. He subsequently moved – or was moved – from one diocese to another. The revolutions of 1917 displaced him several times, and in 1920 he was in Crimea with the White forces under Petr Wrangel. Evacuated later that year to Constantinople, he then moved to Serbia in 1921 but continued his support, to the extent that that was possible, for the counter-revolutionary forces. In these later years, he expressed anti-Semitic opinions, which were not in evidence in his earlier years. He died in Yugoslavia and was buried in Belgrade.

As with his friend Antonij, Mikhail M. Gribanovskij (1856–1898) did not remain long at the Petersburg Academy. Unlike his friend, Gribanovskij came from a traditional background, his father being a priest and his mother the daughter of a priest. Entering the Petersburg Academy in 1880, he finished the four-year program with a *kandidat*'s thesis on "The Religio-Philosophical Worldview of the Philosopher Heraclitus."[32] In that same year 1884, he, like Antonij, became a monk, simply taking the name Mikhail, and began teaching basic theology that year as well at his alma mater. He probably began writing a thesis for the *magister*'s degree soon afterward, for in 1887 it was already complete even though the defense did not take place until April of the following year. Mikhail (Gribanovskij), already displaying symptoms of tuberculosis in 1889, resigned from the Academy, and on the advice of doctors to seek a warmer climate he left for Crimea. He was fortunate to receive an appointment to serve as rector of the embassy church in Athens in 1890 where he remained until 1894, but he never returned to scholarly endeavors. Although still ill, he served upon his return to Russia as bishop at several locales, but he finally succumbed at the age of forty-two.

---

31 Antonij (1888), 61.
32 Mikhail's choice of an apparently philosophical topic for this early thesis should not be taken as indicative of a dominant interest in him. As with Antonij, Mikhail's concern with abstraction was short-lived.

Already before finishing the course of study at the Academy, Mikhail (Gribanovskij) sketched his bold philosophical project in a diary entry in January 1883:

> To comprehend Christianity philosophically is the greatest goal today, as outlined by Schelling. ... The dogmas of the greatest, the absolute religion must be the greatest, truest philosophy. We simply must understand and penetrate into them by philosophical analysis and synthesis. There is as yet no Christian philosophy; it needs to be created.[33]

It is this project that Mikhail set out to fulfill, even if only partially as a first step with his *magister*'s thesis, which bore an imposing and promising title: "An Attempt at a Clarification of Basic Christian Truths by Natural Human Thought. Issue 1: The Existence of God."[34] Unfortunately, its extended argument is nothing that we have not previously seen, albeit with Mikhail there is a "twist." He dismissed the cosmological argument, finding it to be incomplete in that it does not provide a link from the observed world to the Christian conception of God. The argument seeks to determine the nature of the Deity through our empirical intuition of all that surrounds us, but in doing so it confuses the two. The most we could conclude from the cosmological argument would be pantheism, but it also makes God an accomplice to the evil in the world.

Mikhail (Gribanovskij) agreed with Kant concerning the defect in Anselm's ontological argument for God's existence. That formulation would have the alleged proof be an analytic judgment, and any judgment involving existence must be synthetic. But the failure of Anselm's argument does not constitute the impossibility of the ontological proof in general. Rather, it should be based on the indubitability of our self-consciousness.[35]

Our minds, he asserted, host a myriad of varied and discordant representations, but we find in consciousness a formal unity of this manifold. Additionally, "we immediately see and necessarily sense in the formal unity of one's own consciousness that there must be in truth the same unity harmoniously embracing all

---

33 Quoted in Florovskij (2009), 542.
34 Mikhail clearly intended the words "The Existence of God" to be merely a subtitle for his extended project of "clarifying the basic Christian truths."
35 Mikhail (2005), 48. We are here supplementing Mikhail's argument for God's existence as found in his *magister*'s thesis with the often more detailed treatment found in lecture notes from his class in theology during the 1888–1889 academic year. A copy of these notes were given to the rector of the Kazan Academy after Mikhail's death and published in the Kazan journal *Pravoslavnij sobesednik* [*Orthodox Interlocutor*] in 1899. They have been reprinted since.

of this content."³⁶ The more we seek to understand logically what is given to us, the more we must ascribe to this content a unitary form, which also must lie in objectivity, in truth. Mikhail claimed it would be more correct to see self-consciousness as a reflection, however partial and/or imperfect, of the absolute self-consciousness. Mikhail regrettably does not offer why this is more correct or provide evidence for this assertion. He merely stated that the absolute character of self-consciousness testifies to the fact that "self-consciousness is the image of the Unconditional. It is the form of the Unconditional, and through this form I intuit the world."³⁷ This "logical" requirement that an image must be an image of something and thus for the existence of God must agree with our immediate awareness of His existence. Indeed, the demand for a harmonious unity in consciousness is a translation into the language of epistemology – though Mikhail does not use that term – of our awareness of God as an absolutely perfect moral being.³⁸

Of most interest is that, like Antonij, Mikhail (Gribanovskij) wished to progress from the "I" of subjective self-consciousness to the objective existence of the "Unconditional," which he identified as the Christian conception of God.³⁹ Mikhail found that we have within our consciousness a conception of the Unconditional, but, he asked, whether it is that of the Unconditional that objectively exists. Of course, without the slightest hesitation, Mikhail responds that *"the real being of the Unconditional is comprehensible to our subjective consciousness. There is no impenetrable abyss* between the nature of the *subject* and the nature of *reality*."⁴⁰ All that is in the conscious mind must be attributed to objective being. Our awareness of this fact, our self-consciousness, is just a gradual clarification to ourselves of the Unconditional. Thus, our own self-clarification coincides with a comprehension of the Unconditional. To resist this clarification is to resist reason and truth. Our moral obligation is to comply with this striving.

Mikhail (Gribanovskij) asserted that his discussion of consciousness and self-consciousness falls under what he called "Christian psychology." It helps answer

---

36 Mikhail (1990), 19. Mikhail faulted Kant for viewing self-consciousness as set against "being," the thing in itself, posited outside consciousness. According to Kant, in Mikhail's reading, self-consciousness is an unalterable and eternal category of reason.
37 Mikhail (2005), 48.
38 Mikhail added that his assertions "completely coincide with the features that in Christian doctrine form the concept of God." Mikhail (1990), 40. The conclusion of his presentation is, at best, a monotheism. However, the *Christian* conception is far more than that. More specifically, no argument is offered for the Trinity; no reference is given to the doctrines contained in the Nicene Creed.
39 Indicative of his future use of "self-consciousness" in an argument for the existence of God was one of Mikhail's first publications already in March 1882 entitled "The Development of the Representation of the 'I' in Humanity."
40 Mikhail (1990), 75.

the metaphysical question of God's existence and shows the truth of the Christian conception of God's existence, i.e., that this concept fully corresponds to the Unconditional Being as it is in itself."[41] But in the final analysis the Orthodox Christian faithful need no empirical proofs. In the speech he delivered before the defense of his *magister*'s thesis, Mikhail became harshly dogmatic, even nationalistic. "The foundations and dogmas of the Orthodox faith must be for us the bases and dogmas of our national existence."[42] All who wish to be truly human and understand their true humanity must accept Orthodox teaching.[43]

A classmate at the Petersburg Academy and who remained there as a professor was Aleksandr P. Vysokoostrovskij (1860–1912). Graduating in 1885, he was appointed to teach logic and psychology the following year. With Debol'skij's departure from the Academy and his own distaste for teaching psychology, Vysokoostrovskij applied for the newly-opened position teaching metaphysics and logic. The application was successful, and he held the professorship until his death. Unfortunately, he published little, and information on him is comparatively scarce.[44] He did pen several short pieces on Karpov, which given Vysokoostrovskij's teaching of logic suggest that he too took a psychologistic approach. On the other hand, his resounding disinterest in teaching psychology suggests he sought to distance himself from the subject. Thus, whether he personally held a psychologistic view of logic or taught it in class must remain open for now.

8.4 Serebrenikov on Psychology and Mirtov Against Nietzsche

Svetilin's illness, mentioned in Chapter 5, forced him to step aside from teaching, resulting in an interruption in the instruction of psychology at the Academy. Debol'skij took it over in September 1884 on a temporary basis. Entrusting a basic required course to a visiting lecturer was an unusual occurrence, but the need was pressing. When Debol'skij left the Academy, Vysokoostrovskij assumed the teaching of psychology, but he soon in 1886 solicited for a new graduate of the Academy to

---

41 Mikhail (1990), 80. The question remains unaddressed whether this Unconditional Being is the *Christian* conception of God.
42 Mikhail (1888), 730.
43 The virulent nationalism in Mikhail's remarks, particularly charging all those who do not accept Orthodox Christianity of lacking humanity, is not just deeply disturbing in light of much recent history, but quite outrageous from one who called himself a "Christian."
44 "[Vysokoostrovskij] wrote little and could not even defend a *magister*'s thesis, but he was a good lecturer and an indulgent mentor." Karpuk (2016), 15.

take on the job.⁴⁵ Vitalij S. Serebrenikov (1862–1942), who had just graduated with a *kandidat*'s thesis on "English Psychology and the Question of Innate Principles of Knowledge and Activity" and had an outstanding record, was thought by all concerned, particularly Vysokoostrovskij, to be the specialist needed to teach psychology. Serebrenikov went on to defend a *magister*'s thesis in 1892 on "Locke's Doctrine of Innate Principles of Knowledge and Activity" – clearly an expanded version of his previous *kandidat*'s work. The Holy Synod approved Serebrenikov's application to study in Germany and France for one year, from August 1892.⁴⁶ Spending an entire semester with Wundt in Leipzig, he saw the experimental techniques employed there.⁴⁷

Although Serebrenikov did write on early modern philosophy, his work was largely of an expository character. He rejected a traditional designation of Locke as a sensualist on the grounds that Locke accepted that the mind had faculties of understanding and reflection in addition to that of sensation. Locke objected not to innate faculties and desires, but to innate concepts and knowledge.⁴⁸ Serebrenikov wrote that a Christian firmly believes that Revelation provides the absolute truth about the nature of the human mind. Thus, to know whether Locke's psychological views of the mind are correct we must simply compare them, with their supposedly scientific character, to Christian doctrine, and Serebrenikov concluded that Locke's *basic* theses do fully agree with Revelation. This concurrence, however, did not extend to Locke's views on morality, which were largely egoistic, and freedom of the will, which he conceived to be an empty apparition. Christian doctrine views the moral aspiration as *sui generis*, irreducible to egoism, and the free will is a creative force, by means of which the human individual develops a moral character. In these matters as well as in that of the materiality of the human mind, Locke's opinions contradict the Christian conception.⁴⁹

In the early years of the twentieth century, Serebrenikov further developed his interest in modern philosophy, shifting his focus slightly from Locke to Leibniz. He held that a number of German commentators on the Locke-Leibniz dispute, such

---

45 Stebenev (2017), 99.
46 That Russian secular philosophers were not totally oblivious to the scholarship emanating from the theological academies is shown again by Aleksej Kozlov's broadly sympathetic review of Serebrenikov's thesis/book. See Kozlov (1892).
47 In late 1908/early 1909, Serebrenikov submitted to the Academy a dissertation on "Leibniz and His Doctrine of the Human Mind" for the degree of doctor of theology. Of the twelve people present at the deciding meeting, three objected, arguing that the dissertation had little, if any, theological content. Nonetheless, the majority favored awarding the degree. Shindarov (2011), 177.
48 Serebrenikov (1892), 488–489.
49 Serebrenikov (1892), 492.

as Kuno Fischer, accepted a prejudice, stemming from Leibniz himself, that saw Locke and the German philosopher as holding quite different views on innate ideas. For Serebrenikov, however, the dispute rested on a misunderstanding, but the bases of that misunderstanding had been provided by Locke himself.[50] In short, Serebrenikov was a conscientious scholar of the history of philosophy, but he contributed nothing of significance to Russian philosophy, as such, and certainly nothing to world philosophy.

Nevertheless, Serebrenikov's principal interest was psychology, not philosophy, and he was particularly enthralled with the development of experimental psychology. Many of his writings were a defense of it against possible objections from traditionalists, who would rely solely on Scripture buttressed by introspection. Serebrenikov expressed the hope in one of his essays for the house organ of the Petersburg Academy that experimental investigations would affirm and elucidate the existence of the personal soul and that these investigations would attest to the veracity of Revelation. One particular facet of this affirmation, which he believed materialistic and positivistic theories of the mind rejected, was the unity of the individual consciousness as an irreducible entity. Even a portrayal of thought processes as mechanical presupposes a personal unity.[51] All of us are aware that we are individuals with a creative potential, that our thoughts, feelings, and desires are manifestations of our selves, but that they do not exhaust our selves. We are more than them though they are part of us. To be sure, however, introspection, which Serebrenikov termed "self-revelation," is our sole means of obtaining immediate knowledge of our personal mental life and through its mediation we obtain knowledge of mental activity in others.[52] He, thereby, implicitly endorsed an analogical argument for knowledge of others' minds.

Serebrenikov had very little to say about the traditional issues plaguing philosophy. In particular, one searches in vain for his own informed treatment of psychologism, despite a commemorative essay from 1898 on Karpov, which summarizes the latter's views without critical comment.[53] In light of this neglect, Serebrenikov appears on the fringes of our concern here. His work, however valuable for the

---

[50] Serebrenikov (1901), 690.
[51] Serebrenikov (1897a), 389–390.
[52] Serebrenikov (1897b), 439.
[53] A contemporary scholar, A. V. Shevcov, writes, "It is clear from Serebrenikov's works and from those of other scholars that they still understood logic and the theory of cognition as belonging together with psychology, something Serebrenikov clearly showed through the example of Karpov's logic." Shevcov (2017), 269. Shevcov merely references Serebrenikov's writings without page references, let alone demonstrating through Serebrenikov's words that he believed logic should be held "as part of a behavioral theory."

spread of experimental psychology in Russia, must be evaluated in terms of its scientific merit, not for its contribution to Russian philosophy. An active member of the St. Petersburg Philosophical Society founded in 1897, Serebrenikov also was named a professor of psychology at the Psycho-Neurological Institute, located in the capital. After the October Revolution, he held various teaching and research positions in psychology and even for a time in the history of philosophy. These, in time, all ceased, and with the increasing repression and the abrupt termination of a pension and any teaching or research opportunities, Serebrenikov left Petersburg for his native Vyatka region, where he worked at a local library until his death in January 1942.[54]

We turn lastly to Dmitrij P. Mirtov (1867–1941), who also came from a clerical background. He entered the Petersburg Academy in 1887 and graduated four years later, presenting as his *kandidat*'s thesis a work entitled "Clement of Alexandria, as Moralist." Mirtov would in time expand this into a *magister*'s thesis, changing the title ever so slightly to "The Moral Doctrine of Clement of Alexandria." Immediately after his graduation from the Academy, he began teaching philosophy, logic, psychology, and pedagogy at a theological seminary, where he remained for three years until December 1894, when he began teaching at the Petersburg Academy. He obtained a doctorate in theology in 1914 with a dissertation entitled "Lotze's Doctrine of the Human Spirit and the Absolute Spirit." With the closing of the theological academies in the wake of the events of 1917, Mirtov began teaching at Petrograd University (1919–1921) and then at the city's Pedagogical Academy. His main source of income, though, was working at the city's public library, where he served first as a cataloger, then in time as a librarian. He retired in 1929, applying and receiving a pension, and died in 1941 during the blockade of Leningrad.

Mirtov's interests, unlike some other figures, hardly ventured beyond the history of philosophy.[55] Judging from the topics of his thesis and dissertations, he remained throughout his teaching career at the Academy an uncontroversial figure who upheld Church doctrines and attitudes. Turning to an address he delivered in 1905 at the Academy, we can surmise that he, consistent with the official Orthodox Church policy, saw the political disturbances of the day in ethical terms. In this address he contrasted Kant's ethics to that of Nietzsche. Whereas Kant wrote that duty and absolute norms superseded personal desires, inclinations, and instincts,

---

54 For more biographical information, see Shindarov (2011), 181–184.
55 Of some interest is Mirtov's summary of Solov'ëv's philosophical writings published in 1900 following Solov'ëv's death. Even those within the Orthodox Church could not withhold according some recognition to him despite whatever reservations they may have harbored of the orthodoxy of his views. Mirtov called Solov'ëv "the most popular representative of Russian philosophical thought in the past quarter century." Mirtov (1900), 620.

Nietzsche, according to Mirtov, the most popular and most stirring German philosophical mind of the day, would have it the other way round.[56] Mirtov asked: "What does this new theory of moral autonomy provide? Does it replace what Kant had established? Here too as in theoretical philosophy the appeal should be repeated: 'Back to Kant'!"[57] Kant's ethical views stand close to both Christian morality and generally accepted morals, whereas Nietzsche's views can be summed up as a rejection of God, truth, the moral good, or, in short, against everything on which the entire moral structure of contemporary society rests.[58]

Much of the Russian philosophical community during Mirtov's time reacted in horror at the influence Nietzsche's thought had acquired. It attacked their cherished metaphysical beliefs and ethical values. The community's fear was rooted not so much in the logic of Nietzsche's thought as a philosophical doctrine, as in what they saw as its potential cultural significance, that it could loosen the grip of traditional political and religio-moral values. Mirtov, in reaction, raced to Kant, whom he saw not as creating a new moral theory, but a new foundation or way of looking at the Gospel message of love and justice. Mirtov was doubtlessly intrigued with Kant's dichotomy between theoretical and practical reason, which allowed for the free will and thereby morality. Additionally, Mirtov expressed support for Kant's view that the pure moral will, a will unhindered by desires and inclinations, is the source of the moral law and that it, as moral, found its fulfillment in respect for duty. Mirtov summarized his seemingly unqualified support for Kant with the closing words of his three-part address to the Petersburg Academy thus:

> If philosophy actually enters onto this path, it can successfully and productively undertake it, having returned to Kant, who determined the *a priori* forms and laws of cognitive, aesthetic, and moral activity. He, in particular, advanced the primacy of practical reason or the will.[59]

The tragedy for Russian philosophy is that Mirtov kept his Kantian convictions so quiet without developing or advocating for their acceptance.

The wake of the Revolution in 1905 brought to the four academies new "Provisional Regulations," which were intended to produce calm to all institutions of higher learning within the Russian Empire. The academies were no longer bound to the Holy Synod, which some saw as liberation and some as a victory for liberalism. Following the rules of the Provisional Regulations, a vote for the rectorship was held for the first time in the Petersburg Academy's history in April

---

56 Mirtov (1905a), 313–314.
57 Mirtov (1905a), 314.
58 Mirtov (1905a), 318.
59 Mirtov (1905b), 608.

1908. Censorship was also relaxed after 1905, allowing for the free discussion of the reforms in higher education and the problems arising from them. For example, the usually silent Vysokoostrovskij published in 1906 an essay "On the Right of the Theological Academies to Award Scholarly Degrees in Philosophy."[60] Such a topic could not possibly have been raised in a public arena earlier.

Whether viewed with rejoicing or dread, however, the liberal period was short-lived. Already in 1908–1909 the Holy Synod initiated an inspection of the four academies, resulting in the dismissal of three professors from the Petersburg Academy, a most unusual turn of events. The mood in both the country's higher educational institutions and in society was to change rapidly in response to the pace of the political reaction and hastened even more by world events.

---

60 See Vysokoostrovskij (1906).

Chapter 9
Philosophy at the Moscow Academy Under the Third Charter

We saw in the last chapter that any image we might have of Russian seminarians and academy students as being quite apolitical and socially conservative needs to be adjusted. On the whole, the picture of academic complacency is, indeed, compelling. However, it would also be incorrect to think that any politicization of the student body that occurred in the theological academies was due *solely* to the spreading of some socio-political "infection" from outside agitation. By no means did a large number of the students succumb or were even susceptible to an externally transmitted political virus. Rather, there were endemic causes for unrest within these higher educational institutions. In the mid-1890s, some high-placed church officials turned their attention and criticism to scholarly works emanating from the academies, which they regarded as unacceptable. For example, Pobedonoscev and some members of the Holy Synod were displeased with the very topic of a *magister*'s thesis by Mikhail M. Tareev, a Moscow Academy graduate, on "The Temptations of the Divine Man" and rejected in 1893 his application for the degree.[1]

Tareev's case was but one instance. There had already been others.[2] As mentioned, not all parties were pleased with the new 1884 Charter, but tensions only increased with a decree from the Holy Synod in February 1889 entitled "Rules for the Examination of Works Presented for Academic Degrees." These rules stipulated that theses submitted for the degrees of *magister* and doctorate had to agree with the spirit and teachings of the Orthodox Church and not present an incorrect view on the origin, character, and significance of the Church's institutions, customs, and traditions.[3] Pobedonoscev became particularly incensed in 1894/95 with the scholarly work contained in the journals and dissertations emanating from the academies. However, he was not alone in expressing dissatisfaction with the state of affairs at the academies. In September 1895 a new rector attempted to institute discipline at the Academy, resulting in further student disruption.

---

[1] Sukhova (2006), 10. Tareev's writings will be discussed later in this chapter.
[2] Evgenij E. Golubinskij (1834–1912) in December 1880 defended a dissertation for a doctorate in theology in a marathon session at the Moscow Academy. Pobedonoscev, who had only recently been appointed to his position, held up the degree for a half-year. Nikolaj F. Kapterev (1847–1917) successfully defended his dissertation for a doctorate in church history in 1885, but Pobedonoscev overturned the decision by the Academic Council of the Moscow Academy.
[3] Sukhova (2006), 8f.

The Holy Synod sent a member of its Educational Committee to investigate. Petr I. Nechaev (1842–1905), himself a graduate of the Petersburg Academy, managed only to further inflame tensions in Moscow. He charged, for one thing, that the students were lax in class attendance and at certain church services. He also found irregularities in the financing of the Academy. Nechaev's resulting report was found to be insulting by thirteen of the Academy's professors, who sent their objections to the Holy Synod. Pobedonoscev took these professorial remarks as itself evidence of lax morality and decreed that students absolutely must attend lectures and professors must seek to inspire and maintain students' attention. In the eyes of the chief procurator, the professors' objections had set a poor example to students of "illegal democracy."[4]

9.1 Ostroumov and Sokolov on German Idealism and Faith

As with many figures we have already seen, Mikhail A. Ostroumov (1847/48–1920)[5] taught for only a few years at the Moscow Academy, lecturing on the history of philosophy and basic theology from 1884. He was invited by the Academy in 1883 to apply for the position to teach the history of philosophy. One requirement, which he duly attended to, was to present and defend a *magister*'s thesis. Another requirement was to give two lectures, one of his own choosing and another specified by the Academy, the lectures serving as a test of his suitability for the teaching position. The surely hastily composed thesis, "History of Philosophy in Relation to Revelation," held that philosophical systems could be viewed as a succession of chains, the links in these chains being internally connected and dependent on each other.[6] Each system contained some truth in speaking of the same object, but they differed in presenting different points of view.[7] For the first of the two

---

[4] Sukhova (2006), 14.
[5] According to the Julian calendar then in use in Imperial Russia, Ostroumov was born on 30 December 1847, which is 11 January 1848 by today's Gregorian calendar.
[6] Given the sophistication of the thesis in terms of argument and style it is unlikely that Ostroumov did *all* the work involved in preparing his thesis in one year before its defense in March 1884 or even in the two-three year period before its journal publication in 1886. He, most likely, already had extensive notes assembled from his previous teaching positions and publications on the history of philosophy.
[7] Denisov (1906), 10. Denisov also reported that Andrej P. Smirnov (1843–1896), who taught at the Academy, offered several objections at the thesis defense. Smirnov, as a quite conservative defender of Orthodox religious teachings and of the Bible, could not abide such a magnanimous outlook on the history of philosophy. Denisov also relates that Ostroumov became acquainted with Vladimir Solov'ëv during the latter's occasional visits, presumably during the early to mid-1880s, to the

test lectures, Ostroumov spoke on "The Significance of Socrates in the History of Philosophical Doctrines," and the second lecture, the one of his choosing, was "Kant's Doctrine of Reason." Clearly, he performed satisfactorily, for he was offered and accepted the job.

Coming from a clerical background, Ostroumov in his youth took the unusual step, though certainly one not without precedent, of enrolling at St. Petersburg University. He soon transferred, however, to the Medical-Surgical Academy and then to the Moscow Theological Academy in 1870. Upon completion of the program there, he taught at various seminaries. His 1879–1880 two-volume *Obzor filosofskikh uchenij* [*Survey of Philosophical Doctrines*] came to the attention of the Holy Synod and was selected as an approved textbook for seminary use. Its importance laid not in its acknowledged influence on others – there is scant reference either to it or to Ostroumov himself in the secondary literature up to the present – but as its detailed and understandable treatment of the history of philosophy with a particular emphasis on theories of cognition and metaphysics.[8] Particularly noteworthy is the absence of a direct subservience of philosophy to religion and religion in general to Orthodoxy. Ostroumov held that both religion and philosophy seek the same goal: to know about God, the world, and the human being. The difference between the two lies in their means of acquiring such knowledge. "Religion forms its worldview directly and originally, creatively producing basic ideas about the soul, God, and creation. Philosophy accepts these ideas as ready-made and seeks to assimilate, understand, and prove them rationally."[9] That they have two different approaches shows that one cannot replace the other. Both are equally necessary, since a more comprehensive possession of truth is always better than a one-sided possession. Moreover, since both are necessary and should exist along parallel tracks independently of each other, both should recognize the other's right to access and reveal the truth. Both should recognize that the existence of the other is mutually beneficial.

Moscow Academy. In one evening conversation in Solov'ëv's hotel room, Ostroumov expressed his idea to Solov'ëv that there should be a philosophical journal similar to the theological journal at the Moscow Academy and that just as the Academy had an ongoing publishing series "Works of the Holy Fathers in Russian Translation with Supplements," so too could there be a series "Works of Philosophers in Russian Translation with Supplementary Philosophical Investigations." Denisov (1906), 17. Could Ostroumov's suggestion be behind Solov'ëv's suggestion to Nikolaj Grot that a "Philosophical Library" be established along with *Voprosy filosofii?* For the suggestion, see Nemeth (2019), 54. Denisov also relates that Solov'ëv gave Ostroumov a copy of his *Religious Foundations of Life* with the inscription "To a Sympathizer in the Heresy of Development."

8 "The first question that should and does concern philosophy is that of the veracity of our cognitions." Ostroumov (1879), 45.

9 Ostroumov (1879), 6f.

Another concern of Ostroumov's was quite topical in his day, namely that of the role of philosophy with the rapid expansion and advances of natural science. Again he supported philosophy as an independent inquiry, claiming it concerns itself with aspects of its object that none of the sciences do. This, he advanced, should not strike us as strange. Physiology deals with the workings of the human organism, whereas anatomy deals with its structure. Philosophy takes the results of the natural sciences and seeks to explain their common connection. It, thereby, views the sciences on the whole in their dependence on the absolute.[10]

Ostroumov's stance on the independence of philosophy was neither particularly striking nor uncommon, but as the title of his two-volume work indicates the main focus of that work is the history of philosophy. We cannot, of course, illustrate, let alone comment, on all of the figures and movements Ostroumov discussed ranging from the Greeks to his own day. Still, it is interesting to note that whereas in his first volume he devoted approximately nine pages each to Descartes and Hume, he devoted 34 to Kant. Ostroumov eloquently presented in clear terms what we could call the classic Russian Orthodox critique of Kantian epistemology. He thought the weak point lies in its quite arbitrary separation of the forms of cognition from its content or manifold. As a result of this unwarranted dichotomy, Kant, in effect, fell into the same skepticism that Hume did, even though the former thought he had refuted the latter. One certainly can agree with Kant that certain forms are always necessarily and universally given with the content of our intuitions. But Kant drew from this erroneous conclusions. Kant did not provide the grounds to deduce that those forms cannot be just as objective as the content. "The fact that the universal and necessary is given *a priori* and the particular and contingent *a posteriori* shows only that they are given by different means. But these different means of givenness do not prevent us from relating to cognitive objects."[11] The Kantian forms of cognition can be seen as all the more objective since they are universal and necessary unlike other perceived qualities of objects, which, being contingent, can vary depending on, for example, the lighting or the physical condition of the perceiver. The objectivity of the Kantian forms is clearly revealed in the fact that unlike *a posteriori* qualities the forms always appear to us as objective. That they always appear as objective clearly reveals their objectivity. Since perceived things have objectivity and the Kantian forms are that in which these things exist, the forms are as objective as are the things themselves. They are not, as Kant held, merely forms of our cognitive faculty.

---

10 Ostroumov (1879), 11.
11 Ostroumov (1879), 157.

Having cavalierly dispensed with Kant does not mean that Ostroumov accepted, as did so many Russian philosophers of the time, a reliance on some mystical epistemic faculty or a direct intuitivism. If we substitute some direct givenness of externality via a mystical intuition to our cognitive faculty at the expense of our five senses and reason, we abandon the trustworthiness of experience, for there is no means of verifying such alleged cognition.[12] Surely our observations and our reasoning are often wrong, but these errors arise from the use of our faculties and not from the very nature of observation and of reason. To appeal to some immediate intuition in place of our traditional modes of inquiry is to open ourselves up to an arbitrary interpretation and understanding of the facts. "Owing to the substitution of the subjective for the objective, the real world appears to the mystic not as it is, but as one imagines it on the basis of purely subjective suggestions of one's personal feeling."[13] Moreover, it is quite impossible to dispel the mystic's self-delusion, for he determines truth not by evidential facts, but by an allegedly direct, subjective intuition.

Although quite dissatisfied with both Kantianism and intuitivism, Ostroumov recognized that the human mind cannot embrace all of existence at once. The basis of the formation of a single coherent worldview must lie outside it. Certainly, our minds are inherently prone to analysis, but not to synthesis.[14] In this, Ostroumov distinguished himself from so many in that he not only cherished science, but saw the scientific endeavor as an essential human one. Left on one's own, the human being analyzes, whereas one needs synthesis as well. Ostroumov concluded that such a unification of analytic elements and the principle behind it can be found in religion, which presents to us a direct revelation of the absolute. Thus, both science and religion are necessary for a harmonious human life.

Ostroumov's *magister*'s thesis, like his earlier *Obzor*, is much too large to examine in detail here, but there is no need to do so. Ostroumov sought to show that the development of both ancient philosophy and modern philosophy (essentially up to his own day, albeit with major lacunae) came to recognize religious revelation as the source and the outcome of all cognition. Dividing the history of modern philosophy as well as ancient philosophy into periods, Ostroumov found that

---

12 Ostroumov (1879), 211.
13 Ostroumov (1879), 212. For Ostroumov, an appeal to direct intuition, such as that proposed later by N.O. Lossky is a form of mysticism.
14 Ostroumov, in the second volume of his work, criticized Schelling for his unscientificity, for identifying things in the absolute. "Merging the differences between things or their properties does not mean explaining these differences, but, on the contrary, it means making things indistinguishable ... and eliminating any possibility of representing or explaining them." Ostroumov (1880), 72.

philosophy in its first period sought to understand cognition by turning to the workings of the mind. In its second period, philosophy referred the mind to the idea of an absolute.[15] Presumably, Ostroumov meant that the human mind is to be understood as a finite form of an absolute subject, the self-consciousness from which all objects of cognition ultimately ensue. He gives here J.G. Fichte as an example, thereby understanding Fichte's relentless project of a *Wissenschaftslehre* as ontological, indeed an abstract theological one, rather than epistemological. In this telling, the absolute is next understood not as a subject but as an object, an absolute object that dynamically develops to ground the finite. This stage in the historical development of philosophy is represented by Schelling before the emergence of Hegel's mature system, which then finally sees the absolute as an idea. In each of these cases, the absolute enters into the finite human self-consciousness as forms. Given its finitude, the human self-consciousness cannot hold more than this of the absolute.[16]

Ostroumov concluded that the philosophical endeavor in both antiquity and in the modern period passed from a somewhat narrowly conceived philosophical sphere to a religious sphere. For him, the speculative philosophies of German Idealism and even onward to his own day, represented, for example, by such a figure as Immanuel Fichte, were only interpretations of religion. Ostroumov could not conceive the philosophical enterprise outside this veritable intellectual straitjacket. He viewed philosophy and its entire history as a choice between skepticism or the acceptance of religious revelation as a philosophical principle around which all else devolved. "Skepticism, however, cannot serve as an independent philosophical principle. Therefore, the religious worldview remains for our time the sole refuge and can alone provide a point of support."[17] A study of the history of modern philosophy shows that philosophers have gradually realized this and have endeavored to seek assistance in religion just as they did in antiquity. Ostroumov made no mention of Solov'ëv in this context. Thus, whether the former's view was influenced in any way by the latter's *Crisis of Western Philosophy* or was "in the air" at the time must remain conjectural. Nevertheless, the theme of a termination of philosophical development in religion would surely have received approval in theological circles.

After merely three years at the Moscow Academy, Ostroumov in 1887 accepted a position at Kharkov University teaching church law in addition to logic and the

---

15 Ostroumov (1886), 166.
16 Ostroumov (1886), 167.
17 Ostroumov (1886), 168.

history of philosophy and with that he falls outside the scope of our study here.[18] He managed to publish a number of other works, including a sizable tome in 1893 *Introduction to Orthodox Church Law*, which represented his doctoral dissertation. This and his other works were largely unrelated to philosophy. He had a distinguished career in Kharkov which included many additional administrative and honorary functions. In the early years of the twentieth century, Ostroumov forcefully championed conservative, monarchist political policies and opposed any reformist concessions believing that they could only lead to social disintegration. Shortly before his death, he was appointed a professor of church law at the newly formed Taurida University in Crimea.

Ostroumov was just one of several figures who at this time while teaching at the Moscow Academy wrote on topics traditionally conceived under the rubric of philosophy. Another such person was Pavel P. Sokolov (1863–1912), who entered the Academy in 1884 and completed his studies there four years later. He was retained through a fellowship for one year and then appointed to lecture on psychology. In successive years, he also taught French. He defended in 1906 his *magister*'s thesis, which he had already published serially in the journal *Voprosy filosofii i psikhologii* in 1902. As we can see from these brief biographical facts, Sokolov's primary interest was in psychology, not philosophy, but given the blurred line separating the two disciplines at the time it was not unusual to write on both. Indicative of this are two works from the early 1890s.

Published over three issues (February, March, and April) of the journal *Pravoslavnoe obozrenie* [*Orthodox Review*] in 1890 and written while in Germany the previous year, Sokolov examined a broad gamut of philosophical thought that included Schopenhauer and von Hartmann, Lotze and Wundt and even devoted several pages to the budding neo-Kantian movement and its various factions, which he found to have only undeveloped, contradictory and disparate theoretical views on the Kantian thing in itself.[19] Sokolov concluded his detailed survey of recent German philosophy with the pronouncement that it was progressing toward the truth. Given his preference for experimental psychology, we may not be surprised that he valued its turn to experience and the natural sciences, its inherent scientificity and logical precision, all qualities which he thought could be found in Lotze.[20]

---

[18] While still teaching at the Moscow Academy he wrote an essay on Thales, which appeared in the journal *Vera i razum* in December 1887. Of course, by this time he had already departed for Kharkov.
[19] Sokolov (1890)), 623.
[20] Sokolov (1890), 640.

What his colleagues at the Moscow Academy may have thought of Sokolov's conclusions is unrecorded, but they must have had firm misgivings. However, a work of his a few years later would surely have returned him to their good graces. His "Doctrine of the Holy Trinity in the Latest Idealistic Philosophy" serialized between 1893 and 1896 juxtaposed the Christian conception of the Trinity to its treatment in Fichte, Schelling, and Hegel.[21] Sokolov minced no words in writing that German Idealism, despite wishing not to reject Christianity outright, contradicts it in principle. "In fact, what can be found more alien to the spirit and doctrine of Christianity than the systems of the latest German Idealism?"[22] These German philosophers obfuscate the issue by asserting that Christianity is the true philosophy, because their own philosophies are the true understanding of Christianity. Sokolov will have nothing of this. German Idealism presents neither the idea of a transcendent, personal God nor that of an independent, immortal human soul. Additionally, there is nothing in any of these philosophical systems that corresponds to the idea of a relation between God and the human individual.

Without remarking on the dissemination of similar ideas to those of the German Idealists by Russian philosophers of the time, Sokolov condemned what he saw as the decidedly un-Christian and pantheistic conception of the Absolute propounded by the Germans. Their conception is an empty abstraction devoid of content. Their god is both everything and nothing, since it is not the Christian God, but merely an aggregate of empirical, finite phenomena. Sokolov questioned why these idealists did not recognize their departure from Christianity and did not stand forthwith in opposition to it as did their proclaimed descendants such as Feuerbach.

The German Idealists with the partial exception of Schelling cared little about the genuine meaning of the Trinity and found it unnecessary to harmonize their

---

21 Years later at an address before the defense of his *magister*'s thesis in 1902 – but published only in 1906! – Sokolov wrote that this work on the Trinity was left incomplete – apparently he initially intended it to be his thesis – and was an elaboration of his undergraduate (*kandidatur*) thesis. See Sokolov (1906), 270. One reason he gave for the abandonment of completing the work was his full-throated opposition to writing on heretical and false doctrines. Sokolov found it incomprehensible how one could search for truth if one could not point out errors. If the purpose of this prohibition "was supposed to serve as a quarantine against any kind of mental infection, then the question arises: whose minds are being protected from heretical microbes? The minds of readers of theological theses? But who reads theological theses? After all, they are read in most cases, of course, by specialists, that is, people who have acquired complete immunity from mental infection. Or, perhaps, the minds of the authors of these learned works themselves? ... Is this not similar to the idea of forbidding physicians from writing about cholera for fear that they might contract it?" Sokolov (1906), 271.
22 Sokolov (1893s), 351.

own views with church teachings. They simply ignored the dogma of the Trinity, which was to be taken verbatim and obligatory for Christians, and saw it as a formula that could be interpreted in various ways. From their viewpoint, official Church doctrine, whether it concerned the Trinity or other matters, was a misunderstanding that could find its "true" sense in philosophy, provided, that is, that it be their own philosophy.[23] All Christian dogmas were but empty forms, the content of which they and only they could fill as they thought fit. A distinctive difference with official Christianity in general is that whereas the Church believed the Trinity was to be taken on faith, the Germans believed it could be the object of philosophy and comprehended by clever machinations.

> The task of philosophy in unraveling the dogma of the Holy Trinity is not, in the opinion of the German Idealists, to bow before the authority of faith and follow its instructions, but to examine the reality behind the symbolic images of faith, to cognize the Divine essence behind the subjective appearances.[24]

Sokolov saw the development of German Protestant theology up to his own day as based on the principles and ideas promulgated by the Idealists. However heretical he may have seen the Christianity professed by the German Idealists, he also ventured that once their philosophical constructions were stripped of terminological obfuscations and wordplay anyone would surely notice that they were devoid of philosophical depth. Indeed, these constructions would lose all sense.[25]

Whereas his publications in the 1890s forcefully conveyed his rather negative attitude toward German Idealism, Sokolov delivered his overall assessment of the philosophical endeavor in general only in his address before his thesis defense in 1902. He, with his self-identification as a psychologist, contrasted philosophy to natural science but first stated that both sought to explain the universe. They otherwise diverged, however, in terms of their objects and their respective means of explaining. Science seeks explanations through observation to establish properties, causes, and laws.[26] Philosophy, though, seeks to understand the ideal meaning of phenomena, to establish their bases, goals, and norms. Being directed toward ideals not facts, philosophy cannot prove that something considered absolutely valuable is absolutely real. Kant showed that what lies beyond experience is thereby un-

---

23 Sokolov (1893b), 406.
24 Sokolov (1893b), 414. Again, although Sokolov does not mention Solov'ëv by name, it is hard not to wonder whether the former had the latter in mind. For more on Solov'ëv's own "philosophical" treatment of the Trinity, see Nemeth (2014), 91, 107. Also see Soloviev (2013), 195–202.
25 Sokolov (1893b), 427.
26 Sokolov (1906), 284.

knowable and cannot be firmly discussed except in terms of faith. Kant's invocation of the "thing in itself" was the greatest misunderstanding in his first *Critique*, and with it he restored a dualism of thought and reality found in earlier metaphysical systems.[27]

Sokolov's colleagues at the Academy must have been distressed with his outright declaration that the age of ontological metaphysics had irrevocably passed. Metaphysics cannot be a theory of what is, but a theory of values. "It must clarify not the factually given, but the theoretically necessary; not what is, but what should be; not the real, but the ideal."[28] Thus, the goal of philosophy is the elucidation and clarification of values, of their absolute necessity in life. We must believe in the traditional trichotomy of truth, goodness, and beauty in order to make life true, good, and beautiful.

9.2 Three Moral Theorists in Moscow

Not all works devoted to issues traditionally labeled philosophy and emanating from the theological academies were written by instructors of philosophy. Given the traditional and popular linkage between the implementation of the religious message and "practical philosophy," i.e., ethics, we can hardly be surprised that many theology instructors at the academies took it on themselves to write not just commentaries on select portions of the Bible and on the Church Fathers, but also on morality. One such figure was Ivan V. Popov (1867–1938), a student of the Moscow Academy from 1888–1892, who then was retained for one year on a fellowship. In 1893 he began to teach patristics. With the successful defense of his *magister*'s thesis, "Natural Moral Law," his position was raised from acting docent to docent.[29] He spent a year at the universities of Berlin and Munich in 1901–1902. In later years, he also taught the history of Patristics at Moscow University and elsewhere.

Popov's participation in the development of Russian philosophy, however modest, was largely expressed by his thesis, a highly scholarly treatise that relied on many historical figures, but comparatively few Russian ones. Nonetheless, from its very start we can find Popov's unexpressed allegiance together with the later Solov'ëv on the innateness of the moral law in the human individual, i.e., the moral law written in the human heart. "This hidden impulse in human nature

---

27 Sokolov (1906), 287–288.
28 Sokolov (1906), 295.
29 His thesis was first published serially in the house organ of the Moscow Academy, *Bogoslovskij vestnik*, in 1896–1898.

made virtue possible among peoples who did not know Revelation."³⁰ As did Solov'ëv, Popov appealed to St. Paul's authority for his claim. To a qualified extent, then, Popov too could affirm the independence of morality from religion. Whereas, however, the assumption of unmistakably religious theses undermines Solov'ëv's assertion of the autonomy of ethics, Popov, by not venturing into normative ethics or even developing a narrowly confined metaethics to the extent that Solov'ëv did, could remain unscathed by the objection. Popov held that the Jew, pagan, or atheist could not appeal to ignorance when confronting God's justice for his iniquities. The sinful non-Christian, just like the Christian, must be mindful of the "inner voice" of one's conscience and will be condemned for not heeding it at the Last Judgment. The Church Fathers indicated the existence within each of us of this innate impulse to goodness and showed that the doctrine of natural moral law is found in the Holy Scriptures. They sought to explain the meaning of natural law and its relation to the revealed law of morality.

Popov considered the theory of evolution to be a new weapon in the arsenal of those who denied both moral absolutes and the innate character of at least a rudimentary moral law. These evolutionists, in his eyes, upheld the contingency and relativity of morality, a position contrary not just to religion but also to public morality. He claimed, however, that the basis of the evolutionists' view rested on misunderstandings and a superficial knowledge of primitive cultures and their languages. Anthropologists have found that even the most primitive peoples exhibit a rather high level of moral development. Thus, in terms of his overall attitude toward evolution Popov supported a most conservative position, although it must be said that he limited himself to what he took to be the moral consequences of it as interpreted largely by such a figure as Herbert Spencer. In this, Popov stood in marked contrast to Solov'ëv, for whom Darwin was to be commended for singling out that human beings have an innate moral feeling and for disengaging aesthetics from utilitarianism in the animal world.³¹

Popov believed that the theory of evolution denied the innate character of the moral law and for this reason remained incompatible with Christian doctrine but was consistent and, indeed, intimately connected with utilitarianism. According to Christian doctrine, our recognition of the supremacy of the moral law over our in-

---

30 Popov (1897), xii. Revelation, nevertheless, is necessary since the "quiet voice" of conscience is only too often drowned out or distorted by that of the passions. In the absence of reference, we can again only conjecture whether Popov was aware of Solov'ëv's similar introduction of St. Paul's invocation of the innate character of the moral law. However, what became the "Introduction" to Solov'ëv's *Justification of the Moral Good* first appeared in late 1894 as an essay in the very popular journal *Vestnik Evropy*, roughly three years earlier than Popov's work.
31 Solov'ëv (2015), 167–168.

nate sinfulness, as a result of the Fall, involves suffering. Thus, the achievement of goodness, contrary to utilitarian teaching, cannot be an empirical calculation of the maximum pleasure between competing alternative courses.

Popov also rejected in addition to utilitarianism Kant's ethical theory owing to its very formalism. No moral principle lacking a goal can determine how one should act. It is the persistence in attaining the goal of moral activity that imparts to individual actions and intentions their moral value. The fundamental moral goal is the unity of rational beings in thought, feeling, and will.[32] It is expressed in the feeling of love, the essence of which is the merger of the lover with the beloved in thought, feeling, and desire.[33] This unity is the objective side of morals, whereas love is its subjective side. As the goal of moral activity, the ideal of unity is the duty of all rational beings, and as such it is what they must strive to attain. "Only that will can be called good, which sincerely seeks unity with other beings with all of one's being."[34] This unity is also, in other words, an aspiration for harmony and order, and its attainment provides a pleasant feeling.[35] Utilitarianism's notion of harmony is a state of affairs when competing interests are reconciled. But even if such a reconciliation were possible, it would have a purely external character and could not be a unity of wills. The germ of disunity and enmity would still lurk in the hearts and minds of those involved. Egoism, in other words, would still lurk, only temporarily and superficially dispelled.

Our sense of duty is based on the "pressure" (*davlenie*) that the idea of the moral ideal exerts on our human will when there is within the will a conflict

---

[32] Popov (1897), 454.
[33] Solov'ëv had already published his work *The Meaning of Love* (*Smysl ljubvi*) serially in *Voprosy filosofii* between 1892–1894. Yet Popov oddly made no mention of it despite a similarity in theme and in its estimation of what love is. He became an active member of the Moscow Psychological Society, under whose auspices *Voprosy filosofii* was published, in 1897, which shows that he was interested in contemporary secular philosophy. Being such, Popov surely could have availed himself of Solov'ëv's the work when writing *Natural Moral Law*. His silence most likely was indicative of the official Church's wish to keep Solov'ëv at arm's length – preferably even farther. Solov'ëv wrote, "The meaning of human love, speaking generally, is the *justification and salvation of individuality through the sacrifice of egoism*. ... A human being (in general and every individual being in particular) ... may *become* all, only by doing away in his consciousness and life with that internal boundary which separates him from another." Solovyov (1985), 42, 45.
[34] Popov (1897), 455.
[35] Popov's introduction of feeling in this connection raises the issue whether the moral agent seeks harmony and unity for its own sake or for the sake of this "pleasant feeling." It is unclear how he could avoid a relapse into some form of eudaimonism. If, as he claims, the Christian doctrine of virtue is connected with suffering, must we not discount the pleasantness of harmony and order? But if we do so, are we not returning in effect to Kantian ethics?

with lower instincts and feelings stemming from externality.[36] The lesson Popov drew from these reflections based on his reading of the Bible is that an essential feature of human nature is a deep aspiration for a living unity with other rational and sensible creatures, manifested subjectively in love and objectively in a universal harmony of human wills.[37] Popov's metaethical beliefs were surely put to an extreme test in light of his subsequent fate.

Popov published in 1916 a large, comprehensive work on St. Augustine that he submitted as a doctoral dissertation and which he defended in 1917 at the Petersburg Academy. He continued to teach at the Moscow Academy until its closure in 1919. Popov taught philosophy for a time at Moscow University until that too became impossible. He was subsequently arrested several times receiving prison sentences for three years in each instance. His 1931 arrest resulted in a sentence of three years to internal exile. Whether because of his age and poor health or as rumored because no one else could be found to translate Latin for a planned publication, he was back in the vicinity of Moscow in 1932. The reprieve was short. In October 1937, he was again arrested on fabricated charges and summarily shot in February of the following year.

Popov's younger colleague by four years, Nikolaj G. Gorodenskij (1871–1906) taught moral theology, not philosophy, at the Moscow Academy until 1902. After that, he taught literature. He completed the course of studies at the Academy in 1895, receiving a *kandidat*'s degree and owing to his academic record he could seek a *magister*'s degree without having to sit for oral examinations. During the following academic year he remained at the Academy to prepare himself for filling one of the open vacancies. During that year, the school's academic council decided he should fill an opening in moral theology, and after reading two test lectures he began teaching in August 1896.[38]

During the first years after his appointment, Gorodenskij authored a number of studies leading up to his *magister*'s thesis. He demonstrated a special concern with innate ideas, which, as we saw, was of particular interest to Popov as well, even though the latter's focus was on morality. His individual essays on Descartes, Locke, and Leibniz are purely secondary studies and are of little interest to posterity. They scarcely reveal their author's own position. Of more interest is Gorodenskij's review of Solov'ëv's *Justification of the Moral Good* that had just appeared in a second edition. Gorodenskij charged Solov'ëv with attempting to coordinate his

---

[36] Popov (1897), 594. The naturalist could object here again that the moral agent dutifully acts in order to relieve this pressure and not out of a moral feeling at all.
[37] Popov's conception of love, while remarkably similar in the abstract to Solov'ëv's, differs from the latter's in its absence of a stress on sexual love.
[38] Iz akademicheskoj (1903), 575.

own thought with Christian doctrine, but he failed to recognize the irreducibility and essence of love in Christian teaching. Solov'ëv proclaimed love to be the goal of morality, not realizing that it is its fundamental principle. Instead, he asserted that love by itself has no moral value and thereby approached apostasy from the Christian standpoint.[39] Solov'ëv attempted to deduce morality from the feelings of shame, pity, and respect, but at least with regard to shame, his position is foreign to the words of both Jesus and St. Paul.[40]

In arguing against Solov'ëv and in support of love as the fundamental principle of morality, Gorodenskij also supported the primordiality of morality in human nature. Of course, in all of this he can be seen as one with Popov. But already in 1896, and thus during the year before the publication of Popov's thesis, Gorodenskij published a remarkable article that, in effect, already went one step beyond Popov. Whereas Popov was content to argue against, above all, the empiricists and the evolutionists, Gorodenskij, assuming human beings have morality and religion written in their hearts, invoked a psychological analysis of the subjective foundations of the link between morality and religion, a link that he held was necessary and not contingent. Religion did not impose a particular morality or moral code on humanity as a whole, but rather the individual religions intrinsically determine forms of morality such that the different religions are accompanied by particular forms of morality.[41] Gorodenskij was quick to point out that a specific set of metaphysical beliefs did not logically predetermine a certain moral code. Both metaphysics and morality are ultimately based on the spiritual make-up of a people, but once morality and religion are established within a society morality is subordinate to the religion. To deny this is to reject the most general of psychological laws. The foundations of religion and morality are, to a certain extent, the same in each of us, namely a dissatisfaction with empirical reality. This dissatisfaction is the main psychological basis of natural religion.[42]

Both religion and morality pose ideals. Religion strives for the ideal of being, and the latter for the ideal of activity. Both require faith in something apart from reality, a faith that demands reality submit or conform to it. At the same time, the religious ideal is placed in a superior position. "Since a person wishes that the ideal in life not turn out to be illusory and deceptive, one must find a basis for it in objective being."[43] A person wants to elevate the significance of one's ideals. Moral ideals are construed as objective laws that even the gods must heed. Such is,

---

39 Gorodenskij (1899), 318.
40 Gorodenskij (1899), 303–304.
41 Gorodenskij (1896), 196–197.
42 Gorodenskij (1896), 201.
43 Gorodenskij (1896), 202.

according to Gorodenskij, the established, i.e., proven, psychologically necessary connection between morality and religion. For a moral duty to become efficacious in practice, a moral agent must believe that that duty is part of the objective moral world order, that in addition to the physical laws governing the world there is a higher, albeit imperceptible, law that if followed will lead to the ultimate victory of the moral good over evil. This belief or faith is a major element in religious faith. "Confidence is needed for moral activity, and complete unconditional confidence is needed for its complete success. Such certainty is characteristic only of religion."[44]

In linking morality and religion and seeing the object of each as ideals, Gorodenskij has in effect provided ample grounds for us to conclude that for him all traditionally conceived religions are products of a fertile human imagination and nothing more, that even the Judeo-Christian conception of God is itself just a projection emanating from the human psyche, an ideal created to satisfy our longing for a better state of affairs. Such a reading would not be too dissimilar from that offered over a half-century earlier by Ludwig Feuerbach. We cannot help but be startled then when he asserts that the confidence required for fully successful moral activity can only be had with a firm conviction in the moral world order, which in turn can *only* be obtained through what he termed "constant spiritual communion with the supreme Source of this moral order."[45] The question Gorodenskij left unanswered here is how he transitioned from viewing the moral order as a psychological projection to an objectively existing order and then to talk of communion with the Source of that order. The only plausible answer based on what he wrote is that there is no logical transition, that he either glossed over it in order to satisfy his own metaphysical convictions – or those of his employers.

Since morality and religion go hand-in-hand with the former in a subordinate position, different religious views offer different moral views. A severance of the linkage between morality and religion is psychologically not going to happen. Thus, if we seek a harmony of moral outlooks, the difference in religions among humanity must be eliminated. Gorodenskij conjectured that although a complete convergence of religious views is an ideal, further religious developments should result in a closer alignment of moralities. His ecumenical spirit certainly was in keeping with a long Christian tradition going back at least to St. Paul but manifested most clearly in the writings of the early Solov'ëv. What is missing or quietly neglected here is recognition of the historical disputes that took place over doctrine, as though ethical precepts were at the heart of religious differences and thus were

---

44 Gorodenskij (1896), 211.
45 Gorodenskij (1896), 211.

all that really mattered. In this again, we find a similarity with Solov'ëv, albeit now with ideas expressed in his later writings, a similarity in what both neglected to take into account.

What Gorodenskij's colleagues and superiors at the Moscow Academy thought of his article is unclear. His transfer from teaching moral theology to literature and literary theory in 1902 may possibly have been prompted by or is at least an indication of some dissatisfaction with the ideas expressed. Another possible indication of the reaction to his ideas becomes apparent by comparing the tone of the 1896 article with that of the thesis he defended in 1903. Seeking to contrast the immediacy and irreducibility of a moral sense to the position that would derive it from psychological factors, Gorodenskij held that defenders of the latter, the empiricists, cannot account for why and how a person should act in a particular way. On the other hand, supporters of the former stance are unable to account for the genesis of morality, despite elucidating the essence of duty. Gorodenskij summarized his position as of 1903, writing:

> Moral consciousness cannot be entirely reduced to any need, instinct, or drive, since such a view in the end eliminates the moral point of view, which judges these very needs and consequently stands above them. On the other hand, however, it is an indubitable fact that morality among other things is peculiar to us and is a need that seeks satisfaction and manifests itself as a psychological force with a kind of blind necessity.[46]

Gorodenskij now tried to formulate a middle position between what he called the Kantians and the empiricists. We do have an innate moral sense, but a psychological element is also necessary for its realization in practice. Practical reason passes from abstract potentiality to action with the assistance of a psychological mechanism.

Gorodenskij in 1903 rejected resolving our moral sense to purely psychological or physiological factors. He did, however, conjecture that in time every mental state would be recognized as the result of a physiological process. Nonetheless, morality, strictly speaking is not illusory, but is a viewpoint. He averred that this position is one that Kant had already espoused and sought to substantiate. Kant erred in treating the "thing in itself" as a metaphysical entity, but he was correct in asserting the presence within us of an inner, rational causality.[47] "Kant's entire antinomy between freedom and causality is essentially based on his arbitrary nar-

---

[46] Gorodenskij (1903b), 566.
[47] Kant wrote that "reason has causality, or that we can at least represent something of the sort in it." Kant (1997), 540 (A547/B575). Gorodenskij surely took Kant's statement to heart and pinned his own "phenomenological" interpretation of Kant's intent around it.

rowing of the latter concept, reducing it to external causality."[48] Yet, Kant in his moral philosophy sought not to explain the emergence of our moral sense, but to link and elucidate known propositions concerning that sense.[49]

Having successfully defended his thesis, Gorodenskij continued teaching literature at the Moscow Academy until 1910. A new charter instituted that year effectively eliminated his position, and he was dismissed.[50] He then taught philosophy for a time at Moscow University as well as at the Higher Courses for Women in Tiflis. After the 1917 revolutions, he taught at various educational institutions, but published little if anything after a 1913 work on Bacon.

Gorodenskij's successor in teaching moral theology was Mikhail M. Tareev (1866–1934). The author of numerous works, the vast majority of them belonging to theological studies rather than to philosophy, Tareev studied at the Moscow Academy from 1887–1891. After receiving the *kandidat*'s degree, he remained at the Academy during the following school year with a fellowship, writing what would become his *magister*'s thesis, and then taught religious subjects as well as French and Latin at the Pskov Theological Seminary. Tareev completed and published his thesis in 1892 and defended it in 1893. Despite its unwieldy title, "The Temptations of the Divine-Man as the Single Redemptive Feat of the Entire Earthly Life of Christ, in Connection with the History of Pre-Christian Religions and the Christian Church," the defense proceeded successfully.[51] However, the Holy Synod, whose approval was necessary for the actual conferring of the degree, had reservations. The Synod "suggested" Tareev change the title and review the entire essay, seeking guidance from the Scriptures and the Patristics. After having done so, he was advised to resubmit the work for consideration. Tareev did as rec-

---

48 Gorodenskij (1903b), 572. Gorodenskij held that contemporary psychology has shown that reason can be causally efficacious, something that Kant in his own day could not see. Gorodenskij (1903a), 166.

49 One of the official opponents at Gorodenskij's thesis defense, Mikhail Tareev, questioned the efficacy of practical reason, which he saw Gorodenskij affirming. Our innate moral sense is too ambiguous to serve as a guide. See Iz akademicheskoj (1903), 586. Tareev in his lengthy remarks, surprisingly given the venue, also mentioned Solov'ëv's "remarkable" book, the *Justification of the Moral Good*, particularly Solov'ëv's final chapter where the author contended that the complete realization of morality would have to be on a universal scale. See Iz akademicheskoj (1903), 581. The second opponent, Popov, apparently refrained from giving preliminary remarks but raised numerous questions for Gorodenskij, some, but not all, of which were answered to Popov's complete satisfaction.

50 One fairly recent secondary work states that Gorodenskij's dismissal was actually a result of his "progressive" views. Golubcov (1999), 34. Unfortunately, Golubcov provides no additional information or the basis of his claim.

51 For a report on Tareev's defense of his thesis, see Sokolov (1893), 192–198.

ommended, finishing a second edition with a suitably altered title in 1895.⁵² The revision met with approval and was recognized as satisfactory for the degree, though only in July 1898. The revised work was not published until 1900.⁵³ It was not until the end of December 1901 that the Academy officially took up Tareev's petition for the formal conferring of the degree and gave its approval in February 1902.⁵⁴ He was appointed to the professorship in moral theology at the Moscow Academy in May.

Tareev upheld a most unusual position for an instructor at a Russian theological institution. Unlike Solov'ëv, he openly disparaged the Patristics. "Between the image of Christ in the Gospels and our conceptions stands the apostolic-patristic doctrine, which obscures from us the simplicity of the truth of the Gospels. In general, this shield leans toward the theological side of Christ's work and teaching over its human and historical side. Dogmatic formulas in their usual understanding make the truth of the Gospels in its historical purity inaccessible to many."⁵⁵ The culprit, in other words, for Tareev was the theological tradition created by the ancient Greek Church Fathers.⁵⁶

Tareev wrote morality emerged historically from the demands that society imposed on the individual as a necessary condition for the persistence of both society and the individual. However, the social and the moral sphere are not conceptually coincident. That which binds the individual in society, viz., law, is not that which binds the individual to others. Solov'ëv, in Tareev's opinion, correctly affirmed that law is a certain minimum of morality. But law concerns the external actions of an individual, whereas morality deals with inner motives. The final goal of morality is not the good of society, but of the individual, i.e., the spiritual good of the subject. This spiritual good is to be attained through the spiritual self-preservation of the human individual within society, but social life tends to crush the individu-

---

52 For Tareev's own account, see Zhurnaly Soveta (1902), 320–321.
53 The title of the revised work was *The Temptations of Our Lord Jesus Christ*. It had a brief, one paragraph "Preface" that, as the author himself noted, was from 1895.
54 B[eneman]skij (1902), 371–372.
55 (Tareev), 1908: 7. Tareev held this position to the end, writing nearly a decade later: "Dogma is the very first element in church life, but it is not the most important in Christianity. The most profound and complex element in Christianity, the first, original element in Christian life, is the intimate spiritual life, the reason of which is contained in Scripture, in Christ's words." Tareev (1917b), 178.
56 Florovskij writes that Tareev "gradually came to an acute doubt about the acceptability of the Greek-Eastern conception of Christianity." Florovskij (2009), 562. Although Florovskij is certainly correct, we could add that as the years advanced and with the growing nationalism, particularly with the start of a world war, Tareev's increasing recognition of a distinctly Russian religious tradition did so too.

al's sense of individuality.[57] In other words, the goal of morality is the preservation of the individual's spiritual freedom within one's social world. Yet, for Tareev the goal of religion is the "self-preservation of the spirit in the world on the whole."[58] From the individual's perspective, then, religion and moral activity are homogeneous and differ only from an objective viewpoint. Therefore, religion and morality have a certain affinity despite having different objects. The influence of Solov'ëv's *Justification of the Moral Good* is again apparent here in that human beings for both have an inherent sense of morality, a "general idea of the good as an unconditional norm."[59] We each have a God-given conscience and an innate knowledge of good and bad.

Inasmuch as morality and religion each have value and yet are independent of each other, they can ally when convenient and part when deemed desirable. Religion has not always preached a course of action that from the rational standpoint is ethical. In these instances, natural feelings have determined what seemed to be the religious course. The Old Testament gives examples of religiously inspired acts of slaughter of defeated enemies and even in one instance of a near sacrifice of one's own son. Still, Tareev finds these acts to be outside the sphere of ethical evaluation, since, though cruel to us, there is no evidence of approbation or censure from a moral consciousness. The moral law and religion itself was revealed to us by God, but the former is ultimately based on our own moral consciousness, which in primitive humanity was still undeveloped and indistinct. The religious point of view cannot seriously object to the subjective primacy of the moral consciousness.[60] But apart from such considerations, it is impossible to determine through the historical record whether the emergence of religion influenced morality or vice versa.

Since religion and morality are, in the final analysis, independent of each other, each human individual has a right to reject a particular religious form if it does not satisfy his/her conscience and concomitantly does not adhere to the dictates of the religious authorities.[61] "The true direction of religion, its development

---

57 Tareev (1904a), 305–306.
58 Tareev (1904b), 395.
59 Solov'ëv (2015), 3. The influence of Solov'ëv on Tareev would not stop here. Solov'ëv earlier argued for the objective independence of morality from religion, writing "moral philosophy has an object of its own (viz., moral norms) independent of positive religion (in a certain sense, the latter even presupposes these norms)." Solov'ëv (2015), 8.
60 Tareev (1904b), 398. Presumably, Tareev took the expression "moral consciousness" as synonymous with "conscience."
61 Berdjaev already during Tareev's scholarly career accused him of interpreting Christianity as "a form of Protestant individualism." Berdjaev (1909), 55f.

with which it happens to be a living force, consists of moving from external obedience to the Absolute, to the inner absoluteness of the spirit."⁶² The sphere of faith is larger than merely that of the morally good, for, as we saw, the two are different. Some, such as Kant, in Tareev's estimation, saw morality as a religion, the only religion of the rational human being. Kant was one example of an advocate of an ethical religion, and Leo Tolstoy was another. Yes, Kant held that the eternal, invariable, and universal moral law leads to the assumption of God's existence, but such a religion is "heartless."⁶³ That is, it lacks the subjective certainty that accompanies resolute faith, religious absoluteness. Only such absoluteness can not only serve as the principle motivating our behavior directed at both personal and social improvement, but also provide us with a meaning of life. With these claims, Tareev expressly leaves behind moral philosophy, writing that Christianity is "above" morality. He provided no specific, i.e., rational, critiques of Kant – or of Tolstoy, for that matter – for none was necessary, for any such critique would be objective and thus contrary to his subjective approach to Christian teaching.

Years later, Tareev, further elaborating his thought, asserted that the Christian moral doctrine is the implementation of a subjective, moral method, This moral doctrine, or "practical theology," was something entirely new in contrast to the "old" dogmatic theology of Christianity. Tareev himself traced the idea of a contrast between the abstract-objective method and a moral-subjective method to Dilthey, Wundt, Münsterberg, and the Baden School of neo-Kantianism in Germany and to Lavrov, Mikhajlovskij, and Kareev in Russia. Whereas these figures applied the distinction to contrast the methodology used in studying nature to the methodology of the social sciences, Tareev wished to set off the subjective method of determining spiritual truth from other truths. The utilization of such a method forms a spiritual science.⁶⁴ Through the subjective method, Christian philosophy extracts its content from the word of God. Church dogma is determined by ecumenical councils, not by patristic teachings and opinions.

In a bow to the fervent nationalism rampant throughout Europe and elsewhere in the years of World War I, Tareev sought to renew again his distaste for the patristic tradition but enhance and enlarge it with an attack on the West through a metaphor. "The philosophy of the heart is our Russian philosophy as opposed to Western rationalism. This is not enough. The philosophy of the heart dis-

---

62 Tareev (1904b), 403.
63 To be more precise, Tareev recognized that Kant called the existence of God (along with the soul's immortality) a postulate of pure practical reason. However, Tareev then wrote, "Therefore, according to Kant the moral law leads to the *assumption* of God's existence, i.e., to religion." Tareev (1904b), 419.
64 Tareev (1917a), 11.

tinguishes the Russian genius from the old Greek spirit with its intellectualism and Gnosticism."[65] Tareev remained at the Moscow Academy until the end, and even after that continued to live in the vicinity of the Academy, located in Sergiev Posad, until 1927, when he moved to Moscow proper. He continued to write with a particular interest focused on the history of Russian theology. The manuscript for this reportedly was near completion already in January 1919 but was never published. Whatever works he may have prepared in his later years were apparently lost due to the family's negligence.[66]

9.3 Two Historians of Philosophy in Moscow

Two individuals who taught the history of philosophy at the Moscow Academy represented two quite dramatically different, or at least contrasting, viewpoints on Russian philosophy and implicitly on the general political atmosphere of the time. Aleksej I. Vvedenskij[67] (1861–1913) completed the course of studies at the Moscow Academy in 1886 and immediately afterward began teaching Latin at the Vologda Seminary. He was selected already the next year to teach the history of philosophy at the Moscow Academy. Upon the death of Viktor Kudrjavcev, Vvedenskij was designated in 1892 his successor in the chair of logic and metaphysics. With a deep sense of tradition as an ethical value, he saw himself as Kudrjavcev's "philosophical" disciple. Vvedenskij published his *magister*'s thesis, *Faith in God, Its Origin and Foundation*, in 1891 and his doctoral thesis, *The Religious Consciousness of Paganism*, in 1892. Vvedenskij twice went on study trips (1891/92 and 1896/97) to France and Germany to investigate how the history and philosophy of religion were taught there. His impressions of the conditions in Western Europe would stand in marked contrast to another as we shall see.

Vvedenskij did manage to write and publish a great deal. Yet, he only gingerly embarked on presenting his own thoughts except in terms of broad generalizations.[68] A deeply religious individual, he saw philosophy as a mediator between the natural sciences and a religious view of the world.

---

65 Tareev (1917a), 53.
66 Golubcov (2010), 486. In the 1910s, Tareev composed a critique of Marxist socialism.
67 Aleksej should not be confused with Aleksandr I. Vvedenskij, the neo-Kantian professor at St. Petersburg University, a confusion that we find even occasionally in Russian-language secondary literature. The two professors held quite different views on the viability of Kant's philosophical project.
68 Zenkovsky wrote that Vvedenskij was "prolific but unoriginal" and "in general followed his teacher Kudrjavtsev" except that in epistemology he "tended toward the 'collective [*soborny*] epis-

Philosophy is of value only insofar as it contributes to the achievement of this goal, the goal of the spiritual self-preservation of the human being, the development of one's normal type, of moral self-improvement. Everything else comes after this. Philosophy is nothing other than the desire for a correct understanding of life based on a true understanding of the world.[69]

We see with this proclamation, delivered in an introductory lecture on the history of philosophy, that Vvedenskij's primary concern was of an ethical or anthropological nature but one grounded on his Orthodox Christian faith. Vvedenskij was quite dismissive of attempts to establish an ethical system without the invocation of a belief in God. It, and not religion, was, he said, one of the deepest and most widespread prejudices today. The attempt to construct an areligious morality arose out of a pagan point of view in an effort to justify an immoral life-style without facing the consequences of such a dissolute path.[70] Vvedenskij saw no particular need for the traditional (Western) proofs of God's existence. The historical proof, namely that the vast majority of peoples over time have believed in God, is the best proof. The image of God "appears before our consciousness with all the evidence of a universal scientifically justified experience."[71]

Vvedenskij seldom ventured beyond metaphysics, as he himself surely would have acknowledged, since for him metaphysical issues constitute the philosophical sphere, properly speaking. Nonetheless, with that in mind he did *propose* on one occasion to investigate space as a constituent element of the world (metaphysically) but only after having dispensed with a psychological and an epistemological inquiry. Vvedenskij believed that the representation of space acquired by our vision is fundamentally different from that obtained through tactile impressions. This, he thought, undermines all theories of space, including Kant's, that make claims in some fashion as to its singular essential character, regardless of whether that character be considered an intuition, a representation, or other. "The difference between our 'visual space' and our 'tactile space' tells us only that our spatial knowledge is not given to us in a ready-made form from the start."[72] What our spatial

---

temology of Prince S. N. Trubetskoi, though without adequate grounding of his views." Zenkovsky (1953), 585.
69 Vvedenskij (1908), 167.
70 Vvedenskij (1900), 121.
71 Vvedenskij (1901), 270.
72 Vvedenskij (1906a), 417. In his discussion Vvedenskij refers not just to Helmholtz but to Chelpanov as well. He could also have – and perhaps should have – referred in this connection to the work of the neo-Kantian Alois Riehl, who wrote: "Sight and touch are two languages, which grasp the same meaning using two entirely different words. Therefore, the ability to translate one of them into the other must be learned with effort – regardless of the anatomical connection

representations do not eliminate is the distinct possibility that we have from birth a predisposition to form a representation of space with the content supplied *a posteriori*.

Vvedenskij did publish a second installment of his investigation thereby completing his proclaimed *psychological* treatment of the idea of space. He summarized that treatment writing that our idea is formed from external material but "according to an *a priori* law or schema" that takes place also in conjunction with the category of unity in our consciousness.[73] Thus, space is our creative product, but not a product from nothing. Unfortunately, Vvedenskij never published a continuation of his investigation, thus leaving us somewhat in the dark as to his most mature reflections on the nature of our idea of space from an epistemological and a metaphysical viewpoint.

Of greatest interest to us is not Vvedenskij's critique of Kant's conception of space, but his view of it along with and as an element of Western philosophy. Unlike a number of others who returned from a period of study in Germany, Vvedenskij did not return to Russia enamored with the philosophical systems he heard there. He recognized already in 1891 that criticism of what he thought to be the one-sided character of Western thought did not alone amount to the construction of a truer system. Vvedenskij recognized that Russian philosophy up to that time had not yet contributed much. The Slavophiles and Russian philosophy in general had critiqued the mistakes of others but offered nothing significant. The time had come, though, to begin the development of Russian philosophy.[74]

Vvedenskij returned to the issue of the possibility of a distinct Russian philosophy in 1893 this time importantly in the secular *Voprosy filosofii* rather than in the smug confines of the in-house theological journal. He held that there had been epochs during which philosophy had completely neglected its central, i.e., metaphysical, tasks. These periods were characterized by dogmatism and skepticism, philosophical attitudes that stemmed from a predominant interest in life's

---

between the two senses." Riehl (1879), 139. Vvedenskij was well aware of Riehl's discussion of space and praised his efforts.

73 Vvedenskij (1906b), 709. Vvedenskij's invocation of unity as a cognitive category is tantalizing but vague. We know, however, that he, following his predecessors, objected not so much to the Kantian categories, as to their exclusive subjectivity. The categories are subjective, to be sure, but they are also objective. A decade earlier in 1895, Vvedenskij wrote, "According to Kant (and, completely in his spirit, also the latest neo-Kantians) space exists only for us and other beings with a similar organization. Undoubtedly, if our own or a similar intuitive sense faculty is a necessary condition for representing space, what follows from that? ... The conclusion about the subjectivity of space does not in any way follow." Vvedenskij (2005), 409. The collection of essays that includes Vvedenskij's essay on Kant also inexcusably misattributes it to *Aleksandr* Vvedenskij..

74 Vvedenskij (1891), 326.

practical concerns. When such concerns do not completely occupy a people's interest, when thinking is free, it proceeds "bravely and resolutely" into philosophy.[75]

Vvedenskij without mentioning names wrote that the possibility of an independent Russian philosophy and of the very philosophical ability of the Russian people has often recently been discussed with some voicing a negative opinion. He holds, though, the contrary view. Those who maintain an opinion contrary to Vvedenskij do not see – or wish to see – that philosophy can adopt a different model, that Russian philosophy lies in probing philosophical anthropology, viz., the meaning and value of life. Much like other philosophies, Russian thought does seek to solve all philosophical problems. However, unlike all others it seeks such solutions with respect to a philosophical anthropology. All other philosophies that concerned themselves with the value of life settled with either an optimistic or pessimistic solution. A third possible path is that on which Russians have embarked, namely submission to the will of God, a religious road perfectly in keeping with their Orthodox Christian faith. The Russian "suffers evil but does not accept it. He does not elevate it into a principle and does not justify it. On the contrary, he energetically condemns it and constantly fights it. He wants to correct it motivated by faith in the optimistic ideal of the coming kingdom of heaven."[76] What is distinctively Russian, as against distinctively religious, in this remains a mystery – unless one claims religiosity is a distinctively Russian characteristic, whereas other nationalities are at least partially devoid of it.

Vvedenskij saw himself proposing a different understanding of the unique characteristic trait of Russian philosophy from that of the Slavophiles. In his eyes, they saw Russian philosophy as different from the West by not limiting their investigations of the mind to its theoretical functions. They wished to look at the mind's practical functions which took into account our feelings and the human will in the single act of faith. For Vvedenskij, the Slavophile proposal was not sufficiently Russian, since "calls for such a synthesis are heard now even among German thinkers and philosophers, not to mention the French, whose philosophy has always been characterized by a practical, moral-aesthetic tendency."[77] Vvedenskij wrote, rather, that the originality of Russian thought should be sought in the principle of life, i.e., in the nation's traditions, understood as including not just the external characteristics of the Russian way of life (religious, historical), but also psychological and biological elements. However, the predominant element in this mix is the religious, which sets Russia off from the West

---

75 Vvedenskij (1893b), 129.
76 Vvedenskij (1893b), 150.
77 Vvedenskij (1893b), 154.

and leads Vvedenskij to claim the nation's traditions to be the "collective consciousness" (*sobornost' soznanija*) of the Russian people. The concept of tradition should be recognized as the fundamental principle of Russian philosophy.[78] Regrettably, he does not show how all of these elements in a nation's way of life are to be taken into account in solving philosophical problems or in what way the resulting solution would differ from those offered by other less enveloping means. Nor does Vvedenskij broach the issue whether the rejection of a nation's traditions amount to a rejection of one's ethnicity. If, say, someone of purely Russian ethnic stock were to uphold eliminative materialism and/or atheism, would that be tantamount to rejecting one's "Russian-ness," perhaps even being a traitor?

Vvedenskij was aware of the possible charge against him of relativism stemming from his nationalism. He was dismissive of it, however, saying that all philosophical methods, even a synthesis of them, cannot avoid a measure of relativism and subjectivity. We can ask of him, then, what becomes of the philosophical quest for truth as paramount. Vvedenskij's primary interest was not so much in seeking answers to puzzling questions as it was to finding a means to distinguish the originality of Russian thought set against other philosophical currents. His answer proved to be a leap away from philosophy into a highly speculative excursion into the sociology of knowledge.

A second historian of philosophy at the Moscow Academy was Pavel V. Tikhomirov (1868–1937), who though clearly a competent professor, passes virtually unnoticed in the pages of Russian philosophy. Coming from a typical clerical background, he finished the course of studies at the Moscow Academy in 1893 and then spent the 1894/95 academic year at Moscow University studying natural science. He was appointed docent at the Moscow Academy teaching Hebrew and Biblical archaeology in 1895 and two years later began teaching the history of philosophy. He continued teaching at the Academy until 1906, but he also taught during the previous year as a *privat-docent* at Moscow University. Tikhomirov appeared content teaching and writing on the history of philosophy including on contemporary philosophy without delivering extended remarks on his own views.[79] He did

---

78 Vvedenskij (1893b), 155. Vvedenskij fully acknowledged a debt to Sergej Trubeckoj for the expression. Vvedenskij's train of thought here is replete with illogical transitions. Is he arguing that Russian philosophy to his day is objectively distinguished by this principle or that it should be viewed by us as embodying this principle? On what basis are we to validate his assertion? If his is to be understood as an objective claim, he provided no evidence. By what criterion are we to know whether we have viewed Russian philosophy properly? And just which philosophies are to be counted as Russian?

79 For example, in an essay entitled "The Problem and Method of Kant's Critique of Cognition," Tikhomirov wrote, "A detailed evaluation of Kant's critical enterprise was not part of the task

provide hints, though, in many writings of his general outlook, which was deeply appreciative of the current Western philosophical path.

Tikhomirov held that in order to make "progress" in philosophy a thinker must take into account the historically offered solutions to the problems that beset contemporaneity. The study of these solutions should form a necessary propaedeutic to one's own attempt at resolving the problem. Without such a study, an individual runs the risk of merely repeating what others have written, committing their mistakes or idly spending one's time repeating what is already known. With such a concern in mind, i.e., not to repeat needlessly paths already well-trodden, Tikhomirov specifically embarked on what he termed a "historico-critical" study of epistemological positions.[80] What he presented was not particularly original, taking as its starting point the divisions presented by such German figures as Friedrich Paulsen, Eduard von Hartmann, and Alois Riehl. What is interesting is that Tikhomirov had not a word to say about the supposed Russian paradigm offered by the Slavophiles or Solov'ëv.

Tikhomirov provided a hint at his position – unfortunately, no more than that – in an essay published in the Moscow Academy's journal in 1908. He there wrote that epistemology does not answer whether metaphysics is possible. However, if we would have a completely elaborated epistemology, it would "almost certainly" have an answer to the question within it. The elaboration of an epistemology should not be undertaken expressly in the pursuit of whether metaphysics is possible.[81] With that aside, what, then, is epistemology? If its concern is with cognition as a fact, how does it differ – or does it? – from psychology? Tikhomirov distinguished the two, writing that psychology deals with the natural laws of thinking whereas logic details the conditions of correct thinking, i.e., its normative laws. His own delimitation of epistemology, however, is deeply disappointing, despite his recognition that it is fundamentally different from psychology. Tikhomirov wrote, "By its normative character, epistemology differs from psychology, and by the fact that it investigates the final foundations, the most remote assumptions of cognition, it differs from logic. ... Epistemology, by definition, is the union of logic with psychology for a very definite, special purpose, namely, the investigation

---

of the present study. We want, above all, to present a correct understanding of his doctrine." Tikhomirov (1899b), 53. Nevertheless, he concluded that Kant's acknowledgment of the absolute validity of mathematical and scientific cognition represents his unquestionable dogmatism.

80 Tikhomirov (1900), 334.

81 Tikhomirov did not state that he had in mind here the Kantian project, but such a reading is surely possible. We can find a basis for such a reading of Kant in the second edition "Introduction" to the first *Critique*. See Kant (1997), 147–148 (B21–B22).

of the 'final bases and assumptions' of cognition."[82] Tikhomirov concluded his essay stating that epistemology resolves the issue of the possibility of metaphysics if we merely adopt the viewpoint just given. How it does that remains totally obscure.

Tikhomirov was more lucid in attempting to differentiate philosophy in general from the natural sciences. In general comments for his course on the history of philosophy at the Moscow Academy in September 1898, he affirmed that philosophy is a "science," independent of others in that it differs from them in its treatment of general questions including that of life on the whole. Whereas the natural sciences can reveal at most conditional knowledge, philosophy seeks absolute truth.[83] Of course, we could understand such pronouncements as being religiously-inspired and virtually necessary given their time and setting. Yet, a decade later under different circumstances he reiterated the same view, albeit with a helpful clarification. The natural sciences accept quite dogmatically certain general concepts and principles, which they view as necessary for their endeavor. These form their *a priori* assumptions, and the practicing scientist feels no need to reflect critically, i.e., philosophically, on them. Philosophy, on the other hand, does investigate them and thereby strengthens and further grounds the particular science.

The theme of the relation between philosophy and science played a large role in yet another essay from the following decade and after Tikhomirov's return from a period of study in Germany. In 1905, he stated that philosophy flourishes when the results of the natural sciences conflict with traditional beliefs and socially predominant positions. The need to resolve this contradiction and thereby revise the accepted worldview results in the activity of philosophizing. "Philosophy cannot appear where there is no contradiction between the new knowledge and the old ideals."[84]

Tikhomirov's elucidation of philosophy's distinctive character is neither particularly original nor insightful, but it at least marks a turn toward a secular understanding of its concerns and tasks. He retained, however, the idea that philosophy along with the natural sciences is progressing toward Truth. In yet another essay, this one from 1907, he *faulted* Hegel for viewing the history of philosophy as a "steady movement toward a consistent elucidation of truth from various sides."[85] Still, Hegel was basically correct in viewing the historical changes in phil-

---

82 Tikhomirov (1908), 705–706. Tikhomirov did not provide a reference for the embedded quotation here. He may have simply been quoting himself.
83 Tikhomirov (1899a), 75.
84 Tikhomirov (1905), 78.
85 Tikhomirov (1907), 12. Tikhomirov's booklet appeared first over two issues of the journal *Bogoslovskij vestnik* in 1907.

osophical doctrines to be a consistent, connected, and regular approximation to truth. Hegel was wrong in demanding a monotonous regularity. In requiring such regularity leading ultimately to his own system, he distorted their true character by forcing them into his preconceived schema. The ultimate end to the philosophical quest for the absolute truth lies at an infinite time in the future. Hegel's schema was also incorrect in looking at history impersonally, as if the developments proceeded without the input of personal and socio-historical factors. These too must be taken into account, but they can have no more than an auxiliary significance in accounting philosophically for the changes in philosophical systems. In the absence of specifics with concrete examples, Tikhomirov's points, however well-taken, are again extremely vague.

Tikhomirov offered little to Russian philosophy apart from a sober, mature, and professional voice. Writing from that perspective, he was one of the very few who, with a thorough familiarity with the history of modern philosophy, publicly acknowledged the poverty of philosophy in his homeland. He likened philosophy to a delicate plant that cannot flourish in the absence of air and a favorable soil. As we saw with Vvedenskij, Tikhomirov too believed that there have been entire historical eras during which many lived who thought of themselves as philosophers but whose doctrines hardly deserve the appellation "philosophy." The Renaissance was just one such era, but contemporary Russian philosophy in Tikhomirov's view was another. He asked, "What have we given that is valuable and independent to philosophy? – Little more than nothing."[86] Russian philosophy to his day had hardly contributed more than critical and historical secondary works. It has presented no thoroughly original systems that could be ranked on a par with those of Descartes, Hume, Kant, and Hegel. It has given nothing comparable even to Herbart and Fechner. In comparing the lack of academic freedom in Russia to the state of affairs in Germany, Tikhomirov linked, not very subtly, the poverty of the Russian philosophical scene to the country's repressive politics.

> None of the obstacles that usually hinder philosophical creativity is as strong in Germany as, for example, in our country. The main brake, the lack of confidence in one's right to express freely one's convictions and the feeling of the constant risk of being subjected to disciplinary action for scientific or philosophical opinions, is completely absent among the Germans, whereas among us it creates at times an unbearably heavy mood that paralyzes mental ingenuity.[87]

---

86 Tikhomirov (1905), 81.
87 Tikhomirov (1905), 84.

The main incubators of philosophical thought, higher educational institutions, in Russia lack academic freedom compared to Germany. For Tikhomirov, then, the lack of philosophical originality in Russia could hardly be surprising. In this, he stands in stark opposition to Vvedenskij.

Tikhomirov taught philosophy from 1907–1917 at the university in Kyiv as well as at the Higher Women's Courses and at the Kyiv Commercial Institute in the city. After the Bolshevik Revolution, he served for a time in an administrative capacity at a newly organized Institute of Public Education in Odessa charged with preparing teachers. Unfortunately, there is little additional concrete information concerning his life during the early years of the Soviet Union.[88]

Contrasting the views of Vvedenskij and Tikhomirov on Russian academic life, we can hardly be surprised that the latter left the Moscow Academy. Vvedenskij obviously celebrated the religiosity there, whereas Tikhomirov found it to be chafing and unnecessarily restrictive. The theological academies in general were clearly not monolithic institutions with just one theological and philosophical direction. The same can be said of the political views of the professoriate. As time progressed, their attitudes toward the swirling events around them often became more pronounced and manifest.

---

[88] The available secondary literature regrettably avoids details of Tikhomirov's remaining years under the Bolshevik regime. We find the briefest possible indication that he taught some unspecified subject for some unspecified period at Leningrad University and upon his death was buried in an Orthodox cemetery in that city. How that could possibly have come about in 1937 of all Soviet years is also left unanswered.

Chapter 10
Philosophy at the Kyiv and Kazan Academies Under the Third Charter

The early years of the twentieth century saw an upsurge in scholarship at the Kyiv Academy. During the first five years a total of eighteen *magister*'s theses were defended, a number that exceeded all other academies.[1] Yet not all was well in the theological academies and not in Kyiv in particular. Although instruction in philosophy was not directly affected by the 1884 Charter, other innovations had unintended consequences. Offerings in languages, both ancient and modern, became elective and were often given at the same time as the history courses, thus forcing students to choose. There had already been significant rioting at the Kazan Academy during the 1886–1887 academic year and disturbances at the Moscow Academy in 1895, but the year 1905 particularly stood apart from the others.

The massacre in St. Petersburg associated with "Bloody Sunday" in January 1905 initiated nation-wide labor unrest on a previously unparalleled scale but even reverberated through the Russian university system. The increasingly radicalized student movement there did not pass unnoticed in the country's theological academies. The seminaries had already in 1903 experienced individual disturbances, leading to the initiation of an underground publication and an underground congress, which was held at the seminary in the city of Vladimir. The ineffectiveness of student demands only led in time to more radical demands that came to include political ones as well. At the academies, the movement largely sprung from a long-simmering discontent with the 1884 Charter, and as at the seminaries the general political situation in the country only intensified the emotional state of the aggrieved parties. The changes introduced that year in the running of the secular universities which strengthened their independence further encouraged demands for similar changes at the academies. An indefinite student strike initiated at the start of the 1905 academic year at the Kyiv Academy soon spread to all Russian academies.[2] A few weeks after the boycott of classes started at Kyiv, students at the other three academies declared that they too would not "attend classes until such time as the academies were given autonomy," largely meaning non-interference in the administrative affairs of the academies by bishops and the bureaucrats of the Holy Synod.[3]

---

[1] Sukhova (2011a), 142–143.
[2] Tkachuk (2011), 86; Sukhova (2011a), 144.
[3] Valliere (1976), 121.

Wishing to prevent the situation at the Kyiv Academy from getting out of hand, the rector Platon (Porfirij F. Rozhdestvenskij) in October convened an elected commission that presented a set of desired changes to the academy's structure. A draft expressing the general mood was adopted after heated discussion in the Academy's Council. The document stated the aspiration that the theological academies be managed along pedagogical and scholarly principles closer to those of the universities. The draft also expressed the desire to reduce the role of the bishop to one of "honorary patronage," to allow for the election of the rector, and to establish the academies as open educational institutions, albeit, of course, devoted to the development of theological scholarship and education, both in an Orthodox Christian spirit. The draft, in effect, largely amounted to a return to the 1869 Charter. It called for a return to public defenses of doctoral dissertations and the awarding of the *magister* and doctoral degrees in church history, church law, and philosophy, none of which according to the present charter were allowed. The not-so-subtle bone of contention here was again the role of the theological academies vis-à-vis the secular universities. In short, the preeminent question remained: To what extent were the academies to be theological research institutions or mere training-grounds for future church administrators?

Three elected representatives from the Kyiv Academy were sent to a meeting with colleagues from the other academies to determine their attitudes toward the draft document, and, as may be expected, opinions varied widely.[4] Nonetheless, the meeting did result in proposals that would form the basis of what became known as the Provisional Rules for the Academies. In November 1905, a delegation of the professors arrived in St. Petersburg to work out these rules with the Holy Synod. Some professors were to be disappointed that the rectorship had to be filled with someone from the first estate, rather than, as they desired, any qualified person, but a consolation was that the rector could be chosen by the faculty. Other draft provisions that were accepted included the direct subordination of the academies to the Holy Synod with the diocesan bishops being reduced to supervisors. The Provisional Rules – in effect amendments to the 1884 Charter – were approved late that month and came into effect in early 1906.[5]

---

[4] One differing opinion concerning the state of the theological academies at the time was given by Bishop Antonij (Khapovickij) in 1905. He proposed that the academies be theological schools in a narrow sense, eliminating all non-theological subjects with the exception of philosophy and Russian literature, the latter being retained for nationalistic purposes. Sukhova (2011a), 147. Also see Sukhova (2006), 24.

[5] Sukhova (2011a), 146.

10.1. Linickij Under the Third Charter

We already introduced Petr Linickij and his philosophical thoughts under the second charter in Chapter 7. Since, however, his service and prolificity at the Kyiv Academy was so great over the span of more than a single charter with so little secondary literature, let us at least briefly look at some of his works written while the third charter was in effect. We just saw that the Kyiv Academy was not totally immune from the disturbances and disruptions occurring throughout the Russian higher educational system. The events of late 1905 at Kyiv University were upsetting enough, but that his own students at the Academy were engaging in political discourse was beyond Linickij's comprehension. In January 1906, Linickij openly opposed student participation in what he viewed as revolutionary action.[6] This aroused the indignation of the students and erected a wall of distrust between them and Linickij that remained in place until his death later that year.[7]

Unless one were to devote an entire monograph, even though brief, to Linickij it would be impossible to examine all of his individual post-1884 writings in detail. Fortunately, we need not do so. As remarked previously, many, if not most, of Linickij's writings throughout his long career consisted, on the one hand, of historical sketches from a decidedly religious standpoint and, on the other hand, of superficial, introductory texts written for pedagogical purposes rather than for a professional audience.

As we have seen, philosophers in late-Imperial Russia were particularly keen on addressing the challenge posed to their Christian faith from positivism and the rapid advances in science. To mount an effective offense, Linickij sought again and again to demarcate philosophy from natural science while harboring a distinct role, as he saw it, for reason apart from faith. He was alarmed by what he took to be the substitution of faith in scientific omniscience for religious faith. Linickij interpreted the rise of positivism in his day as stemming from this belief in science. Whereas religious faith is concerned with the relation of finite beings to God and our destiny in the afterlife, scientific faith is concerned with finite beings alone and the satisfaction of our temporal needs.

> Knowledge and faith, science and religion not only do not exclude and cannot replace one another, but on the contrary are both necessary. Through religious faith, the dignity of science

---

6 Mozgovaja (2012), 12.
7 Shortly after Linickij's death, Petr Kudrjavcev, who also taught philosophy at the Kyiv Academy published a lengthy obituary summarizing Linickij's philosophical position. See Kudrjavcev (1906).

rises, and the need for knowledge turns into an impartial and sublime love of truth. With the help of science, religious faith is cleansed and deepened.⁸

How science has historically done this is left unsaid, though religion has surely attempted to "cleanse" science as we can readily see from Christian-Church attacks on heliocentrism and on the theory of evolution. If science deals with the contingent, the natural, and religion deals with the eternal, the supernatural, then what is the concern of philosophy? Is it a science or a religion?

Writing in 1881, Linickij held that the primary object of philosophical investigation is the idea of being. It is the simplest and logically the most fundamental idea, and since experience shows that one thing causally arises from another it is "natural" to assume that there is something that is not caused. There is a hierarchy of beings with essences being independent in comparison to appearances, the latter being causally dependent on the former. Whereas appearances are the object of the empirical sciences, essences of things up to the fundamental, original being are and have always been assumed to be the proper object of philosophy.⁹ But the goal is a philosophical system, a unified worldview, which requires the consistent unification of the only two possible opposing philosophies: empiricism and rationalism. Kant attempted a synthesis, but his conclusion was a skepticism. Hegel picked up from Kant but proceeded by attempting to construct an absolute system that would include empiricism and rationalism. This too, however, would prove impossible.¹⁰

Having said all this, namely that philosophy is concerned with the idea of being, that it aims for a coherent and all-encompassing worldview, what were Linickij's proposed solutions to enduring philosophical problems? Do we have a solution, say, to how *a priori* synthetic judgments are possible? Does he present how the mind constitutes the very notion of objectivity or how the mind distinguishes between a really existing object from a mere mirage? Does he offer a refutation of psychologism? And what about a theory of linguistic meaning and reference? Re-

---

8 Linickij (1892) 27. The essay from which this quotation is taken originally appeared in 1889 in the journal *Vera i razum* and entitled "What Distinguishes Faith from Knowledge?" ["Chem razlichaetsja vera ot znanija?"].
9 Linickij (2012), 61. Of course, Linickij provided no substantiation for his claim, and his very reading of the history of philosophy is highly selective, seeing in it only what he wished to see at the expense of all else.
10 Linickij demonstrated some familiarity with Solov'ëv's *Critique of Abstract Principles* already at this early date, writing that it represented the first Russian-language attempt at such a philosophical synthesis. In the end, though, it was nothing more than a Hegelianism. Linickij (2012), 177.

grettably, he had no answers to any of these questions, but there are hints, though undeveloped and unclarified to be sure.

Linickij recognized mathematics to be an *a priori* science. The natural sciences rely on experience or observation for data. Mathematics, as one of what he termed the "speculative sciences," relies on the understanding. Instead of observations, mathematics appeals to intelligible quantities or geometrical figures. Inasmuch as philosophy does not depend on outer experience, but on thought, which belongs to the understanding, it belongs among the speculative sciences. However oddly and in apparent, though unstated, contrast to Kant among others, Linickij held that *a priori* disciplines, such as pure mathematics, "do not so much give us actual knowledge as techniques of thinking and the mental skills that serve as necessary tools for acquiring knowledge."[11] All empirical sciences need the help that the *a priori*, or speculative, disciplines can supply. How they are to do this is left unsaid.

Linickij did not state outright whether, for example, mathematics consists of synthetic judgments, but he did immediately go on to say that philosophy "similarly" does not provide knowledge.[12] He, thereby, implies that neither pure mathematics nor philosophy yields knowledge, yet both consist of *a priori* concepts. The basis of philosophical knowledge revolves around the ideas of God, the soul, and the world, which, though vague, are part of our *a priori* mental equipment. Moreover, unless one, contrary to the psychological evidence, contends that only empirical science is possible, philosophy must be developed and constructed deductively utilizing these *a priori* ideas. However vague these ideas may be, they are neither the result of intuition nor are they representations, as are mathematical objects. Indeed, having declared that human beings have them as part of our mental equipment, Linickij conceded at one point that not everyone has an idea of the Deity. Additionally, he tells us that philosophy is concerned first with the essence of things as well as self-consciousness, then with the essence of being, but without specifying what he means by "being."[13] Does not an investigation of essences, whether it be those of things or of being, provide knowledge? In any case, Linickij continued by claiming that *every* philosophy is either materialistic or spiritualistic, depending on how that particular philosophy construes essences. But this entire discussion flatly contradicts his claim that whereas the scientist is focused on

---

11 Linickij (1894a), 153–154.
12 The caveat to accepting Linickij's statement without reservation is that he also on the same page wrote of the objects of philosophical knowledge. How can one speak of the objects of philosophical knowledge if there is no philosophical knowledge? Linickij (1894a), 154.
13 Linickij (1894a), 170, 175. Surely, one could conceivably find a way to reconcile Linickij's statements, but the fact remains that he gave no definition for "being," leaving it to the reader to make sense of his claims.

some object or phenomenon, the philosopher concentrates on the process involved in the investigation or observation. That is, the philosopher seeks to account for how the faculty of thinking operates.[14] In short, we have here a series of hopeless confusions.

If philosophy is concerned with understanding the external world through reflection on it and with the use of fundamental *a priori* principles, then physics, in a sense, is the fundamental natural science. Likewise, turning inward we would have to say that psychology is the fundamental science of the inner world. Since mental processes are involved in *all* scientific activity, including the study of externality, can we say that psychology is the fundamental science? Linickij did not address this issue directly, but gave every indication that his answer would be in the affirmative. He was quick to add, however, that this does not imply psychologism, which would entail placing psychology as the basis of philosophy. No, psychology deals with facts, though of the inner world. As such, it is an empirical science, and as such depends on philosophy for its basic principle.

As we see, Linickij was in the last instance a foundationalist. Philosophy cannot obtain its fundamental principle from external experience, but only from thought itself. Without a thorough examination, he stated that there is a unity of thought, which, in turn, demands a single principle from which all others are derived. That principle serves as the ground of what Linickij termed the three separate philosophical "sciences," or disciplines: logic, epistemology, and ontology. The designation for the loftiest such science is metaphysics, i.e., the science of the unconditional.[15] Linickij's attempt to connect again all the threads he had unraveled is rushed and incomplete, leaving an edifice that while it may stand as a testimony to his diligence is unable to withstand even the slightest critical scrutiny. Regardless of how he fared in the classroom, his expositions left much to be desired. He attempted to address and systematize the history of philosophy according primacy within it to a battle between empiricism and rationalism, understood as spiritualism, but already in his day the battle was taking place elsewhere leaving him alone even in the eyes of his contemporaries to tilt at windmills.

10.2 Linickij's Successors: Bogdashevskij and P. Kudrjavcev

In 1887 and before the start of the academic year, Linickij requested a change from teaching the history of philosophy to that of logic and metaphysics. This was grant-

---

14 Linickij (1894a), 169.
15 Linickij (1894b), 8–9.

ed, creating a vacancy that was immediately filled by Dmitrij I. Bogdashevskij (1861–1933), a student of Linickij's. Bogdashevskij, the son of a priest, graduated at the top of his class at the seminary he attended and received a scholarship to study at the Kyiv Academy in 1882. On the completion of the program there in 1886, he was retained on a fellowship to prepare for a professorship, which as just mentioned, conveniently opened up the following year. In 1890, he was awarded a *magister*'s degree and received a promotion. Upon his request, he took on the role of teaching the New Testament in 1897. He received a doctorate in 1904 and was ordained a priest in 1910, after which he rose steadily in rank.[16]

Bogdashevskij penned many works, but few in philosophy and all of them were while he taught the subject at the Academy. Based on student accounts from the time and his swift departure from philosophy to theology, a picture emerges that, while he was sincere and diligent, Bogdashevskij was not terribly interested in philosophy, which made his teaching of the subject much less effective than it could and should have been.[17] His early 1892 work entitled "In Defense of a Metaphysics of the Mind" actually was a review of a recently published book *Philosophy of Phenomenal Formalism* by Nikolaj Debol'skij, whom we saw in Chapter 5. Entirely in praise of Debol'skij's effort, Bogdashevskij concluded his review, writing "We cannot help but express in conclusion our wish for the soonest possible publication of further installments of this work, which is undeniably good and useful."[18] And again in another review the following year, this time on Linickij's 1892 *Textbook for the Study of the Problems of Philosophy*, Bogdashevskij had virtually nothing but praise for it apart from some quibbling on the order of some of the presentations. He thought Linickij had presented the most important problems of philosophy and provided "everywhere a firm, definite solution." When tackling each problem, Linickij paused and advanced the essential and interesting side.[19]

In an address at the Kyiv Academy in late September/early October 1894, Bogdashevskij presented the arguably most direct statement of his meta-philosophical position, which, as it turns out, largely coincided with Linickij's. Published in the house organ of the Academy as well as separately under the title "On the Relationship between Philosophy and Natural Science," Bogdashevskij claimed that the sciences do not address the most important question: What is knowledge? Not only do they not attempt to answer it, but they cannot without transgressing their own de-

---

16 For a highly informed biography of Bogdashevskij, see Tkachuk (2012).
17 Tkachuk (2002), 48.
18 Bogdashevskij (1892), 650.
19 Bogdashevskij (1893), 137.

limited spheres. Even to ask for the conditions and limits of knowledge is beyond their scope. This does not mean, however, that philosophies are to be erected in their entirety *a priori*. "It is impossible to construct a theory of cognition without attention to the factual realities of thinking. It is impossible to create an ethics that renounces the factual actions of the will."[20] On the other hand, if the natural sciences attempt on their own to solve philosophical problems, they go astray. Bogdashevskij's basic thesis was that philosophy is a thoroughly independent discipline, one that does not contradict or oppose the natural sciences. On the contrary, it works along with the sciences, influencing them and vice versa. It should be kept in mind, though, that Bogdashevskij conceived philosophy as metaphysics pure and simple. In reconstructing the history of the interrelations between philosophy and the sciences, Bogdashevskij mentioned only the positive interactions, particularly those that occurred in antiquity and in early modern thought when scientists were characterized as "natural philosophers." Wishing to establish his thesis, he of course found that metaphysics has rendered important services to science more than once, though these were usually overlooked.

Even though the threat posed to his religious fervor and metaphysics in general from Comtean positivism had long receded, Bogdashevskij pleaded for tolerance by scientists. Metaphysical philosophy without science loses sight of the objective world, but science without it is "unable to contribute to the genuine exaltation and ennoblement of the spirit, which surely must be the goal of knowledge."[21] Without the ideal element that metaphysics provides, the sciences become purposeless and fragmented spheres of knowledge.

Bogdashevskij's lengthiest and most concentrated piece of philosophical writing was an 1898 exposition and critique of Kantian philosophy. As with virtually all Russian theologians of the time, Bogdashevskij simply could not grasp the fundamental distinction between transcendental and empirical idealism, although he apparently recognized Kant had made such a distinction. His Kant is a phenomenalist who denies the "real" existence of space, time, and causality. But the Achilles heel of Kantianism, as we hear over and over, is its supposition of unknowable things in themselves. If there are such "things in themselves," as Kant claims, they must be substances. And without such a supposition it is impossible to explain how we have sensations, a sensible manifold. Since sensations in the plural affect us, they must also have qualities that allow us to distinguish one from another. "Consequently, quantity and quality cannot be merely simple forms of our under-

---

20 Bogdashevskij (1894), 14.
21 Bogdashevskij (1894), 42.

standing."²² We need not linger on Bogdashevskij's criticisms. They offer little, if anything, to the criticisms have seen and can expect to see. He did not accept Kant's contention that existence is not a predicate, but Bogdashevskij was willing to concede that the cosmological and teleological proofs of God's existence taken separately cannot establish the existence of a personal Being. Taken together, however, as he believed they should be, the proofs complement one another. Bogdashevskij's critique remained an isolated effort, hardly recognized outside the narrow confines of the Russian academies. Surely, some students at those academies would have found its pages useful for its succinct summaries, but it contributed nothing to international Kant-scholarship.²³ In any case, it marked Bogdashevskij's swan song in philosophy, after which he authored numerous tracts that belong in the sphere of Biblical scholarship. He rapidly rose within the ranks of the Orthodox Church from his ordination to the priesthood in 1910, to bishop, and then to archbishop.

The last philosophy professor at the Kyiv Academy during the era of Imperial Russia was Petr P. Kudrjavcev (1868–1940), not to be confused with Viktor D. Kudrjavcev, whom we met earlier. A graduate of the Kyiv Academy in 1892, he remained there to prepare for a professorship. However, in 1893 he secured a position at the Polodsk Seminary, teaching philosophy, and a position at a Polodsk school for women teaching literature and pedagogy. With Bogdashevskij's transfer to New Testament studies, Kudrjavcev welcomed the opportunity to return to the Academy in 1897 to teach the history of philosophy. He remained a professor there until the Academy was closed in 1919. While he taught at the Kyiv Academy, he supplemented his salary by concurrently teaching as well at other institutions in the city.

Kudrjavcev was among, if not the leader of, a small group of progressive Academy professors who welcomed the events of 1905 hoping that increased political freedom would lead to increased academic freedom. He participated in composing the Provisional Rules mentioned earlier and believed that the academies should be institutions devoted to theological scholarship, not just schools for the training of priests.²⁴ The measured success of 1906 would not be repeated or even last long. The election by secret ballot of a new rector in 1907 was blocked by the Holy Synod, which insisted on a different figure. Then, in early 1908 Khropovickij, who had become Archbishop Antonij, conducted an audit of the Kyiv Academy and submitted his report to the Synod. In it, he accused the progressive professors,

---

22 Bogdashevskij (1898), 109.
23 For another short account of Bogdashevskij's critique of Kant, see Nemeth (2017), 203–205.
24 Pastushenko (2007), 167.

which of course included Kudrjavcev, of sympathizing with the goals of the revolutionaries, prompting them to address the accusations directly.

Kudrjavcev is another figure from the annals of Imperial-Russian philosophy who has received little attention. Lossky in his single-volume *History of Russian Philosophy* made no note of him. Even Zenkovsky, who had studied in Kyiv, albeit at the secular university there, did not so much as mention Kudrjavcev in his two-volume *History*. The likely reason is not hard to find: Zenkovsky thought Petr Kudrjavcev offered little of note to Russian philosophy. The former, in his separate recollections of "outstanding" people he had encountered, wrote: "Kudrjavcev's main talent lay not in the sphere of scholarship or philosophy, but in the sphere of morals. In matters of conscience, he was profound, rigorously truthful, and uncompromising. Among the professors of the Kyiv Academy, he was their conscience."[25] Zenkovsky went on to remark that Kudrjavcev authored only one good work in philosophy, but it contained not even a single hint of the author's own position.

Kudrjavcev's teaching duties as a professor of the history of philosophy surely did not logically entail that he had to expound his own philosophical stand on traditional issues, and as a matter of fact he did not. But he did offer his personal interpretation of that history as a continuous battle between what he took to be absolutism and relativism. He tells us that absolutism is the recognition of absolute norms, goals, and values, whereas relativism is the simple denial of those absolutes.[26] Indeed, he held that this battle ran throughout history, throughout the whole of humanity, and is even the defining element in the life of the human individual. The historical struggle between absolutism and relativism became at times especially acute due to conditions external to the struggle. These moments have served as historical turning points in the political and cultural lives of nations and continue to do so.[27]

One way in which the age-old struggle between absolutism and relativism has manifested itself, according to Kudrjavcev, is in that between idealism and realism. Without giving precise definitions to his terms, he correctly observed that Kant intimately tied the absolute dignity of the human individual to his idealism, a position Fichte, as his successor, loudly endorsed. Idealism entered Russian thought in the early nineteenth century as a philosophy of liberation. Kudrjavcev considered it odd, though, that philosophical idealism became associated with political conservativism and reaction, and the extreme realist philosophy of materialism in the

---

25 Zenkovskij (1994), 47.
26 Kudrjavcev (2012), 325.
27 Kudrjavcev (2012), 74.

1860s took up the banner of human liberation.[28] Writing in 1908, Kudrjavcev, believed a new generation of idealists had emerged, arguing for political progressivism and denouncing materialism as its enemy. These progressive thinkers found the theoretical views of their immediate political predecessors untenable and sought the philosophical foundation of their views elsewhere. Some found it in the "pure empiricism" of Mach and Avenarius, while adhering to the methodological significance of materialism as F.A. Lange did. These progressive thinkers believed the opposition to metaphysics that lay at the heart of empiricism logically led to relativism and the rejection of absolute ethical ideals. In other words, an attachment to any philosophical position short of metaphysical idealism led ultimately in their view to the opposite political position that they sought to uphold.

In light of his teaching position, we cannot be surprised that Kudrjavcev's publications concerned the history of philosophy. He sought to trace the tension between faith and scientific knowledge back at least to the ancient Greeks, among whom he found there to be only a gradual demarcation between the two faculties. The perceived opposition between faith and knowledge received scholarly attention in Russia only in the nineteenth century and found its starkest expression in the dispute between the Slavophiles and the Westernizers.[29]

Despite his praise for Kant's view of the recognition of human dignity, Kudrjavcev was no Kantian. He offered no insight into Kant's arguments on the impossibility of transcending the bounds of sensible experience, but chastised those of his contemporaries, particularly in Germany, who sought a way to resolve the problems Kant introduced through his admission of an unknowable thing in itself. Kudrjavcev viewed it as an ineliminable concept in Kant's system, one that would require excising at least a third of the text.[30] In their futile effort to expunge the thing in itself from Kant's texts and despite their differences with the positivists, the neo-Kantians reduced all aspects of the Absolute to the functions of a transcendental mind but could not help move toward subjectivism and relativism. The Absolute in neo-Kantianism is merely a function of this transcendental mind but not something that enables the absolute principle of reason. For all his progres-

---

28 Kudrjavcev may have found it "odd," but to the student of Russian intellectual history it certainly is not. The political banner associated with the Enlightenment was condemned by the Orthodox Church which preached political conservativism, if not reaction, coupled with religious idealism. Kant and Fichte were condemned, leaving only the "materialists" defending political progressivism. Kudrjavcev's inclusion of those at the academies as idealists is philosophically accurate, but most were not by any means politically progressive. Quite the contrary.
29 Kudrjavcev (1991), 41. Kudrjavcev's article originally appeared in 1901 in the journal of the Kyiv Academy.
30 Kudrjavcev (2012), 174.

sivism, Kudrjavcev remained a deeply committed adherent of Orthodox Christianity. This prevented him from openly dissociating himself from his predecessors and teachers at the theological academies who, like him, advocated a religio-philosophical idealism but, unlike him, in practice championed reactionary political and social stands. With Kudrjavcev, philosophy at the Kyiv Academy demonstrated it had exhausted its creativity and vitality.

Something should be said of Kudrjavcev's later years. The years of political tumult between 1905 and 1917 had neither altered nor diminished Kudrjavcev's general progressive stance. In April 1917, he told a gathering of clergy and laymen in Kyiv that they bore some responsibility for the ordinary workers' anger and resentment toward themselves for their passivity in confronting governmental abuses. Those assembled could not rightly expect workers either to forgive them for their past indifference or trust them now to be sincere. In the 1920s with the closing of the Kyiv Academy, he held a number of different positions in the Ukrainian state, as it all-too-briefly existed. He also taught Russian and Russian literature before his arrest and sentencing to a labor camp. His term was commuted after three years owing to a heart condition. He was employed for a time in an agricultural laboratory before being arrested again in 1938. Released again eight months later allegedly on lack of evidence, Kudrjavcev died of a heart attack in mid-1940.

10.3 Snegirev Under the Third Charter

As was the case with Linickij's tenure at the Kyiv Academy, that of the Kazan Academy professor Veniamin Snegirev, whom we also encountered in Chapter 7, spanned longer than the mere fifteen-year duration of the second charter. During his later years he taught psychology, logic and philosophy, although he is primarily remembered as a psychologist, and a proponent of the introspective approach at that. A number of his lectures, some of which he was preparing for publication upon his death in 1889, were edited and presented by his brother Aleksandr. The most direct statement of Veniamin's philosophical position was presented in a lengthy essay that appeared in 1891 under the title "On the Nature of Human Knowledge and Its Relation to Objective Being." Knowledge, Snegirev tells us, is a social product. Certainly, it can be had only by self-conscious beings motivated, to be sure, by curiosity and a desire for it. However, we must not disregard its importance, indeed its necessity, as a tool in the struggle for survival. Were it not for the mutual cooperation of self-conscious human individuals, knowledge would not have developed and progressed. In this sense, it is the property of societies.

We should note here Snegirev's disquieting talk upfront of knowledge as a property of societies, which he understands as individual nations or peoples.[31] Each such nation has a special character and concomitantly, given his other claims, a unique form of knowledge. The potentially relativistic implications of such an assertion are tempered, fortunately, by his admission that knowledge spreads gradually, uniting, not dividing, nations and loses its original one-sidedness, becoming common possession of many societies. Thus, Snegirev notably refrains from any hint of sociologism.

Genuine knowledge can be had of objective reality by the natural sciences but also of the cognizing subject through reflection on one's inner states. Snegirev had no doubts that introspection provided an accurate picture of the human mind, a picture that was inaccessible to others through the techniques employed in the natural sciences.[32] Without so much as the slightest hesitation, Snegirev here identified the discipline associated with the employment of introspection not as psychology – as we might expect – but as philosophy, and it reveals the sphere of the supersensible, spiritual being within us. This supersensible order includes thought and reason, which, to Snegirev's religiously-trained frame of mind, are the highest manifestations of existence, and as such philosophy "naturally" seeks them in exteriority, in the physical world, as a certain order.[33] To the two sources of knowledge already mentioned, viz., external feelings and inner ones, Snegirev added a third, a religious feeling that reveals the infinite to us.

As with all the figures we have discussed, Snegirev is dismissive of the Kantian "thing in itself," considering it to be a pure fiction, since its acceptance would preclude in his eyes seeing God's handiwork in the universe, the meaning and purpose of it all. Snegirev did not offer a philosophical argument for his rejection of the unknowable thing in itself, which in the Kantian scheme presents itself owing to the *a priori* formal intuitions of space and time. Rejecting that scheme, Snegirev believed the ultimate foundations of the universe can be known from the appearances themselves and "are accessible to a certain extent from the perspective of the appearances rooted in those foundations by simply studying them more deeply, without the need of intuiting them from the opposite perspective."[34] And with this

---

[31] Snegirev (1891), 10.
[32] Snegirev stipulates, however, that we can know the states of others insofar as they are similar to our own through analogy. Unfortunately, he did not linger on this issue without detailing either how such an analogous procedure differs essentially from the techniques of experimental psychology or how the analogy is accomplished.
[33] Snegirev (1891), 18.
[34] Snegirev (1891), 22.

total elimination of unknowable things in themselves, the connection between "philosophy" and natural science is restored. How this restoration takes place is left unsaid.

Another aspect of Snegirev's thought is his epistemic foundationalism. He thought all human knowledge must be based on an absolutely valid truth, a truth concerning a *"real"* being that is discovered immediately to be a real being.[35] The proposition that asserts this truth is: thinking exists. Here, "thinking and the being that is thought coincide and envelop each other without a remainder."[36] The object of thought is thought itself, which alone has absolute certainty in the scope of human knowledge. All other known truths ultimately rest on the assumption of the truth of the being of thinking. At this point, Snegirev is not explicitly endorsing a Cartesian ego as emanating from this thinking, but only the thinking itself as existing. He does acknowledge, however, that thinking is intentional. That is, thinking requires an object, an object that appears to the thought-process as "other." Owing to its need for an intentional object, there would be no thought if there were no object. Otherness, in short, is a basis of thought, as a type of being. Snegirev construed this logical dependence of thought on otherness as ontological and causal. The object produces thought, and even in reflection on itself, on its own being, "thought necessarily intuits its dependence on otherness."[37] Thinking cannot think of itself or of anything without that process being caused. In this way, the causality is an *a priori* law, a law that extends to and throughout the spheres of both the psychic and the material. We find its applicability immediately in thought and as absolutely valid throughout. "Therefore, if ideas and the senses exist, they also have a respective cause, and this cause is obviously real – it actually exists – just as they themselves do. Just as sensations and ideas arouse thought, so too parts of external reality arouse sensations and ideas."[38] There can be no doubt that Snegirev was acquainted with Kant's writings and, in fact, with much of modern philosophy. From what we have just seen, he was quite dismissive of it too. Perhaps more importantly, he certainly could not have abided Husserl's transcendental re-

---

[35] Thus, for those familiar with Husserlian terminology Snegirev insists that the fundamental being from which philosophy starts be both *reell* and *real*.
[36] Snegirev (1891), 41.
[37] Snegirev (1891), 46. Although he does not comment on the immediacy of the ego's presence in thought, the inference is clear. Just as the thinking process requires an "other," the ego of the thinking process is just as immediate. However, this does not mean that the ego's logical persistence is greater than that of transcendent objects.
[38] Snegirev (1891), 47.

duction and exhibited not so much as an inkling of the need for a theory of meaning.[39]

In the posthumously published compilation of his lectures on psychology delivered from 1884/85–1888/89, Snegirev expounded on the applicability of the law of causality, such as in the example above. It is immediate and obvious, requiring no traditionally conceived philosophical proof. He thought of the existence of reality, transcendent to the cognizer and the cognizing process, as an immediate truth. Indeed, no "philosophical proof" was either possible or necessary. The lack of a developed theory of meaning places Snegirev in a puzzling position. For while he insists on the immediacy of externality he also asserts that all we truly know of the properties of material objects is by way of our sensations, which are after all our inner states. These states form an idea of the object in our minds. If all we truly know are our inner states, how does the sense of objectivity, of the transcendency of the causes of sensations, arise? This is a question Snegirev did not pose, let alone answer.

Snegirev sought to oppose the Kantian scheme in its entirety and, thus, also took exception with its account of space and time as *a priori* forms of sensible intuition. He held that the key to the formation of our idea (*ideja*) of space is found in the structure of our human sense organs, particularly touch and vision. It arises in our minds in exactly the same way as other ideas we have and attach to external objects – color, temperature, sound, etc. Since it is only by virtue of space that we can characterize an object as external, the psychic "constitution" of our intuition of space must have a certain priority over the other attributes mentioned. Regrettably, Snegirev did not elaborate on this theme. Instead, he held that given the universal applicability of the causal law something transcendent to consciousness must produce our "idea" of space, as is the case with our other sensations. "There-

---

[39] Snegirev devoted little, if any, attention to the technical issues in philosophy that were swirling in professional philosophical circles at the time. In his posthumously published essay "Metaphysics and Philosophy," he abruptly criticized German neo-Kantianism for its negative stand toward metaphysical issues. Snegirev opined that it in its entirety was subject to all of the objections that could be leveled against Kant's philosophy. Referring presumably, but without explicit acknowledgment, to Cohen, Snegirev held that the identification of philosophy with the quest for the foundations of natural science entailed the abandonment of any meaningful sense of knowledge. Snegirev (1890), 53. Snegirev, as did so many others we have seen, identified philosophy with metaphysics. The object of philosophy is the entire world, all that is. "Its task is to explain this whole just as the individual sciences explain its various parts. ... The goal is to give a scientific worldview, revealing as much as possible the inner sense of the entirety of existence and of human life." Snegirev (1890), 74. On the other hand, neo-Kantianism "creates only a surrogate for philosophy, presenting to a hungry society a simple phantom, an elusive ghost consisting of negations." Snegirev (1890), 53.

fore, space, on the one hand, exists outside us. On the other hand, it is our state, just as a color actually exists outside us and is at the same time our state."[40]

Snegirev devoted some attention to time, i.e., to our consciousness of the flow of time, which he viewed as analogous to our consciousness of space. Whereas we speak of the measurement of the space occupied by an object as its length or size, we speak of the measurement of the time of a phenomenon as its duration. And although Snegirev realizes that time can be divided into smaller and smaller durations, which we call "moments," he failed to connect his observations concerning inner time-consciousness, which he called "subjective time," with the constitution of higher order conceptions as did Kant and Husserl, in particular, in enormous detail. Snegirev, clearly, was aware that "subjective time" lurks behind our conceptions of singularity and distinctiveness, but he viewed it primarily and explicitly as serving a negative function, namely to establish the opposition between the external and the internal, the psychic and the corporeal.[41] His analysis stopped precisely just where his philosophical analysis should have begun. Snegirev's way into philosophy was through mundane psychology, but the goal was philosophy understood as metaphysics, particularly a theistic metaphysics.

10.4 The Summit of Imperial Russia's Academic Religious Philosophy

Another often unjustly overlooked figure in secondary studies of philosophy in Imperial Russia is Viktor I. Nesmelov (1863–1937).[42] Upon graduating from the Saratov Seminary in 1883, he enrolled at the Kazan Academy. Apparently, his record there was outstanding, and a term paper he wrote on Gregory of Nyssa was deemed to be of such merit that he was urged to submit it as a thesis for the *magister*'s degree, which he did, and defended in February 1888.[43] He then was ap-

---

40 Snegirev (1893), 318.
41 Snegirev (1893), 323.
42 Berdjaev for a time hailed Nesmelov as "the most profound phenomenon" to emerge from the theological academies. Berdjaev (1910a), 187. Berdjaev's essay was originally written for the famous collection *Vekhi*. In another essay from 1909, Berdjaev hailed Nesmelov as a "bold, deep, and original thinker," who in certain respects is more interesting than Solov'ëv. Berdjaev (1910b), 276.
43 Nesmelov remained at the Kazan Academy upon graduation in 1887, receiving a fellowship to help prepare for assuming a teaching position in metaphysics there. Snegirev prepared a program for him in order to become acquainted with the works of ancient and modern metaphysicians after which he should pass from the historical perspective to the psychological. At the end of the academic year, Nesmelov submitted a report demonstrating that he had worked on Snegirev's program, but he also handed over a substantial treatise of his own. Snegirev wrote a review in

pointed a docent in metaphysics and promoted to extraordinary professor in late December 1895. Nesmelov, in typical Russian fashion, began the serial publication in 1895 of what became the first volume of his principal work *Nauka o cheloveke* [*The Science of the Human Being*], for which he was awarded a doctorate in theology in 1898. The second volume appeared in 1903, but generally speaking Nesmelov published little compared to a number of others.

Nesmelov proceeded from the view that all psychic activity can be investigated through self-reflection or introspection. He was quite dismissive of the notion of unconscious mental processes, holding that a belief in the unconscious was the result of pure misunderstanding and that it would lead only to a crude naivety. What sort of "naivety" he had in mind is unclear. Nonetheless, Nesmelov contended that were it not for the interactions between the mind and the world our conscious processes would be chaotic. Isolated from any interaction with the world, they would be independent of each other, "without order and meaning."[44] If our mental processes were always different, our mental life would also be nothing but nonsense.

Unlike Kant, Nesmelov turned not to *a priori* forms and categories to establish order in cognition, but to the phenomena themselves, which enter successively into consciousness. The determination of some similarity between the phenomena is the work of thought, but a mundane thought-process, not, as in Kant, a transcendental one. Indeed, we see that much of Nesmelov's epistemological investigations are an attempt at a psychological explanation of cognition, endeavoring to offer a competing theory to Kant's transcendental idealism, if not an outright refutation of it. To do so, Nesmelov appealed to the British empiricists' procedure while refusing

---

which he pointed out the treatise's positive aspects as well as what he considered to be its shortcomings, which, nevertheless, did not reduce the value of the work. Snegirev's treatise had long been thought to be lost, but recently a copy was found in the national archives of Tatarstan. We are told very little concerning the particulars of the document. For example, how much editing was required? Since Nesmelov's treatise was never published, we must be cautious, but the points he made offer an insight into his frame of mind at the time. Being only a student work, Nesmelov followed his teacher's lead in confusing epistemological concerns with ontological ones. Unlike his teacher, however, he attempted a philosophical proof of the objective world. "Since the beginning of experience refers to a time when the subject as such did not exist and it is self-determined only through and from experience, experience clearly does not belong exclusively to the subject. Thus, we must assume the existence of an object as its real foundation." Nesmelov (2020), 21. Also like his teacher, Nesmelov inexplicably held that space and time are created by the cognizing subject: "We know that the objective world is a world of similar and different things and phenomena. The subject creates for its being the form of space and for its life the form of time." Nesmelov (2020), 35. Further explication of this bizarre statement is not to be had.

44 Nesmelov (1905), 27.

to accept certain assumptions about the nature of sensory impressions, on the one hand, and the mechanics of cognition, on the other.[45]

Nesmelov attempted to construct the origin of the child's conception of objectivity on the basis of the genetic psychology of his day. Certainly, we can commend him for doing so instead of merely taking the conception for granted as most of the figures we have discussed did. Nesmelov saw the first step in the process of objectification as the localization of sensory impressions.[46] Unfortunately, instead of examining how kinaesthetic localization becomes our complete conception of objectivity, Nesmelov was content with asserting that the latter is merely the result of a complex processing of the former. "The entire difference between these processes consists solely in that one gives a *local* determination of impressions within the organism itself, whereas the other goes further in this direction and posits a *spatial* determination of impressions outside the organism."[47]

Having dispensed with an approach to objectification via genetic psychology, Nesmelov turned to a structural approach. Objectification requires two different moments. The first is a synthesis, by which a complex of sensory impressions is formed. In other words, how is an object, as a unified set of impressions, possible? In this, we can see the influence of Kant, for whom also "synthesis" is the action of combining different representations into one cognition.[48] The second moment of objectification is "analysis," by which the product of synthesis is objectified. Nesmelov remarked that each instance of analysis always represents the necessary conclusion of a synthesis, but in doing so he omitted any consideration of intentional but merely imaginary objects, such as of Pegasus or Polyphemus.[49] Nesmelov recognized that Kant had already posed the problem of how a real intentional object is possible but admonished him for hastening to a different problem, name-

---

[45] Nesmelov, for example, conceded to the British empiricists that the mind of a baby at the time of birth is a "blank slate," Locke's *tabula rasa*, but already by the end of the first day the child can make crude and the simplest distinctions. "But once the act of distinguishing has taken place, consciousness has opened, and spiritual life has begun." Nesmelov (1905), 36.

[46] Of some interest to us is the comparison of Nesmelov's treatment of the localization of sensations to Husserl's in *Ideas II*, where in §36 Husserl lingers, though not unnecessarily, on its role in the constitution of the corporeal Body. See Husserl (1989), 152–155.

[47] Nesmelov (1905), 39. There is a vicious circle here in that objectification involves spatial determination, but Nesmelov was trying to elaborate on the constitution of the individual's conception of space. Fortunately, he was aware of the issue, writing that a complete objectification requires the association of an entire series of impressions. However, he did not provide the needed elaboration of how such an association leads to the desired goal.

[48] See Kant (1997), 210 (A77/B103).

[49] The qualification here is that Nesmelov's language does not always reveal that in using the term "object" he meant a real (objectified) object, not merely an intentional object.

10.4 The Summit of Imperial Russia's Academic Religious Philosophy — 279

ly how synthetic judgments are possible *a priori*. Not recognizing how Kant's formulation of the central problem arises from his acceptance of time and space as *a priori* intuitions, Nesmelov viewed the essence of the epistemological problem to be how objective judgments in general are possible. Nevertheless, he saw that the solution to the problem lies explicitly not in a transcendental inquiry, but a psychological one. The objectification of sensory impressions is a result of the unification of impressions as spatial localizations, since all impressions cannot be had in consciousness simultaneously. For Nesmelov, then, the spatiality of impressions is a result of cognition's inability to be aware of all at the same time. How this differs from saying that our conception of space is an *a priori* form is unclear. He wrote:

> If we would consider these processes only with respect to their content, i.e., quite independently of all other conscious states, then the organization of the chaotic world of consciousness alone would express their entire significance. Therefore, their entire application would be limited to just the world of given impressions alone.[50]

The formation and objectification of representations is dependent on the formation and unification of impressions, which in turn depends on the relation of the subject to externality. Nesmelov's contention is surely quite vague.

Having seemingly established that cognition can result only from an interplay between the subject and sensory impressions causally induced from exteriority, Nesmelov adopted a different approach that patently offers little room for a correspondence theory of truth. He wrote:

> The formation of any cognition directly depends not on any objective foundations, but only on the subjective and harmonious position of the cognition within the content on hand of the mind. Both the person in everyday life and the scholar equally affirm as cognition only those thought-constructions in which there is harmony in the mental content, and they equally hold to these cognitions only as long as this harmony exists. ... Therefore, all cognition, by its very nature, is always and necessarily subjective.[51]

At the time of writing the *Nauka*, Nesmelov followed the lead of Snegirev in rejecting the possibility of a philosophical, i.e., rational, proof of objectivity. We have, undoubtedly, a large quantity of cognitions that refer to objectivity. That is, they have the sense of emanating from an objective world, but in fact all mental processes, as

---

50 Nesmelov (1905), 78.
51 Nesmelov (1905), 84.

mental, are subjective.⁵² Thus, that we attribute their source to objective reality "is not a cognitive phenomenon, but a phenomenon of faith, which however is affirmed to be a real cognition."⁵³ Lacking a complete theory of intentionality, of sense-constitution, Nesmelov opted to ascribe the sense of objectivity ultimately to a faculty that lies outside explication, namely faith. By invoking a faculty of faith, Nesmelov thought he could solve – and in fact had solved – an otherwise intractable epistemological problem.

Nesmelov affirmed that faith and cognition are intimately connected. If, however, faith is involved in every act of objective cognition, how can we have faith but no cognition and cognition of inner states without faith? Nesmelov's answer is that faith and knowledge (*znanie*) are not two different forms of cognition (*poznanie*), but two different moments (*momenta*) of the cognitive process. Owing to the difference of these moments, the cognitive process is both a development of faith and of the formation of knowledge. The latter, knowledge, is the final ideal of the cognitive process, whereas faith is the actual state of the aspiration for knowledge. The vast bulk of human knowledge is actually not knowledge, but only faith. Having said that, Nesmelov believed he had shown that there is no collision, no dispute between faith and knowledge and that there cannot be one. To assert the contrary is a result of a blatant misunderstanding. Knowledge is faith, albeit a *complete* faith or confidence in the agreement of one's thought with reality.⁵⁴

Nesmelov faulted Kant for attempting to prove in his "Refutation of Idealism" the existence of objects in space outside me by arguing from the temporal persistence of something in perception. Nesmelov held to the Cartesian standpoint that self-consciousness is the only fully rational certainty we can have of that something exists, viz., the "I," the cognizing subject. Thus, only based on the fact of self-consciousness and the deduction from it that I certainly exist, can I affirm the existence of something else. The persistence that Kant found in perception is only a seeming phenomenon. Within the sphere of all that is cognizable and even conceivable, only the existence of the cognizing subject is persistent. That

---

52 He clarifies slightly further on, writing "the whole process of cognizing objective reality is obviously only the process of a person believing in the objective significance of one's judgments about reality, and therefore all the propositions comprising one's knowledge are really only different expressions of one's faith." Nesmelov (1905), 103.
53 Nesmelov (1905), 85.
54 To ascribe the sense of objectivity to sensory impressions, to a "moment" of cognizing, namely faith, as Nesmelov did, hardly resolves the issue of the constitution of that sense; it merely shifts the issue. We can still ask how "faith" accomplishes the constitution. Does it just in a single instant attribute objectivity to sensory impressions? How do we account for why some impressions appear more "real" than others?

is, the subject *introduces* persistence into the world in one's representations and concepts. Nesmelov held it to be only logical, then, that temporal forms can be determined to the subject's satisfaction quite independently of the objectivity of the external world. These forms, as intuitions, refer only to the connection between the sense data, not the data themselves.

> Consequently, a subject can never at all intuit itself in the intuitive form of time, because conscious activity stands outside this form, and in itself this activity says absolutely nothing about time, space, or any objective existence. Therefore, Kant's entire account of the origin and significance of the intuitive form of time is an indubitable result of a pure misunderstanding.[55]

We should bear in mind here that Nesmelov rejected the Kantian position that space and time are *a priori* forms of intuition, as though those forms were exclusively part of the mechanism of the subject's cognitive faculty. Kant's greatest error, though, lay in his distorted view of the significance of self-consciousness, ascribing an exaggerated importance to sense experience. The subject's sensations and representations are the subject's states. Nesmelov held that sensations and representations inform the subject of what one has and of occurrences within oneself, but not of what exists externally. Nesmelov's conclusion here is not dissimilar from Fichte's, namely, that the subject affirms the existence of a world external to oneself through and only because of the subject's affirmation of its own existence in the world. Since the subject's self-consciousness is identical with its existence, its conscious activity as acting in the world is, then, actually acting in the world. By acting in the world, the subject affirms its own real existence. What we have in thought is not the thing in itself, but a symbol of the actual thing. By virtue of the constancy and necessity of our representations, that they cannot change whimsically, but only by either our own actions or by apparent forces known to us, they naturally acquire the sense of objectivity.

Much more can be said even in simply summarizing Nesmelov's large book. To the extent that it has garnered attention it is not for the points we have just seen, but for its religious anthropology, which represents a general worldview rather than a response to traditionally conceived philosophical questions. But one such question, which for many is an essential component of a worldview, is the religious factor, more specifically the existence of God. Many of the philosophical theologians we have studied here rejected the Feuerbachian view that the human conception of God is of purely human origin, that that conception is of a Being with infinite attributes. Nesmelov, perhaps surprisingly, saw a measure of truth here. All of our conceptions of God are necessarily man-made, since they are all con-

---

[55] Nesmelov (1905), 125.

ceived in the finite human consciousness. We cannot truly have a conception of the infinite and thus also not of God. By attempting a philosophical argument that our conception of God corresponds to God in reality, the theistic philosopher already loses to his/her opponents. Not only is the theist's argument unsatisfactory on its own terms, but it raises another question as to the origin of the human conception of God and, as such, plays into the hands of Feuerbachians.

Viktor Kudrjavcev years before realized that to ask for the origin of our conception of God as an all-perfect being poses difficulties. Finding no satisfactory answer, he concluded that God Himself had directly given it to us. Nesmelov opined that "it is impossible in fact to attach serious significance to such an argument."[56] Rather, if we cannot find the origin of our conception of God from any available source, the only logical conclusion we can draw is an agnostic one. To say that "the idea of God arises in us from God Himself is not at all the logical conclusion from the given premises, but a simple logical trick that can only evoke a smile from serious people and in no case convince them of what we want."[57] Apparently, then, we come to a quite indefinite position. Neither the arguments of the empiricists nor those of their opponents can stand critical scrutiny.[58]

Nesmelov was, of course, not a religious agnostic and certainly not an atheist. Only faith in God is justified. But philosophy can help explain and justify the need for religious faith, that is, explain it as a rational need, for the individual alone. Rational proofs one way or another are of no avail. This is not to say, of course,

---

56 Nesmelov (1905), 249.

57 Nesmelov (1905), 249. Nesmelov defended his position quite frankly against that of Kudrjavcev, stating "It is quite natural that with such a pseudo-empirical explanation of the idea of God any genuine empiricist can quite freely and boldly advance and defend a purely naturalistic explanation of this idea. For although only assumptions are expressed, they are nevertheless based on the actual facts of experience and not on facts invented for the sake of some magical transformation of ignorance into knowledge." Nesmelov (1905), 250.

58 Nesmelov was certainly aware of the traditional cosmological and ontological proofs for the existence of God, but predictably found them wanting in that they have God operating inexplicably within the empirical world. In doing so, Kudrjavcev's argument, is a concession to the opponents of God's existence that potentially leads to pantheism or outright atheism. Nesmelov (1905), 347. More specifically, although a theological explanation of the universe in the teleological argument is obviously quite consistent with the existence of God, it alone cannot lead to such an acknowledgment unless one is first inclined to see the hand of God in the world. Nesmelov (1905), 343. And as to the cosmological argument, Nesmelov wrote, "we obviously have a right to speak only of the *necessary* concept of a first cause but not at all of the *actual existence* of such a cause. For in reality we encounter only secondary causes and not first causes anywhere. We not only do not know a first cause, but cannot at all conceive of one." Nesmelov (1905), 345. The moral argument, which sees God as the perfect ethical legislator, potentially leads to the erection of the saint as the equal of God, and the ontological argument leads to the posing of the source of our idea of God.

that Nesmelov himself found no value in disputing God's existence. Far from it, he agreed with those who proclaimed the idea of God lies within us, but this idea is neither the result of some reflection on conscious phenomena nor is it given through non-sensible exterior experience. Rather, it is "factually realized as an object within a person by the nature of one's own individuality (*lichnost'*) as the living image of God."[59] And with this assertion Nesmelov left the sphere of rational discourse. If one were to dispute Nesmelov's contention, saying that there is no such image of God within oneself, Nesmelov could hardly point to empirical evidence for it. By his own admission, no such evidence can be had.

> Whether there is another world apart from the presently given one no one knows or can know. That, however, within the bounds of the presently given world there is not just sensible matter, but also a supersensible individual connected with it is something of which we are immediately aware and know for certain in a cognition of ourselves.[60]

The human individual finds within one's consciousness the idea of God, the details of which present themselves as valid cognition of God's existence and nature. Nesmelov cautions us not to take his statements as an explanation of what is quite inexplicable, but only that we have within each of us an awareness of God's infinite being and absolute nature. This "psychological" proof, although not a complete and rigorous proof, holds that a spiritual, supersensible world lies within us, a world that evokes the individual's religious and moral aspirations. Clearly, Nesmelov has moved far beyond what we can discuss in purely rational terms. But, as he remarked, "there is no other way to a justification of an awareness of God, and the psychological proof is the only proof that by a direct and genuinely scientific path leads a person to a reliable cognition of God."[61]

This by no means concluded all that Nesmelov had to say in his large two-volume work. The second volume, entitled *The Metaphysics of Life and Christian Revelation*, first appeared in 1903. As the title suggests, it proceeded entirely from an Orthodox Christian standpoint, and after its appearance he published little apart from a text based on lectures delivered in August 1912 and published the following year. Again seeking to accommodate modern scientific advances with an overall religious outlook, Nesmelov asserted that a scientific conception of the world based on purely empirical cognition can be had, but it can neither exhaust the

---

59 Nesmelov (1905), 256.
60 Nesmelov (1905), 264. Of some interest in understanding his point, Nesmelov approvingly quoted Fichte's *The Vocation of Man*. Indeed, Nesmelov quoted from Fichte's corpus a number of times in his work.
61 Nesmelov (1905), 352.

full scope of human judgments nor express the depth of our spiritual relationship to the world. For one thing, science cannot tell what the goal of the world's development is, a development that science observes but the meaning of which is insoluble within the bounds of an empirical study of nature. The role of philosophy lies in providing rational considerations for the solution to these issues.

Collapsing philosophy with faith, Nesmelov found no dispute between science and religion. They adopt different viewpoints and, therefore, cannot contradict each other. As long as science adheres to the discovery of the operative laws of nature, it cannot so much as illuminate let alone eliminate the mystical revelations found in religious intuitions concerning, for example, the origin and final destiny of the world. As astonishing as it may sound to us today, Nesmelov asserted that religion and science only very seldom come into actual conflict for the simple reason that they only rarely attempt to transgress their respective domains.[62] In his view, religion – presumably his personal understanding of his religion – "does not speak of how in reality these empirical things and phenomena exist, but only about that on which their real existence depends."[63] Thus, science need no longer fear unwanted intrusions into its domain by religious thinkers, but the tables have turned. Theologians have to relentlessly struggle against scientific advances into their transcendent sphere. Unfortunately, this is a burden theologians must bear, for scientists, as human beings, cannot help themselves psychologically from posing the ultimate questions. Kant offered a practical solution, but it is unlikely to satisfy either the scientist or the theologian. Nesmelov concluded that in light of the situation we must seek a completely different path for the reconciliation of faith and knowledge.

Whereas the path for the study of the possibility of knowledge, epistemology, has established its foundations and logical conditions, the study of faith has not yet discovered its way forward. If faith presents itself as a theoretical faculty that reveals truth – and of course this was Nesmelov's position – then the path taken in epistemology should also yield results for the study of faith even if it has remained obscured owing to the thick fog cast by Kant's inquiries. Nesmelov also added, though, that the relation of sensory perception to objective reality has not been

---

[62] Nesmelov did note, however, that the authorities in the *Western* church quite futilely attempted to link scientific thought to their understanding of physical nature as presented in Biblical texts. The reference here is to the conflict between Galileo and the Catholic Church regarding heliocentrism. See Nesmelov (2015), 21. Nesmelov "conveniently" overlooked, however, those within his own Russian Orthodox Church who quarreled with Darwinism not on scientific grounds, but on the basis of a reading of the Bible.

[63] Nesmelov (2015), 24.

fully explained. Whatever the solution to the problem of the sense of objectivity may be, it will be found only on the basis of a psychological analysis of the mind.

Like Descartes, Nesmelov viewed the act of self-reflection as the original expression of perceiving something as existing. For this reason, he saw it as the ultimate foundation for any inquiry about being. But he also reaffirmed the pivotal Kantian contention – one that he had already mentioned in 1905 – that in the absence of self-consciousness all mental phenomena would present themselves in consciousness chaotically without a possessor. That is, we would have a myriad of bewildering impressions in consciousness without being aware of them. "They would, therefore, not belong to anyone and would not express anything."[64] Implicit in *any* perceptual judgment is a relation to the I or ego. The subject of all mental activities perceives those activities as one's own, not as someone else's.[65] The cognizing subject can in each act of perception turn one's mental gaze from "the moment of perception of objective reality" to oneself as perceiving, i.e., "the moment of the conscious perception of one's own life." Both perceptions are equally fundamental. Additionally – and here Nesmelov was on the cusp of the concept of sense-constitution even though he ultimately refrained from advancing further – the meaning of conscious phenomena as perceptions of existing states of affairs is determined by what he calls special judgments about them determined not by their order in consciousness, but by the creative subject of consciousness, namely, the I. Nesmelov saw Kant as advancing much of this, but the latter saw the cognition of reality limited to the sphere of sensory perception alone without specifying the reason for this restriction.[66]

Nesmelov paused at this point to elaborate on the nature of the cognizing subject, which reveals itself to itself in two ways: in an intuition as a freely rational being seeking the fulfillment of goals of its own choosing and, secondly, in sense perception as a corporeal being who is part of a given environment. He drew from this a positively odd conclusion reminiscent of Descartes that we have as it were two different "essences": one spiritual, the other material. Thus, we are both a material thing and a person (*lichnost'*). On the one hand, we are part of the physical and chemical worldly processes and, on the other hand, independent free agents in the world. How can the obvious contradictions from this duality be resolved? Here, the influence of Kant is quite apparent. The logical inconsistency of these two views of the subject does not in the least result in the elimination of one

---

64 Nesmelov (2015), 56–57.
65 Nesmelov (2015), 58.
66 Nesmelov had regrets that Kant had not proceeded to investigate cognition of non-sensory representations, but in turn we can regret that he, Nesmelov, did not attend to senseful, though non-objectifying, mental acts. The focus of his attention lay elsewhere.

or the other. In our everyday life, we can alternately maintain one or the other depending on the current concern or need. We can regard the issue as another riddle of existence, the final solution to which may lie at the end of our scientific quest.

Nesmelov recognized that many natural scientists had already decided that the only means to resolve the mind-body problem is through the universal adoption of a thoroughly naturalistic viewpoint. But Nesmelov proposed addressing the problem by way of a return to the problem of how cognition is possible. He suggested revisiting the neglected exclusion of all non-sensory impressions. Rather than simply saying that we have an extra-sensory intuition, Nesmelov proposed that the dilemma can be resolved *psychologically* through a two-fold manner of intuiting the world.

> We can intuit worldly existence from the only point of view possible for us, from that of our own real existence. But from this one point of view we can intuit existence from two different sides: with respect to its visible superficiality in the sensible world of appearances and with respect to its invisible foundations in the supersensible world of substances. These different sides of existence are revealed to us in different ways by the two means by which we perceive ourselves, so that these two means in reality are not only different ways of perceiving ourselves, but also different ways of obtaining real cognition of existence.[67]

Just as the cognizing subject can perceive of oneself and the world quite naturalistically, so too can the subject perceive one's genuine individuality and ability to initiate action freely and see other transcendent beings in the same light.

In writing of two points of view, Nesmelov did not mean that they are *merely* different mental attitudes toward one and the same object. There is, in addition to the naturalistic viewpoint based on sense perception, the viewpoint based on an immediate mental intuition. As such, it makes no use of our five senses. It is completely independent of the external, physical conditions and is intrinsically personal, so that its result cannot be shown or pointed out to another for corroboration by others. Consequently, it cannot serve as a link between people, as a means to adjudicate disputes. We have, thus, a double sense of the intentional object: one based on empirical data, the other on a different, an immediate intuition. The different paths taken by our cognitive activity using different data result in different aspects of existence. Both yield knowledge, understood in a broad sense as we saw previously when discussing Nesmelov's earlier work, but he now preferred to characterize as "faith" that which arises from following the path of intellectual intuition and as "knowledge" that which follows from the path of empirical intuitions. "Therefore, faith has as its object the sphere of transcendent being, whereas

---

[67] Nesmelov (2015), 69.

knowledge concerns only the empirical sphere of the world of appearances."[68] Both faith and knowledge are subjective, mental phenomena. The objects in both cases are transcendent to the cognizing subject. Our empirical senses provide details about external objects, but an analysis of the logical structure of the cognitive process gives no information as to how objectively existing things become the subjectively ideal objects in cognition. Nonetheless, we know of the real existence of sensed objects "not from the evidence of our sense organs, but only by virtue of their immediate givenness to us."[69] Therefore, faith, as a form of knowledge through intuition, completely corresponds to science, which provides a form of knowledge through the empirical senses. The sphere of faith, which includes all that is grasped by the immediate intuition that he also calls "intellectual intuition," is the sphere of religious intuition and through it we have an immediate knowledge of God.

Since all cognitions concerning the sphere of transcendence are unprovable, they cannot be admitted into scientific knowledge, which demands only provable judgments. And since we have no means of explaining the sense of objectivity that the objects of our empirical senses have, we face a philosophical impasse and with this our inquiry ends. Nesmelov chose a resignation into religious faith over the pursuit of a phenomenological inquiry into the constitution of sense. He also stated at the start of his 1912/1913 paper that a purely scientific-philosophical outlook on the world would never prove satisfying, would never exhaust the richness of human judgments about the world, but by his own admission he did not and never would be able to show that these were more than subjective, psychologically-rooted deficiencies and needs.

Nesmelov remained at the Kazan Academy through the years. In 1918, the buildings were occupied by different groups and for a time used as a military hospital treating those with typhoid. Some professors attempted to give lessons in their residences and were paid miserly salaries by the Provisional Government. Some, unable to sustain themselves and their families, simply quit the Academy; some died from the typhus raging around them. One of Nesmelov's three sons, a Bolshevik, was killed that year by peasants when he and some others invaded a monastery. In 1921, the Kazan Academy was officially closed, leaving Nesmelov

---

68 Nesmelov (2015), 76.
69 Nesmelov (2015), 81. Sadly, Nesmelov rushed to attribute the sense of objectivity to perceived objects by means of some mysterious act of "faith" without reflecting on what distinguishes perceptions from hallucinations. The perception in both cases is the same, but there is something different. At approximately the same time as Nesmelov was dwelling on these matters, Husserl did too, calling a belief in a perceived object's existence the appearance's act-quality. For this and to compare Husserl's treatment of the same issue, see Husserl (2004), 11 ff.

without employment. He apparently worked for a time teaching at Kazan University, but his application for a regular appointment in psychology went nowhere.[70] He also served as an assistant to the head of the provincial bureau of statistics. In 1930, Nesmelov was arrested on the charge of being a leader of a counter-revolutionary group. The investigation lasted almost two years, at the end of which he was released but placed under house arrest, this apparently being his "reward" for fathering a martyred Bolshevik. In 1932, he was again arrested on the charge of recommending in private conversations with students the study of Hegel rather Marx. After a short time, he was released. Nesmelov lived for another five years, escaping the Siberian fate of so many of his friends, former colleagues, fellow theologians, and students.

Nesmelov's writings, coming at the end of an era, marked arguably the zenith of philosophical approaches to theology in Imperial Russia. However faulty and incomplete we may regard his work, he attempted to take modern philosophy through Kant seriously by facing the challenges it posed for Orthodox theology.

---

70 Konstantin (1998), 24.

Part IV: **Under the 1910 Charter**

Chapter 11
Philosophy at the Academies Under the Fourth Charter

The adoption of the Provisional Rules in 1906 proved to be a short-lived victory for the liberal forces. The Rules were not intended to be more than a stop-gap measure. In the general political turbulence that swirled in the country at the time, the fate of even the theological schools could not be divorced from that of secular institutions. By 1908, the pendulum had decidedly begun swinging in the opposite direction with further reforms not just being postponed, but reversed. The Holy Synod called for a review of the academies in 1908, and as could be expected the auditors, who were by no means impartial observers, found that a spirit of secularism and liberalism had pervaded the schools at the expense of discipline and church spirit. We have already seen that Archbishop Antonij (Khropovickij) submitted a report that year admonishing the academies – in particular the one in Kyiv – for a collapse of the traditional religiosity of the curriculum there. A commission established in 1909 that included Antonij and Archbishop Sergius (Stragorodskij) held that pastoral work rather than original scholarship be the focus of training at the academies and therefore that most secular sciences be excluded from an integrated curriculum. Antonij, being among the most reactionary members of the commission, questioned the utility of instruction in non-theological subjects. The commission's work fulfilled its purpose when in 1910 the charter of 1884 was in effect completely restored, freed of any hint of secularism and liberalism.[1] The newly adopted 1910 Charter called for the academies to be closed theological colleges with the purpose of training young men for a pastoral ministry. The governing of the academies in all respects was to be subordinate to the Holy Synod and the local bishops, thereby eliminating any hope of autonomy. Instruction in the natural sciences was to be conducted only from a theological point of view. Secular instructors were to be gradually eliminated, and the teaching of philosophy was deemed mandatory with the required hours being increased to 15 per week. However, as with the sciences, instruction in it was "to follow the traditional rule that its higher principles and scholarly conclusions must go hand in hand with theology, philosophy serving as a propaedeutic to the latter."[2] The Charter was further

---
[1] Pavlov (2017), 273.
[2] Ustav (1910), 50. The 1910 Charter specifically stated: "The teacher of the history of philosophy should direct the attention of the students to the philosophical thoughts in history most closely related to the concerns of theologians." Ustav (1910), 51. This charter mentioned in particular Plato

strengthened in a conservative direction by "Alterations" enacted in 1911. Certainly, not everyone was happy with the latest charter, but it would remain in effect until 1917.

The pendulum swung yet again this time in the opposite direction with the February 1917 Revolution. In its aftermath, the Provisional Rules were once again introduced with a proviso for the direct election of the rector and assistant rector. The Council of each academy was granted the power to award *magister*'s and doctoral degrees. This "liberal" period was again short-lived. In the fall of 1918, the theological *system* was officially abolished, although attempts were made by each academy to continue in one way or another. The St. Petersburg Academy, for example, ceased to exist in December 1918 after attempting unsuccessfully to join with the University there, hoping to form in effect a separate department or school under the aegis of the University. The Kazan Academy, like its counterpart in Moscow, tried in 1918 to unite with the city's secular university but, again like in Moscow, the hopes never came to fruition. Given the political situation, with few regular publications appearing for financial reasons, let alone legally permitted, the required publication requirement for new dissertations was rescinded. The Kazan Academy continued to function as a private educational institution, operating in a helter skelter fashion, until March 1921.

The situation in Kyiv was somewhat more complicated. The world war already had made pressing demands on the military to requisition the Academy's facilities in 1915 and with the possibility of Kyiv being occupied, the Holy Synod decided to evacuate. With the shifting governments in the region after the October Revolution, the Academy was never quite able to return to normal functioning, particularly since government funding ceased. As in Kazan, the authorities at the Kyiv Academy attempted to transform the school into a private institution, holding classes in the apartments of the instructors. This could only be a temporary measure but was hardly a long-term solution particularly given the socio-economic conditions at the time. Nonetheless, an attempt was made to formulate a new charter for the school in 1921 that called for a three-year curriculum consisting of only theological subjects. The school, holding on as long as it could, completely ceased in 1923.[3]

---

and Neoplatonism, but also the thought of Aristotle, given its importance for understanding Catholic theology and scholasticism, as well as that of Kant, since it embodied Protestant theology.
3 Sukhova (2013a), 74–76.

11.1 Philosophy at the Petersburg, Kyiv, and Kazan Academies

The last decade or so of the academies under the Imperial Russian regime were turbulent years that hardly lent themselves to patient philosophical reflection even for the best of minds, and the academy tradition and culture would hardly have nurtured any who may have appeared. Of course, some secondary literature did emerge. At the St. Petersburg Academy, for example, Dmitrij P. Mirtov (1867–1941), whom we briefly discussed previously, published his work on Lotze in 1914, which was accepted as a doctoral dissertation in theology without the traditional need of a defense. Mirtov published additionally a number of other works but never attempted to present a detailed picture of his own position, if, of course, he had one. Much the same could be said of Vitalij Serebrenikov whom we also saw in Chapter 8. He wrote nothing of note at the Academy during the period of the 1910 Charter. Later with the closing of the school, he held a position at the University teaching experimental psychology and other institutions in the city. When that became impossible, he worked at the city library in Kirov (Vyatka). Aleksandr I. Makarovskij (1888–1958) studied at the Petersburg Academy from 1909–1913 writing a *kandidat*'s thesis on Kant's theory of human moral nature from the viewpoint of Christian psychology. Upon graduating, he remained at the Academy with a fellowship in psychology, but from March 1914 until August 1918 he held a position teaching logic, psychology, philosophy, and pedagogy at the Pskov Theological Seminary. He too wrote nothing of note in either philosophy or psychology.

Another figure who taught at the Petersburg Academy during the twentieth century's second decade was Viktor A. Beljaev [1883-?]. Beljaev was a graduate of the Academy in 1908 and studied in Leipzig and Berlin in 1910. He taught in Petersburg until the Academy closed, and then taught at the University until 1921, when the philosophy department was summarily eliminated. After this, he worked at the public library until 1929. His *magister*'s thesis in 1914 on Leibniz's refutation of Spinoza's pantheism met resistance from the Holy Synod, which refused to grant his degree, doubting the depth of Beljaev's religiosity. Three years later, the Synod changed its mind.

Beljaev's sole work revealing his personal position to any significant extent was an essay published in 1914 entitled "On the Relationship Between Epistemology and Metaphysics." Beljaev proceeded from the claim that Kant's Critical philosophy has showed that epistemology has a logical priority over metaphysics, that a fully developed theory of cognition will accord a firm setting for metaphysics. Once we know the limits of our cognitive faculty, metaphysics can acquire the character of a complete and finished science. However, the elucidation of epistemology encounters enormous difficulties, leading to an entire series of problems. Beljaev claimed that for one thing epistemology amounts to an ontology. If following

Kant, we determine that space and time are *a priori* forms of sensible intuition, this already states something about the structure of our cognitive faculty, namely how it is. Thus, in spite of its intention a theory of cognition becomes an ontology. But, we can ask, what are we to make of these claims? Are they not themselves knowledge-claims? It appears we have a vicious circle here. Our investigation proceeded from asking how cognition is possible but found that the very answer presupposed the possibility of cognition.[4]

None of Beljaev's arguments against epistemology as first philosophy is particularly original. He himself appealed to Hegel, and, more importantly for our purposes here, Beljaev found the difficulties that accorded primacy to the theory of cognition stemmed from assumptions concerning the distinct duality of subject and object. His proposed solution was to secure the closest internal unity between the subjective and the objective orders – or at least a strict correspondence. This can be done only by assuming a new higher principle in which the two orders are united while at the same time allowing for their independence. The specifics here are not entirely clear, but his theological message is clear. The assumption of this "higher principle" is a leap indeed into metaphysics, and Beljaev recognized this to be the case and that the assumption makes epistemology dependent on metaphysics. "Such is the genuine conclusion of the present investigation. It, however, does not, of course, exclude the proposition that metaphysics needs assumptions with an epistemological character. Thus, we must ultimately recognize a reciprocity between epistemology and metaphysics as well as a mutual dependence on each other."[5] Metaphysics with its greater resemblance to religion than natural science has as its object the absolute, which does not allow for an exhaustive study by finite beings. Metaphysics "must remain only a more or less approximate expression of absolute truth."[6] In this, we see that Beljaev was strongly indebted not just to Hegel, but to Solov'ëv's critique of modern philosophy. We can also see why the Holy Synod questioned Beljaev's religiosity. His conception of God was a philosophical construct based on an explicit assumption made to avoid a difficulty in philosophy. In other words, his conception of the Deity is hardly that presented in Judeo-Christian revelation.

Beljaev was arrested in 1936 on the fabricated charge of counter-revolutionary activities. He received a sentence of three years of "corrective work" at the Karaganda Corrective Labor Camp, one of the largest in the Gulag system. Amazingly, he survived and was released. During the 1950s he lived in Leningrad, and in 1953 ob-

---

4 Beljaev (1914), 526.
5 Beljaev (1914), 537–538.
6 Beljaev (1914), 540.

tained a *kandidat*'s degree for a work on Aristotle's logic. His subsequent fate is not recorded.

Turning to the Kyiv Academy, we have already seen much that can be said about the state of philosophy there under the fourth charter. Petr Kudrjavcev taught there until the Academy was closed, and Bogdashevskij abandoned philosophy for Biblical scholarship earlier. In short, philosophical inquiry had exhausted itself. The sole figure to emerge in these years was Ivan P. Chetverikov (1880–1969), who taught psychology at the Academy from 1909 until 1917. A graduate of that institution in 1900, he defended a *magister*'s thesis "On God as a Personal Being" in 1904, the very title showing the influence on him of Russian Academic speculation of the time, particularly the thought of Viktor Kudrjavcev, and his personal distancing from philosophy. Chetverikov made much of a distinction between the human person and the "absolute person," his euphemism, of course, for God, Who is both a personal *and* an absolute Being and makes moral activity possible. The human individual has both an empirical personhood and an ideal one, the latter manifested in one's moral aspirations and which stem from the Absolute Person. In surviving notes from a course in psychology at the Academy in 1911–1912, Chetverikov connected free will with the ideal aspect each of us has without a further defense for his position.[7]

Chetverikov's own personal fate may be of some interest. He studied in Germany (Leipzig, Göttingen, and Munich) from 1906–1908. Whether he encountered the early phenomenological movement while there is unrecorded. He taught briefly in 1917 at Kyiv University, and with the Bolshevik Revolution and Civil War he was evacuated to Crimea. Subsequently, he lived in Moscow and was an active member of GAKhN (State Academy for the Study of the Arts) from 1922 until that institution was closed. Arrested in 1933, Chetverikov was sentenced to a three-year exile in Kazakhstan. Toward the end of World War II, he apparently and voluntarily retreated with the invading German troops and managed not to return to Soviet Russia. He taught for a time at an Orthodox institution in Paris and died in Stuttgart in 1969.[8] In any case, while at GAKhN, Chetverikov concerned himself with the Platonic view of aesthetics.

The Kazan Academy exhibited a measure of intellectual vibrancy during the fourth charter, which was sorely lacking in Petersburg and Kyiv, arguably owing to the continuing presence of Nesmelov. Teaching at the Academy only briefly while under the fourth charter, Nikolaj V. Petrov (1874–1956) completed the four-year

---

7 Chetverikov (1997), 343.
8 Stojukhina and Mazilov (2016), 35–36. The reader should keep in mind, however, that the secondary accounts of Chetverikov's biography are not in full agreement. The details are quite sketchy.

curriculum there in 1898. He, then, taught the history of philosophy and the New Testament at the Academy from 1900–1912, but moved over to the secular university while also remaining at his alma mater. A theologian, not a philosopher despite his teaching duties, Petrov's works used the anthropologically-oriented ideas of Nesmelov, Khrapovickij, and others to see knowledge, feeling, and the will as three functions of a single free human spirit. Apart from this, however, he falls outside the scope of our study here. He was repeatedly arrested in the 1920s. In 1930, he was sentenced to a three-year exile in Kazakhstan, but apparently survived the Stalinist years.

Finally, another shadowy figure who virtually disappeared from the pages of history in the years after the consolidation of the Soviet Union was Matvej N. Ershov (1886-?), a graduate of the Kazan Academy in 1911. He too remained there on a fellowship upon graduation. But he soon afterward began teaching the Old Testament. He published and defended a *magister*'s thesis in 1914 entitled *The Problem of Our Knowledge of God in Malebranche's Philosophy*, and in September of that year began teaching the history of philosophy.[9] In November 1916 Ershov applied for a position teaching philosophy at Kazan University, which apparently was successful. He remained in Kazan through much of 1917, but he was already in 1918 found actively participating in the creation of a liberal arts faculty for the Imperial Eastern Institute in Vladivostok. It would become the State Far-Eastern University in 1920 after a reorganization.[10]

However unoriginal Ershov's position, as set forth in his thesis, may have been, it is worth summarizing for its recapitulation at this late date of a common-enough attitude prevalent at the theological academies of the time.[11] Ershov's thesis is primarily a secondary study of the French Oratorian occasionalist, but Ershov was clearly sympathetic to his portrayal of Malebranche's thought. Seeking, as others we have discussed in these pages, a way of synthesizing the God of Christian Revelation with the Absolute discussed by philosophers, he found a possible solution in the writings of Malebranche. For Ershov, the first question to be an-

---

[9] He also published in 1914 a translation of Malebranche's *Dialogue between a Christian Philosopher and a Chinese Philosopher on the Existence and Nature of God*.

[10] Both how Ershov got to the Russian Far East is unclear and why he went there at all are unknown. Whatever the case, he did not remain in Vladivostok, since later in the decade (1926) he was with the law faculty of the Higher Russian School in Harbin, China, a city at the time teeming with Russian exiles from the Soviet Union. His subsequent fate is quite unclear.

[11] "It is impossible to find anything that would be considered original in comparison with Nesmelov's ideas, except for his work on Malebranche's texts. At the same time, Ershov in emigration completely left behind questions of epistemology, ontology, and began the study of philosophy of education, psychology, and pedagogy." Solov'ev (2021b), 158.

swered in this matter was what is it that we cognize when we have a cognition of God. He believed the path we seek is through a comparison of the mystical elements in Malebranche's thought with the analogous elements in Patristic philosophy.[12] We find in both Malebranche and in the doctrines of the early Christian thinkers beginning with Justin Martyr the same combination of rationalism and mysticism along with the Biblical teaching of the image and likeness of God in human beings. In all of the sources Ershov investigated, he found that God cannot be the object of rational cognition, but only of an intellectual intuition. The organ of this intuition, however, is the mind. The object, God, cannot be fully grasped in rational terms but must be intuitively perceived, since the Deity is indefinite and incomprehensible to rational thought.[13] Ershov, thus, based on the comparisons he adduced, claimed that with Malebranche's belief in a mystical cognition of God and the doctrines of the early Eastern Church Fathers there is a universal religious experience. Moreover, we can enter into an immediate spiritual unity with God. This mystical path of intellectual intuition cannot be rationally justified. For this reason the Church Fathers turned to the dogmas of the Christian faith.

In Vladivostok, Ershov published *The Developmental Paths of Philosophy in Russia*, a comparatively small book (64 pages of text) drawn from his lectures at the university there in 1920–1921. It, taken alone, is of little importance adding nothing new or distinctive to the various histories now available to us. Given his background at the Kazan Academy, it may be surprising how little attention Ershov gave in his book to the philosophies and personalities in the theological academies. On the other hand, it may not be surprising given Ershov's own intellectual evolution from his concerns while at the Kazan Academy to his isolation in the Far East in the Russian Civil War. Ershov began to espouse a "philosophical sociologism," a variant of nominalism whereby the dominant philosophies of countries are conditioned by a national intellectual tradition or make-up, which in turn was deeply influenced by one's language. Philosophical constructions, in this scheme, are dependent on the national characteristics of the nation's philosophers. In this way, it is meaningful to speak of "German philosophy" or "Greek philosophy" not as a purely geographical designation of the philosophers as individuals, but as distinct ways of engaging in philosophizing. Each philosophical system reflects a national element found in the minds of its creator. He wrote, "There is another typical feature that to a large degree characterizes philosophy as distinct from science. ... This is the dependence of philosophical constructions on the national mind-set, their dependence on the national characteristics of the philosophers, the creators of

---

[12] Ershov (1914), 3.
[13] Ershov (1914), 201.

these constructions."[14] The fundamental difference in philosophical systems is primarily due to this national element, which serves as their principal constitutive feature.

Ershov tells us that in his *Developmental Paths* he deliberately focused on philosophy in the Russian universities, not the academies, in order to emphasize what he considered to be the consistent growth of a Russian philosophical consciousness since the re-introduction of philosophy into the universities in the 1860s.[15] The development of a Russian philosophical tradition could then begin without the many overt political restraints that it had endured earlier during the reign of Tsar Nicholas I. Ershov's thinking remained little known even in Russia, let alone in the West. In any case, he set out his thesis without much elaboration and in relative isolation. Still, the sociologistic idea he expressed would independently be taken up by many in his homeland. An idea deeply rooted in Russia's sense of intellectual inferiority and soul-searching became a standard feature of much of its scholarship lingering on into the present day.

11.2 Philosophy at the Moscow Academy: Glagolev

Unlike at the other theological academies, the Moscow Academy retained or produced at least two individuals who continued to publish notable works during the tumultuous decade following the adoption of the Provisional Rules. The senior-most figure there whom we shall discuss in this chapter was Sergej S. Glagolev (1865–1937). Of course, he himself was a graduate of the Moscow Academy in 1889, after which he taught at the Vologda Seminary. He received a *magister*'s degree in 1894 after the successful defense of a thesis, "On the Origin and Original State of the Human Race." However, as we saw the Holy Synod had to approve the awarding of all such degrees, and for this reason Glagolev was not "officially" awarded the degree until the following year. He was certainly already at this time teaching theology at the Moscow Academy. During the years 1898–1899, Glagolev did research in the libraries and museums of Paris and Berlin, and in 1900 he published

---

[14] Ershov (1990). This quotation is taken from Ershov's *Introduction to Philosophy* based on lectures in Vladivostok in 1921.

[15] Ershov (1922), 61. A contemporary scholar Artem Solov'ev writes that Ershov ignored mentioning the views of his own teacher Nesmelov "due to the fact that he perceived Nesmelov as a theologian, and not as a philosopher." Solov'ev (2021b), 159. This, as we see, is not quite accurate. Ershov purposely wished to highlight the views of university professors to show the existence of a Russian philosophical tradition that could emerge when unrestrained by institutional measures, be they governmental or other.

a book *Supernatural Revelation and the Natural Cognition of God Outside the True Church*. He submitted and defended this work as a doctoral dissertation the following year. Glagolev remained a professor of theology at the Moscow Academy as long as that was possible. During the 1920s, he managed to teach mathematics at various institutions. Arrested in 1928 on the charge of being a member of an anti-Soviet group, he was sentenced to internal exile in Penza for a term of three years, but in 1931 he was again charged, this time with being a member of a monarchist organization and given a sentence of five years in a labor camp. Although he was eventually released, he was again charged with counter-revolutionary activities in June 1937, receiving the death sentence, which was carried out in October.

Insofar as Glagolev is remembered, it is chiefly for his stubborn defense of Biblical, and therefore Church, teachings, in particular against evolutionary theory with respect to the emergence of the human race from "lower" animal life. We should point out that Glagolev was above all a theologian, not a philosopher. Nevertheless, his writings, of which there are many, are most often in the sphere of Christian apologetics in confrontation with the natural sciences of his day. He already set forth in one of his earliest pieces the principal task to which he would devote his scholarly life. His declared intent was "to show that the Biblical doctrine of the origin of the human being and the Biblical view of humanity and of our vocation do not contradict the indubitable data of the positive sciences concerning the human being."[16] The task of science was to clarify and supplement, through additional data, the condensed Biblical account of the origin of the world and of the human race, but not to infringe into its sphere by giving an alternative account.

Singling out the Darwinian conception of the survival of the fittest for criticism, Glagolev held that that principle had to be rejected for, if nothing else, its sheer ambiguity. If organisms best adapted to their environment are the most likely to survive and reproduce, then those that best correspond to this principle are those that do so with the least expenditure of effort and with the greatest success. Glagolev reasoned that this description fits best those at the lowest rung of the biological ladder, not the highest. Such are single-celled organisms that do nothing but feed and reproduce. "One can only wonder why all organic life does not exist in such or similar forms."[17] On the other hand, the human being, which the Bible hails as residing at the other, the highest, end of the biological ladder on Earth, should be seen as at the dead end of organic development based on the Darwinian model. We humans have acquired a faculty and function quite unnecessary for self-preservation and reproduction, viz., the mind, which encourages the creation of

---

16 Glagolev (1894b), 171.
17 Glagolev (1912), 89.

culture in various forms, all of which are at the expense of reproduction and have nothing to do with self-preservation. That we have developed also a conscience, that we question our actions, particularly those by which we overcome obstacles and the contrary efforts of other creatures, be they lower animals or inferior human beings, seemingly counts against the Darwinian scheme. "Yes, in fact, if the evolutionary factor were the experience of those fittest for existence, there would be no evolution at all."[18] The presence of a conscience in each of us is a result of the Biblical Fall. In this way, the theory of evolution does not explain reality and actually contradicts the demands of our moral consciousness, which "thirsts for redemption."[19] As Glagolev remarked already in 1894, in his eyes Darwin's theory is not truly a theory of evolution. To evolve means to progress, to develop, but Darwin's theory indicates no principle in the human being that proceeds from a state of less perfection to greater perfection.[20]

Glagolev did not entirely reject heredity, provided that is that it allowed ample room for a Christian interpretation, an interpretation that allows for the fulfillment of God's plan. Glagolev granted that physical features, such as the color of eyes, the shape of nose and chin, can and often are passed from one generation to another. In this regard, Glagolev was particularly appreciative of what he took to be Mendel's positivism, i.e., experimental and repeatable findings without the introduction of metaphysical explanatory principles – principles that forsake religious tenets. "If the Mendelists would attempt to give a doctrine about the essence of the factors that govern heredity, they would enter the slippery slope of being carried away by bad metaphysics. But Mendel did not embark on this path."[21] Against this, Glagolev held that despite its inability to explain fully the origin and development of organisms, the science of his day was absolutely convinced that it could be done scientifically, without invoking religious principles. But when science attempts to do this, viz., to explain the world beyond empirically obtained data it engages in metaphysics. It attempts to establish the human being's proper relation to the world. Far from renouncing metaphysics, science claims it alone has the method and the key to the solution of metaphysical problems.[22]

We see, then, that Glagolev had a rather positivistic conception of the scientific endeavor. It coupled with his conception of Biblical Revelation as the conveyance of

---

[18] Glagolev (1912), 89.
[19] Glagolev (1912), 101.
[20] Glagolev (1894a), 275–276.
[21] Glagolev (1914), 198.
[22] Glagolev (1914), 97. For a more complete discussion of the reception of the Darwinian theory of evolution, which also discusses Glagolev's treatment, see Vucinich (1989). For an overview of Glagolev's attitude toward Darwinism, see Kline (1967), 321–325.

the Truth, which in turn is transmitted in the Orthodox faith means that science does not and cannot discover the Truth, which is eternal and infinite. Science deals with what can be measured, but infinity cannot be measured.[23]

We can hardly be surprised to see a professor of theology at an explicitly theological school defend as best he could the importance of his subject-matter. And as we have seen, Glagolev was by no means unique in fearing encroachments into it by natural science. What separates him from many of his colleagues was the effort he exerted to familiarize himself with the natural science of his day, even though he was by no means impartial in his selections. He sought out, in particular, those writings that at least leaned in his own direction or could be readily interpreted as doing so. Again this should be of little surprise to us. Still, already at the start of his academic career he, in effect, asked his students to follow his lead in studying science with an eye toward then defending Christianity from an informed standpoint. If they would do so, "more people would be attracted to their side and the sooner the anti-religious direction would disappear from natural science."[24] Whether that would be the case is another matter. However harshly one might wish to judge Glagolev's understanding of the biological sciences of his day, he at least made a decided effort to familiarize himself with some literature. He should also be applauded for accepting a symbolic, non-fundamentalist reading of the Creation story in the Bible, unlike so many even in our own time. When God inspired the words found there, God knew that many would not understand them if He gave a totally accurate account. "The story of creation was proclaimed to humanity not for the purposes of the natural sciences, but for those of religion. And it was proclaimed in a form most understandable to us, but at the same time, undoubtedly, using expressions most suitable to the truth."[25] The Bible describes scientific phenomena purposely in a language that would be comprehensible to both the most intelligent and the simplest at the time.

---

[23] Glagolev (1908), 2, 11–12.
[24] Glagolev (1892), 390. This was originally presented in a lecture in August 1892 to students, colleagues, and officials at the Moscow Academy. However, a few years later Glagolev urged theologians not to rush too quickly into the apologetic task of defending Orthodox doctrines in confronting the latest scientific developments. "We think that in most cases there is no need to hurry either with a rejection of scientific assumptions or with adapting our dogma to a new worldview." Glagolev (1900), 77. Reflecting on the non-Euclidean geometries of Lobachevsky and Riemann, Glagolev found them to be "strange facts" that lead to scientific skepticism, since they utterly contradict each other. However, the religious person finds that they "serve as the basis for a cautious attitude toward scientific conclusions and proofs." Glagolev (1908), 35. Glagolev concluded that scientific conclusions must always be taken guardedly.
[25] Glagolev (1900), 77–78.

Glagolev was not particularly interested in wrestling with traditional philosophical problems and certainly not with the intricacies of epistemology. However, at least on one occasion he turned to the ontological argument for God's existence, which he found to rest on the assumption of existence as a perfection. According to the argument, anything merely conceived and that does not exist is imperfect, but if it does correspond to something that does exist, it is thereby more perfect. Glagolev (and many others, particularly Kant) rejected the argument. "Existence is a more general concept than either perfection or imperfection. Existence is neither one nor the other."[26] One argument he gave – though he gave more – is that if existence were a perfection, then of two conceivable deeds, both of which being equally vile, the one actually carried out would be less vile than the other. "Therefore, it is impossible to consider existence a perfection, and the ontological argument which is based on this assumption is wrong."[27] Nonetheless, Glagolev believed that we always seek stability in the ever-changing flux of things and events. We assume that despite all the changes of and in our minds we each retain a personality. Likewise, we assume that the world too, despite its changes, has a stable physical foundation. Behind the phenomenality of the world, we seek the basis, the one real basis, behind this phenomenality, this merely "seeming"; we wish to lift the Schopenhauerian veil of Maya to reveal the Truth. Glagolev believed that the conclusion from this is that there is one true and absolute being, viz., God. If everything is in flux, there must be some substratum of everything that belies everything. Such an absolute is the Deity.

Consumed with theology, Glagolev saw everything through its lens. He held, for example, that philosophy was the philosophy of religion, the clarification and grounding of religious tenets. But, make no mistake, the object of both theology and philosophy is the same, what he termed "the highest and all-encompassing truth."[28] But are there no other objects? What else is the concern of philosophy, even if it be only an intermediate and not the ultimate truth? Glagolev devoted little attention to answering such questions, but he did single out logic – Aristotelian logic, which he also called "European logic" – for study.[29] He claimed that its independence from religious and metaphysical principles was merely illusory. The study of logic will lead us to conclude that behind it is an entire metaphysical system. And with this claim, we enter what from a philosophical standpoint is the most troubling aspect of Glagolev's thought. In his text on logic from 1910, he claim-

---

26 Glagolev (1910), 191.
27 Glagolev (1910), 191.
28 Glagolev (1915), 152.
29 Glagolev (1915), 170. Glagolev apparently remained in total ignorance of the work of Frege, Russell, and others that would utterly transform the logic he knew.

ed that logic is the study of thinking as a tool of cognition. Thinking, being a mental activity, is the subject matter of psychology. What, then, is the relationship of logic to psychology? Psychology does not concern itself with the relation of thinking to any other existence than itself. Logic, as Glagolev conceived it, concerns itself with the relation of thinking to existence alone, not thinking by itself. Since logic obtains its "material" from psychology, viz., from thought, it is "only the development of one part (*otdel*) of psychology and is the application of this part to achieve practical goals."[30] He concluded that logic, therefore, is subordinate to psychology.

The utility of logic stems from the correspondence of thought to reality. If there were no such correspondence, it would be impossible for us to know and utilize life itself. For logic is an essential tool in our thinking processes. Logic is, in this respect, akin to any science and to any practical human activity. Thus, as we saw from his puzzled, if not incomprehensible, reaction to non-Euclidean geometries, he could not comprehend any abstract, formalized discipline that did not explicitly deal with concrete existence. Glagolev displayed no sign of understanding the train of thought that became modern symbolic logic. His rigid philosophical anthropology would have made it impossible for him to escape the relativistic consequences of psychologism except by way of an appeal to religion. Whether he consciously realized this or not, it is what he, in fact, did.

11.3 Florenskij's Critique of Kant

With the death of Aleksej Vvedenskij in 1913, his position in philosophy and logic fell to Fedor K. Andreev (1887–1929), who taught at the Moscow Academy until its closure in 1919. He then taught Russian literature in a Moscow school until 1921. He himself was a graduate of the Moscow Academy in 1913 submitting his *kandidat*'s thesis on the Slavophile Jurij Samarin and began preparing a *magister*'s thesis on the religious and philosophical investigations of the early Slavophiles. The rector appointed Glagolev as one of the two reviewers. There the trail ends. "Unfortunately, there is no official information about the fate of this work or of the reviews of these persons."[31]

Among the best known instructors at the Moscow Academy, even if he taught there only for a short time, was Sergej M. Solov'ëv (1885–1942), the nephew of Vladimir Solov'ëv. Sergej lived a most tragic life, the details of which we need not recount here. Perhaps best known today for his biography of his uncle, Sergej also

---

30 Glagolev (1910), 2.
31 Golubcov (2010), 477.

wrote much poetry and produced many translations of world literature including works by Seneca, Virgil, and Aeschylus. Completing his studies at Moscow University in 1911, he enrolled four years later as a student at the Moscow Academy, apparently being allowed to skip the first year of studies there. He received a *kandidat*'s degree in 1918 with a thesis on the Gospel According to John. However it came to be, Solov'ëv taught the Western Church Fathers for a short time before the Academy was closed in 1919. He converted to Catholicism in the early 1920s. Of course, his open profession of faith could not be tolerated for long, and in 1931 he was sentenced to ten years in a labor camp. Whether his mental health collapsed naturally or owing to his interrogation, he was released from serving his sentence, but assigned to a psychiatric hospital. He died in 1941.

The last figure to whom we turn is, without doubt, the most well-known of all the figures we have discussed in this work. He has garnered considerable attention even in the West from theologians and literary scholars for his wide-ranging and eccentric writings and for his open defiance of Soviet authority. Since biographical information is readily available,[32] we need not linger long on it. Pavel Florenskij (1882–1937), was born in Azerbaijan to an Armenian mother and a Russian father, who worked as a railroad engineer. He studied mathematics and philosophy at Moscow University, graduating in 1904. He reportedly could have continued there as a graduate student in mathematics but instead chose to enroll at the Moscow Theological Academy. We find in his many extant writings that he paid considerable attention to the set theory of Cantor and later to certain developments in physics. Florenskij's interest in these matters from his earliest university years onward was always in using them as an instrument in service to his religious, spiritual outlook. How much he understood of the physics and mathematics he routinely invoked, given the conclusions he drew from them, is questionable.

Already while at the University, Florenskij showed his predilection for the supernatural and mystical side of religion in his 1903 "On Superstition and Miracle" ("O sueverii i chude"), which he published in the short-lived symbolist journal *New Way* (*Novyj put'*).[33] He demonstrated at this time an interest in the mystical, not the philosophical, aspects of Vladimir Solov'ëv's writings, aspects that the Russian symbolist movement at the time also noted and emphasized.

---

[32] For those interested in much more biographical information, the obvious first choice in English is Pyman (2010). There are others, such as Slesinski (1984). Additional, albeit shorter and less detailed, accounts are readily available.

[33] Igumen [Father Superior] Andronik (A. S. Trubachev), one of the editors of a four-volume edition of Florenskij's works, writes that Florenskij noted at the end of the published article that it was originally written in January 1902. See Florenskij (1994), 704.

Florenskij was also interested during this period in translating Kant much as was Solov'ëv in his early university years, but there the similarity ends. The latter was interested in Kant as a philosopher, whereas Florenskij saw Kant's work as a support for and as a stepping stone to, a spiritualistic viewpoint. Unlike Solov'ëv, who viewed Kant's philosophy as a dialectically and historically necessary stage in philosophy's development, leading ultimately to a recognition of the end of abstract Western philosophy, Florenskij saw Kantianism simply as a failed and incorrect philosophy that would lead not to religion, but to skepticism and a rejection of religion. Some historical background may be helpful. On the initiative of Sergej Trubeckoj, a Historico-Philological Society was created at Moscow University in early 1902.[34] One of the Society's stated aims was a publishing program that included translations as well as original works. A philosophy section of the Society proposed that its first publication consist of a collection of Kant's Latin works in Russian translation and that Florenskij would contribute a translation of Kant's 1756 *Physical Monadology*. The collection as such never appeared, but Florenskij did complete the translation and had it published in the house organ of the Moscow Academy in 1905.[35] He made it clear in his introduction to the piece that the dynamic theory of matter developed by Kant represented "the final and unavoidable presupposition of physics and of the other sciences of the external world, as long as these sciences remain sciences and are not replaced by pure metaphysics."[36] The dynamic model represented the last word in the sciences of external nature.

Completing the course of studies at the Moscow Academy with a *kandidat*'s thesis "On Religious Truth" and impressing all those there with his erudition and sheer zeal, Florenskij was asked to stay on as a teacher. One of the requirements was to present two public lectures, the topic of one of which was to be of the candidate's own choice whereas the other was assigned. In one entitled "The Cosmological Antinomies of Immanuel Kant," Florenskij demonstrated he had absorbed totally the Orthodox Church's emphasis on (Neo-)Platonic philosophy

---

[34] The Society's existence was short-lived. It was only with great persistence and Trubeckoj's family name – his title was "Prince" – that the government allowed the Society to come about in the first place. Trubeckoj's health deteriorated significantly in 1903, forcing him to seek rest in western Europe. Without his devoted efforts to mediate between the increasingly radicalized student body and the government, the latter dissolved the Society in 1904.

[35] Žust writes, "Under the influence of Vvedensky, Florensky during his first year of study [at the Moscow Academy] became very interested in Kant's philosophy." Žust (2002), 88. Žust's claim is somewhat incorrect although it is possible that once at the Academy Vvedenskij urged and helped Florenskij to publish his translation in *Bogoslovskij vestnik*.

[36] Florenskij (1905), 97.

and the interpretation of it in the works of the Greek Church Fathers. To view the human mind as an epistemological legislator would undercut the role of the Deity and as such had to be rejected. Kant's treatment of the cosmological antinomies as found in the Transcendental Dialectic of his first *Critique* leads to metaphysical skepticism and serves as the battleground for the two giants of philosophy, viz., Kant and Plato.

Florenskij started his presentation of "The Cosmological Antinomies," naturally enough, with a short summary of what Kant called a "transcendental illusion" and the givenness of the infinite in experience.[37] Whereas how we are to understand Kant's assertions concerning that givenness is contentious in Kant-scholarship, Florenskij, wasting no time, held that at least for Kant only the finite, not the infinite, is experientially given.[38] Reason, however, always asks for more; it seeks a unity, completion, which experience alone cannot provide. Florenskij criticized Kant for introducing the idea of the world in his discussion when his proof is limited to how we conceive space and time. "It follows from this that if he indeed proved an antinomic character, it was only of the forms of intuition, not of the idea of the world. It is not the properties of things that are contradictory, but only the properties of *space and time*."[39] This, Florenskij finds "strange" given Kant's initial claim, in the former's eyes, that the idea of the world is contradictory, which is what Kant should have shown in Florenskij's eyes. We need not and, in fact, should not engage in whether Florenskij's point is correct, particularly given the ambiguity here of Kant's use of the word "world." Kant, in any case, drew the conclusion from this as well as the other antinomies that the spatio-temporal world cannot be taken as a thing in itself, but only as an appearance. For space and time are representations, not things. But since we must represent all the things of experience as in space and time, then those things are never given in themselves, but only as appearances.[40] Thus, while we can credit Florenskij for noticing that Kant did not pose the world as having an antinomic character, he did not recognize that the antinomic character of space and time was a basis of Kant's distinction between the realms of the in-itself and appearances. Owing to this oversight, Florenskij without the slightest hesitation charged Kant with the strange contention that contradictions arise when we think of the world as a thing in itself. Florenskij did not rec-

---

37 For Kant's understanding of a "transcendental illusion," see Kant (1997), 384–387 (A293/B349–A298/B355).
38 Florenskij (1996a), 5.
39 Florenskij (1996a), 26.
40 Kant (1997), 511–512 (A492/B520 –A 493/B521).

ognize the guiding thread of Kant's argument. Instead, Florenskij charged Kant with inserting the thing in itself into his proof "out of the blue," so to speak.[41]

Florenskij's chief criticism of Kant was the latter's rejection, in his eyes, of the idea of an actual infinity,[42] an idea that formed the central focus of Florenskij's philosophical musings, such as they were. Already while an undergraduate studying mathematics, Florenskij was introduced to Georg Cantor's idea and formulation of set theory. Florenskij claimed that Kant had come to his position through reasoning that a given magnitude can be obtained only by means of a series of finite syntheses, but an infinite magnitude would then require an infinite number of finite syntheses.[43] However, now relying on Cantor and without further argument, Florenskij rejected that the given must be finite and that the infinite cannot be given. An actual infinity, which is not exhausted by an infinite series of syntheses, can, indeed, be given.[44] Florenskij concluded his presentation, with what from today's perspective with our focus on Kant's Transcendental Deduction, is the odd claim that the discussion of the antinomies represents the deepest and also the most fruitful of Kant's ideas, while being the most precarious in the first *Critique*.

The second of the two public lectures that Florenskij gave at the Moscow Academy in September 1908 bore the title, at least in its published version, "The Universal Human Roots of Idealism." Florenskij in it stressed the platonic heritage of the Russian academies as well as his highly idealistic understanding of Plato's teachings. It was not a particularly scholarly treatment, did not address or make references to issues stemming from the scholarship on Plato at the time, and, above all, presented no logical arguments. Florenskij espoused his allegiance to a Solov'ëvian-like "all-unity" and, in particular, "integral knowledge," which, he claimed, Plato had already clearly outlined but which had ceased to guide science beginning at some unspecified date, assuming, of course it ever did. Florenskij rejected the pro-

---

41 Florenskij (1996a), 26. Florenskij wrote there, "Just as strange is Kant's assertion that contradictions result from the fact that we conceive the world not as an appearance, but as a thing in itself. This would indeed be the case if the concept of the thing in itself entered anywhere in the scope of the proof. However, nowhere is there such an inclusion in the proof of the thing in itself."
42 Florenskij based his assertions regarding Kant entirely on a reading solely of the first antinomy, but rather surprisingly gave no textual reference for this assertion.
43 Florenskij appears to have relied on Kant (1997), 474 (A432/B460) for his reading of Kant. He did recognize that Kant in the Transcendental Aesthetic also mentioned that space is represented as an infinite given magnitude. Florenskij, however, made no further use of this claim. See Kant (1997), 175 (B39). Kant scholars have spent considerable time attempting to resolve an apparent contradiction.
44 Florenskij wrote, "I will not develop this idea for you." Florenskij (1996a), 27. But he asked his listeners and readers to bear in mind that all of contemporary mathematics has been reconstructed on the idea of actual infinity.

liferation of scientific disciplines, which have lost contact with the world, in favor of "Science" – note the capital "S." There are no longer polymaths among us, only spiritual atoms, which have consumed and destroyed the modern soul.[45]

Merely to conclude our brief discussion here of Florenskij's relationship to Kant, we find that the advancing years did not temper his attitude. In May 1918, he lectured at the Moscow Academy contrasting Plato to Kant, having completely absorbed traditional Orthodox Christianity's critique and particularly that of Pamfil Jurkevich given some fifty years earlier at Moscow University. Florenskij acknowledged the brilliance of Kant's philosophical system, but at the same time held it to be most "hypocritical" and "cunning." "Every proposition, every term, every train of thought in it is neither a 'yes' nor a 'no'."[46] Kant, in this telling, speaks of appearances in which nothing appears and of supposedly meaningful noumena but that are incomprehensible. The things in themselves are neither things nor in themselves. Again echoing a charge not unknown among Russian philosophers, Florenskij saw Kant as a Protestant "to the bone," who employs philosophical tricks in order to conceal the subjectivity of his outlook.[47] In contrast to Plato, for whom the supreme principle is the idea of the good, Kant held that it is the subjective idea of obligation notably without any specificity.

11.4 Florenskij's *Magnum Opus*

Florenskij's *kandidat*'s thesis from 1908 would prove to be the first edition of what became his principal work. He originally intended to submit as a *magister*'s thesis a translation of the works of the Neoplatonist Iamblichus along with commentary. Apparently, Florenskij's progress on this did not proceed as rapidly as the Academy wished and accepting Vvedenskij's suggestion, he prepared and submitted in 1912 a revision of his earlier thesis. Now bearing the title "On Spiritual Truth," the thesis underwent significant changes in order for it to be approved by the Holy Synod.[48] This "second edition" underwent further changes, and an, in effect, "third edition" was published in 1913, which Florenskij was able finally to defend in May 1914 with Glagolev and the then-rector of the Academy F. K. Andreev serving as opponents,

---

45 Florenskij (2000), 148.
46 Florenskij (1977), 122.
47 Florenskij (1977), 123. For a far more detailed and complete presentation of Florenskij's view of Kant's philosophy, see Haney (2001).
48 In a review of Florenskij's book, Arkhimandrit Nikanor, whom we shall see again shortly, questioned whether Florenskij's *magister*'s thesis represented a "significant revision" of his *kandidat*'s thesis, as was required. See Nikanor (1996), 320.

Vvedenskij having died the previous year. Florenskij's successful defense led a few weeks later to his election to be a professor effective from the day of the dispute. It took, however, several months for final, formal approval of the degree by the Holy Synod.[49]

Set out as a set of twelve letters to an unidentified addressee, the final text, in effect a fourth edition, *The Pillar and Ground of the Truth* published in 1914 differed from the version published and submitted as a *magister*'s thesis by the omission of the final three "Letters."[50] In light of other theses we have discussed in these pages, it is nothing short of amazing that *The Pillar* was accepted as a thesis and that the Holy Synod also did so. It bears little similarity to other efforts either in tone or scholarship. But as Georgij Florovskij, a noted Orthodox theologian and scholar, remarked concerning the book, it is "the most characteristic monument of the pre-War [I] era."[51] However one may view *The Pillar*, there can be no mistake that it is not a work in philosophy, but in speculative theology. To claim otherwise would be not just self-delusional and constitute a disparagement of philosophy as a discipline, but also of reason itself. This is not to say, though, that it should be simply dismissed out of hand. There are seeming philosophical propositions, claims, and conclusions in it that can be explored, and it is to these that we turn.

The second "Letter" entitled "Doubt" will surely remind the reader, whether it was Florenskij's intention or not, of Fichte's own "Doubt" in the title of the first "book" of his slim *Die Bestimmung des Menschen* (*Vocation of Man*). Whereas Fichte, however, was concerned at the time of its writing with the conflict between our unshakable conviction in our free will and the determinism of the natural order, Florenskij was interested here in the givenness of evidence as a criterion of truth and in interpreting the logical law of identity as having metaphysical significance. The doubt of which Florenskij wrote is not one that can be surmounted with either empirical evidence or rational thought alone. But, make no mistake, Florenskij offered neither new arguments nor even recounted traditional ones. He did hold, though, that however tenuous the ultimate validity of what each independently provides, there are three forms of experience: (1) external, sensible

---

49 The powerful and influential bishop of Kharkov and member of the Holy Synod Antonij (Khrapovickij) approved Florenskij's thesis, but he publicly disapproved of Florenskij's "name-worshipping," which was in vogue among a small circle of Orthodox theologians. See Pyman (2010), 102, 249.
50 Florenskij wrote in a copy of the book given to a friend that it represented his state of mind when he "decided to transfer to the Academy, i.e., during my fourth year at the University." Quoted in Andronik (1990), 829. Andronik's essay provides considerably more detail on the composition of the book and the differences between the various editions for the interested reader.
51 Florovskij (2009), 626. He continued, "Florenskij's book is intentionally and deliberately subjective. ... This is a book by a very self-absorbed writer. Loneliness is always felt in his reflections."

experience, (2) internal experience of rational thought, and (3) mystical intuition. Each of these claims for itself validity, but none can provide certainty and their respective claims are quite unjustified. Our demand for certainty in their alleged veracity demands proof from each of them. We cannot accept their truth-claims without proof, but "at the same time the very proposition 'not to accept anything without proof' must itself be proved."[52] Thus, in Florenskij's eyes, philosophical foundationalism rests on a dogmatic presupposition, for that very presupposition cannot be proved but must be accepted on faith.

Florenskij, not unlike the Jena Fichte of 1794, came to what the latter called "the absolutely first, purely and simply [schlechthin] unconditioned foundational principle of all human knowledge."[53] Whatever interpretation Fichte may have given to the law of identity A=A, Florenskij imparted to it and employed it for an explicitly theological purpose. He wrote that if there is absolute Truth – note the capitalization – "Truth" being his euphemism for God,[54] the law of identity will find its basis and justification therein. Does this mean that if there is no God, then the law of identity would lack foundation? Of course, Florenskij would never have countenanced the mere possibility of there being no God. But unlike Fichte, for whom the law of identity is absolutely certain and without any ground, let alone one independent of reason, Florenskij found querying for the ground of the law of absolute identity to be meaningful. In his usual cryptic style, he wrote, "To the question, Why is A A? we answer, A is A because, eternally being not-A, in this not-A it finds its affirmation as A. ... Thus, the law of identity will receive its grounding not in its lower, rational form, but in its higher, reasonable form."[55] Florenskij unavoidably here invited interpretation, lest his words be dismissed as pure gibberish. The "A," the "not-A," and their unity symbolically represent that the knower and the one known, although empirically distinct, are yet one within the all-unity. Knowing is "a real unification of the knower and what is

---

[52] Florensky (1997), 30–31. For the sake of convenience for the reader, references to Florenskij's best-known work is to its English-language translation. However, the translation is by no means a critical edition. No indication is given of the changes and additions the author made over the course of its various editions. The most egregious fault, however, is the incorrect rendering of the implication sign "⊃" as "⊂." See, for example, Florensky (1997), 425 and cf. Florenskij (1914), 601 and Florenskij (2003), 462.
[53] Fichte (2021), 200.
[54] Florenskij in his fifth "Letter" identifies "Truth" with "consubstantiality of the Holy Trinity." Florensky (1997), 81. He thereby makes clear that his discussion is a theological, not a philosophical, one.
[55] Florensky (1997), 36.

known."⁵⁶ Florenskij's message is not philosophical, but theological and even mystical. In his conception, the laws of logic are not rooted in a psychologism, but in a reductionistic theologism. In this way, Florenskij avoided relativism, but at the cost of raising the issue whether God could render the laws of logic differently. In this fourth "Letter," he simply, as it were, posits that Truth, Good, and Beauty – note again the capitalizations – are three different points of view on a single principle of spiritual life. Together these points of view form a metaphysical triad. Spiritual life seen in another's immediate action is the good, and when objectively intuited "by a third" – a third what is unclear – is beauty.⁵⁷ Florenskij notably gives neither rules of conduct for ethical behavior, for making ethical decisions, nor principles by which one can even hold an object to be a work of art.⁵⁸

Florenskij's sixth "Letter" makes clear that his criticisms of Kant's treatment of the antinomies were not meant to be understood as rejections of the antinomies as though there are no such antinomies and that Kant merely misunderstood the implications of what he was describing. Yes, Kant in Florenskij's opinion did not understand the antinomies, but the misunderstanding was not that our reason, as a faculty, had to be curbed, but that the world itself, the world as it really is, is antinomic. "Here, on earth, there are contradictions in everything; and they can be removed neither by social organization nor by philosophical argument."⁵⁹ Certainly, Florenskij saw the rational mind, in looking at the world, finds contradictions present everywhere. To claim otherwise, namely that antinomies are limited to one sharply delimited sphere of existence would amount to, in effect, a rejection of the all-unity of existence. "The thesis and the antithesis together form the expression of truth. In other words, truth is an antinomy, and it cannot fail to be such."⁶⁰ Since reason cannot deduce on its own the Solov'ëvian-like "all-unity" or, as here in

---

56 Florensky (1997), 55. He asserted that this affirmation of all-unity is "the fundamental and characteristic proposition of Russian and, in general, of all Eastern philosophy." He, thus, left open whether Russian philosophy is a branch of Eastern philosophy or merely shares with the latter its fundamental characteristic.
57 If one would have queried Florenskij as to the difference between the Good and the good, between the Truth and the truth, his reply certainly would have been as he wrote in *The Pillar*, "In heaven, there is only one Truth. But here, on earth, we have a multitude of truths, fragments of the Truth, noncongruent to one another." Florensky (1997), 117. Presumably, Florenskij would have said that the mental activity exemplified seen in science and mathematics is the truth.
58 In this way, if Kant is to be faulted for the indeterminacy of the categorical imperative, so much more so must we fault Florenskij.
59 Florensky (1997), 117. Offering a different assessment, Pawel Rojek writes that Florenskij was not clear how far the antinomies extended, presumably because Florenskij "spoke mainly on religious truths, expressed in Holy Scripture, dogmatics or liturgy." Rojek (2019), 519.
60 Florensky (1997), 109.

The Pillar, integral fullness, it must be postulated. Nonetheless, there are two worlds. Access from one of them to the "other" world is by means of faith, which can "overcome" the antinomies of one of these worlds – our world.[61] Through faith, we escape the confines of reason, which thereby becomes a "new" reason. With his deprecation of reason to penetrate beyond our antinomic world, we understand why he offered no rational proofs for God's existence. Indeed, he felt that a "rational" faith, a religious faith based on reason and rational proofs is "a slander against God, a monstrous product of human egotism,"[62] for it would be tantamount to subordinating God to reason. Florenskij believed that such a faith would amount to a kind of atheism.

It should be clear by now that Florenskij with his religious anti-intellectualism had next to nothing to contribute to philosophy as understood today and even as understood by many, if not most, in the Imperial Russian academies. His Neoplatonism offered little beyond what others, such as Jurkevich, had developed, and who directed their energies to the problems of the day such as reductionist materialism. Employing various literary devices, such as symbolism and poetry, presumably to convey his thoughts, he made it impossible for anyone to contest his claims, although there is no evidence that he sought to convince others of the accuracy of his viewpoint.[63] Everything is taken for granted.[64] He devoted no particular attention to ontology apart from this speculation of two worlds and none to epistemology apart from a 1908 manuscript composed as an introduction to a course on the history of ancient philosophy. In that 1908 composition, he posited that the subject-object duality of the cognitive process had to be destroyed in favor of a monistic model. How that was to be accomplished was left unsaid.[65] Although he taught philosophy, Florenskij's published works while at the Moscow Academy do not belong to the discipline of philosophy, but, to be charitable, to theology.

---

61 Florensky (1997), 344.
62 Florensky (1997), 48.
63 Presumably, this is what Florovskij meant by writing as we saw in a previous footnote, that Florenskij was very self-absorbed.
64 For a far more charitable approach and reading of Florenskij's book than that presented here, see Foltz (2013). Despite Foltz's sophisticated presentation, Florenskij's thought remains speculative theology, not philosophy.
65 Florenskij (1996b), 34. This piece was not published until 1913 in the Moscow Academy's house journal *Bogoslovskij vestnik*.

11.5 Florenskij's Critics

Unlike the vast majority of works emanating from Imperial Russia's theological academies, *The Pillar* was recognized – and rather quickly – by several eminent figures among Russia's established intellectual community outside the religious institutions. Let us note first, however, the reaction within the Moscow Academy. Aleksandr V. Pozdeevskij (1876-?), who took the monastic name Feodor, singled out Florenskij's concern with the antinomy – note the singular – of human understanding. Pozdeevskij found Florenskij's treatment of its role in the history of ancient and modern philosophy to be excellent. Pozdeevskij accepted Florenskij's speculative contention that the antinomy of the understanding was a result of the fragmentation of being itself, and thus also of the understanding, as the result of sin, presumably meaning the Biblical Fall.[66] Another figure within the Moscow Academy and who served as one of Florenskij's thesis examiners was Sergej Glagolev, who also had nothing but praise for Florenskij's book, finding it to be an exceptional phenomenon. The book's contents were unusual but original, capturing the author's exceptional individuality, and resolved the problem of epistemology by turning it into a religious problem. Glagolev held that Florenskij, viewing the world through platonic eyes, saw a contradiction between being and thinking. Whereas thought can operate only with immovable objects or facts, the world around us is a process, in unceasing motion. As for Florenskij himself, Glagolev found him to have "an amazing and comprehensive breadth of scientific knowledge. A mathematician by specialty, he has studied mechanics and physics deeply."[67] Judging from his closing remarks, Glagolev found *The Pillar* as presenting an original deeply Orthodox worldview that offered, unlike that of Eduard von Hartmann, an optimistic work filled with faith, hope, and love. It was unusual in form but as such stepped outside the regular confines of scholarship. Even though submitted as a thesis for a *magister*'s degree, Glagolev seriously contemplated nominating *The Pillar* as a doctoral thesis.

More surprising than the reaction to *The Pillar* within the Moscow Academy is that it received notice outside the Academy's walls in secular society, an unusual though not quite an unprecedented occurrence.[68] Nikolaj A. Berdjaev (1874–1948), a name well-known in the West for his peculiar Christian existentialism,

---

[66] Feodor (1914), 175.
[67] Glagolev (1916), 77. Since Florenskij had but an undergraduate background in mathematics, that Glagolev thought this made Florenskij a mathematician speaks volumes as to Glagolev's own knowledge of mathematics and physics.
[68] That Florenskij received such notice is most likely due to his friendship while at Moscow University with the Symbolist poet and literary figure Andrej Bely, whose real name was Boris Bugaev.

published remarks on Florenskij's work soon after it appeared in its final form in 1914. Finding it to be an exciting and refined book unique in Russian theological literature, Berdjaev also opined that it represented an Orthodoxy not in ascendancy, but in decline.[69] Stressing the theme of freedom that we see throughout his many popular works, Berdjaev found Florenskij's book lacked precisely a concern with the free search for truth and divine wisdom. Florenskij viewed religion as dogma to be accepted without hesitation and uncritically. "The most painful and unpleasant thing in Florenskij's book is his dislike of freedom, an indifference toward it, a lack of understanding of Christian freedom, of freedom in the Spirit. ... His religion is not a religion of freedom; the pathos of freedom is alien to him."[70] But Berdjaev did not view *The Pillar* entirely negatively. He remarked that the best pages of the book were those devoted to Florenskij's doctrine of antinomy. Religious life is indeed antinomic, and reason does find therein contradictory theses. Florenskij, however, did not consistently pursue these theses, straying instead onto a completely different path. The note on which Berdjaev ended his review is quite consistent with his general attitude. "Nobody needs Florenskij's book; it is only a document of a soul running away from itself. ... The spirit of freedom is so foreign, so unknown to Florenskij."[71]

Another figure who looked at Florenskij's work and who was firmly planted in Imperial Russia's small secular philosophical circle was Boris Jakovenko (1884–1948). In his March 1914 review of *The Pillar*, Jakovenko expressed the view that the work was an imposing and quite striking composition but that it could be intelligible only to someone with an emotional and nervous personality. Otherwise, one would lose one's mind in the work's futile search for truth. Being so emotionally charged, Florenskij did not realize the proximity of his ideas to German Idealism. His subjective manifestations of despair turn quickly in the book into a principled objective despair rooted in a belief that neither the immediate data of sense intuition nor the deductions of the understanding are in any way the means to truth. Florenskij's faith, however in Jakovenko's view, is "not strong enough to stand alone on its own two feet, to be unafraid of the understanding and not think constantly of the danger from that side."[72] Florenskij with ever greater theoretical despair revealed these theoretical constructions as the volume progresses. They lead either to an infinite regress or appeal to a blind intuition. Whichever way Florenskij would choose would lead to his original skepticism. Regrettably,

---

69 Berdjaev (1914), 110.
70 Berdjaev (1914), 112.
71 Berdjaev (1914), 125.
72 Jakovenko (1996), 264.

Florenskij's despair had progressed so far that he could not see the failure of his endeavors.

The last secular figure to whom we turn is Evgenij N. Trubeckoj (1863–1920), a follower and friend of Vladimir Solov'ëv and upholder of his late friend's legacy. He presented his first summary and view of Florenskij's book in a report at a meeting of the Religio-Philosophical Society in late February/early March (new style) 1914, a report that appeared in print in May. Trubeckoj claimed that Florenskij had accomplished one thing that had eluded Solov'ëv, namely, the use of long-standing Orthodox religious service for the development of religious doctrine. Trubeckoj parted, though, with Florenskij's view of modern philosophy. The two men agreed on the diagnosis that the human understanding was sick. Trubeckoj viewed the inner contradictions in our understanding as shown in the history of modern philosophy to be an obstacle to that understanding. However, in Trubeckoj's eyes, Florenskij saw, at least at times, that truth itself, not just the human understanding, harbored inner contradictions. "Is it the dogma itself or our imperfect understanding of dogma? On this point, Florenskij oscillates and wants it both ways."[73] Trubeckoj's judgment is that Florenskij's attitude toward reason is inconsistent with his basic Christian worldview.

Trubeckoj followed up this early 1914 report with another look at Florenskij's book in his 1918 work *The Meaning of Life*.[74] Combining Florenskij, Berdjaev, and Vladimir Ern (1882–1917) as representatives of what he termed "mystical alogicism," Trubeckoj charged that if, as they held, there is no logically justified transition from thought to revelation, then any conceptual attempt to find the meaning of life is patently futile. Were they correct, doubts in such a meaning could not be addressed by reasoned argument, but they can be removed by demonstrating that they conflict with necessary assumptions of thought as well as with the very nature of religious faith. Lest we conclude from this remark that Trubeckoj will offer a reasoned philosophical argument, he, as a disciple of Solov'ëv, presented no such thing. Trubeckoj countered Florenskij's position, writing that human knowledge is obtained by means of communion with God, i.e., only through the revelation of the absolute consciousness in the finite human consciousness. Thus, we know only insofar as some aspect of the divine is revealed to us. Such revelation, however, is distinct from purely religious revelation. But, "to deny the *possibility* of revelation means, therefore, to renounce thought itself, its necessary metaphysical assumption."[75] This does not contradict the essence of the Christian faith. In fact, it

---

[73] Trubeckoj (1914), 37.
[74] For a general summary of Trubeckoj's position in English, see Trubetzkoy (1917–1918).
[75] Trubeckoj (2011), 272.

is an affirmation of that faith. The denial of a bridge between thought and faith is the heretical position. In this way, Trubeckoj subtly accused Florenskij of preaching heresy.

Trubeckoj also rejected Florenskij's blatant anti-intellectualism, which we can see as a corollary of his dissociation of thought from faith. Trubeckoj admonished Florenskij for his neglect of the connection between ancient Athenian philosophy and the divine revelations beheld by Abraham, Isaac, and Jacob. If Florenskij were correct, all those not of the Christian faith would be condemned. St. Paul, however, reminded us that such revelation is "more or less available to everyone, even to pagans."[76] In this way, Trubeckoj drew not only from Solov'ëv, but, more immediately, from St. Paul's encounter with the Areopagus council in Athens as told in the Christian Bible's Acts of the Apostles.

As we saw, most at the Moscow Academy were entranced by Florenskij's display of symbolism and logic, his literary style and his knowledge of the Church Fathers, his debt to the Slavophiles and his familiarity with modern secular philosophy, whereas Russian secular intellectuals had their reservations. There was at least, though, one individual from the Academy who had seemingly nothing good to say about *The Pillar*. Nikolaj P. Kudrjavcev (1884–1923), who took the monastic name Nikanor (Kudrjavcev), attended the Moscow Academy graduating in 1909. Thus, since their time at the Academy overlapped by three years, they must have known, or at least been acquainted with, each other. In an article published in January 1916, Nikanor (Kudrjavcev) agreed with the secular philosophers that *The Pillar* sought salvation from earthly despair by an abject appeal to the Triune God and Truth, transcendent to knowledge. Nikanor (Kudrjavcev) held that despite Florenskij's overt criticism of Kant, his method was reminiscent of Kant's moral postulation of the Deity.[77]

Florenskij certainly lived for a number of years after the consolidation of the Soviet Union and into the Stalinist era. He paid considerably for that fact as did a number of others. An account of his arrests, internment in a labor camp, and then execution outside St. Petersburg in December 1937 needs no further elaboration. However, in the 1920s and thus while he was still able to walk the streets, he pre-

---

76 Trubeckoj (2011), 274.
77 Nikanor (1996), 334. Whether one agrees with this assessment is an open question, but Nikanor's most damning charge against Florenskij was surely his accusation of plagiarism. The former claimed that the "true author" of *The Pillar* was not Florenskij, but the monk Arkhimandrite Serapion (secular name Vladimir M. Mashkin), who died in 1905. Nikanor (199,6), 350. Serapion had studied at the Moscow Academy from 1892–1896. Upon his death, the bulk of his manuscript writings passed to Florenskij. An assessment of Nikanor's severe judgment, of course, is well beyond the scope of this work, even if it were possible.

sented in writing highly imaginative, even fanciful, interpretations of the theory of relativity and of the edge of the universe. The mere fact that he would entertain such speculations, unfortunately, does not speak well of his understanding of the recent developments in physics.[78]

---

[78] For more on these speculations, see Chase (2015).

Chapter 12
Concluding Remarks

The reader surely knows of the ultimate fate in general of the theological academies, and with it in particular of philosophical instruction there, in the wake of the Bolshevik *coup d'état* by a relatively small cadre of professional revolutionaries. A governmental decree in early 1918 stipulated the separation of church and state. This meant that the academies would henceforth receive no public funding, requiring them to become private institutions. Already, however, during the previous year, the securing of funds for the payment of salaries and student scholarships ranked as the major concern of the academies' administrations.[1] The Bolsheviks also commandeered many of the academies' buildings, forcing instructional activities to take place often in the residences of the instructors. However, in the absence of a defined institutional structure there could be little unity and dynamism and no means to attract new students.[2]

We mentioned in several previous chapters some particulars concerning the respective fates of certain academy philosophy professors. The literally absurd accusations against these individuals followed by sentencing to inhuman labor camps cannot and certainly should not in any way be excused or even passed over in silence. Of course, we cannot know how philosophy might have fared and developed in the academies had political events not forced their closing. A sad twist of fate is that the few professionally trained philosophers from the Imperial Russia era who survived, Aleksej F. Losev being the most notable example, had to commit to scholarly work on the Greeks – the further back in time from Marx the better – which the philosophical tradition in both the secular universities and the theological academies idolized anyway. Although a new generation of philosophers in the academies may have come along and in some manner rejuvenated philosophical teaching and doctrine there, the prospects from the vantage point of 1917 did not look promising. Philosophy in neither the Petersburg nor the Kyiv Academies had any promising young acolytes who, in this alternate non-Bolshevik reality, could have steered it in a new direction away from sheer metaphysical speculation. The Kazan Academy did, admittedly, have Nesmelov. His great work *Nauka o cheloveke* did mark the summit of a particular metaphysically-oriented branch of academic philosophy in Imperial Russia, but it appeared already more than a dec-

---

1 Golubcov (2010), 450.
2 For more information on how the academies fared in the late 1910s-1920s, see Sukhova (2013a), 75–76.

ade before the apocalyptic events mentioned above. Nesmelov in the decade following the appearance of his *magnum opus* produced nothing particularly substantial and gave no reason for us to think he would have contributed significantly if the circumstances had been different. Moreover, he had no distinguished students. In Moscow, the advent of Florenskij's works with their expansive symbolism and pseudo-scientific conjectures further testifies to the sheer poverty of reasoned and restrained academic thought at the end of the Great War. Much as the early Vladimir Solov'ëv in 1874 had ridiculously claimed that Western philosophy had culminated with Schopenhauer and von Hartmann, we can assert that with Nesmelov speculative philosophy in Imperial Russia's theological academies had reached its climax and termination, not just historically but philosophically. That tradition had exhausted its options much as Solov'ëv himself thought had happened with Western philosophy.

To be sure, philosophical life in the theological academies was forcibly, even violently, extinguished by political forces in the aftermath of the Bolshevik Revolution. Nonetheless, there were already few signs of much philosophical vitality. Indeed observing from the perspective of the second decade of the twentieth century, the future looked dim for academic philosophy if there were no external infusion of ideas. In this sense, we can turn Solov'ëv's thesis "on its head." That is, one way forward for academic philosophy had it not been completely obstructed by political events lay in an enrichment from Western-oriented philosophies in general – and not just philosophies of religion – that would have avoided the shoals of speculative thought. We can see that Karinskij had approached such a path with his attention to logic and analyticity in examining philosophical texts.[3] The upsurge in nationalistic feeling, which was never confined solely to the political sphere, made that possibility, however, virtually inconceivable in the immediate decades after his work. We must not overlook, though, that the pursuit of a more inclusive path was, in any case, impeded or hindered from the start by an emergence of a stultifying intellectual "apartheid," which we can see was and is actively manifested and promoted, for example, in the very characterization of the country's religious faith as the *Russian* Orthodox Church. In this way, the Russian Church had set itself apart, and emphatically continues to do so, not merely from the West, but even from other Orthodox Churches. Ershov's "philosophical sociologism" was but a forthright expression of an attitude that had its roots in a largely xenophobic national tradition that persists to this day.

---

3 From an historical perspective, we see that the vitality of nations, both economically as well as intellectually, is often greatly enhanced with an infusion of foreign sources. An isolated nation becomes stagnant, relying, as it were, on incestuous relationships with the past.

The linear dead-end path of Russian academic philosophy, however, does not mean that it remained hermetically sealed within the walls of the four academies, not influencing or being influenced by Imperial Russian secular philosophy. Yes, during much of the first half of the nineteenth century there was limited communication between the theological and the secular intellectual communities. This was virtually inevitable given the socio-political circumstances and the nascent character of the intellectual sphere. Nonetheless, as we saw, Belinskij had some knowledge of works emanating from the academies, and with the re-introduction of philosophy into the secular universities in the 1860s Jurkevich, for one, was able to introduce academy philosophy into the secular Moscow University. Solov'ëv, as Jurkevich's disciple of sorts, built upon his mentor's teachings, producing a distinctive religious philosophy that resounded through Moscow University in the coming decades, finding notable successors.[4] Jurkevich, of course, was not the only example of a prominent figure within academy walls to accept a teaching position in one of the empire's universities. Upon Jurkevich's death, his colleagues at Moscow University seriously considered Karinskij to fill the vacancy. And although Karinskij's works were unknown to them, they were not at all dismissive of his candidacy solely because he came from a theological academy. We also saw that Sidonskij, whose background was clearly at an academy, had even earlier in the 1860s begun teaching at St. Petersburg University. There were other examples, indeed a number of them, such as Sylvestr S. Gogockij, who moved from the Kyiv Academy to the university in the city. With the passing of the years, the migration of professors from the academies to the universities increased, even if only in an adjunct capacity in order to supplement their meager salaries.

---

[4] George Kline wrote, "no priest, no professor in a theological academy, however learned or 'intelligent,' was admitted into association with the secular intelligentsia (assuming he sought such admission), even to the extent of being permitted to publish in radical or liberal journals." Kline (1967), 308. In a sense, Kline is correct. However, if he suggests that the entire secular intelligentsia sided with the stands of the radical or liberal journals, he exaggerates. That there was some communication between the academic and the secular communities is clear from Solov'ëv's serialized publication of his *Crisis of Western Philosophy* as well as other early articles and reviews in *Pravoslavnoe obozrenie*, the journal of the Moscow Academy. That academy professors published in their own journals, rather than in "radical or liberal journals," may have been due to considerations other than some unbridgeable intellectual gap. The academies, understandably, wished through their journals to demonstrate and to promote the scholarship of their faculty. We should also keep in mind that the number of "radical or liberal" journals at the time was quite small, and they depended on public subscriptions for their continuance. It is not unreasonable for us to ask, then, whether it would be advantageous for these journals to publish technical articles on German Idealism and the Church Fathers.

In terms of intellectual influence from the theological academy to the secular world, there was in addition to the Jurkevich-Solov'ëv connection the significant influence by Archbishop Nikanor on Nikolaj Grot (1852–1899), who was instrumental in establishing the Moscow Psychological Society. While Grot and Nikanor resided in Odessa, they were in communication, and the latter was largely responsible for Grot's move away from positivism to idealism.[5] Finally, we observed that Florenskij's *Pillar* received significant attention from figures within secular society, such as Berdjaev, and Florenskij, in turn, was very much a part of the bohemian and secular Symbolist movement that flourished at the time. Thus, while the radical intelligentsia certainly nourished a hostile attitude toward those at the academies for what they perceived as its narrow religious parochialism, not all of secular Imperial Russian society felt disdain and contempt for academic philosophy and philosophers. A more accurate characterization of secular society's attitude throughout the period we have covered here would be that of indifference, which led to ignorance. The concerns of the academies were seen as arising from the specific needs of the first estate, which had little direct impact on the rest of society.

Just as secular philosophers in Imperial Russia had a certain amount of knowledge of philosophy in the academies and were nourished by it, so too did academic philosophers display some knowledge of secular philosophical developments when these developments intruded into their domain. As we saw, a number of academic philosophers certainly knew the religious writings of Solov'ëv, and we saw Linickij's 1881 detailed reply to Chicherin's *Science and Religion*. Perhaps an even more poignant example is the extensive exchange between Karinskij and Aleksandr Vvedenskij on Kantian epistemology. In this way, we find that when philosophers from one social sector happened to veer in the direction that the other considered its own, each certainly was aware of that fact. In short, then, Russian academic philosophy died an intellectually natural death, having in its old age exhausted itself of its own insular powers. Yet, it did have offspring in the form of the classical Russian idealism launched in the secular sphere by Solov'ëv and continued by the Trubeckoj brothers, in one direction, and Florenskij and Losev in another. The highly metaphysical idealism presented by these individuals persisted for a time until it was forcibly extinguished by those who opposed any form of critical thinking other than their own. That, however, is another story. Whether it is worth telling, whether it too from a contemporary Western perspective can only belong to the past, having reached a dead end, is left to the reader.

---

5 For Grot's own account, see Grot (1886), and for a recent informed account of the influence of Nikanor on Grot, see Solov'ev (2014).

Bibliography

Akvilonov, Evgenij (1905a): *Ob istinnoj svobode i nravstvennom dolge*. St. Petersburg: Tip. Uchilishcha glukhonemykh.
Akvilonov, Evgenii (1905b): *O fiziko-teleologicheskom dokazatel'stve bytija Bozhija*. St. Petersburg: Tip. I. V. Leont'eva.
Akvilonov, Evgenii (1907): *Iudejskij vopros. O nevozmozhnosti predostavlenija polnopravija russkim grazhdanam iz iudejskago naroda*. St. Petersburg: Tip. M. Merkusheva.
Andronik, Igumen (1990): "Iz istorii knigi *Stolp i otverzhdenie istiny*". In Florenskij, Pavel (1990): *Stolp i utverzhdenie istiny*. Tom I, chast' II. Moscow: Izd. Pravda, pp. 827–837.
[Anonymous] (1840): "Sovremennaja russkaja bibliografija". *Syn Otechestva*, tom III, kn. IV, p. 723.
Antonij, Ieromonakh (1888): *Psikhologicheskija dannyja v pol'zu svobody voli i nravstvennoj otvetstvennosti*. St. Petersburg: Izd. I. L. Tuzova.
Antonij, Episkop (1900): *Polnoe sobranie sochinenij*. Tom 1. Kazan: Tip. Imperatorskago Universiteta.
Arsen'ev, Vasilij S. (2005): *Vospominanija i dnevnik*. M. V. Rejzin and Andrej I. Serkov (Eds.). St. Petersburg: Izd. N. I. Novikova.
Askochenskij, V. (1863): *Istorija Kievskoj dukhovnoj akademii, po preobrazovanii eja v 1819 godu*. St. Petersburg: Tip. Eduarda Vejmara.
Avgustin (Nikitin), Arkhimandrit (2018): "Ignatij Fessler (1756–1839) – filolog, filosof, bogoslov". *Trudy kafedry bogoslovija Sankt-Peterburgskoj dukhovnoj akademii*, no. 1 (20), pp. 178–194.
Avsenev, Feofan (1869): *Iz zapisok po psikhologii*. Kiev: Tip. Kievskago Gubernskago upravlenija.
Avsenev, Petr S. (2016): *Sochinenija*. A. G. Volkov (Ed.). Kyiv: NGU im. M. Dragomanova.
Bazhanov, V. A. (2012a): "Logika v Rossii i pravoslavnaja cerkov". *Logicheskie issledovanija*, no. 18, pp. 5–25.
Bazhanov, V. A. (2012b): "Prepodavanie logiki v dorevoljucionnoj Rossii: vklad svjashchennosluzhitelej". *Vysshee obrazovanie v Rossii*, no. 1, pp. 144–148.
Beck, Lewis White (1969): *Early German Philosophy: Kant and His Predecessors*. Cambridge, MA: The Belknap Press of Harvard University Press.
Belinskij, V.G. (1840): "Russkaja literatura". *Otechestvennyja zapiski*, tom XI, otd. VI, pp. 2–5.
Belinskij, V.G. (1941): *Izbrannye filosofskie sochinenija*. Moscow: Ogiz.
Belinskij, V.G. (1955): *Polnoe sobranie sochinenij v 13 tomakh*, Moscow: Izd.-vo AN SSSR. Tom 8.
Beljaev, Viktor A. (1914): "K otnosheniju mezhdu gnoseologiej i metafizikoj". *Khristianskoe chtenie*, no. 4, pp. 523–542.
B[eneman]skij, [Mikhail I.] (1902): "Iz akademicheskoj zhizni". *Bogoslovskij vestnik*, tom 3, no. 11, pp. 365–389.
Berdjaev, Nikolaj A. (1909): "Opyt filosofskogo opravdanija khristianstva". *Russkaja mysl'*, g. 13, kn.ix, pp. 54–72.
Berdjaev, Nikolaj A. (1910a): "Filosofskaja istina i intelligentskaja pravda". In *Dukhovnyj krizis intelligencii*. St. Petersburg: Tip. tovarishchestva "Obshchestvennaja Pol'za", pp. 171–192.
Berdjaev, Nikolaj A. (1910b): "Opyt filosofskago opravdenija khristianstva". In *Dukhovnyj krizis intelligencii*. St. Petersburg: Tip. tovarishchestva "Obshchestvennaja Pol'za", pp. 274–298.
Berdjaev, Nikolaj A. (1914): "Stilizovanoe pravoslavie". *Russkaja mysl'*, tom 35, kn. 1, pp. 109–125.
Bogdashevskij, Dmitrij I. (1892): "V zashchitu metafiziki uma". *Trudy Kievskoj dukhovnoj akademii*, tom 1, no. 4, pp. 644–650.
Bogdashevskij, Dmitrij I. (1893): "Zdravaja metafizika". *Trudy Kievskoj dukhovnoj akademii*, no. 5, 125–138.

Bogdashevskij, Dmitrij I. (1894): *O vzaimnom otnoshenii filosofii i estestvoznanija*. Kiev: Tip. G.T. Korchak-Novikago.
Bogdashevskij, Dmitrij I. (1898): *Filosofija Kanta*. Kiev: Tip. Imperatorskago universiteta.
Bugrov, Konstantin D. (2020): "Providenie i vlast': politicheskaja mysl' Feofana Prokopovicha". *Izvestija Ural. Feder. Universiteta*, ser. 2, tom 22, no. 1, pp. 99–111.
Bulgakov, Makarij (1843): *Istorija Kievskoj akademii*. St. Petersburg: Tip. Konstantina Zhernakova.
Charipova, Liudmila V. (2006): *Latin books and the Eastern Orthodox clerical elite in Kiev, 1632–1780*. Manchester: Manchester University Press.
Chase, Michael (2015): "Pavel Florensky on Space and Time". *ΣΧΟΛΗ*, vol. 9, no. 1, pp. 105–118.
Chechin, Sergij (2005): "Mitropolit Stefan Javors'kij ta Get'man Ivan Mazepa". *Nizhins'ka starovina: Naukovij istoriko-kul'turologichni zbirnik*, vyp. 4, pp. 78–102.
Chetverikov, Ivan P. (1997): "Iz lekcij po obshchej psikhologii". In *Russkaja religioznaja antropologija*, tom II. N. K. Gavrjushin (Ed.). Moscow: Moskovskaja dukhovnaja akademii, pp. 335–343.
Chicherin, Boris (1999): *Nauka i religija*. Moscow: Izd. "Respublika".
Chistovich, Ilarion (1857): *Istorija S. Peterburgskoj dukhovnoj akademii*. St. Petersburg: Tip. Jakova Treja.
Chistovich, Ilarion (1876): *Kurs opytnoj psikhologii*. St. Petersburg: Tip. Departamenta Udelov.
Chistovich, Ilarion (1889): *S.-Peterburgskaja dukhovnaja akademija za poslednija 30 let (1858–1888gg.)*. St. Petersburg: v sinodal'noj tipografii.
Chizhevskij, Dmitrij I. (1930): "Platon v drevnej Rusi". In *Zapiski Russkago istoricheskago obshchestva v Prage*, kn. 2. Prague: Société Historique Russe à Prague, pp. 71–81.
Chizhevs'kij, Dmitro (2005): *Filosofs'ki tvori u chotir'okh tomakh*. Kyiv: Smoloskip.
Chizhevskij, Dmitrij I. (2007): *Gegel' v Rossii*. St. Petersburg: Nauka.
Chrissidis, Nicolaos (2016): *An Academy at the Court of the Tsars: Greek Scholars and Jesuit Education in Early Modern Russia*. DeKalb, IL: Northern Illinois University Press.
Chubarov, Igor M. (1997): "Predfenomenologicheskaja tradicija v russkoj filosofija konca XIX veka". In *Antologija fenomenologicheskoj filosofii v Rossii*. I. M. Chubarov (Ed.). Moscow: Russkoe fenomenologicheskoe obshchestvo, izd. Logosa, pp. 7–27.
Cinger, Vasilij Ja. (1874): "Tochnye nauki i pozitivizm". In *Otchet i rechi, proiznesennye v torzhestvennom sobranii Imperatorskogo Moskovskogo universiteta 12 janvarja 1874 g*. Moscow: Univ. tip., pp. 38–98.
Collins, Randall (2002): *The Sociology of Philosophies: A Global Theory of Intellectual Change*. Cambridge, MA: Belnap Press of Harvard University.
Collis, Robert (2012): *The Petrine Instauration: Religion, Esotericism and Science at the Court of Peter the Great, 1689–1725*. Leiden: Koninklijke Brill NV.
Cracraft, James (1978): "Feofan Prokopovich and the Kiev Academy". In *Russian Orthodoxy under the Old Regime*. Robert L. Nichols and Theofanis George Stavrou (Eds.). Minneapolis: University of Minnesota Press, pp. 44–64.
Cracraft, James (1981): "Did Feofan Prokopovich Really Write *Pravda voli monarshei?*". *Slavic Review*, vol. 40, no. 2, pp. 173–193.
Cvyk, Irina. V. (2013): "Prepodavanie filosofii v Moskovskoj dukhovnoj akademii XIXv.". *Vestnik RUDN*. Serija filosofija, no. 1, pp. 44–57.
D. P. (1869): "Biograficheskaja zametka". In Avsenev, Feofan (1869): *Iz zapisok po psikhologii*. Kiev: Tip. Kievskago Gubernskago upravlenija, pp. i-xvi.
Debol'skij, Nikolaj G. (1880): *Filosofskie osnovy nravstvennogo vospitanija*. St. Petersburg: Tip. V. S. Balasheva.

Debol'skij, Nikolaj G. (1882): *Filosofija budushchago*. St. Petersburg: Tip. Kotomina.
Debol'skij, Nikolaj G. (1886): *O vysshem blage ili o verkhovnoj celi nravstvennoj dejatel'nosti*. St. Petersburg: Tip. Obshchestvennaja pol'za.
Debol'skij Nikolaj G. (1916): "Nachalo nacional'nostej v russkom i nemeckom osveshchenii". *Zhurnal Ministerstva narodnago prosveshchenija*, no. 2, pp. 183–207.
De Horn, Jean (1843): *Mémoire sur ma carrière civile et militaire en Russie*. London: J. Mitchell et Cie.
Denisov, Jakov A. (1906): *Professor Khar'kovskago universiteta M.A. Ostroumov*. Khar'kov: Tip. Gubernskago Pravlenija.
Drozdov, Aleksej (1835): *Opyt sistemy nravstvennoj filosofii*. St. Petersburg: Tip. I. Glazumova.
Ershov, Matvej N. (1914): *Problema bogopoznanija v filosofii Mal'bransha*. Kazan: Central'naja tip.
Ershov, Matvej N. (1922): *Puti razvitija filosofii v Rossii*. Vladivostok: Izd. Gosudarstvennago dal'nevostochnago universiteta.
Ershov, Matvej N. (1990): "Vlijanie lichnosti filosofa na filosofskoe postroenie". In *Na perelome. Filosofskie diskussii 20-x godov*. P.V. Alekseev (Ed.). Moscow: Politizdat, pp. 103–106.
Feodor, Ep. (A.V. Rozdeevskij) (1914): [Review of] *O dukhovnoj Istine. Opyt pravoslavnoj teodicei*. *Bogoslovskij vestnik*, tom 2, no. 5, pp. 140–181.
Fichte, J. G. (2021): *Foundation of the Entire Wissenschaftslehre and Related Writings (1794–95)*. Daniel Breazeale (Trans.). Oxford: Oxford University Press.
Filaret (1885): *Sobranie mnenij i otzyvov Filareta, Mitropolita Moskovskago i Kolomenskago, po uchebnym i cerkovno-gosudarstvennym voprosam*. Tom 1. St. Petersburg: Synodel'noj tip.
Florenskij, Pavel A. (1914): *Stolp i utverzhdenie istiny: Opyt pravoslavnoj teodicei*. Moscow: Izd. Mamontov.
Florenskij, Pavel A. (1905): "Ot perevodchika". *Bogoslovskij vestnik*, tom 3, no. 9, pp. 95–99.
Florenskij, Pavel A. (1977): "Iz bogoslovskogo nasledija". In *Bogoslovskie trudy*, vyp. 17, pp. 85–248.
Florenskij, Pavel A. (1994): *Sochinenija v chetyrekh tomakh*. Tom 1. Moscow: Mysl'.
Florenskij, Pavel A. (1996a): "Kosmologicheskie antinomii Immanuila Kanta". In *Sochinenija v chetyrekh tomakh*. Tom 2. Moscow: Izd. "Mysl'", pp. 3–33.
Florenskij, Pavel A. (1996b): "Predely gnoseologii (Osnovnaja antinomija teorii znanija)". In *Sochinenija v chetyrekh tomakh*. Tom 2. Moscow: Izd. "Mysl'", pp, 34–60.
Florenskij, Pavel A. (2000): "Obshchecheloveskie korni idealizma (filosofija narodov)". In *Sochinenija v chetyrekh tomakh*. Tom 3(2). Moscow: Izd. "Mysl'", pp. 45–168.
Florenskij, Pavel A. (2003): *Stolp i utverzhdenie istiny: Opyt pravoslavnoj teodicei*. Moscow: OOO Izd. AST.
Florensky, Pavel (1997): *The Pillar and Ground of the Truth*. Boris Jakim (Trans.). Princeton: Princeton University Press.
Florovskij, Georgij (2009): *Puti russkogo bogoslovija*. Moscow: Institut russkoj civilizacii.
Florovsky, Georges (1979): *Ways of Russian Theology*. Robert L. Nichols (Trans.). Belmont, MA: Nordland Publishing Company.
Foltz, Bruce (2013): "The Fluttering of Autumn Leaves: Logic, Mathematics, and Metaphysics in Florensky's *The Pillar and Ground of the Truth*". In *Logic in Orthodox Christian Teaching*. Andrew Schumann (Ed.). Frankfurt: Ontos Verlag, pp. 174–203.
Frege, Gottlob (1986): *The Foundations of Arithmetic*. J. L. Austin (Trans.). Evanston, IL: Northwestern University Press.
Gavriil, Arkhimandrit (1840): *Istorija filosofii*. Chast VI. Kazan: Universitetskaja tip.
Glagolev, Sergej S. (1892): "Ob otnoshenii filosofii i estestvennykh nauk k nauk. Vvedenie Bogoslovie". *Bogoslovskij vestnik*, tom 3, no. 12, pp. 370–390.

Glagolev, Sergej S. (1894a): *O proiskhozhdenii i pervobytnom sostojanii roda chelovecheskago.* Moscow: Tip. A. I. Snegirevoj.
Glagolev, Sergej S. (1894b.): "Potrebnost' v apologiticheskikh trudakh v nostojashchee vremja". *Bogoslovskij vestnik,* no. 8, pp. 167–180.
Glagolev, Sergej S. (1898): *Protoierej Feodor Aleksandrov Golubinskij (Ego zhizn' i dejatel'nost').* Sergiev Posad: Tip. A. I. Snegirevoj.
Glagolev, Sergej S. (1900): *Religija i nauka v ikh vzaimootnoshenii k nastupajushchemu XX stoletiju.* Svjato-Troickaja Sergieva Lavra: Sobstvennaja tipografija.
Glagolev, Sergej S. (1908): *Istina i nauka.* Sergiev Posad: Tip. Sv.-Tr. Sergievoj Lavry.
Glagolev, Sergej S. (1910): *Po voprosam logiki.* Khar'kov: Tip. Gubernskago Pravlenija.
Glagolev, Sergej S. (1912): *O proiskhozhdenii cheloveka. (Razbor teorii Vasmanna).* Sergiev Posad: Izd. M. S. Elova.
Glagolev, Sergej S. (1914): *Estestvennonauchnye voprosy, v ikh otnoshenii k khristianskomu miroponimaniju.* Sergiev Posad: Izd. M.S. Elova.
Glagolev, Sergej S. (1915): "Filosofija i svoboda". In *V pamjat' stoletija (1814–1914) Imperatorskoj Moskovskoj Dukhovnoj Akademii. Sbornik statej.* Chast' pervaja. Sergiev Posad: Tip. Sv.-Tr. Sergievoj Lavry, pp. 152–200.
Glagolev, Sergej S. (1916): "Otzyv na knigu o. Pavla Florenskogo *O dukhovnoj Istine*". *Zhurnal sobranij Soveta Imperatorskoj Moskovskoj Dukhovnoj akademii za 1914 goda.* Seregiev Posad: Tip. Sv.-Tr. Sergievoj Lavry, pp. 76–85.
Golubcov, Sergij (1999): *Moskovskaja dukhovnaja akademija v nachale XX veka.* Moscow: Izd. Martis.
Golubcov, Sergej. (2010): "Moskovskaja dukhovnaja akademija v revoljucionnyj period (1917–1918)". *Bogoslovskij vestnik,* no. 11–12, pp. 443–509.
Golubinskij, Fedor A. (1884a): *Lekcii filosofii,* vyp. 1. Moscow: Tip. L. F. Snegirev.
Golubinskij, Fedor A. (1884b): *Lekcii filosofii,* vyp. 2. Moscow: Tip. L. F. Snegirev.
Golubinskij, Fedor A. (1884c): *Lekcii filosofii,* vyp. 3. Moscow: Tip. L. F. Snegirev.
Golubinskij, Fedor A. (1884d): *Lekcii filosofii,* vyp. 4. Moscow: Tip. L. F. Snegirev.
Golubinskij, Fedor A. (1898): *Lekcii filosofii. Metafizicheskaja psikhologija.* Moscow: Pechatnja A. I. Snegirevoj.
Gorodenskij, Nikolaj G. (1896): "Otnoshenie nravstvennosti k religii". *Bogoslovskij vestnik,* tom 4, no. 11, pp. 194–215.
Gorodenskij, Nikolaj G. (1899): "Nravstvennaja filosofija Vl. S. Solov'ëva". *Bogoslovskij vestnik,* tom 1, no. 2, pp. 287–321.
Gorodenskij, Nikolaj G. (1903a): *Nravstvennoe soznanie chelovechestvo.* Sergieva Lavra: sovstvennaja tipografija.
Gorodenskij, Nikolaj G. (1903b): "Rech' pered zashchitoju dissertacii 'Nravstvennoe soznanie chelovechestva'". *Bogoslovskij vestnik,* tom 2, no. 7/8, pp. 564–574.
Grot, Nikolaj Ja. (1886): "O napravlenii i zadachakh moej filosofii. Po povodu stat'i arkhiepiskopa Nikanora". *Pravoslavnoe obozrenie,* 12, pp. 792–809.
Gurvich, Georgij (1915): *"Pravda voli monarshej" Feofana Prokopovicha i eja zapadnoevropejskie istochniki.* Jur'ev: Tip. K. Mattisena.
Hamburg, Gary M. (2016): *Russia's Path Toward Enlightenment: Faith, Politics, and Reason, 1500–1801.* New Haven, CT: Yale University Press.
Haney, Frank (2001): "Pavel Florenskij und Kant – eine wichtige Seite der russischen Kant-Rezeption". *Kant-Studien,* vol. 92, no. 1, pp. 81–103.

Hesse, Mary B. (2005): *Forces and Fields: The Concept of Action at a Distance in the History of Physics.* Mineola, NY: Dover Publications, Inc.
Husserl, Edmund (1982): *Ideas pertaining to a Pure Phenomenology and to a Phenomenological Philosophy.* F. Kersten (Trans.). The Hague: Martinus Nijhoff.
Husserl, Edmund (1989): *Ideas Pertaining to a Pure Phenomenology and to a Phenomenological Philosophy. Second Book.* Richard Rojcewicz and Andre Schuwer (Trans.). Dordrecht: Klkuwer Academic Publishers.
Husserl, Edmund (1997): *Psychological and Transcendental Phenomenology and the Confrontation with Heidegger (1927–1931).* Thomas Sheehan and Richard E. Palmer (Trans.). Dordrecht: Kluwer Academic Publishers.
Husserl, Edmund (2004): *Wahrnehmung und Aufmerksamkeit. Texte aus dem Nachlass (1893–1912).* Thomas Vongehr und Regula Giuliani (Ed.). Dordrecht: Springer.
Ikonnikov, V. S. (1884): *Biograficheskij slovar' professorov i prepodavatelej Imperatorskago universiteta sv. Vladimira (1834–1884).* Kiev: Tip. Imperatorskago universiteta sv. Vladimira.
Ismajlov, Filipp F. (1860): *Vzgljad na sobstvennuju proshedshuju zhizn'*. Moscow: Univ. tip.
Ivanov, Vladimir (1986): "Stanovlenie bogoslovskoj mysli v Moskovskoj dukhovnoj akademii (1814–1870)". In *Moskovskaja dukhovnaja akademija 300 let (1685–1985).* Moscow: Izd. Moskovskoj patriarkhii, pp. 113–147.
Ivanov, Andrey (2020a): "Escape from Rome: Teofan Prokopovych and Ukrainian Orthodox Ties to the Eternal City, 1650–1721". *Harvard Ukrainian Studies,* vol. 37, no. 102, pp. 47–81.
Ivanov, Andrey (2020b): *A Spiritual Revolution. The Impact of Reformation and Enlightenment in Orthodox Russia.* Madison, WI: The University of Wisconsin Press.
"Iz akademicheskoj zhizni: Magisterskij disput i.d. docenta Akademii N. G. Gorodenskago" (1903): *Bogoslovskij vestnik,* t. 2, no. 7/8, pp. 575–587.
Jakovenko, Boris (1996). "Filosofija otchajanija". In *P. A. Florenskij: pro et contra.* K. G. Isupova (Ed.). St. Petersburg: RkhGU, pp. 254–265.
Jakovenko, Boris (2003): *Istorija russkoj filosofii.* Moscow: Respublika.
Jastrebov, Mitrofan F. (1897): Novaja tochka zrenija v sisteme nravstvennago bogoslovija. *Trudy Kievskoj dukhovnoj Akademii,* no. 11, pp. 367–399.
Jastrebov, Mitrofan F. (1900): "Vysokopreosvjashchennyj Innokentij (Borisov), kak professor bogoslovija Kievskoj dukhovnoj Akademii". *Trudy Kievskoj dukhovnoj Akademii,* no. 12, pp. 522–566.
Jurkevich, Pamfil D. (1861): "Dokazatel'stva bytija boga". *Trudy Kievskoj dukhovnoj Akademii,* kn. 3, pp. 327–357.
Jurkevich, Pamfil D. (1990): *Filosofskie proizvedenija.* Moscow: Izd. Pravda.
Kadosov, Svjashchennik Pavel (2016): "Illarion Alekseevich Chistovich: uchenyj, prepodavatel', gosudarstvennyj dejtel'". *Khristianskoe chtenie,* no. 4, pp: 56–72.
Kadosov, Svjashchennik Pavel (2019): "Professor Sankt-Peterburgskoj dukhovnoj akademii I. A. Chistovich i ego rodnye". *Vestnik Istoricheskogo obshchestva,* no. 1(3), pp. 53–71.
Kant, Immanuel (1996): *Practical Philosophy.* Mary J. Gregor (Trans.). Cambridge: Cambridge University Press.
Kant, Immanuel (1997): *Critique of Pure Reason.* Paul Guyer and Allen W.Wood (Trans.). Cambridge: Cambridge University Press.
Karinskij, Mikhail I. (1873a): "Kriticheskij obzor poslednego perioda germanskoj filosofii". *Khristianskoe chtenie,* no. 1, pp. 70–132.

Karinskij, Mikhail I. (1873b): "Kriticheskij obzor poslednego perioda germanskoj filosofii (Prodolzhenie)". *Khristianskoe chtenie*, no. 3, pp. 525–557.
Karinskij, Mikhail I. (1873c): "Kriticheskij obzor poslednego perioda germanskoj filosofii (Prodolzhenie)". *Khristianskoe chtenie*, no. 4, pp. 658–737.
Karinskij, Mikhail I. (1873d): "Kriticheskij obzor poslednego perioda germanskoj filosofii (Prodolzhenie")". *Khristianskoe chtenie*, no. 6, pp. 210–258.
Karinskij, Mikhail I. (1875): "K voprosu o pozitivizme". *Pravoslavnoe obozrenija*, October, pp. 345–374.
Karinskij, Mikhail I. (1878): "Javlenie ii dejstvitel'nost'". *Pravoslavnoe obozrenie*, April, pp. 659–704.
Karinskij, Mikhail I. (1892): "Recenzii sochinenij, udostoennykh Svjatejshim Sinodom premij mitropolita Makarija v tekushchem godu. 'Idealizm i realism'". *Khristianskoe chtenie*, no. 11–12, pp. 645–677.
Karinskij, Mikhail I. (1893): *Ob istinakh samoochevidnykh*. St. Petersburg: Tip. V. S. Balashev.
Karpov, Vasilij N. (1839): Predislovie perevodchika. In Genrikh Ritter. *Istorija filosofii drevnikh vremen. Chast pervaja*. St. Petersburg: Tip. I.Glazunova, pp. iii-ix.
Karpov, Vasilij N. (1840): *Vvedenie v filosofiju*. St. Petersburg: Tip. I. Glazunova.
Karpov, Vasilij N. (1855): "Obshchij kharakter filosofii i prichina razlichnykh ee napravlenij v mire khristianskom". In Kucenko, N. A. (2005): *Dukhovno-akademicheskaja filosofija v Rossii pervoj poloviny XIX veka*. Moscow: Rossijskaja Akademija Nauk, Institut filosofii, pp. 101–104.
Karpov, Vasilij N. (1856a): *Sistematicheskoe izlozhenie logiki*. St. Petersburg: Tip. Jakova Treja.
Karpov, Vasilij N. (1856b): "Vzgljad na dvizhenie filosofii v mire khristianskom i naprichiny razlichnykh eja napravlenij". *Zhurnal Ministerstva narodnago prosveshchenija*, chast' XCII, otd. II, pp. 167–198.
Karpov, Vasilij N. (1860a): "Filosofskij racionalizm novejshego vremeni". In Karpov, Vasilij N. (2013): *Sochinenija v trekh tomakh. Tom 1*. Melitopol': Izd. dom Melitopol'skoj gorodskoj tip, pp. 130–254.
Karpov, Vasilij N. (1860b): "O samopoznanii". In Karpov, Vasilij N. (2013): *Sochinenija v trekh tomakh. Tom 1*. Melitopol': Izd. dom Melitopol'skoj gorodskoj tip, pp. 256–271.
Karpov, Vasilij N. (1865): "O samopoznanii". In Mejson, Dzhon (John Mason) (1865): *O samopoznanii*. Professor Karpov (Trans.). Moscow: Univ. tip., pp. 207–231.
Karpov, Vasilij N. (1868): "Vstupitel'naja lekcija v psikhologiju". In Karpov, Vasilij N. (2013): *Sochinenija v trekh tomakh. Tom 1*. Melitopol': Izd. dom Melitopol'skoj gorodskoj tip, pp. 308–339.
Karpuk, Dmitrij A. (2016): "Bogoslovskaja nauka v Sankt-Peterburgskoj Dukhovnoj Akademii (k 295-letiju so dnja osnovanija i 70-letiju so dnja vozrozhdenija". *Khristianskoe chtenie*, no. 6, pp. 10–30.
Kashuba, Marija V. (1979): *Georgij Konisskij*. Moscow: Mysl'.
Kashuba, Marija V. (2006): "Etika jak akademichna disciplina v Kievo-Mogiljanskij Akademiï". *Kiïevs'ka Akademija*, vyp. 2–3, pp. 98–104.
Kashuba, Marija V. (2014): "Etika v filosofskikh kursakh professorov Kievo-Mogiljanskoj akademii". *Eticheskaja mysl'/Ethical Thought*, no. 14, pp. 217–239.
Kassow, Samuel D. (1989): *Students, Professors, and the State in Tsarist Russia*. Berkeley: University of California Press.
Katanskij, Aleksandr I. (2010): *Vospominenija starogo professora. S 1847 po 1913 god*. Nizhnij Novgorod: Tipografija Rido.
Kedrov, I[van] (1838): *Opyt filosofii prirody*. St. Petersburg: Tip. departamenta vneshnej torgovli.
Kedrov, Ivan (1844): *Kurs psikhologii*. Jaroslavl: Tip. Gubernskago Pravlenija.

Khomenko, I. V. (2012): "Logika v Kievskoj akademiceskoj i universitetskoj filosofii XIX-nachala XX v.". *Epistemologija & filosofija nauki*, tom XXXIV, no. 4, pp. 179–190.

Khrisanf, Archim. [Retivcev, Vladimir N.] (1860): "Vzgljad na mnenie novejshikh racionalistov o sushchestve religii". *Pravoslavnyj sobesednik*, tom 3, pp. 162–195; 446–480.

Kireevskij, I. V. (1972): "On the Necessity and Possibility of New Principles in Philosophy". In Peter J, Christoff: *An Introduction to Nineteenth-Century Russian Slavophilism*. Vol. 2. The Hague: Mouton, pp. 345–375.

Kirik, D. P., and V. M. Nichuk (1979): "Problemi piznannja v trorakh F. Prokopovich". In Prokopovich, Feofan: *Filosofs'ki tvori*. Tom I. Kyiv: Naukova dumka, pp. 36–62.

Kline, George L. (1967): "Darwinism and the Russian Orthodox Church". In *Continuity and Change in Russiab and Soviet Thought*. Ernest J. Simmons (Ed.). New York: Russell & Russell, pp. 307–328.

Kocjuba, V. I. (2012): "O nekotorykh aspektakh zhizni i filosofii protoiereja F. A. Golubinskogo". *Vestnik PSTGU. I: Bogoslovie. Filosofija*, vyp. 2(40), pp. 32–45.

Konstantin (Gorjanov), Arkhiepiskon (1998): "Zhizn' i eligiozno-filosofskaja antropologija Viktora Nesmelova". *Khristianskoe chtenie*, no. 16, pp. 5–25.

Korb, Johann-Georg (2013): *Diary of an Austrian Secretary of Legation*. New York: Routledge.

Korzo, M. A. (2011): *Nravstvennoe bogoslovie Simeona Poloskogo: Osvoenie katolicheskoj tradicii Moskovskimi knizhnikami votoroj poloviny XVII veka*. Moscow: IFRAN.

Korsunskij, Ivan N. (1890): "Professor V. N. Potapov: Nekrolog". *Pribavlenija k Tvorenijam sv. Otcov*, chast' 46, kn. 3, pp. 142–176.

Korsunskij, Ivan N. (1893): "Viktor Dmitrievich Kudrjavcev-Platonov". In Kudrjavcev-Platonov, Viktor D. (1893): *Sochinenija*. Tom pervyj, vyp. pervyj. Sergiev Posad: Izd. Bratstva Prepodobnago, pp. 1–56.

Kozlov, Aleksej A. (1892): [Review] Serebrenikov. *Uchenie Lokka o prirozhdennykh nachalakh znanija*. *Voprosy filosofii i psikhologii*, kn. 13, pp. 49–59.

Kozlovs'kij, Viktor (2007): "Markelin Olesnic'kij pro vitoki i npirodu praktichnoï filosofii". *Kiïvs'ka Akademija*, vyp. 4, pp. 109–129.

Kozlovs'kij, Viktor (2011): "Vol'fians'ka Sistema filosofs'koï osviti ta iï recepcija vikladachami Kievo-Mogiljans'koï akademiï". In *Filosofs'ka osvita v Ukraïni: Istorija i suchasnist'*. Kyiv: NaUKMA, pp. 29–65.

Kruglov, A. N. (2009): *Filosofija Kanta v Rossii v konce XVIII – pervoj polovine XIX vekov*. Moscow: Kanon.+.

Kucenko, N. A. (2002): "Ivan Mikhajlovich Skvorcov – pervyj professor filosofii v Kievskoj dukhovnoj akademii". In *Istorija filosofii*, no. 9. Moscow: IF RA, pp. 43–51.

Kucenko, N. A. (2008): *Professional'naja filosofija v Rossii pervoj poloviny-serediny XIX veka: process stanovlenija i vidnejshie predstaviteli*. Moscow: IF RAN.

Kudrjavcev, Pëtr P. (1899): "Professor Dmitrij Vasil'evich Pospekhov". *Vera i cerkov*, tom II, otd. II, pp. 786–812.

Kudrjavcev, Pëtr P. (1905): "Professor Markellin Aekseevich Olesnickij". *Trudy Kievskoj dukhovnoj akademii*, kn. 4, pp. 675–704.

Kudrjavcev, Petr P. (1906): "Professor Petr Ivanovich Linickij". *Trudy Kievskoj dukhovnoj akademii*, kn. 2, pp. 737–771.

Kudrjavcev, Petr P. (1991): "Glavnye momenty v istorii voprosa ob otnoshenii very k znaniju". *Khristianskoe chtenie*, no. 4, pp. 29–50.

Kudrjavcev, Petr P. (2012): *Absoljutizm ili reljativism?* In *Sochinenija v dvukh tomakh*. Tom 1. A. G. Volkov (Ed.). Melitopol': Izdatel'skij dom MGT.

Kudrjavcev-Platonov, Viktor D. (1857): "O edinobozhii, kak pervonachal'nom vide religii roda chelovecheskogo". *Pribavlenija k Tvorenijam sv. Otcov*, chast' 16, kn. 3, pp. 328–416.
Kudrjavcev-Platonov, Viktor D. (1860): "O pervonachal'nom proiskhozhdenii na zemle roda chelovecheskago". In Kudrjavcev-Platonov, Viktor D. (1894): *Sochinenija*. Tom tretij, vyp. vtoroj. Sergiev Posad: Izd. Bratstva Prepodobnago Sergija, 196–247.
Kudrjavcev-Platonov, Viktor D. (1861): "O religioznom indiferentizme". In Kudrjavcev-Platonov, Viktor D. (1892): *Sochinenija*. Tom vtoroj, vyp. vtoroj. Sergiev Posad: Izd. Bratstva Prepodobnago Sergija, pp. 62–103.
Kudrjavcev-Platonov, Viktor D. (1864): "Ob istochnike idei bozhestva". In Kudrjavcev-Platonov, 1898: 1–34.
Kudrjavcev-Platonov, Viktor D. (1870): "Religija, eja sushchnost' i proiskhozhdenie". *Pravoslavnoe obozrenie*, no. 4: 417–464; no. 5: 773–800; no. 6, pp. 895–939.
Kudrjavcev-Platonov, Viktor D. (1874): "Religija i pozitivnaja filosofija". In Kudrjavcev-Platonov, Viktor D. (1898): *Sochinenija*. Tom tretij, vyp. pervyj. Sergiev Posad: Izd. Bratstva Prepodobnago Sergija, pp. 320–350.
Kudrjavcev-Platonov, Viktor D. (1890): "Znachenie dokazatel'stv bytija Bozhija". *Pravoslavnoe obozrenie*, no. 1, pp. 3–26.
Kudrjavcev-Platonov, Viktor D. (1892): *Sochinenija*, tom vtoroj, vyp. vtoroj. Sergiev Posad: Izd. Bratstva Prepodobnago Sergija.
Kudrjavcev-Platonov, Viktor D. (1893a): *Nachal'nyja osnovanija filosofii*. Moscow: N. I. Osesireyj.
Kudrjavcev-Platonov, Viktor D. (1893b): *Sochinenija*, tom pervyj, vyp. pervyj. Sergiev Posad: Izd. Bratstva Prepodobnago Sergija.
Kudrjavcev-Platonov, Viktor D. (1894a): *Sochinenija*, tom pervyj, vyp. tretij. Sergiev Posad: Izd. Bratstva Prepodobnago Sergija.
Kudrjavcev-Platonov, Viktor D. (1894b): *Sochinenija*, tom tretij, vyp. vtoroj. Sergiev Posad: Izd. Bratstva Prepodobnago Sergija.
Kudrjavcev-Platonov, Viktor D. (1898): *Sochinenija*, tom tretij, vyp. pervyj. Sergiev Posad: Izd. Bratstva Prepodobnago Sergija.
Kudrjavcev-Platonov, Viktor D. (1908): *Vvedenie v filosofiju*. Sergiev Posad: Tip. Sv.-Tr. Sergievoj Lavry.
Kutnevich, V. I. (1864): "Vstupitel'nja filosofskaja lekcija (po studencheskoj zapisi)". *Pribavlenija k Tvorenijam sv. Otcov*, chast' 23, kn. 5–6, pp. 635–646.
Laskeev, P. M. (1898): "Dva proekta pravoslavno-khristianskoj filosofii". *Khristianskoe chtenie*, no. 5, pp. 732–756.
L[evickij], R[oman] I. (1880): "O nravstvennom uchenii khristianstva". *Pravoslavnoe obozrenie*, kn. 9, pp. 13–28.
Linickij, Petr I. (1874): *Obzor filosofskikh uchenij*. Kiev: Tip. S. T. Eremeev.
Linickij, Petr I. (1881): *Ob umozrenii i otnoshenii umozritel'nago poznanija k opytu*. Kiev: Tip. G. T. Korchak-Novickago.
Linickij, Petr I. (1892): *Posobie k izucheniju voprosov filosofii*. Kharkov: Tip. Gubernskago Pravlenija.
Linickij, Petr I. (1894a): "Filosofija kak nauka". *Vera i razum*, kn. 2, no. 4, pp. 151–176.
Linickij, Petr I. (1894b): "Filosofija kak nauka (Okonchanie)". *Vera i razum*, kn. 2, chast' 2, pp. 1–12.
Linickij, Petr I. (1898): "Otzyvy ekstraordinarnogo professora M. Iastrebova i zasluzhennogo ordinarnogo professora P. Linickogo o sochinenii ekstraordinarnogo professora M. Olesnitckogo". *Trudy Kievskoj Dukhovnoj Akademii*, no. 4, pp. 304–336.
Linickij, Petr I. (2012): *Osnovye voprosy filosofii*. In *Sochinenija v pjati tomakh*. Tom 1. Melitopol': Izdatel'sklij dom MGT, pp. 40–182.

Lopatinskij, Feofilakt (1997): *Izbrannye filosofskie proizvedenija*, ed. A. V. Panibratcev. Moscow: Institut filosofii, Rossijskaja Akademija Nauk.
Lossky, N. O. (1951): *History of Russian Philosophy*. New York: International Universities Press, Inc.
Luk'janov, S. M. (1916): *O Vl. S. Solov'ëv v ego molodye gody. Materialy k biografii*, kn. pervaja. Petrograd: Senatskaja tipografija.
Mejson, Dzhon (John Mason) (1783): *Poznanie sebja samago*. I. P. Turgenev (Trans.). Moscow: Univ. tip.
Mejson, Dzhon (John Mason) (1865): *O samopoznanii*. Professor Karpov (Trans.). Moscow: Univ. tip.
Michelson, Patrick Lally (2020): "Russian Orthodox Thought in the Church's Clerical Academies". In *The Oxford Handbook of Russian Religious Thought*. Caryl Emerson, George Pattison, and Randall A. Poole (Eds.). Oxford: Oxford University Press, pp. 94–110.
Mikhail (Gribanovskij) (1888): "Rech', proiznesennaja pered zashchitoj dissertanii na stepen' magistra bogoslovija". *Khristianskoe chtenie*, no. 5–6, pp. 727–731.
Mikhail (Gribanovskij), Ieromonakh (1990): "Istina bytija Bozhija. Opyt ujasnenija osnovnykh khristianskikh istin estestvennoj chelovecheskoj mysl'ju". In *Bogoslovskie trudy*, tom 30. Moscow: Izd. Moskovskoj Patriarkhii RPKhI, pp. 5–82.
Mikhail (Gribanovskij), Arkhiep (2005): *Lekcii po vvedeniju v krug bogoslovskikh nauk*. St. Petersburg: Ob-vo pamjati Igumenij Taisii.
Miloslavskij, Petr A. (1875): "Sovremennoe uchenie o substancijakh (Probnaja lekcija po metafizike)". *Pravoslavnyj sobesednik*, tom II, pp.401–421.
Miloslavskij, Petr A. (1878): *Tipy sovremennoj filosofskoj mysli v Germanii*. Kazan: Tip. Imperatorskago Universiteta.
Miloslavskij, Petr A. (1879a): "Pozdnee slovo o prezhdevremennom dele. Stranica v istorii russkoj filosofskoj mysli". *Pravoslavnoe obozrenie*, tom I, pp. 265–292.
Miloslavskij, Petr A. (1879b): "Proiskhozhdenie i znachenie filosofii". *Pravoslavnoe obozrenie*, tom III, pp. 232–266.
Miloslavskij, Petr A. (1883): *Osnovanij filosofii kak special'noj nauki*. Kazan: Tip, Imp. universiteta.
Mirtov, Dmitrij P. (1900): "Filosofija "cel'nogo znanija"". *Khristianskoe chtenie*, no. 10, pp. 620–628.
Mirtov, Dmitrij P. (1905a): "Nravstvennaja avtonomija po Kantu i Nicshe". *Khristianskoe chtenie*, no. 5, pp. 313–337.
Mirtov, Dmitrij P. (1905b): "Nravstvennaja avtonomija po Kantu i Nicshe". *Khristianskoe chtenie*, no. 5, pp. 587–608.
Morozov, A. A. (1971): "Metafora i allegorija u Stefana Javorskogo". In *Poetica i stilistika russkoj literatury*. M. P. Alekseev (Ed.). Leningrad: Izd. Nauka, pp. 35–44.
Mozgovaja, N. (2012): "Zdravaja metafizika Petra Linickogo". In Petr I. Linickij, *Sochinenija v pjati tomakh*. Tom 1. A. G. Volkov (Ed.). Melitopol': Izd. Dom MGT. 5–39.
Mozgovaja, N. (2016): "Psikhologicheskij idealizm Petra Avseneva". In Petr S. Avsenev. *Sochinenija*. A. G Volkov (Ed.). Kyiv: NGU im. M. Dragomanova, pp. 5–23.
Nadezhdin, N. I. (1914): "Iz zapisok Moskovskago Protoiereja N. I. Nadezhdina. (1832–1833gg.)". In *U troicy v akademii. 1814–1914gg. Jubilejnyj sbornik istoricheskikh materialov*. Moscow: Tip. T-va I. D. Sytima, pp. 42–79.
Nadezhin, Feodor S. (1837): *Ocherk istorii filosofii po Rejngol'du*. St. Petersburg: Tip. departamenta vneshnej torgovli.
Nemeth, Thomas (2014): *The Early Solov'ëv and His Quest for Metaphysics*. Cham, Switzerland: Springer International Publishing.

Nemeth, Thomas (2016): "Solovyov's *Crisis* and Positivism in Late Imperial Russia". *Solov'ëvskie issledovanija*, vypusk 2(50), pp. 65–80.
Nemeth, Thomas (2017): *Kant in Imperial Russia*. Cham, Switzerland: Springer International Publishing.
Nemeth, Thomas (2018): "Gustav Shpet's Implicit Phenomenological Idealism". *Husserl Studies*, vol. 34, pp. 267–285.
Nemeth, Thomas (2019): *The Later Solov'ëv. Philosophy in Imperial Russia*. Cham, Switzerland: Springer Nature.
Nesmelov, V.I. (1889): "Pamjati Veniamina Alekseevicha Snegireva". *Pravoslavnyj sobesednik*, no. 5, pp. 97–151.
Nesmelov, V. I. (1905): *Nauka o cheloveke*. Kazan: Central'naja tipografija.
Nesmelov, V. I. (2015): *Vera i znanie s tochki zrenija gnoseologii*. St. Petersburg: Obshchestvo pamjati igumenii Taisii.
Nesmelov, V. I. (2020): *Problema znanija. Opyt issledovanija prirodnogo nachala i formy filosofskogo znanija*. Vladivostok: Izd. Dal'nevostochnogo federal'nogo universiteta.
Nichols, Robert L. (1978): "Orthodoxy and Russia's Enlightenment, 1762–1825". In *Russian Orthodoxy under the Old Regime*. Robert L. Nichols and Theofanis George Stavrou (Eds.). Minneapolis: University of Minnesota Press, pp. 65–89.
Nikitenko, A. V. (1840): "Vvedenie v Filosofiju g. Karpova". *Syn Otechestva*, tom III, kn. IV, pp. 701–722.
Nikanor, Arkhiepiskop [Brovkovich] (1871): "Mozhno li pozitivnym filosofskim metodom dokazyvat' bytie chego-libo sverkhchuvstvennago-boga, dukhovnoj bezsmertnoj dushi i t. d.?". *Pravoslavnyj sobesednik*, tom 2, pp. 41–110.
Nikanor, Arkhiepiskop [Brovkovich] (1875): *Pozitivnaja filosofija i sverkhchuvstvennoe bytie*. Tom 1. St. Petersburg: Obshchestvennaja pol'za.
Nikanor, Arkhimandrit [Kudrjavcev] (1996): "Recenzija na kn.: Stolp i utverzhdenie Istiny". In *P. A. Florenskij: pro et contra*. K. G. Isupova (Ed.). St. Petersburg: RkhGU, pp. 316–354.
Nikolaev, P. A. (Ed.) (1989): *Russkie pisaateli 11–20 vv.* Tom 1. Moscow: Izd. Sovetskaja enciklopedija.
Nikol'skij, Aleksandr (1907): "Russkaja dukhovno-akademicheskaja filosofija, kak predshestvennica slavjanofil'stva i universitetskoj filosofii v Rossii. (Prodolzhenie)". *Vera i razum*, no. 3, pp. 352–365.
Obolevitch, Teresa (2015): "Galileo in the Russian Orthodox Context: History, Philosophy, Theology, and Science". *Zygon*, vol. 50, no. 4, pp. 788–808.
Olesnickij, Markellin A. (1882): *Istorija nravstvennosti i nravstvennykh uchenij*. Kiev: Tip. G. T. Korchak-Novickago.
Olesnickij, Markellin A. (1884): "Nravstvennyj progress". *Trudy Kievskoj dukhovnoj akademii*, no. 12, pp. 453–486.
Ostroumov, Mikhail A. (1879): *Obzor filosofskikh uchenij. Dlja dukhovnykh seminarij. Pervaja polovina*. Moscow: Tip. E. Lissner I Ju. Roman.
Ostroumov, Mikhail A. (1880): *Obzor filosofskikh uchenij. Dlja dukhovnykh seminarij. Vtoraja polovina*. Moscow: Tip. E. Lissner I Ju. Roman.
Ostroumov, Mikhail A. (1886): "Istorija filosofii v otnoshenii k otkroveniju". *Vera i razum*, tom II, chast' II, pp. 159–181.
"Otchet imperatorskoj S. Peterburgskoj akademii nauk o chetvertom prisuzhdenii uchrezhdennykh kamergerom P. N. Demidovym premij za 1834 god". (1835). *Zhurnal Ministerstva narodnago prosveshchenija*, July, chast' 7, pp. 84–110.

Ovchinnikova, Elena A. (2012): "Etika v universitetskoj tradicii v Rossii XVIII-XIX vv.". In *Diskursy etiki. Al'manakh: Vyp. I.* V. Ju. Perova (Ed.). St. Petersburg: Izd. Russkoj khristianskoj gumanitarnoj akademii, pp. 32–46.

Panibratcev, A. V. (1997a): *Filosofija v Moskovskoj Slavjano-Greko-Latiinskoj Akademii (pervaja chetvert' XVIII veka).* Moscow: Rossijskaja Akademija nauk. Institut filosofii.

Panibratcev, A. V. (1997b): "Filosofija v Rossii nachala XVIII veka i preemstvennost' i perspektivy razvitija". In Lopatinskij, Feofilakt (1997): *Izbrannye filosofskie proizvedenija.* A. V. Panibratcev (Ed.). Moscow: Institut filosofii, Rossijskaja Akademija Nauk, pp. 3–18.

Pastushenko, Liudmyla (2007): "Petro Kudriavtsev u religiĭno-filosof'komu zhytti Kyieva pochatku XX stolittia". *Kyivs'ka akademiia,* vyp. 4, pp. 166–179.

Pavlov, A. T. (2017): *Filosofskoe obrazovanie v Rossijskoj imperii.* Moscow: Izd. Borob'ev A. V.

Pipes, Richard (1979): *Russian under the Old Regime.* Harmondsworth, Middlesex: Penguin Books Ltd.

Pocci [Pozzi], Vera (2018): "'Institutiones Metaphysicae' I. Ja. Vetrinskogo i Sankt-Peterburgskaja dukhovnaja akademija (chast' I)". *Istorija filosofii,* tom 23, no. 1, pp. 56–66.

Poljakova, I. A. (2009): *Fedor Fedorovich Sidonskij (1805–1873): pravo na biografiju.* St. Petersburg: RkhGA.

Popov, Ivan V. (1897): *Estestvennyj nravstvennyj zakon.* Sergiev Posad: Tip. A. I. Snegirevoj.

Potapov, V. (1880): "O vzaimodejstvii veshchej. Filosofskij ocherk". *Pribavlenija k Tvorenijam sv. Otcov.* Chast' 26, kn. 1, pp. 136–146.

Pozzi, Vera (2017): *Kant e l'ortodossia russa. Accademie ecclesiastiche e filosofia in Russia tra XVIII e XIX secolo.* Firenze: Firenze University Press.

Proekt ustava dukhovnykh akademij (1823): St. Petersburg: Tip. V. Plavil'shchikova.

Prokopovich, Feofan (1961): *Sochinenija,* ed. S. S. Volk. Leningrad: Izd. Akademija nauk SSSR.

Prokopovich, Feofan (1980): *Filosofs'ki tvori.* Tom II. Kyiv: Naukova dumka.

Pypin, A. N. (1902): *Istorija russkoj literatury.* Tom III. St. Petersburg: Tip. M. M. Stasjulevicha.

Pyman, Avril (2010): *Pavel Florensky: A Quiet Genius.* New York: Continuum International Publishing Group.

Radlov, Ernest L. (1895): "Uchenaja dejatel'nost' Mikhaila Ivanovich Karinskogo". *Zhurnal Ministerstva narodnogo prosveshchenija,* January, chast' CCXCVII, pp. 406–429.

"Raznyja izvestija" (1874): *Pravoslavnoe obozrenie,* tom III, March, pp. 157–172.

Riasanovsky, Nicholas (1969): *Nicholas I and Official Nationality in Russia, 1825–1855.* Berkeley and Los Angeles: UCLA Press.

Riehl, Alois (1879): *Der philosophische Kriticismus und seine Bedeutung für die positive Wissenschaft.* Zweiter Band, erster Teil. Leipzig: Wilhelm Engelmann.

Rojek, Pawel (2019): "Pavel Florenskij's Theory of Religious Antinomies". *Logica Universalis,* vol. 13, no. 4, pp. 515–540.

Rostislavov, Dmitrij I. (1872): "Petersburgskaja dukhovnaga akademija do grafa Protosova – Vospominanija. (Okonchanie)". *Vestnik Evropy,* tom 5, Sept.-Oct., pp. 152–207.

Saltykov, Svjashchennik Aleksandr (1986): "Kratkij ocherk istorii Moskovskoj dukhovnoj akademii". In *Moskovskaja dukhovnaja akademija 300 let (1685–1985).* Moscow: Izd. Moskovskoj patriarkhii, pp. 73–112.

Sbornik lekcij byvshikh professorov Kievskoj dukhovnoj akademii (1869): Kiev: Tip. Gubernskago Upravlenija.

Sbornik postanovlenij i rasporjazhenij po censure s 1720 po 1862 goda (1862): St. Petersburg: Tip. Morskago Ministerstva.

Scanlan, James P. (1970): "Nicholas Chernyshevsky and Philosophical Materialism in Russia". *Journal of the History of Philosophy*, vol. 8, no. 1, pp. 65–86.
Semikras, V. V. (2019): "Etiko-pravovi ideï v Kievo-Mogiljans'kij akademiï XVIII st.". *Ukraïns'ki kul'turologichni studiï*, 2(5), pp. 36–40.
Serebrenikov, Vitalij S. (1892): "Rech', proiznesennaja pred zashchitoj magisterskoj dissertacii". *Khristianskoe chtenie*, No. 5–6:, pp. 487–492.
Serebrenikov, Vitalij S. (1897a): "Mekhanicheskoe vozzrenie na dushevnuju zhizn' pered sudom sovremennykh strogo nauchnykh psikhologicheskikh issledovanij". *Khristianskoe chtenie*, no. 3, pp. 373–390.
Serebrenikov, Vitalij S. (1897b): "Samootkrovenie dukha kak istochnik ego poznanija". *Khristianskoe chtenie*, no. 3, pp. 424–439.
Serebrenikov, Vitalij S. (1901): "Leibnic i Lokk po vopros o prirozhdennykh idejakh". *Khristianskoe chtenie*, no. 5, pp. 661–680.
Ševčenko, Ihor (1985): "The Many Worlds of Peter Mohyla". In *Harvarad Ukrainian Studies*, vol. 8, no. 1/2, pp. 9–44.
Shakmatov, M. V. (1930): "Platon v drevnej Rusi". In *Zapiski Russkago istoricheskago obshchestva v Prage*. Kn. 2. Prague: Société Historique Russe à Prague, pp. 49–70.
Shevcov, Aleksandr V. (2017): "Logiko-gnoseologicheskoe napravlenie filosofii v Sankt-Peterburgskoj dukhovnoj akademii (1870–1918)". *Khristianskoe chtenie*, no. 1, pp. 263–284.
Shindarov, Sergej B. (2011): "Uchënaja i uchebnaja dejatel'nost' professora SPbDA V.S. Serebrenikova". *Khristianskoe chtenie*, no. 3(38), pp. 169–195.
Ship, N. A. (2010): *Kiïvs'ka dukhovna akademija v kul'turno-osvitjans'komu prostori Ukraïni (1818–1919)*. Kyiv: Feniks.
Shkurinov, P. S. (1992): *Filosofija Rossii XVIII veka*. Moscow: Vysch. shk.
Shpet, Gustav. 1914. "Filosofskoe nasledstvo P. D. Jurkevicha". *Voprosy filosofii i psikhologii*, kn. 125(V), pp. 653–728.
Shpet, Gustav (2008): *Ocherk razvitija russkoj filosofii. I.* Moscow: ROSSPEN.
Sidonskij, Feodor (1833): *Vvedenie v nauku filosofii*. St. Petersburg: Tip. Konrad Vingebera.
Simchich, Mikola (2009): *Philosophia rationalis u Kievo-Mogiljanskij akademiï: Monografija*. Vinnytsia: O. Vlasjuk.
Simchich, Mikola (2016): "Kievo-Mogiljans'kij aristotelizm u konteksti drugoï skolastiki". *Kiïvs'ka akademija*, vyp. 13, pp. 11–32.
Simeon Polockij (1953): *Izbrannye Sochinenija*. Moscow-Leningrad: Izd. Akademii nauk SSSR.
Skvorcov, Ivan M. (1835): "O filosofii Plotina". In Skvorcov, Ivan M. (2014): *Sochinenija v dvukh tomakh*. Tom 1. N. G. Mozgovaja, A. G. Volkov (Eds.). Kyiv: NPU im. M.P. Dragomonova, pp. 55–64.
Skvorcov, Ivan M. (1838): "Kriticheskoe obozrenie Kantovoj religii v predelakh odnogo razuma". In Skvorcov, Ivan M. (2014): *Sochinenija v dvukh tomakh*. Tom 1. N. G. Mozgovaja, A. G. Volkov (Eds.). Kyiv: NPU im. M.P. Dragomonova, pp. 86–119.
Skvorcov, Ivan M. (1863a): "Khristianskoe upotreblenie filosofii ili filosofija sv. Grigorija Nisskogo". In Skvorcov, Ivan M. (2014): *Sochinenija v dvukh tomakh*. Tom 1. N. G. Mozgovaja, A. G. Volkov (Eds.). Kyiv: NPU im. M.P. Dragomonova, pp. 33–54.
Skvorcov, Ivan M. (1863b): "O metafizicheskom nachale filosofii". In Askocheskij, Viktor I. (1863): *Istorija Kievskoj dukhovnoj akademii po preobrazovanii eja v 1819 godu*. St. Petersburg: Tip. Eduard Vejmar, pp. 49–67.
Skvorcov (Skvorcev), Ioanna (1869): *Zapiski po nravstvennoj filosofii*. Kiev: Tip. Guberskago Upravlenija.

Skvorcov, Ivan M. (2014): *Sochinenija v dvukh tomakh*. Tom 1. N. G. Mozgovaja, A. G. Volkov (Eds.). Kyiv: NPU im. M.P. Dragomonova.
Skvorcov, Konstantin I. (1868): *Filosofija otcov i uchitelej cerki*. Kiev: Tip. Kievskago Guberiskago Upravlenija.
Slesinski, Robert (1984): *Pavel Florensky: A Metaphysics of Love*. Crestwood, NY: St. Vladimir's Seminary Press.
Smirnov, Sergej (1855): *Istorija Moskovskoj slavjano-greko-latinskoj akademii*. Moscow: Tip. V. Got'e.
Smirnov, Sergej (1879): *Istorija Moskovskoj akademii do eja preobrazovanija. (1814 – 1870)*. M: Univ. tip.
Snegirev, Veniamin A. (1871): "Spiritizm, kak filosofsko-religioznaja doktrina". *Pravoslavnyj sobesednik*, tom 1, pp. 12 – 41.
Snegirev, Veniamin A. (1875): "Son i snovidenija". *Pravoslavnyj sobesednik*, tom III, pp. 208 – 226.
Snegirev, Veniamin A. (1876a): "Nauki o cheloveke". *Pravoslavnyj sobesednik*, tom III, pp. 62 – 89.
Snegirev, Veniamin A. (1876b): " Psikhologija i logika kak filosofskie nauki". *Pravoslavnyj sobesednik*, tom II, pp. 427 – 451.
Snegirev, Veniamin A. (1890): *Metafizika i filosofija*. Khar'kov: Tip. Gubernskago Pravlenija.
Snegirev, Veniamin A. (1891): *O prirode chelovecheskago znanija i otnoshenii ego k bytiju ob"ektivnomu*. Khar'kov: Tip. Gubernskago Pravlenija.
Snegirev, Veniamin A. (1893): *Psikhologija*. Khar'kov: Tip. Adol'fa Darre.
Sokolov, Nafanail P. (1861): "Vzgljad na filosofiju Gegelja". *Pravoslavnyj sobesednik*, chast' pervaja, pp. 306 – 332.
Sokolov, Pavel P. (1890): "Filosofija v sovremennoj Germanii". *Pravoslavnoe obozrenie*, April, pp. 612 – 640.
Sokolov, Pavel P. (1893a): "Uchenie o svjatoj troice v novejshej idealisticheskoj filosofii". *Vera i razum*, tom II, chast' II, no. 20, pp. 351 – 382.
Sokolov, Pavel P. (1893b): "Uchenie o svjatoj troice v novejshej idealisticheskoj filosofii". *Vera i razum*, tom II, chast' II, no. 21, pp. 406 – 428.
Sokolov, Pavel P. (1906): "Problema very s tochki zrenija psikhologii i teorii poznanija". *Bogoslovskij vestnik*, tom 2, no. 6, pp. 270 – 301.
Sokolov, Vasilij A. (1893): "Magisterskie disputy". *Bogoslovskij vestnik*, tom 2, no. 4, pp. 192 – 206.
Sokolov, Vasilij A. (1916): "Gody studenchestva (1870 – 1874)". *Bogoslovskij vestnik*, tom 1, no. 2: 246 – 275; tom 2, no. 5, pp. 3 – 36.
Soloviev, Vladimir (1889): *La Russie et l' église universelle*. Paris: Albert Savine.
Soloviev, Vladimir (2013): *Russia and the Universal Church*, William G. von Peters (Ed.). Chattanooga, TN: Catholic Resources.
Solovyov, Vladimir (1985): *The Meaning of Love*. Thomas R. Beyer, Jr. (Trans.). Hudson, NY: Lindisfarne Press.
Solovyov, Vladimir (1996): *The Crisis of Western Philosophy (Against the Positivists)*. Boris Jakim (Trans.). Hudson, NY: Lindisfarne Press.
Solov'ev, Artem P. (2013): "Istochniki dlja issledovanija filosofii arkhiepiskopa Nikanora (Brovkovicha)". *Vestnik PSTGU, I: Bogoslovie. Filosofija*, vyp. 2(46), pp. 88 – 102.
Solov'ev, Artem P. (2015): *"Soglasit' filosofiju s pravoslavnoj religiej": idejnoe nasledie arkhiepiskopa Nikanora (Brovkovicha) v istorii russkoj mysli XIX-XX vekov*. Ufa: Izd. Slovokhotov A. A.
Solov'ev, Artem P. (2017): "Filosofskie issledovanija v nauchno-bogoslovskom zhurnale Kazanskoj dukhovnoj akademii "Pravoslavnyj Sobesednik" (1855 – 1918)". *Khristianskoe chtenie*, no. 2, pp. 272 – 295.

Solov'ev, Artem P. (2021a): "Idei P.A. Miloslavskogo v kontekste Kazanskoj dukhovno-akademicheskoj filosofii". *Khristianskoe chtenie*, no. 4, pp. 274–284.
Solov'ev, Artem P. (2021b): "Ucheniki V.I. Nesmelova i filosofsko-teologicheskie issledovanija v Kazanskoj dukhovnoj akademii 1910-kh gg.". *Khristianskoe chtenie*, no. 3, pp. 152–164.
Solov'ëv, Vladimir (1911): *Pis'ma Vladimira Sergeevicha Solov'ëva*, tom III. St. Petersburg: Tip. t-va Obshchestvennaja Pol'za.
Solov'ëv, Vladimir (1913): *Sobranie sochinenij Vladimira Sergeevicha Solov'ëva*, tom devjatyj. St. Petersburg: Knigonadatel'skoe Tovarnshchestvo Prosveshchenie.
Solov'ëv, Vladimir (1914): *Sobranie sochinenij Vladimira Sergeevicha Solov'ëva*, tom chetvertyj. St. Petersburg: Knigonadatel'skoe Tovarnshchestvo Prosveshchenie.
Solov'ëv, Vladimir (2000a): *Sochinenija*, tom pervyj 1873–1876. Moscow: Nauka.
Solov'ëv, Vladimir (2000b): *Sochinenija*, tom vtoroj 1875–1877. Moscow: Nauka.
Solov'ëv, Vladimir (2015): *Justification of the Moral Good*. Thomas Nemeth (Trans.). Cham, Switzerland: Springer.
Solov'ev, Vladimir (2019): "On the Philosophical Works of P. D. Iurkevych", Richard Hantola (Trans.). *East/West: Journal of Ukrainian Studies*, vol. VI, no.2, pp. 177–197.
Stebenev, Aleksandr S. (2017): "Istorija razvitija psikhologii v Sankt-Peterburgskoj dukhovnoj akademii v dorevoljucionnyj period". In *XI Sretenskaja nauchno-prakticheskaja konferencija "Psikheja i Pnevma" 16–17 Febralja 2017 g*. D. V. Shmonin (Ed.). St. Petersburg: Izd. Russkoj Khristianskoj gumanitornoj akademii, pp. 96–102.
Stojukhira, Natal'ja Ju. and Vladimir A. Mazilov (2016): "Chetverikov Ivan Pimenovich i dannye biografii #1". *Istorija rossijskoj psikhologii v licakh: Dajdzhest*, no. 4, pp. 34–50.
Stratij, Jaroslava (2002): "Georgij Shcherbac'kij i kartezianstvo v Kyivo-Mogiljans'kij akademiï". In *Religijno-filosofs'ka dumka v Kyivo-Mogiljans'kij Akademiï: Evropejs'kij kontekst*. V. S. Gors'kij, et al. (Ed.). Kyiv: K M Akademija, pp. 151–174.
Student semidesjatykh godov. (1914): "Kratkija vospominanija o Moskovskoj dukhovnoj akademii v period 1876–1880 g." In *U troicy v akademii. 1814–1914 gg*. Sergiev Posad: Izd. byvshikh vospitannikov MDA, pp. 172–201.
Subtelny, Orest (2009): *Ukraine: a history*. Toronto: University of Toronto Press, Inc.
Sukhova, N. Ju. (2006): "Nesostojavshajasja dukhovno-uchebnaja reforma 1890-x godov". *Vestnik PSTGU II: Istorija. Istorija Russkoj Pravoslavnoj Cerki*, vyp. 3(20), pp. 7–26.
Sukhova, N. Ju. (2009a): "Pravoslavnye dukhovnye akademii v 1850–60-x gg. i reforma 1869 g". *Vestnik Moskovskogo gosudarstvennogo oblastnogo universiteta. Serija "Istorija i politicheskie nauki"*. no. 4, pp. 23–28.
Sukhova, N. Ju. (2009b): "Znachenie svjatejshego sinoda v istorii nauchno-bogoslovskoj attestacii (1839–1917)". *Vestnik cheljabinskogo gosudarstvennogo universiteta*, no. 38(176). Istorija, pp. 101–109.
Sukhova, N. Ju. (2010a): "Dissertacionnye disputy kak forma nauchnoj raboty v pravoslavnykh akademijakh Rossii v 1869–1884 gg.". *Vestnik Pravoslovnogo Svjato-Tikhonovskogo gumanitarnogo universiteta. II: Istorija. Istorija Russkoj Pravoslavonoj cerki*, vyp. 3(36), pp. 21–35.
Sukhova, N. Ju. (2010b): "Zapiski svjatitelej Innokentija (Borisova) i Filareta (Drozdova) o dukhovnykh shkolakh". *Filaretovskij al'manakh*, vyp. 6, pp. 43–91.
Sukhova, N. Ju. (2011a): "Bogoslovskoe obrazovanie v Rossii v nachale XX v. (na primere Kievskoj dukhovnoj akademii)". *Trudy Kievskoj dukhovnoj akademii*, no. 15, pp. 141–155.

Sukhova, N. Ju. (2011b): "Dukhovno-uchebnyj proekt svjatitelja Innokentija (Borisova) 1830-kh gg.". *Vestnik Pravoslovnogo Svjato-Tikhonovskogo gumanitarnogo universiteta. II: Istorija. Istorija Russkoj Pravoslavonoj cerki*, vyp. 2(39), pp. 18–34.

Sukhova, N. Ju. (2013a): *Dukhovnye shkoly i dukhovnoe prosveshchenie v Rossii (XVII-nachalo XX v.)*. Moscow/St. Petersburg: Uchebnyj Komitet RPC.

Sukhova, N. Ju. (2013b): *Russkaja bogoslovskaja nauka (po doktorskim i magisterskim dissertacijam 1870–1918 gg.)*. Moscow: Izd. PSTGU.

Sukhova, N. Yu. (2017): "The 'Idea of the University' in the Russian Theological Academies (19th and Early 20th Centuries)". *Slověne*, no. 2, pp. 400–412.

Svetilin, Aleksandr E. (1871): *Uchebnik formal'noj logiki*. St. Petersburg: Tip. A. Transhelja.

Svetilin, Aleksandr E. (1874): [Review] Vladislavlev. Logika. *Zhurnal Ministerstva narodnogo prosveshchenija*, August, chast' CLXXIV, otd. 2: 184–298; October, chast' CLXXV, otd. 2, pp. 209–252.

Svetilin, Aleksandr E. (1878): "Umerennyj materializm". *Khristianskoe Chtenie*, no.3/4, pp. 561–584.

Svetilin, Aleksandr E. (1880): *Uchebnik logiki*. St. Petersburg: Tip. F. G. Eleonskagoj & Ko.

Tareev, Mikhail M. (1904a): "Religija i nravstvennost'". *Bogoslovskij vestnik*, tom 3, no. 10, pp. 296–317.

Tareev, Mikhail M. (1904b): "Religija i nravstvennost' (Prodolzhenie)". *Bogoslovskij vestnik*, tom 3, no. 11, pp. 395–421.

Tareev, Mikhail M. (1908): *"Unichizhenie Khrista"*. In *Osnovy Khristianstva*. Tom I: *Khristos*. Sergiev Posad: Tipografija Sv.-Tr. Sergievoj Lavry, pp. 7–134.

Tareev, Mikhail M. (1917a): "Novoe bogoslovie". *Bogoslovskij vestnik*, tom 2, no. 6/7, pp. 1–53.

Tareev, Mikhail M. (1917b): "Novoe bogoslovie (Prodolzhenie)". *Bogoslovskij vestnik*, tom 2, no. 8/9, pp. 168–224.

Tikhomirov, Pavel V. (1899a): "Istorija filosofii kak process postepennoj vyrabotki nauchno obosnovannogo i istinnogo mirovozzrenija". *Bogoslovskij vestnik*, tom 1, no. 1, pp. 57–76.

Tikhomirov, Pavel V. (1899b): "Problema i metod Kantovoj kritiki poznanija". *Vera i razum*, no. 14, pp. 37–64.

Tikhomirov, Pavel V. (1900): "Tipy gnoseologicheskikh uchenij". *Bogoslovskij vestnik*, tom 2, no. 7, pp. 333–366.

Tikhomirov, Pavel V. (1905): "Akademicheskaja svoboda i razvitie filosofii v Germanii". *Bogoslovskij vestnik*, tom 2, no. 5, pp. 65–94.

Tikhomirov, Pavel V. (1907): *Nauchyja zadachi i metody istorii filosofii*. Sergiev Posad: Tip. Sv.-Tr. Sergievoj Lavry.

Tikhomirov, Pavel V. (1908): "Ocherki po gnoseologii". *Bogoslovskij vestnik*, tom 1, no. 4, pp. 693–706.

Tkachuk, Marina L. (2002): "Iak vyvchalyi storiu filosofiï v Kyïv'skoï dukhovnoï akademiï XIX-pochatku XX st.". *Magisterium*, vyp. 9. Istoryko-filosofs'ki studiï, pp. 35–51.

Tkachuk, Marina L. (2011): "Filosofija v Kyivskii dukhovniy akademii: osvitnii aspekt". In *Filosofska osvita v Ukraini: istoriia i suchasnist*. M. L. Tkachuk (Ed.). Kyiv: TOV "Agrar Media Grup", pp. 66–94.

Tkachuk, Marina L. (2012): ""Akademiju beskonechno ljublju...": arkhiepiskop Vasilij (Bogdashevskij) kak student, professor i rektor Kievskoj dukhovnoj akademii". *Trudy Kyïv'skoï dukhovnoï akademiï*, no. 16, pp. 27–56.

Todes, Daniel P. (1989): *Darwin without Malthus. The Struggle for Existence in Russian Evolutionary Thought*. Oxford: Oxford University Press.

Troubetzkoy, Prince Eugene (1917–1918): "The Meaning of Life, and of the World, Revealed by the Cross". *The Hibbert Journal*, vol. xvi, no. 3, pp. 353–365.
Trubeckoj, Evgenij N. (1914): "Svet Favorskij i preobrazhenie uma. Po povodu knigi svjashennika P. A. Florenskogo *Stolp i utverzhdenie Istiny*". *Russkaja mysl'*, May, pp. 25–54.
Trubeckoj, Evgenij N. (2011): *Smysl zhizni*. Moscow: Institut russkoj civilizacii.
Tsvyk, Irina. (2010): "Philosophy in the Russian Academies: The Case of Viktor Kudryavtsev-Platonov". In *Philosophical Theology and the Christian Traditions: Russian and Western Perspectives*. David Bradshaw (Ed.). Washington, D.C.: The Council for Research in Values and Philosophy, pp. 147–160.
"Ustav pravoslavnykh dukhovnykh akademij". (1910). *Trudy Kievskoj dukhovnoj akademii*, no. 7–8, pp. 1–60.
Valliere, Paul R. (1976): "The Problem of Liberal Orthodoxy in Russia, 1905". *St. Vladimir's Orthodox Theological Quarterly*, vol. 20, pp. 115–131.
Vladislavlev, Mikhail (1874): "Protoierej Fedor Fedorovich Sidonskij. (Nekrolog)". *Zhurnal Ministerstva narodnogo prosveshchenija*, chast', vol. CLXXI, January, pp. 50–55.
Volkov, Andrej K. (1884). "K voprosy o pessimizme". *Pravoslavnyj sobesednik*, chast' vtoraja, pp. 332–371.
Vucinich, Alexander (1988): *Darwin in Russian Thought*. Berkeley/Los Angeles: University of California Press.
Vvedenskij, Aleksandr (1901): *Filosofskie ocherki*. St. Petersburg: Tip. Balashev.
Vvedenskij, Aleksej I. (1891): "Osnovnye gnoseologicheskie principy posle-Kantovskoj filosofii". *Bogoslovskij vestnik*, tom 2, no. 2, pp. 305–326.
Vvedenskij, Aleksej I. (1893a): "O religioznoj filosofii Viktora Dimitrievicha Kudrjavceva". *Vera i razum*, tom II, chast' I, pp. 52–71.
Vvedenskij, Aleksej I. (1893b): "O zadachakh sovremennoj filosofii, v svjazi s voprosom o vozmozhnosti i napravlenii filosofii samobytno-russkoj". *Voprosy filosofii i psikhologii*, kn. 20(5), pp. 125–157.
Vvedenskij, Aleksej I. (1898): *Professor filosofii Protoierej Feodor Aleksandrovich Golubinskij*. Sergiev Posad: A. I. Snegirevoj.
Vvedenskij, Aleksej I. (1900): "Krasota smerti i smert' krasoty". In *Na sovremennyja temy*. Moscow: Universitetskaja tip, pp. 111–121.
Vvedenskij, Aleksej I. (1901): *Umozritel'nye elementy teisticheskogo miroponimanii*. Vyp. 1: *Zakon prichinnosti i real'nost' vneshnego mira*. Khar'kov: Tip. Gubern. pravlenija.
Vvedenskij, Aleksej I. (1906a): "Analiz idei prostranstva". *Bogoslovskij vestnik*, tom 1, no. 3, pp. 403–430.
Vvedenskij, Aleksej I. (1906b): "Analiz idei prostranstva". *Bogoslovskij vestnik*, tom 1, no. 4, pp. 692–709.
Vvedenskij, Aleksej I. (1908): "Mirovaja tragedija znanija". *Bogoslovskij vestnik*, tom 1, no. 1, pp. 148–182.
Vvedenskij, Aleksej I. (2005): "Uchenie Kanta o prostranstve". In *Kant: pro et contra*. A. I. Abramov (Ed.). St. Petersburg: Izd. Russkoj Khristianskoj gumanitarnoj akademii, pp. 376–415.
Vysokoostrovskij, A. P. (1906): "O prave dukhovnykh akademij prisuzhdat' uchenye stepeni po filosofskim naukam". *Khristianskoe chtenie*, no. 5, pp. 748–777.
Walicki, Andrzej (2015): *The Flow of Ideas: Russian Thought from the Enlightenment to the Religious-Philosophical Renaissance*. Jolanta Kozak and Hilda Andrews-Rusiecka (Trans.). Frankfurt am Main: Peter Lang GmbH.

Zenkovskij, V. V. (1994): Moi vstrechi s vydajushchimisja ljud'mi. In *Zapiski russkoj akademicheskoj gruppy v SShA*. Vol 26. New York: Transactions of the Association of Russian-American Scholars in the U.S.A, pp. 3–64.

Zenkovsky, V. V. (1953): *A History of Russian Philosophy*. George L. Kline (Trans.). London: Routledge & Kegan Paul Ltd.

"Zhurnaly Soveta Moskovskoj Dukhovnoj Akademii za 1901 god" (1902): *Bogoslovskij vestnik*, tom 3, no. 12, pp. 305–352.

Znamenskij, P. V. (1891): *Istorija Kazanskoj dukhovnoj akademii za pervyj (doreformennyj) period ee sushchestvovanija (1842–1870 gody)*, vyp. 1. Kazan: Tip. Imperatorskago Universiteta.

Znamenskij, P. V. (1892): *Istorija Kazanskoj dukhovnoj akademii za pervyj (doreformennyj) period ee sushchestvovanija (1842–1870 gody)*, vyp. 2. Kazan: Tip. Imperatorskago Universiteta.

Žust, Milan (2002): *À la recherche de la Vérité vivante*. Roma: Lipa Srl.

Index

Academic philosophy, exhaustion of 319 ff.
Akvilonov, Evgenij
- biographical sketch 217–218, 220
- free will vs. determinism 218
- proofs of God's existence 217–220
Andreev, Fedor 303, 308
Antonij (Aleksej Khrapovickij)
- biographical sketch 220–221, 223
- free will 221, 222
- primacy of the practical 221
- subjectivism, non-Kantian 221–222
Aristotle 3, 5, 12
- philosophy of 20
Avsenev, Petr
- anthropological generalizations 101–102
- biographical sketch 97–98
- three means of acquiring knowledge of the "soul" 99–100
- three strivings of our worldly efforts 101

Beljaev, Viktor
- biographical sketch 293, 294
- rejection of epistemology as first philosophy 294
Berdjaev, Nikolaj
- criticism of Florenskij's viewpoint in his *Pillar* 313–314
Bible translations x
Bogdashevskij, Dmitrij
- biographical sketch 267
- critique of Kantianism 268
- philosophy and science, relationship between 268

Charter of 1884, reactionary character of 291–292
Charter of 1910
- philosophy under 293 ff.
- restoration of earlier charter 291
Chetverikov, Ivan
- biographical sketch 295
Chistovich, Illarion
- biographical sketch 60, 122–123

- criticism of Kantianism 124
- introspection as technique in psychology 123
- understanding of what philosophy is 124–125
Chizhevskij, Dmitrij 4 f., 25
Church Fathers, increasing recognition of the heritage of 175

Debol'skij, Nikolaj
- aim to show whether ontological knowledge is possible 145–148
- biographical sketch 128–129, 130
- criticism of Hegel 134 f.
- critique of empiricism in his early work 129
- critique of Kantian ethics 135–137
- introduction of "Supreme Reason" 133
- moral activity, concern of 135
- move toward a theistic conception of consciousness 130
- nationality, conception of 137–139
Decembrists ix
Drozdov, Aleksej 44–45

Ershov, Matvej
- biographical sketch 296
- his sociologism 297–298
- Malebranche's philosophy, on 296–297

Fessler, Ignaz
- brief professorial tenure 28
- defense against charges of pantheism 28 f.
Florenskij, Pavel
- actual infinity 307
- allegiance to Solov'ëvian "all-unity" 307
- Kant as thoroughly Protestant 308
- Neo-Platonic criticism of Kant's antinomies 311
- *Pillar and Ground of the Truth*, the, genesis and structure of 309–312
- some biographical information 304
- translation of Kant's *Physical Monadology* 305–306

Galich Aleksandr 40 f.
Gavriil, Arkhimandrit 47 f.
Glagolev, Sergej
- biographical sketch 298 – 299
- conception of philosophy as philosophy of religion 302
- Darwin's theory of evolution, criticism of 299 – 301
- Florenskij's *Pillar* as presentation of Orthodox worldview 313
- ontological argument for God's existence 302
- positivistic conception of science 300 – 301
Golubinskij, Feodor
- biographical sketch 63 – 64
- lectures on philosophy 65 – 66
- position vis-à-vis Kant 67 – 71
Gorodenskij, Nikolaj
- biographical sketch 244, 247, 248
- critique of Solov'ëv's ethics 244 – 245. 248
- Kantian ethics 247
Great Reforms, impact on academic life 119 – 121

Innokentij, Archbishop
- biographical sketch 94
- knowledge of Kant 97 f.
- three kinds of knowledge 95 – 96

Jakovenko, Boris
- critique of Florenskij's *Pillar* 314
Javorskij, Stefan 8, 10, 15, 19
Jurkevich, Pamfil xiii
- biographical sketch 103, 108
- eliminative materialism, criticism of 106 – 107
- Kant's treatment of proofs for God's existence 108
- religious platonism in first publication 104 – 105

Kalinovs'kij, Stefan 11
Karinskij, Mikhail
- analogical argument for the Other's existence 148
- biographical sketch 139 – 140, 149
- commentary on Kant's epistemology 212 – 217

- critique of positivism 144
- on positivism 159
- on post-Kantian German philosophy 140 – 143
- on the "I" of consciousness 147 – 148
- thesis comparison with Solov'ëv's 142 – 143
Karpov, Vasilij
- biographical sketch 48
- connection between philosophy and religion 54
- connection of Protestantism and German Idealism 55, 57 – 59
- nationalism in philosophy 51
- psychologism of 53, 57 – 58
- three realms in his 1840 *Introduction* 48 – 50
Kazan Theological Academy
- dramatic effect of new charter on 109
- establishment of 109
- First Charter, under the 109 ff.
- Second Charter, under the 190 ff.
- Third Charter, under the 272 ff.
Kedrov, Ivan 46 – 47
Khrisanf (Vladimir Retivcev)
- biographical sketch 112, 114
- characterizations of entire peoples 113
- German Idealism linked to Protestantism 113
Khupockij, Petr 153 – 154
Konys'kiy, Hryboriy 21 – 22
Kudrjavcev, Petr
- biographical sketch 269 – 270
- on Kant and neo-Kantianism 270 – 271
- progressive politics of 269, 272
- struggle between absolutism and relativism 270
- Zenkovsky's opinion of 270
Kudrjavcev, Viktor
- biographical sketch 73, 153 – 154
- concepts of reason 157
- ethical theory 169 – 171
- on materialism 76 – 77
- on natural science 155, 166 – 169
- on positivism 84 – 87, 158
- our conception of God 95 – 96
- philosophical method 159 – 160
- proofs for God's existence 163 – 166
- rejection of mysticism 161

- role of philosophy in human inquiry   156
- sub-divisions of philosophy   157–158
- whether a pagan can be moral   75–76
Kurbskij, Andrej   3
Kutnevich, Vasilij   62–63
Kyiv Academy   8, 11, 20, 22
Kyivan Mohyla College   5, 11 f.
Kyivan Rus'
- education in   4–5
- embrace of Eastern Orthodoxy   2
Kyiv Theological Academy
- First Charter, under the   88 f.
- Second Charter, under the   176 ff.
- Third Charter, under the   261 ff.

Leichoudes (Likhud) brothers   7–8, 12
Levickij, Roman
- moral theory of   172–173
- reason-based arguments, role of   171–172
Linickij, Petr
- biographical sketch   182
- Chicherin, criticism of   187–188, 321
- epistemological conceptions of   184–189
- history of philosophy, text on   182
- Kantianism, rejection of   189, 264–265
- mathematics as *a priori* science   265
- opposition to student political expressions   263
- philosophy, conception of   182–184, 264–266
Logic
- teaching of, in the 1850s   114–116
- texts in use in early 19th century Russia   114–115
Lopatinskij, Fedor (Feofilakt)
- doctrine of "two truths"   13–14
- relations with Peter the Great   15
- teaching activities   13

Men of the Sixties   ix
Mikhail (Gribanovskij)
- biographical sketch   223
- proofs of God's existence   224–226
Miloslavskij, Petr
- biographical sketch   192, 198
- idealism ending with Hegel   194
- philosophy, conception of   196

- post-Hegelian German philosophy   194–195
- psychologism, opposition to   197
Mirtov, Dmitrij
- biographical sketch   229, 293
- contrast of Kant's ethics to Nietzsche's   229–230
Moscow Academy   9–10
Moscow Theological Academy
- establishment of   61
- First Charter, under the   61 ff.
- Second Charter, under the   150 ff.
- stability of professorial staff under second charter   150
- Third Charter, under the   232 ff.

Nadezhin, Feodor   45–46
Nashchins'kij, David
- teaching of Wolfffian philosophy   24
Nesmelov, Viktor
- biographical sketch   276, 276 f., 287–288
- critique of Kant's "Refutation of Idealism"   280–281
- faith, role of, in cognition   280, 282, 286
- faith, study of, in epistemology   284
- God, origin of our conception of   282
- introspection as means of investigating mental activity   277
- Objectification, structural analysis of   278–280
- objectivity, child's conception of   278
- science and religion are different viewpoints   284
Nikanor (Aleksandr Brovkovich)
- biographical sketch   198–199
- influence of, on N. Ja. Grot   321
- positive philosophical method   198
- subjective and objective knowledge, contrast between   200–201
Nikanor (Nikolaj Kudrjavcev)
- criticism of Florenskij   316

Olesnickij, Markellin
- biographical sketch   177, 180–181
- Protestantism, conceptual turn toward   177, 180
- psychology, reliance on, in ethical theory   177–179

Orthodox Church
- nationalism of   x
- quiescence of   ix
Ostroumov, Mikhail
- biographical sketch   233–234, 237
- history of philosophy, interpretation of   235, 237
- relation of philosophy to religion and science   234–235

Peter the Great   8, 13, 18, 33
Pipes, Richard   ix, 2f.
Platonic philosophy as pillar of true philosophy   29
Pobedonoscev, Konstantin, counter-reforms of   207, 211
Popov, Ivan
- biographical sketch   241
- Darwinian theory of evolution   242
- Innateness of moral law   241–242
Pospekhov, Dmitrij
- biographical sketch   176
- editorial work and translations   176
Potapov, Vasilij
- attack on British empiricism   151
- biographical sketch   150–151
- on Newtonian action at a distance   151–153
Pravoslavnij sobesednik, journal of Kazan Academy   190
Prokopovich, Feofan   11, 12
- relations to Peter the Great   15–19
- teaching activities   15–17
Provisional Regulations (or Rules) governing the Academies   230, 262, 291
Provisional Rules of February 1917   292, 298
Psychologism among Russian Orthodox thinkers   xiv

Reforms under Alexander I   27–28
Russian Academic philosophy, general characteristics of   xi-xiii

Second Charter of 1869, nature of   119–121
Serebrenikov, Vitalij
- biographical sketch   227, 229, 293
- experimental psychology, interest in   228
- on Locke   227

Shcherbac'kij, Grigorij
- support for Cartesian foundationalism   22–24
Shpet, Gustav   x, 2, 37
- judgment of Sidonskij's *Introduction*   39f.
Sidonskij, Fedor
- advocacy of philosophy as an independent discipline   41–42
- his *Introduction to Philosophy* and its fate   39–44
- professorial career at Petersburg Academy   44
Skvorcov, Ivan
- biographical sketch   88–89
- on Kant's *Religion within the Bounds of Reason Alone*   92
- on space and time   90
- on the "One" of Plotinus   91
Smirnov, Ivan   110
Snegirev, Veniamin
- biographical sketch   190, 272
- epistemic foundationalism   274–275
- logic as empirical science   192
- on introspection   273
- on space and time   273, 275–276
- psychology as preeminent science   191
Sokolov, Nafanail
- biographical sketch   110–111, 190
- criticism of Hegel's philosophy as an absolute atheism   110–111
Sokolov, Pavel
- Christian conception of Trinity in German Idealism   239–240
- pantheistic conception of the Absolute in German Idealism   239
Solov'ëv, Sergej
- at Moscow Theological Academy   304
- some biographical information   303–304
Solov'ëv, Vladimir
- possible attendance in Kudrjavcev's classes   80f.
- possible attendance of, at Kudrjavcev's talk on Comte   84f.
- review of Karpov's logic text   54f.
- review of Nikanor's Positive Philosophy   203, 203f.

Speranskij, Mikhail
– role in the creation of the Academies 27–28
St. Petersburg Theological Academy
– establishment of 33
– First Charter, under the 33ff.
– Second Charter, under the 122ff.
– Third Charter, under the 211ff.
Student strikes in 1905 261
Svetilin, Aleksandr
– relation between logic and psychology 126–127
– relation between psychology and physiology 127
Symeon of Polotsk 3

Tareev, Mikhail
– biographical sketch 248–249, 252
– independence of religion and morality 249–250
– influence of Solov'ëv on 250f.
– Patristics, disparagement of 249
– practical reason, efficacy of 248f.
– rejection of thesis 232
Tikhomirov, Pavel
– biographical sketch 256–257, 260
– epistemology, conception of 257–258
– Russian philosophy, poverty of 259–260
Trubeckoj, Evgenij
– criticism of Florenskij 315–316

Universities, founding of 1

Vetrinskij, Irodian 35–38
Vvedenskij, Aleksandr
– description of Academic life in 1820s 38
Vvedenskij, Aleksej
– biographical sketch 252
– philosophy is metaphysics 253
– Russian philosophy, conception of 254–256
– space, psychological treatment of 254
Vysokoostrovskij, Aleksandr 226, 227
– on awarding of degrees in philosophy 231

Western philosophy, subjectivism of 86, 142, 176, 193, 237, 254, 305, 319f.
Wolffian philosophy
– introduction of, at Moscow Academy 24
– pedagogical hegemony of, at Moscow Academy 25–26

www.ingramcontent.com/pod-product-compliance
Lightning Source LLC
Chambersburg PA
CBHW020219170426
43201CB00007B/260